Hamburg: Halifax-Bomber, 7 Mann, 6 tot

Westdeutschland: Britenbomber, 3 Mann verbrannt

Hamburg: Lancaster-Bomber, 8 Mann, 8 tot

Holland: Lancaster-Bomber, 8 Australier tot

...land: Lancaster-Bomber, 8 Australier tot

Kanalküste: Lancaster-Bomber, 8 Mann, 5 tot

Am Kanal: Liberator-Bomber (USA.), alle tot

Hamburg: Britenbomber, kein Mann gerettet

Hollandküste: Liberator-Bomber, 10 Mann tot

Hamburg: Wellington-Bomber, 6 Mann, 1 tot

Nordfrankreich: USA.-Bomber, alle Mann tot

Hamburg: Rest einer „Fliegenden Festung"

Hamburg: USA.-Bomber, 10 Mann, 9 tot

Hamburg: Britenbomber, in der Luft zerplatzt

Kanalküste: USA.-Jäger, kein Mann gerettet

Holland: Lancaster-Bomber, 8 Mann, 6 tot

Hannover: Britenbomber, 7 Mann, 6 Tote

Nordfrankreich: Britenbomber, 7 Mann, 7 tot

Kanalküste: Das blieb von einem Britenbomber

Kanal: Wellington-Bomber, wird zerlegt

Hannover: Halifax-Bomber, 7 Mann, 6 tot

Kanalküste: Stirling-Bomber, aufschl. zerrissen

Nordfrankreich: Britenbomber, alle Mann tot

Holland: Lancaster-Bomber, 8 Mann, tot

Hamburg: Wellington-Bomber 6 Mann, 4 tot

Hamburg: Lancaster-Bomber, 8 Mann, 3 tot

Hamburg: Britenbomber, alles, was übriglieb

Hannover: Blick in Wellington-Trümmer

Westdeutschland: Britenbomber, 8 Mann, 4 tot

Holland: Liberator-Bomber, 10 Mann, 9 tot

Atlantik-Küste: Britenbomber, 5 Mann, 1 tot

Kanal: 3 im Schlauchboot gerettet

DO YOU REMEMBER ?

Do you remember the ones who died?
Brownie and Bill and Clanger,
And can you remember their faces, their faces
As they laughed with you in the hangar?

And what of the others who also paid
Corker and Charlie and Dinkum ——
And do you remember the drunks, the drunks
We had in the City of Lincoln?

And their popsies too, are they still alive?
Evelyn, Edna and Rose
And are they all married and happy, and happy
Without e'er a thought for their beaus?

And what about those who were married, eh?
Mary and Maggie and Joan
They're widows now; still pining? still pining?
Still travelling life alone?

And what if the Dead asked the living,
Did you build that New World we planned,
We can only reply "We failed you, we failed you
We needed your steadying hand".

And what excuses to offer the Dead,
For losing the peace they won?
We can only show our possessions, possessions
And sadly answer "None".

Dennis Dear

THEIR NAMES WILL NEVER DIE

The first rays of the dawning sun
Shall touch its pillars,
And as the day advances
And the light grows stronger,
You shall read the names
Engraved on the stone,
Of those who sailed the angry sky
And saw harbour no more.
No gravestone in yew-dark churchyard
Shall mark their resting place,
Their bones lie in the forgotten corners
Of earth and sea.

But that we may not lose their memory
With fading years, their monument stands here.
Here, at the heart of England, half way between
Royal Windsor and Lordly London; looking down
Here where the trees troop down to Runnymede.
Meadow of the Magna Carta, field of freedom.
Never saw you so fitting a memorial,
Proof that the principles established here
Are still dear to the hearts of men.
Here now they stand contrasted one alike,
The field of freedom's birth, and the memorial
To freedom's winning.

And, as the evening comes,
And mists, like quiet ghosts, rise from the river bed
And climb the hill to wander through the cloisters,
We shall not forget them. Above the mist
We shall see the memorial still, and over it
The crown and single star. And we shall pray
As the mists rise up and the air grows dark
That we shall wear
As brave a heart as they.

Paul C. Scott
(Engraved on a window at Runnymede)

LANCASTER
AT WAR:5
FIFTY YEARS ON

*'When my Old Lags go over the top, I want to make sure they have something
more effective in their hands with which to fight rather than just a swagger stick'*

Sir Arthur T. Harris, Bt GCB, OBE, AFC, LLD
Air Officer Commanding-in-Chief,
Bomber Command
February 1942 – September 1945

LETHAL LADY

To watch her 'twixt the goosenecks, on the
flarepath rolling fast;
Towards night sky with tail fins high, and a
day's brief dusk long past.
Have you felt a hardstand tremble to four
Merlins' blasting roar?
And seen that tailwheel dancing in the
slipstream's rushing bore?
Ever viewed a Lanc on funnels as she homed on
a misty morn',
Maybe glimpsed her low on the down wind leg,
heard her snarl at the
Coming Down?
Hell's terror at night this lady, as lethal still
by day,
For her beauty concealed grim purpose as the
Lanc had a debt to pay!

J. R. Walsh (June 1986)

LANCASTER AT WAR:5

FIFTY YEARS ON

MIKE GARBETT
AND BRIAN GOULDING

First published 1995

ISBN 0 7110 2397 2

Published by Ian Allan Publishing

an imprint of Ian Allan Ltd, Terminal House,
Station Approach, Shepperton,
Surrey TW17 8AS.

Printed by Ian Allan Printing Ltd, Coombelands
House, Coombelands Lane, Addlestone, Weybridge,
Surrey KT15 1HY.

Design and art direction: Simon Joslin

Front cover:
*Re-creating vividly the wartime atmosphere, this January
1991 shot shows Lancaster B Mk VII NX611 at East
Kirkby with the fully-restored watch-office (control tower) in
the background.*
Brian Goulding

500054383

BATTLE ORDER

(with acknowledgement to the late-lamented Chris Wren, well remembered for his good-humoured contributions to the wartime spirit)

'L' FOR 'LANC'

'Yes, old friend, you were unbeatable in your time, but you are in your declining years now. Amazing-looking aircraft are screaming through the air at speeds which you in your prime could not even have dreamed about.

But those of us who knew you intimately, those whom you bore so faithfully through skies that were not all friendly, will remember well the all-engulfing snore of your four Merlins and the pale-blue flickering flame from your exhausts in the blackness on either side.

...You have droned your way into the immortality of history; and when your work finally is finished, your epitaph may well be:

> High-flying in paths of sunlight
> O'er clouds the moon had kissed
> Black in the blood-red sunset
> Or grey in the morning mist.
> Target or load or distance
> Were all the same to you;
> Through hell and flak you roar'd
> And back
> Above the strato cu'.

(By Doug Gray DFC, former RCAF pilot with No 101 Sqn, No 1 Group Bomber Command, writing in 1954.)

AN OLD-FASHIONED LANCASTER

> Just an old-fashioned Lancy, with old-fashioned wings
> And a fuselage all tattered and torn,
> With old-fashioned engines, that splutter and bang
> All the way there and back to a prang.
> With old-fashioned turrets, and old-fashioned guns,
> That gunners D.I. every morn
> Though she don't look so swell
> - She can battle like hell,
> As the people of Berlin can tell.
> When she's way up on high -
> She's the Queen of the sky,
> That old-fashioned Lancy of mine.

(Popular RAF song, variation of 'Old-fashioned Wimpy', to the tune of 'Old-fashioned Lady'.)

BRIEFING

In the introduction to our first *Lancaster at War*, which was written in 1970, we started by saying: 'It is now over a quarter of a century since the Lancaster last flew operationally during World War 2'. It seems hardly possible that another full quarter century has since sped by, and by coincidence, as these words are written, the 50th Anniversary of VE-Day has just been celebrated, with VJ-Day's soon to take place. So, still on the anniversary theme, next year (1996) will be the 40th since withdrawal of the last Lancaster from RAF service; and last year (1994) was the 30th since its last operational users (the French Navy and Royal Canadian Air Force) retired theirs. It also makes us conscious of the fact that it is now well over 40 years since we started our research, and not much less than that since our partnership was forged. We have felt it appropriate to include some '50 years on' comparisons.

We must make the point that neither of us saw wartime service, for the simple reason that we were then mere schoolboys, born a few years too late. We both, however, recall the war years all too clearly, living as we were with our parents in the industrial midlands of England, spending much of our nocturnal lives in Anderson air-raid shelters, hearing nightly the chilling wail of warning sirens, and then the distinctive throb of German bomber engines, wondering whether they were *en route* to another city, or if it was ours that was to be their target for tonight — you never knew. Then the distant boom-boom of our always seemingly ineffective ack-ack, occasional rattle of shrapnel on the house roofs, but the most frightening of all, the awful whistle and crump-crump of bombs, thankfully usually fairly distant, as often as not having been jettisoned more in hope than expectation by some homeward-bound straggler. Then, after the all-clear, the glow of fires on the horizon, sometimes up to a hundred miles away, depending on whether it had been Sheffield, Manchester, Liverpool, Coventry, etc that the enemy had attacked.

The deprivation and rationing didn't seem to bother us unduly in those days; but actually being machine-gunned by a low-flying German twin-engined intruder one lunchtime did! It was a taste of the terror being experienced nightly by our bomber crews. But we weren't there — and what we write can be based only on the reflections and revelations of those who were, and which are presented in our books as accurately as possible, in good faith, exactly as related to us. We are so grateful to those who have delved into their albums, scrapbooks and store of memories for us over many years. Some of the pictures and stories in this book were donated to us 30 years or more ago, when the events were still fresher in the minds than is perhaps the case today, as age starts to take its inevitable toll.

In our early days our interests were centred very much on the aircraft themselves: serial numbers, squadron codes, markings, etc; but with the passage of time, the interest has swung much more to the men who flew the Lancs, and the men and women who serviced and supported them, and who provided the essential back-up for what was a truly mighty army of the air. It is the stories from such people, all directly involved, which have become of equal, if not greater, importance to us than the intrinsic details of the Lancasters themselves. We feel it is this factor that has perhaps tended to set our books a little apart from others of a primarily reference nature, all of which have their place, of course. We hope we have again paid due tribute to all those lads and lasses of the Lancaster era, and that our efforts will be something of a fillip to them at a time when many of them still feel so badly let down after they'd played such a vital part in our survival.

Have any of those modern-day 'experts' who still seek to denigrate virtually everything Bomber Command did, *any* idea of what it was like to

Right:
MARK OF A THOROUGHBRED
'...When she's way up on high, she's the Queen of the sky...'
Forever relegated to being an also-ran is the Lanc powered by Hercules radials. Never regarded as a contender for quite the beauty of line of the Lancaster fitted with neatly underslung in-line Merlins, the variant was nevertheless a potent weapon and worthy stablemate. Given that a mere 300 production machines were built — hardly more than a blip in total Lancaster production — the BII made no small contribution to Bomber Command's offensive and deserves wider recognition, closer study.

Born of necessity — insurance in the event of supply problems because of the enormous demand for the Merlin — the Hercules-engined BII admittedly had a chequered service life. After 'on the job' operational trials with No 61 Sqn (based at Syerston) during the period October 1942/February 1943, No 5 Group discarded the type; but No 3 Group welcomed it with open arms, anxious to increase its bomb-carrying capability as well as reduce losses incurred with medium-altitude Stirlings and Wellingtons. From March 1943, No 115 Sqn (then stationed at East Wretham) converted to the Lanc II and set about the enemy with renewed determination. Later adding No 514 Sqn (the only squadron actually formed with Lanc IIs) to its battle order, No 3 Group built up a fine record before giving up the trusty variant by the end of September 1944 (the possible Merlin engine-supply problem long since overcome thanks largely to Packard) and changing to the Merlin-Lancaster. However, it was the Canadian-controlled and -manned No 6 Group which truly carved out a proud record on the BII. The Linton-on-Ouse squadrons — No 426 'Thunderbird' and No 408 'Goose' — added their weight to the offensive in June and August 1943 and were joined by No 432 'Leaside' at East Moor from September of that year. By the close of August 1944 the breed was history in so far as No 6 Group was concerned, all three units converting to the like-motored Halifax, a worthy successor.

Stubbornly defying identification is 'Berlin Special' from either the 'Goose' or 'Thunderbird' Squadrons. Anyone out there remember her?
R. J. Russell/via R. R. Smith

Above:
PANOPLY FOR A MOOSE

live in Britain in the early war years when, for months on end, we went to
bed in those dreadful shelters as a matter of course, night-in, night-out?
From what they have to say, and from the documentary films they continue
to produce — which often distort the history they are supposed to portray
— we can only assume they have not the remotest idea. They, of course,
had they been around in 1939, would never have allowed war to happen
anyway. But what would *they* have done about surviving, and taking the war
to the enemy, as was the task of Bomber Command? Had Germany and its
industrial and commercial heartlands not been stopped in its tracks (as it was
solely by Bomber Command's efforts initially, later to be aided in no small
measure by the USAAF), would we ever have been able to set foot on
Europe's shores on D-Day? How many more tens of millions of lives would
it have cost had Germany not been denied much of its industrial might?
How much longer would the war have lasted? Might we even have found
ourselves facing not the Germans across the Channel but the Russians?

No — the job *had* to be done as it *was* done, by the *only* force available
to us at that time — Bomber Command, with its senior officers acting under
orders from the highest levels of Allied Command, not on any personal
whims or preferences as is so frequently implied by postwar armchair
'experts'. Let there be no doubt whatever as to which service it was that
truly paved the way to eventual victory by its ceaseless hammering of the
German war machine.

In reality, was there any other way at that time to slow down the
enemy's own technical development and potential? Even in mid-1944, when
rockets were raining indiscriminately on eastern and southern England, and
on London in particular, it was feared that Hitler was not far away from
getting an atomic warhead, and any lessening of the bombing effort could
still have cost us the war. The systematic destruction of each and every
possible piece of Germany's war production *had* to be undertaken. It was no
good relying on precision bombing, since in each German city, and smaller
towns, there were hundreds of back street/street corner sub-contracting
engineering shops just as there had been in Birmingham, Coventry, Derby,
Sheffield, etc, when they were attacked indiscriminately by the Germans in
the earlier years of the war. Ask any Briton who suffered those raids what

Above:
PANOPLY FOR A MOOSE
'...Maybe glimpsed her low on the downwind leg, heard her snarl at the coming dawn...'
*The last vestige of sunlight as yet undarkened behind a smothering, thickly risen bank of
cloud, forms an imposing backdrop to a BX, cutting a majestic silhouette and soon to pancake at
Middleton St George. It is 19 April 1944 and the premoninantly Canadian crew (with, usually,
a British flight engineer and perhaps wireless op or gunner) will have little opportunity or
inclination for appreciating Mother Nature's splendour as they complete another of a seemingly
endless round of circuits and bumps, cross-countries — you name it. No 419 'Moose' Sqn, newly
converted to Chadwick's masterpiece, must return to the fray without delay. With a combined total
of 2,264 Wellington and Halifax operational sorties behind it, 419 will, in the event, tot up
2,029 on Lancasters — the highest of any No 6 Group Lancaster unit. Set against this, records
tell us that by the cessation of hostilities in Europe the 'Moose' outfit, along with No 408 'Goose'
Sqn, suffered the highest loss overall of any Canadian squadron. A reported 129 aircraft, of
which 47 comprised Lancasters and their crews, were lost on, or as a result of, operations.* The
Public Archives of Canada

they felt when we at last began to hit back meaningfully through Bomber
Command. They will tell you: elation, relief, hope. At times, the USAAF's
bombing was far more intensive and supposedly indiscriminate than that of
Bomber Command, yet their bomber crews were not vilified.

Brave words and promises had failed to make or preserve true peace
after World War 1, when we'd made the mistake of shopping short. It could
not be allowed to happen again and our bombers had to pave the way for
the ground troops at all costs, increasingly urgently as the war progressed to
ensure a political and territorial East/West balance after the war's end. We
have, since the end of World War 2, been persuaded to stop short in several
relatively minor conflicts, eg Suez and the Gulf, and all that has achieved
has been to prolong the real dangers of the situations, with the
troublemakers still in office, usually in positions of even greater power.

Many veterans today, not only of Bomber Command, but of all services,
including our venerable USAAF 8th Air Force partners, ask: 'What did we
fight for?' 'God, King and Country' was the cry as the British and
Commonwealth lads signed up. What has become of those ideals? The old
traditional beliefs have been worn away and ridiculed, the institution of the
monarchy is no longer universally respected, and national sovereignty is

gradually being subsumed by what appears to be an increasingly federalist European Union. Is this *really* what those near-six years of war and millions of deaths were all about?

Never before in any of our seven books have we commented on the politics of war, but we felt it appropriate to air our views in this one, knowing full well the sense of betrayal felt by many wartime veterans who have been branded as warmongers — even war criminals — by some of the more extreme elements in the media. It is incomprehensible how it came to happen, but it is still happening in the inquests into subsequent wars such as the Falklands conflict, so splendidly won.

We hope our books give a true and reasonably accurate record of events. We do not seek to glorify war in any way — on the contrary, we do show the horror side of it, too. But — let there be no doubt whatever of our admiration for those Bomber Command heroes, who fought hard and long for our benefit, and carried the war to the enemy when no other arm of the service could. Their efforts brought us peace for what has been an almost unprecedented 50 years. Let us pray to God that it is not thrown away.

Inevitably, in any book about the bomber force, the lion's share is going to be about aircrew; but we hope the ground staff — civil and military — who supported them so doggedly, have in this volume received fair coverage and will not feel neglected or overlooked. We hope also that full tribute has been given to those Commonwealth airmen, Britons living in many countries round the world, and men of other nationalities, including Americans who joined up through the RCAF, who so readily answered the call from the outset of war in 1939. Such a response is not likely to be seen again. Would

we now spring to *their* aid so unhesitatingly; or would 'commercial' considerations (eg oil) prevail?

Each man who flew with Bomber Command is fast becoming a legend. Each member of each crew is unique, with his own experiences. We can never hope to cover them all, but trust that what we have chosen is a realistic representation of how it was, those 50 and more years back. We weren't there, so we shall never truly know. Those, to whom this book is dedicated, were there, so they *will* truly know.

Below:
JOBS FOR THE BOYS
A picture such as this tells us so much. It is not just that it depicts a mud-spattered, oil-begrimed, exhaust-stained 'Y-Yorker' (BI HK700, 'GI:Y') of No 622 Sqn at Mildenhall one milder than usual February day in 1945.

It is not just that it features a Lancaster whose cockpit-bound engine fitters or mechanics are running-up her port-outer Merlin, whilst a colleague, astride the starboard-outer, tightens or loosens a cowling panel, and a rigger completes removal of Perspex covers.

More, whereby it is a reminder that she is but one Lanc of one flight of one squadron of one group, of five groups by then wholly or partly-equipped.

More, whereby it is but one dispersal on one aerodrome on one day in one month in one year, of a little over three years during which Lancasters were an ever-increasing element in Bomber Command's arsenal as it unceasingly hammered away at Hitler's much vaunted thousand-year Reich.

More, whereby it shows us a few of the many erks whose graft and craft, self-pride and dedication kept those Lancs on the daily battle order. H. E. Pam

ACKNOWLEDGEMENTS

This is our eighth book on the Lancaster 'family', and our fifth in the 'At War' series (including *Lincoln at War 1944–66*). The initial ideas with which we approached Ian Allan Ltd in the late 1960s, and which resulted in the first *Lancaster at War*, the progenitor of the series, appear to have proved highly successful. Our publishers judged there to be room for one more, perhaps, in this year of anniversaries of great events, before the hangar doors are finally closed, and to do it, we have, in effect, been coerced out of at least semi-retirement. It seems appropriate to be able to pay this further tribute in a rather special year, while many of the veterans are still with us, albeit in decreasing numbers.

It is thanks to them (and in some cases the surviving families of those who have 'slipped the surly bonds of earth') that we have been able to put together this book — 'yet another book on the Lancaster' as no doubt some reviewers will say. The pattern may well be similar in many respects to our previous 'At Wars', which seem to have become a fairly well-proven formula, to which we have chosen largely to adhere. The content, however, is all new, including most of the photographs, few of which will have been published before — a feature on which we pride ourselves. Most of the material is from 'those who were there', including the pictures, not all of which will be of modern-day, computer-enhanced quality, but chosen as much for 'atmosphere' as anything and in many cases reproduced from small, faded, yellowing originals, taken on Box Brownies, against all the rules, and at considerable risk of court martial.

The names of those who have contributed to our collection of material over the years would fill a book, but we now make special mention of the main contributors to this volume:

We are particularly indebted to Tom Bailey for his painstaking research at the Public Record Office, Kew, to provide many answers, fill many gaps, solve hitherto long-standing mysteries, with methodical, neat purpose as befits a career schoolmaster and former operational navigator. Evidence of his work is to be seen on many pages, and without Tom's contribution, many details would have remained incomplete, the ends still loose.

The story of Tom's crew also appears, and to all of them, our thanks for their agreement to co-operate so fully; to Tom's wife Joan, also, for her help with research, and considerable tolerance of Tom's regular absences on visits to Kew.

The Public Record Office has revolutionised the research into wartime history in recent years, as official squadron and station records have been made available. We thank the Director and staff for facilities placed at the disposal of our researcher, Tom Bailey. We also thank the Air Historical Branch of the Ministry of Defence for its assistance in past years.

To those who were there, and who have directly contributed stories, and to those others whose help and recollections have been so invaluable in enabling us to present detailed accounts of the events of those momentous years, requiring them to delve deep into their memories:

Charles Cuthill DFC, AFC, former 149 Sqn pilot, who compiled his impressions soon after the war's end when he was trying to come to terms with the modern air force, and used it as a means to get it 'out of the system'.

To the late Dennis Dear DFM, for his stories and poems also composed early postwar to clear his mind and expunge certain feelings from his conscience. It is his drawings which appeared in the RAF Spilsby booklet *Journey's End*, from which several extracts are reproduced, hopefully to raise a smile, as was originally intended.

Alan G ('Buck') Buckley, Desmond Chorley, Bert Dowty and the late Bert Crum DFM, AEM, Tony Duck, the late Bill Endean DFC, Walter Faraday DFC, Sid Giffard, Tom Hall, Vic Huxley, Ron Makinson, Alan Morgan.

The late Frances Thompson and several widows, who spoke so openly on the loss of their loved ones, whose wish for privacy we have observed.

'The Inseparables' could not have been written without the help of some of them — Douglas Webb DFM and George Chalmers DFC, DFM (surviving members of the No 617 Sqn crew), Frank Cholerton, Ken Newby.

Also, our thanks to Iris Wilkinson (widow of Ray), Alastair Nicholson, Malcolm King, Robert Owen (617 Sqn historian) and Ted Wass (Secretary of the No 617 Sqn Association).

For the poems, we have to thank Les Buckell and the late Harry Brown DFM (both rear gunners on Lancs as well as gifted poets), John Walsh (who was too young to serve in the war, so did not experience the happenings, yet whose poems reflect the extent to which he has 'tuned in' to the past).

Also, we give credit to unknown authors of poems etc, taken from scrapbooks, jottings, POW diaries and the like, once penned by men whose identities were either not recorded or long-forgotten even before their gems were donated to us. We hope they will not object to their work appearing here as an intended tribute to them and their peers.

And for two contributors who did not serve, but whose stories have, we feel, made worthy contributions to span the '50 years':

John Delanoy, who responded to our request for a schoolboy's recollections and impressions of the war.

Rob Davis, one of the younger breed trying to recapture the atmosphere of Bomber Command, as have so many in more recent decades, their interest having been stimulated by previous books, and whose enthusiasm has been heightened as the traces of history have receded.

For the drawings, we are grateful to Ken Aitken, ex-RAF, whose enthusiasm and gifted application have, we feel, captured most vividly the atmosphere of life on a wartime Lancaster station, as have the priceless photographs taken at the time by E. Darwin Evans.

We also acknowledge the help given to us over the years by the hard-working, unpaid secretaries of various squadron and air-crew associations; in particular, Shirley Westrup, Secretary of the Elsham Wolds Association, indefatigable organiser of reunions, etc, typical of the WAAF breed, and a hostess much appreciated by many.

For photographic work over the past 30 years, working wonders with old negatives, and copies of aged, yellowing prints, our appreciation to Cyril Parrish; staff of Peter Moss Photography, and the late Bob Roberts; Gerry Raggett and Roy Blackwell.

We express our appreciation generally to all fellow-enthusiasts, authors and researchers, some of whose own books have provided valuable cross-references, such as Bruce Robertson's and Frances K Masons's own Lancaster books, Martin Middlebrook's and Chris Everitt's Bomber Command War Diaries, and other books as specifically mentioned in text and captions.

For general help and support going back more years than we choose to calculate, thanks to: Trevor Allen, Bryan Challand, Tony Duck, Frank Harper, Colin Hill, Harry Holmes, Eric Howell, the late Sandy Jack, John Marshall, Dennis Oldham, Bob Pitt and Charles Waterfall.

Rhonda and Johnny Spiegel: Rhonda for her wizardry on the word processor, for which we'd have been pressed to find an equal, particularly at short notice, and with their house move looming ever closer to our deadline; and to Johnny for considerable support, some proof-reading, and observations of a life-long aviation enthusiast.

To Air Vice-Marshal J. E. (Johnnie) Johnson CB, CBE, DSO, DFC for his Foreword.

To David Shephard OBE, world-renowned artist of wildlife, transport, aircraft, etc, self-confessed 'Lancaster Nut', for his closing words.

And to The Reverend Canon Day DFC (himself a Lancaster pilot with No 156 Sqn, who survived being shot down to become a POW), for his reflections.

Our families: Edna and Arthur Garbett (Mike's parents) for their unstinting support in every respect, particularly when it has mattered the most.

And to Mary (Brian's wife of almost 40 years), who has somehow tolerated many meetings, unscheduled visitors, countless absences, numerous odd diversions on holidays, missed birthdays, lapsed anniversaries, in the interests of what is supposed to be a 'labour of love'.

FOREWORD

by Air Vice-Marshal J.E. ('Johnnie') Johnson, CB, CBE, DSO & 2 bars, DFC & bar, C. Eng,
Belgian Order of Leopold and Croix de Guerre, American Legion of Merit, DFC and Air Medal

In this splendid book Rob Davis, a fluent storyteller, writes about 'that awful time between briefing and take-off' and I well remember that feeling which I experienced one winter's afternoon long ago at Scampton, the big bomber base in Lincolnshire.

At that time my Squadron (616) was also based in Lincolnshire and on that particular day the Kirton Rugby XV had bussed down the old Roman road to take on the bomber boys. It was a bright, cold afternoon and as we drove to the rugger pitch we could see lots of airmen servicing the big Lancaster bombers and long bomb trolleys delivering their lethal weapons. We knew that operations were 'on' that night.

After tea we were invited to attend the Station Commander's briefing given by a well-decorated Group Captain and as he spoke about the long sea crossings, the target, the flak belts and enemy fighters one could sense the tension building-up in that crowded briefing room. Afterwards the crews split up for more specialist briefings for navigators, bomb aimers, air gunners and wireless operators. Thus, the crews had known for hours that once again they would be facing the perils of the night. How vastly different from our fighter world when we sat comfortably in our dispersal hut, reading or writing, and were airborne within two minutes of the call from ops.

Since that day at Scampton I have often thought about what powerful force made the bomber boys press on, sometimes for second and third tours, each of thirty or so missions, where a man stood one chance in three of surviving one tour.

At the end of his first tour Leonard Cheshire wrote: 'From now on, I'm just a has-been; from now on, I've got to sit in the background and live on memories, because never again will I be able to capture the companionship and confidence of men like these...'*

'Of arms, and the man I sing,' wrote Virgil in his great epic about love and war — the very core of human experience; and it was love of their crews that drew back Leonard Cheshire, Guy Gibson, Micky Martin, Gus Walker and their gallant company, some to fly 100-plus missions. The bomber squadron was, indeed, their family and their home and their crews were very close. Flying together gave them tremendous faith in each other. They trusted each other. The squadron and the crews called them back, and when these brave, resolute Wing Commanders and Squadron Leaders returned to the fray and led by example, others followed, and it was at this level that the real leadership in Bomber Command was to be found.

Above:
J. E. ('Johnnie') Johnson.
Douglas Glass

Johnnie Johnson signature

* Leonard Cheshire, *Bomber Pilot* (Hutchinson, London, 1943)

'Johnnie' Johnson, though a fighter pilot by profession, has always held the bomber boys in the highest regard, as expressed in his own excellent books on air warfare; hence our request to him to write the Foreword for this volume, to which he so kindly agreed.

He joined the RAFVR as a weekend flyer in 1939, was mobilised as soon as war was declared, and completed flying training in time to join his first squadron (Spitfires) as the Battle of Britain was ending. Apart from one six-month rest period, he was to continue to fly Spitfires on operations right across Europe to Berlin until VE-Day, by when he had risen to the rank of Group Captain, leading his own large wing of fighters.

He was to finish the war as the top-scoring Allied fighter ace in Europe with 38 confirmed victories, and very highly decorated. He opted to stay in the RAF postwar, despite having to drop back initially to

relatively lowly rank. When the Korean War started in 1950, he was on an exchange posting with the USAF in Tokyo, and was soon back on ops, flying twin-engined A-26 Invaders on reconnaissance and fighter-bomber missions, before returning to the RAF to command a squadron of Sabre jet fighters in Germany. He again rose to the rank of Group Captain and found himself on bombers, as a station commander in the early days of the 'V' Force, one of his tasks being to instil fighter-type quick reaction to alerts, and reduce the hours normally required to get bombers airborne down to minutes.

Subsequently achieving the rank of Air Vice-Marshal, 'Johnnie' Johnson retired from the RAF in March 1966 as AOC Air Forces Middle East. Now living happily in retirement in deepest Derbyshire, he is still very active in the aviation field as writer, speaker and presence at special events. Truly a living legend.

GLOSSARY

AA	Anti-aircraft
A&AEE	Aircraft & Armament Experimental Establishment
AFC	Air Force Cross
A/G	Air Gunner
Airborne Cigar (ABC)	Listening/Jamming Device
Ammo	Ammunition
AOC	Air Officer Commanding
ASR	Air-Sea Rescue
AUW	All up weight
AVM	Air Vice-Marshal
AWOL	Absent without leave
Bf	Alternative designation for Messerschmitt (eg Bf109)
Bind	Nuisance/chore
Bod	Real person. Short for body
Boomerang	An aircraft that returns without dropping its bombs. Also referred to as an early return
Bull	Nonsense. Nonsensical orders
Bumph	Printed papers, orders. Vulgarly said to be fit only for toilet paper!
Cans	Incendiary clusters mounted in boxes/cans
CGM	Conspicuous Gallantry Medal
Circuits and bumps	Flights around the aerodrome and landings performed over and over again by way of practice
Civvy street	Civilian life
Con	Conversion
Cookie	4,000lb blast bomb
CO	Commanding Officer
Corkscrew	Evasive manouevre
Cpl	Corporal
CU	Conversion Unit
DF	Direction Finding
DFC	Distinguished Flying Cross
DFM	Distinguished Flying Medal
DI	Daily Inspection
DRC	Distant Reading Compass
DSO	Distinguished Service Order
ENSA	Entertainment National Services Association
Erk	An aircraftman. Any airman below Corporal rank
ETA	Estimated time of arrival
Fido	Fog clearance system
Fishpond	Fighter warning device
Flg Off	Flying Officer
'Flight'	Flight Sergeant
Flt Lt	Flight Lieutenant
Flt Sgt	Flight Sergeant
FTR	Failed to return
Funnels	Final approach path
Fw	Focke-Wulf
Gee	Navigation aid
Gen	Reliable information
G-H	Navigation/bombing aid
Gong	Medal, decoration
Goose-neck	Paraffin runway lighting flare
GP	General purpose
George	Auto pilot
Greaser	'Three pointer' landing when all three wheels land simultaneously
Gremlins	Mythical mischievous genus of creature, specially invented by the RAF as the cause of anything that goes wrong
Groupie	Group Captain
H_2S	Navigation/bombing aid
Hairy-do	Occurrence that has serious consequences or just escapes them. Also known as a Shaky-Do or Dicey-Do
Halley/Hallies	Handley Page Halifax heavy bomber

HCU	Heavy Conversion Unit
I/C	In charge
IFF	Identification Friend or Foe
LFS	Lancaster Finishing School
Lobbing in	Originally a landing for emergency reasons but extended to cover any unexpected landing
M/B	Master bomber
Me	Messerschmitt
Monica	Fighter warning device
MR	Maritime Reconnaissance
MT	Motor Transport
MU	Maintenance Unit
NAAFI	Navy, Army and Air Force Institutes
NCO	Non-Commissioned Officer
NFT	Night Flying Test
Nissen	Hut of easily-erected type. Originated by Canadian mining engineer Lt-Col P.N.Nissen
Oboe	Navigation/bombing aid
OC	Officer Commanding
OCU	Operational Conversion Unit
OTU	Operation Training Unit
PFF	Path Finder Force
Pit	Bed
Plt Off	Pilot Officer
POW	Prisoner of War
Prang	To damage, destroy, wreck
QFE	Barometric pressure for ground level at airfield
RAAF	Royal Australian Air Force
RAF	Royal Air Force
RCAF	Royal Canadian Air Force
RNZAF	Royal New Zealand Air Force
R/T	Radio Telephone
'Sarg'	Sergeant
Scrub	To eliminate, wash out, cancel
'Second dickey'	Pilot, usually new to operations, flying with a seasoned crew
Sgt	Sergeant
SHQ	Station headquarters
Snag	Defect
SNCO	Senior non-commissioned officer
SOC	Struck off charge
S of TT	School of Technical Training
Sprog	Originally any airman under training but extended to anyone raw or inexperienced
Sqn Ldr	Squadron Leader
TAS/IAS	True airspeed/Indicated airspeed
TI	Target indicator
Tiger Force	Bomber group scheduled to operate against Japan
'Tinsel/Tinselling'	The code name given for the transmission of engine noise to block-out radio transmissions.
USAAF	United States Army Air Force
U/S	Unserviceable
VC	Victoria Cross
VHF	Very high frequency
WAAF	Women's Auxiliary Air Force
Wangle	A fiddle in a mild sort of way. Bypassing the system
WFU	Withdrawn from use
Wg Cdr	Wing Commander
'Window'	Strips of foil to confuse enemy radar (also known as 'Tinsel')
Wingco	Wing Commander
WO	Warrant Officer
W/op	Wireless operator
W/T	Wireless/Telephone
WVS	Women's Voluntary Service (now WRVS)
Y-run	Cross-country training flight using H_2S radar

THEY WHO KNEW AS ONLY THEY COULD KNOW

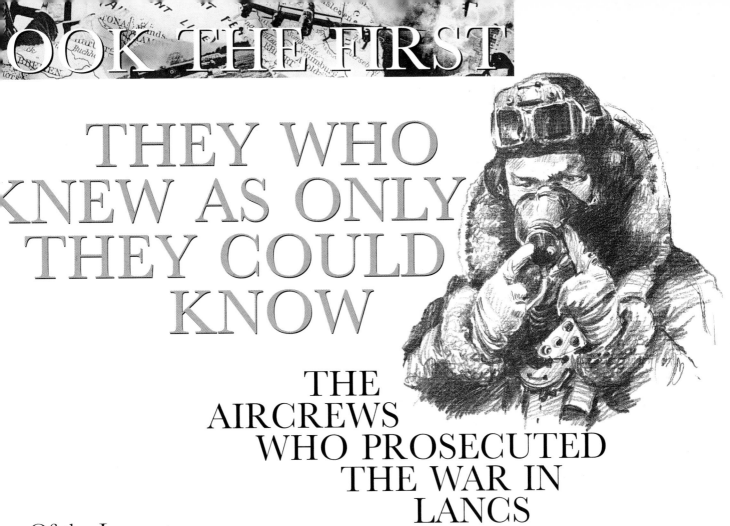

THE AIRCREWS WHO PROSECUTED THE WAR IN LANCS

Of the Lancaster:

This emergency design turned out to be without exception the finest bomber of the war. Its efficiency was almost incredible, both in performance and in the way in which it could be saddled with ever-increasing loads without breaking the camel's back. It is astonishing that so small an aircraft as the Lancaster could so easily take the enormous 22,000lb 'Grand Slam' bomb, a weapon which no other could… carry. The Lancaster far surpassed all the other types of heavy bomber.

Not only could it take heavier bomb loads, not only was it easier to handle, and not only were there fewer accidents with this than with other types; throughout the war the casualty rate on Lancasters was also consistently below that of other types. It is true that in 1944 the wastage of Lancasters from casualties became equal to, and at times even greater than, the wastage of Halifaxes, but this was the exception that proved the rule; at that time I invariably used Lancasters alone for those attacks which involved the deepest penetration into Germany and were consequently the most dangerous.

The Lancaster was so far the best aircraft we had that I continually pressed for its production at the expense of other types… The superiority of the Lancaster also had its effect on our policy in training and the conversion of crews to heavy bombers. I wanted all the Lancasters I could get in the front line, and this meant we had to use Halifaxes and Stirlings for the greater part of the training in the heavy conversion units, with only a brief course at a Lancaster finishing school, as it was called, at the end; in this way large numbers of Lancasters were saved for operations, though at the expense, which was well worthwhile, of some increase in the time taken to train Lancaster crews…'

AITKEN

Of the aircrew regardless of which aircraft they flew:

'...There are no words with which I can do justice to the aircrew who fought under my command. There is no parallel in warfare to such courage and determination in the face of danger over so prolonged a period, of danger which at times was so great that scarcely one man in three could expect to survive his tour of thirty operations; this is what a casualty rate of 5% on each of these thirty operations would have meant, and during the whole of 1942 the casualty rate was 4.1%. Of those who survived their first tour of operations,

between six and seven thousand undertook a second, and many a third, tour. It was, moreover, a clear and highly conscious courage, by which the risk was taken with calm forethought, for the aircrew were all highly skilled men, much above the average in education, who had to understand every aspect and detail of their task. It was, furthermore, the courage of the small hours, of men virtually alone, for at his battle station the airman is virtually alone. It was the courage of men with long-drawn apprehensions of daily 'going over the top'. They were without exception volunteers, for no man was trained for aircrew with the RAF who did not volunteer for this. Such devotion must never be forgotten. It is unforgettable by anyone whose contacts gave them knowledge and understanding of what these young men experienced and faced...'

Who said such eloquent, telling words? He who knew more than anyone: Sir Arthur T. Harris, C-in-C Bomber Command from February 1942 to September 1945, in his classic *Bomber Offensive* published by Collins in 1947. As was confirmed during a well-remembered afternoon spent in his company at his home in leafy Goring-on-Thames one Sunday in 1980, he never wavered in his views, his conviction.

Here follow a series of essays and cameos which, it is hoped, will give a wider public a feel for what it was like to fly in Lancasters, by day as well as by night, the threat of total oblivion ever present.

"THE SPARKLERS"

Charles Cuthill

How quiet the night seems. Germany lies below us under the cloak of darkness and outside, nothing definite can be seen except the stars. We (the crew of Lancaster 'Dog') work in a world of our own.

It is lonely in the nose. The instruments in the unlit cockpit glow coldly. Even the engineer's presence at my side is of little comfort, because we do not talk — no one is talking — but I can feel the reassuring swings of the gunners' turrets. I think of the other crews out there, somewhere in the night — navigating hard, to keep the thousand-bomber stream compact. Our lives depend on it.

Instinctively I watch the instruments which help me to control our aircraft's path, and feed the indicated corrections to the pedals and wheel. I rarely use 'George' — I want to be occupied with the act of flying, and be ready to make a quick manoeuvre... having to disconnect 'George' takes time — time enough to get shot down.

Our wings rock with a startling suddenness — it wakes us up. A plane (one of ours, I tell myself) has left a slipstream in our path. But the thoughts of collision do not worry me, because the more slipstreams we meet, the more confident I am that we are making-good our track – and, anyway, it's so pleasant to have company.

We crossed the Channel an hour ago, flying at a thousand feet, just beneath a 10/10ths cloud-layer. The navigation lights had shone around us everywhere, in a confusion of reds, whites and greens, and I had held station on the white tail-lights ahead. With all those lights, any stray late-comer (or an enemy fighter) could have joined the stream easily.

As we approached the French coast, the navigation lights were switched off and only the nearest aircraft could be seen silhouetted in the dusk. Soon these aircraft, too, became hidden by the night. Since then, we have been navigating on our own... but one set of lights had remained shining. Whether the pilot had forgotten to put the lights out, or had left them on for fear of collision, I do not know. Eventually we saw them no more.

On crossing the coast, we continued to fly low to avoid being detected by the German early-warning radar. We were heading for

the hills (you couldn't see them), and I waited for the navigator to tell me to climb — but on the ground ahead, two large flashes made me pull up early and we went into cloud. I let down again, wondering if the flashes had been caused by aircraft hitting the hills, and continued to fly as low as I safely dared... it only needed one plane flying high for a radar to sound the alert.

Then started the long slow climb to bombing height and we had quickly entered cloud — which was a sanctuary from fighters, perhaps, but not from the watching radars. By now, to upset the radars' vision, every bomber would be scattering 'window' — a fluttering carpet of strips of foil — and, because of it, only the stream's stragglers would have been 'seen' clearly.

At 10,000 feet, we broke cloud and saw the stars. At 18,000 feet, I thought I could see the ground in places. Old 'Dog' had been reluctant to go higher so I had levelled off; and soon — after crossing the 'bomb-line' — we were into enemy territory.

"Navigator to pilot." The voice intrudes on my loneliness. "Turning Point in three minutes. Next course, 108."

"108," I repeat.

A ribbon of light shines over my right shoulder as the navigator gently moves the blackout curtain. Taking the slip of paper he hands me, I turn on the cockpit lighting and read: '108°. ETA 2115.' Then I reset the DRC repeater needle, ready for the next leg, and compare the new course with the one already marked on my 'Captains of aircraft map.'

"Time's up, Skip. Turn on to 108," calls the navigator.

Rolling out on to the new course, I wait a moment, then check the course against the magnetic compass.

"That's OK, Skip," confirms the navigator, having checked his repeater reading. If he catches me flying more than a couple of degrees off, he'll have my guts.

Relaxing a little, I search the sky as continuously as accurate flying will allow. The stars reach to the horizon — but searching is like looking at nothing to find something... I think that the cloud is clearing below us.

I thought I saw a gleam of red. It was ahead and below, slightly to starboard. There it is again! A dull red flash, shining through low cloud or fog... it seems to be stationary on the ground.

The light is clearer now, and closer. It's occulting. I tell the crew what I see, and point out the light to the engineer... I get the feeling that we're drifting off to starboard and that we're going to pass nearer to the light than we need to.

"Is it an airfield ident beacon or a fighter beacon?" I ask the navigator.

"We weren't told about either at the briefing," he replies irritably, "— but tell me when it's abeam and I'll log it."

"OK nav. Can we spare the WOP for the astrodome?"

"Hell, No! He's 'tinselling' — and there's a broadcast-wind in a minute or two."

"Pilot to bomb aimer. Get into the astrodome quickly and watch out for fighters!"

The bomb aimer comes scrambling through — under the engineer's seat — into the navigator's compartment, and sends a blaze of light into the cockpit.

"Christ — the curtain!" I yell. But I only deafen myself and the rest of us — the bomb aimer's off intercom.

"Pilot to engineer. Take over 'windowing' will you — till that beacon's out of sight."

Wink... wink... wink... — the light pulses out into the deep pool of darkness; and slowly we come to the beacon. To keep it in sight, I lean across the empty engineer's seat and the flashes seem to be saying: "There's no escape... no escape... no escape..." Suddenly I feel that we are going to be carried — in one great vortex — around and down towards the beacon.

Shit, it's only a stupid little light! ...

"Pilot to navigator. The beacon's abeam to starboard — about ten miles."

The navigator says he'll log it. Then he tells me I'm flying twenty-five degrees off-course to starboard. Hell, there might be a dozen fighters orbiting that beacon, waiting for orders to kill! and tonight, they could catch our silhouette amongst the stars... I just happen to be looking for fighters, that's all — and he just happens to be sitting in his office wondering what bloody course I'm steering. I'm ready to 'Corkscrew' — fighters may be coming at us any time now!

The beacon is out of sight behind the engines and wing, but the mid-upper and bomb aimer still see it. I start to dip each wing in turn — twenty degrees left, twenty degrees right — so that the mid-upper can see directly below (Oh for a mid-under gun!). The navigator complains that my manoeuvrings will put us off track. I tell him that the swings will cancel out... I reckon he's worried the lurchings will make him sick.

Now the rear gunner can see the beacon, and I only bank when the mid-upper asks me — I don't want an airsick crew tonight.

18,700 feet. I am letting old 'Dog' creep up. She's a crummy high-flyer, and we need all the height we can get for the target. The bomb aimer is 'windowing' again, down in the nose; whilst the engineer has checked the engines and fuel and made up his log.

So I call up the crew to check their intercom and oxygen. All is well... "Navigator to pilot. Turn on to 088, we're drifting off to starboard!"

"088," I confirm, and turn on to it willingly.

The navigator is worrying: his Gee set is being jammed. "I'll have to take some astro, Skip," he says: "there's too much 'grass' now, for a Gee-fix. By the way — we should be coming to a defended area out to starboard, in twenty minutes. Tell me if you see it."

I affirm — settling down to fly as accurately as I can for the next few minutes, to provide a steady base for the navigator's star sights.

"OK, Skip. I'm in the astrodome. Are you ready?"

"Ready, nav." I concentrate, to fly the instruments... if I slip or skid, so will the bubble in his sextant and he'll get a dubious reading..."I've finished, Skip. Relax!" The navigator — he never stops working from take-off to landing — will go back to his table, and work out and plot the sights. With luck, the fix will be accurate to within five to ten miles.

I join the engineer in resuming my scan. We look out into the darkness: ahead and above, to the side, and down... you often catch things more clearly out the corner of your eye — but you must keep them moving! Occasionally, for reassurance, we glance across at the flickering blue glow from the shrouded exhausts. A fighter can home on them... now and again the port-inner gives a pop of yellow flame.

"Navigator to pilot, we're back on track. Turn on to 098 degrees."

I acknowledge, and the navigator says: "Can you get another five miles an hour out of her, we're nearly a minute late?"

"I'll try," I tell him.

We have increased speed and the engineer has completed his log. There'll be enough fuel. I fiddle with the pitch levers, trying to get the engines to run with an even beat... and I think of the streaks of oil and coolant that I saw on the engine cowlings before darkness fell. How far will the streaks reach back now, I wonder?

There's a yellow glow off the starboard bow, a little higher than we are. It hangs in the sky. The glow brightens into a wide circle of light.

Suddenly, another glow... and another and another. They parallel

Below:
TYPICAL

'...It's so pleasant to have company...'

Charles Cuthill and crew line up in front of a spanking-new No 149 'East India' Sqn Lancaster at Methwold, accompanied by the ground staff responsible for keeping their aircraft serviceable.

Completing the Lancaster Finishing School course at Feltwell (3 LFS), the Cuthill septet had a surprise in store, and no little disappointment, on being posted next door to the squadron (No 149) at Methwold: disappointed, because they wanted a change of scenery; surprised, because they knew the squadron had Stirlings. Despite the several Stirlings standing around the edge of Methwold airfield on one wheel and a wingtip when they arrived, and after having to convince the flight commander checking him out that it was possible, with all the confidence of the Skipper's 400hr, to make a three-point landing in a Stirling (the squadron did wheelers), they went ahead and enjoyed what were to be their last flights on this aircraft type. They were to practise their first G-H runs on Ely cathedral. These squadron Stirlings were very different from the battered ones in use at HCU. But even the squadron Stirlings, as far as they were concerned, lived up to their HCU name. On their very last Stirling trip (9 September 1944) they had to

spend 45min circling the drome — the crew winding everything down — before landing. They never operated on Stirlings.

Cuthill's ego was put back a place when the first of the new Lancs arrived. He watched a flurry of red lips and long blonde hair up in the cockpit, and then, after tidying-up time, out stepped two(!) beautiful ATA ferry girls, though Charles never got to meet them for he was but a sergeant pilot! In common with his contemporaries, he had got into the habit of believing that it needed the whole crew to fly an aeroplane!

Baptism of action for the Cuthill complement was a daylight mounted against Cap Gris Nez on 26 September 1944; final offensive sortie was Ludwigshafen on 5th January 1945, also in daylight.

Known identities in our picture (mid-January 1945) are: (left to right)

Rear:
Ground crew? Mid-upper gunner: Sgt Dick Clarke,
Pilot: Flt Lt Charlie Cuthill, Bomb aimer: Flt Sgt Ron Finch,
Wireless operator: Flt Sgt 'Paddy' Fowles, Rear gunner: Sgt Ernie Wilkinson, Flight engineer: Sgt Sam Small,
Front:
Navigator: FS Ken Crawford, RAAF, Corporal I/C ground crew: Cpl Kay? Ground crew? Ground crew?
C. R. Cuthill

our track and light up the sky like a street.

"Fighter flares to starboard!" I yell. "If they're coming, it'll be from port."

I start gently weaving the aircraft from side to side — trying to present an ever-moving target — and at the same time I steadily gain height, then lose it. The navigator says we'll soon be off track again if we continue this jinking. I tell him to 'Wrap up!' as I'm waiting and listening — ready to slam on full aileron and rudder, if a gunner calls 'Corkscrew, port. Go!' (Then, my jinking would become a much more violent affair.)..."

The flares are behind us now, sinking on their parachutes. They brighten, momentarily, then burn out. I stop the jinking when the sky is in darkness again. At briefing they told us we might see some night-fighter 'Mossies,' or even a 'Fort'. Why worry about Jerry?

A column of brilliant white light stabs at the darkness. It points straight at the sky. The brilliance doesn't dim with height — but, above us, it shuts off as if cut with a knife.

"Pilot to crew. Searchlight ahead to starboard — about ten miles! Is that the defended area, nav?"

"Too right!" he says. "I was wondering when we'd see it."

I note the relief in his voice, but I tell him that I think we are off track to starboard again.

The beam begins to swing about — searching. Then, suddenly, it comes toppling towards us like a falling pillar... the light is blinding. I duck down. When I look out again, the beam is back to the vertical. I pray hard that it will stay there.

As we come under the sweep of its arc, the searchlight's beam towers into the night. It is holding steady, like a cat waiting to pounce... but now that we're close, what if it comes swinging towards us again? The ache in my chest is growing. I'll not hold this course much longer...

If it swings towards us, I'll turn away and dive like hell. If it catches us in the dive, I'll turn starboard and zoom... and if it holds on to us and there isn't any flak, I'll expect fighters and corkscrew like hell. And if we're coned, in flak?... (I reckon I'd pull up to lose speed — then roll her over and pull through!)

"Nav. When it's abeam, how far should we be from the defended area?" I ask.

"Fifteen miles."

"I reckon we'll only be three or four. I'm turning port."

"No, hold it!" he counters — he is breathless from calculating — "I'll have a new course worked out in a jiffy."

The beam is dipping away from us. Then suddenly, frighteningly, it sweeps into our half of the sky and stops. A bomber — like a moth in candle-light — is held two-thirds of the way up the beam. Instantly, a dozen fingers of criss-crossing light clutch at the yellow-lit wings. The bomber flies alongside us to starboard; and the cone of lights, holding its victim, leans along with us.

The cone is flattening as the bomber tries to fly out of it. There is a flash, and the plane has disappeared... it could have been us!

In the lights, hangs a thin vertical smoke-trail and the burst of an explosion. Then — except for the original one — the searchlights are dowsed.

"Hey, did you see that, Skip?" says the WOP from the astrodome: "There wasn't any flak."

"The fighters got him," continues the mid-upper. But the navigator is trying to make himself heard above the chat, so I yell, "QUIET!"

"Thank you, Skipper," says the navigator. "Please turn on to 060 degrees for the next turning point."

Silence, at last...

I look back at the solitary searchlight. The beam is swinging around — like a kid with a torch — probing, to 'flick over' another victim. Hell, I've started to spiral... you can't fly along steadily, looking backwards: but I'm so happy to see that searchlight behind us.

There is a continual rushing sound over the intercom. A mike-switch left on — and more! The navigator has a habit of loosening his oxygen mask, to cool his face as he works. He does it without thinking; and the bomb aimer, the engineer, and the WOP — all know to keep a check on him. I have seen him, plotting like hell,

AITKEN

with his mask unclipped and dangling — and us, flying way above the 10,000 foot level (where we are supposed to be on oxygen)... soon — before he passes out on us — he'll be starting to make numerous miscalculations.

"Switch off your mike and tighten your mask, however it is!" That is all I say. There is the sound of clunking, fumbling and mumbling. And, a final Click! then silence...

"Rear gunner to pilot — they've put the searchlight out!"

Apart from the stars there's not a light to be seen. The navigator asks the bomb aimer if he can identify the turning point visually. The bomb aimer can't, so the navigator decides to turn on ETA.

"Navigator to pilot — turn on to 045. Target in fifteen minutes..."

"Here's the can, Skip." The bomb aimer (for my relief) dutifully passes the battered old tin... I've often wondered what he does with the contents. One day I'll ask him.

We are bombing with the second wave at H hour plus six minutes. Our height: 19,000 feet — with the engine-revs set at the top of the cruising range — and that's the highest 'Old Dog's' ever been with a bomb load. She's wallowy. The engineer turns up the oxygen supply and I check the intercom and oxygen with each of the crew... the mid-upper's electrical heating in his flying suit has packed up. I tell him to let me know when he's starting to freeze — but he'll have to stay where he is until we've bombed.

"H hour in three minutes," says the navigator.

The bomb aimer is prone in the nose, carrying out the final checks to his bombing gear; and somewhere ahead in the darkness lies the target.

"Good Luck, blokes!" I call to the crew.

In the distance, slightly to port, a cluster of soft green flares beings to burn on the ground.

"Pilot to crew, the target indicators are down!"

"Huh! Thirty seconds early — PFF must be slipping," says the navigator, almost to himself.

Above the flares and level with us, appears a thin wavering line of bright yellow lights. The lights twinkle like sparklers. The flak has started! Now the green flares have been centred with reds, and seconds later the flares are surrounded by mushrooming flashes. The flashing increases with a vicious intensity and fires are beginning to glow. All the time we are getting closer...

"Target in three minutes!" calls the navigator.

"Pilot to engineer. Twenty-eight fifty." As the engineer brings up the revs, filling the cockpit with sound, I move the throttles back to maintain the airspeed.

I sense the coming barrage... straight through is the safest way. No search-lights yet! My mouth is dry with remembered fear...

"Bomb aimer to pilot. Bombs fused and selected, camera's set. Everything OK. Target sighted... Left, left — twenty degrees!"

"Left, twenty."

The air is filling with flashes around us. My hands are locked to the wheel, so tight that I notice... Christ, what's that carpet of yellow flares for?

"Twenty degrees LEFT, skipper!" the bomb aimer reminds me… it's not that I'd forgotten.

"Make it thirty!"… the target, with growing pools of fire, is disappearing under the nose and the sky has turned crimson.

"Bomb doors open!" says the bomb aimer. his voice has a calm urgency.

"Bomb doors open!" I reply — my left hand moves the lever… the ritual between him and me has begun. the rest of the crew must wait in torment.

"Left… left," he continues — and I'm turning the wheel…

"Steady," he calls again. We are hitting turbulent patches from those ahead — and I'm struggling to keep us level.

"S-T-E-A-D-Y!"… this time it's almost a reprimand.

Rocking, bumping… the smell of explosion, stabs of light… BANG! — I look up. Flak bursting with orange flame — it was right against us! Christ… and there's a Lanc ahead in the target glow. It slips across our bows, amongst the flashes and smoke, and dips out of sight — then I'm fighting the controls again. Please God, just this once… let's get through!

"Right… right. Steady!" the bomb aimer is calling… "Shit, we can't bomb, there's a Halifax below us! No, he's turning… steady… s-t-e-a-d-y… BOMBS AWAY!"

Thump, thump, thump, thump… as each bomb leaves, my heart (with the aeroplane) grows lighter.

"Bombs away! Bomb doors closed," the bomb aimer calls.

"Closing bomb doors," I reply. Keep her straight, for the blasted photo!… sweat in my eyes. Suddenly in the light of the target, like a ghost-turning to come head-on… "There's a 109 just gone underneath us!" I yell to the crew.

The mid-upper has seen the Messerschmitt pull up out of sight. "It's too hot for him down here," he says.

"Photo taken… bomb bay's clear, jettison bars across," calls the bomb aimer: "That's it, Skipper!"

Already I'm turning left, banking steeply and opening the throttles. She's as light and eager to go as we are… we cross over a silhouetted Lanc.

The rear gunner yells: "There's a flamer over the target!… "and one blew up behind us on the run-in," adds the mid-upper. Why don't they shut up…

We descend towards the edge of darkness… homeward, at last.

A big searchlight has lit-up ahead of us to starboard. The beam is shining across our track at a low angle — and it bars the way home. Blast! I warn the crew, and level off from the descent.

To fly round the beam will take time; waste fuel; force us off track — and we'll lose the protection of the stream. I elect to hold our height and course. I hope the rest of the stream is doing the same.

We seem to be approaching the beam so slowly that I increase speed; but the beam just keeps leaning — unmoving. It hasn't moved since we first saw it… but don't move now: or if you do — swing across to another part of the sky! I feel like a thief in the night, wanting to tread, tiptoe. Suddenly the beam is swinging towards us.

Too quick for thought: I lock the wheel over and slam on full-rudder… 'Old Dog' is standing on her port wing-tip, momentarily-suspended over a huge river of silver light.

"They're trying to cone us. I'm going to dive!"

Our nose comes swinging down. The edge of the ray spills into the darkness… night is becoming day. Brighter. The brilliance is hurting! I don't know what is happening, except there is light and I pray for darkness… and we're falling, falling — dazzled and disorientated… then we're through into black space.

Christ, the throttles. I fumble them closed…

Then I'm pulling like hell at the wheel: both hands!

Trim back — she's settling into the dive… more trim. Keep pulling! I see target-fires through the canopy top, moving downwards towards the nose… there's a lot of 'g' now. She's going to come out (if she doesn't break up, first)!

The gyro-instruments are tumbling, so I level the wings on the fires. Then out of the glow comes a Lanc —sliding sideways and upwards towards us. And, as I try to pull the wheel back harder, the

Lanc disappears full-size under the nose, with a 'KER-THUMP!'

We are nearly flying level again: I can tell by the position of the target-fires through the windscreen. I turn up the cockpit lighting, to counter the dazzle left in my eyes. The airspeed indicator is reading 305 and I wait for us to slow down. No one has spoken since I started the dive… how quiet it is. Christ, the engines — I throttled them back! I re-check the speed, then slowly open the throttles… all four engines are running correctly. We need to get the target behind us again as quickly as possible.

Height, 10,400 feet. Turning, now: away from the light towards darkness. The 'artificial horizon' has toppled; and we swing and pitch as I struggle to make it, using the 'turn and slip' indicator… Paddy, in the astrodome, breaks the silence: "Hey, Skip — Didn't we hit a Lanc, back there?"

"I think it was slipstream — I'll get the engineer to check… just let me get back on to course, first."

When I straighten up from the turn, the searchlight is out.

"Pilot to navigator: we're back on course. I'll stay at this height till we're clear of the searchlight. Then I'll climb and rejoin the stream."

"Pilot to engineer. Do your flak-damage check now, and take a good look at our underside. See if we had a collision!"

"Roger, Skip… when it happened, I thought the wings had come off."

"I think we only hit his slipstream."

"No Sir," butts in Paddy. "We hit him!"

"Well, did anyone see what happened to the other Lanc?" I query. Nobody did… the engineer climbs back into his seat. He says he didn't see any damage.

High in the sky to port, a tiny pin-point of light has started to glow. The glow intensifies and becomes fan-shaped. Then it begins falling to earth, leaving a trail of flame…

"Navigator to pilot. You are clear to start climbing."

"Roger, nav — climbing, now."

"Pilot to engineer — twenty-eight fifty, plus nine. Let's get back to the stream and have a hot cup of coffee."

THROUGH ALL THIS TIME

C. R. Cuthill

'…I began to wonder if it had really taken place as I had once described it…' *

Charles Cuthill in reflective mood. One of a surprising number of Halton brats (boy apprentices) who graduated to the ranks of aircrew, he was a 21-year-old sergeant pilot with 403hr 45min of flying behind him when he and his complement of six like-NCOs arrived at Methwold as August was giving way to September 1944.

His log book showed a total of 564hr (of which 125hr were operational — 90hr day; 35hr night) when he left there a day or so after January 1945, by now an acting Flight Lieutenant.

Staying in the service postwar, he retired with effect from 12 May 1961, having added an AFC to his DFC.

* Writing in November 1994 on re-reading his impressions penned more years ago than he cared to remember.

Above:
The Author, Charles Cuthill, pictured early in 1995

TO REAP THE WHIRLWIND

'...Thump, thump, thump, thump... as each bomb leaves, my heart (with the aeroplane) grows lighter...'

Now here's a poser. How many hours... how much effort... how many individuals do you suppose were involved in seeing to it that each squadron of Lancs took part in any bombing raid called for by the powers-that-be?

How many hours... how much effort... how many individuals do you reckon had a hand in supporting 156,308 Lancaster sorties? For that is the figure the statisticians came up with when the facts relating to the war effort were assembled in mind-boggling detail.

Impressive as that total of 156,308 was — near enough 60% of Bomber Command's 261,157 sorties undertaken by its heavy brigade — grasp the fact that Lancs dropped an estimated total of 608,612 tons of munitions of all types — around two-thirds of the Command's 955,044 total tonnage. But what of the effort in human terms? No trade put in more graft, more dedication, more devotion to duty than did the armourers whose task it was to prepare and load those 608,612 tons of bombs, incendiaries, ammo, etc. Let us look in on some of those armourers and their charges.

TO THE ARMOURERS

How often have you sat at home
And heard on the news at nine
That our bombers have raided districts
On and around the Rhine?
And have you thought as you sat there
In the comfort of your easy chair
Of all the blokes who never fly
And so unnoticed get passed by?

No wings or brevets on their breast
In ragged blue they do their best
To load the bombs and fill the guns
To blast the daylight from the Huns.
A job of danger, a job of skill,
The power the aircrews need to kill.

So to the Armourers let us raise
A handshake true and a word of praise
And when victory comes to this fair land
Don't just forget that scruffy band.

Anon

Opposite top:
Here, a part of one bomb dump on one aerodrome on one day in one month in one year spent humping and winching and carting the wares of war, which were the responsibility of armourers. For once, the sun shines at Middleton St George sometime in 1944 as a David Brown tractor driver waits patiently for a train of bomb trolleys to be loaded. Nothing and no one moved quickly in a bomb dump. The very nature of their job precluded that.
If once there was camouflage netting, there is no sign of any now the risk of German attacks has receded.
L. Horne via J. L. Armitage

Opposite centre left:
Moving south several counties from No 6 Group territory let us drop in at Little Staughton (near Bedford), one of the westernmost Lancaster bases, a pathfinder station in No 8 Group, and observe No 582 Sqn preparations for a raid. High capacity (HC) 2,000lb bombs, soon to be loaded, look positively sinister. Move on in time two score years and ten and the technical site, here visible in the background, is still recognisable, and the airfield is still in use by light aircraft.
J. D. Garrick

Opposite centre right:
Consider yourself fortunate you are not an armourer having to load 1,000lb medium capacity bombs into No 156 Sqn's Lancs at rain-soaked Warboys, February 1944.
Only those who were there, working on open dispersals for hour after hour, day after day, or night after night, can know the agonies of chapped lips, fingers and ears and feet without feeling; battling against lung-choking mist or fog, or freezing rain, or snow.
Note how frail the bomb trolley and bomb carriers appear.
W. L. Bagg

Opposite bottom:
Middleton St George again, with much of the clutter to be found on and around any dispersal on any day well in evidence. A wheel chock...a can...engine cowlings...a trolley acc'...a Nissen hut...all set the scene so well. Not yet identified are the men in view, the Lanc X from either No 419 'Moose' or its companion Canadian outfit, No 428 'Ghost' Sqn. The load? Nearest to the tractor is a 4,000lb Cookie blast bomb; foreground are 500lb medium capacity (MC) bombs; barely visible are incendiaries being fitted to their carriers.
L. Horne via J. L. Armitage

Opposite inset:
As anyone who has served in HM Forces will tell you, every item of equipment had a number, be it the humblest washer or a complete Lancaster. What is more it had to be signed for innumerable times during its service life. To think that every bomb aimer had to sign for the privilege of dropping his deadly cargo, having first completed a bombing chit like this one, among several such keepsakes taken home to Canada by Harry Lindhorst and soon lost to view as he put his recent past behind him and looked to his future. Harry served with No 115 Sqn at Witchford and to this day keeps in touch with English wireless operator Sam Wood and fellow Canuck, ex-mid-upper Orville Blouin. Pilot Bill Burnett, also Canadian, along with others from a crew of two Brits and five from the land of the maple leaf flag have long since lost contact.
H. Lindhorst

Above left:
Mindful of the part Lancasters played in the unceasing sea-mining campaign here we see one of the so-called 'vegetables', each weighing 1,500lb, being loaded on to a trolley at Syerston, late October/early November 1942, prior to a 'gardening' sortie, as the minelaying trips were known. Syerston then housed Nos 61 and 106 Sqns, both of whose crews frequently took aloft representatives of the Royal Navy, one of whom is pictured in the foreground to our picture. Also worth a mention is the WAAF tractor driver. Popperfoto

Right:
MUSCLEMAN
'..."Bomb bay's clear, jettison bars across", calls the bomb aimer...'

Big though the Lanc was by the standards of the day, the fuselage was of narrow width with not an inch of space wasted. As the picture clearly illustrates, armourers, positioned above the bomb bay, had little room for manoeuvre. It was a back-aching task and most bombing-up teams operated a rota system whereby armourers took it in turn to manhandle the winches or guide the loads up from ground level.

Imagine working in such cramped confines on a hot summer's day, the sun's rays shafting unmercifully through the cockpit Perspex to create an oven-like atmosphere (it would be little different in the rear of the fuselage). Equally, visualise the same scene on a winter's day, hoar frost coating the Lanc inside and out, steel ice-cold to the touch, breath freezing on the stagnant air.

Here, a candid study taken at Middleton St George by station photographer Len Horne crouching, back to the instrument panel, inside a Canadian BX. Len, we know, has now left this earth but what of the armourer here featured? Who can put a name to him? How crude the winches appear five decades on!/L. Horne via J. L. Armitage

Below:
DUSK IS THE TIME
'...Prepare for death, if here at night you roam, and sign your will before you sup from home...' (Samuel Johnson)

There she stands, at dusk, the time of day to which the Lancaster seems to belong; big and black and sinister, looking like some huge mantis, coiled and ready to spring on an unsuspecting prey.

It is quite dark now and growing chilly, the gathering clouds perhaps suggesting that dirty weather lies ahead and may yet force a scrub. As each man checks his equipment for the umpteenth time, feelings are all mixed up. They wouldn't, given a choice, choose to go, it is something nobody really wants to do in truth, but as long as it has to be done — and it does have to be done — then they may as well get their 30 trips into their log books in the quickest time possible. No more time to ponder. The motors whine and cough into life and the fuselage steadily vibrates as they are revved up, tested for magneto drops, then allowed to slow to idling speed. A final call from the Skipper to his crew before the brake pressure is released with a familiar hiss, and they are moving out of the pan, turning, waddling along the peri-track, heading for the smoking flame of the flarepath dancing in the wind forever fanning across the drome.

Another night of danger, of fear, of excitement, of torment has begun.

Bottesford, November 1943; 467 Sqn RAAF's 'M-Mother' Berlin-bound. RAAF Official

EAST WITH THE NIGHT

'...Under the cloak of darkness...'

The stentorian roar of Merlins rudely disturbs the countryside as the squadrons once more venture forth to rain bombs and incendiaries on Germany with unremitting intensity. Arguably, crews never really got used to the prickly moment of take-off... that nerve-jerking moment when each Lanc, invariably overloaded, lumbered down the runway, shaking, straining in an agonisingly slow way... at first as if hesitant, as if making up her mind about coming unstuck... then, mind made up, eager to fly yet as though restrained like some wild animal at the end of a chain... each crew silently willing her into the air, the boundary fence looming ever nearer, wondering if they might have to 'pull the tit' for full emergency boost.

Be it a summertime take-off in the long, languid evening twilight, or wintertime, well after dark, each kite usually needed the full length of the runway to lurch into the air.

When there was a gale — and during the bitter cold nights in winter there always seemed to be one — crews could be sure of a particularly 'hairy' take-off with a cross-wind adding to the problems of the normal swing — a real muck-sweat. On such occasions it appeared to the crews that the powers-that-be simply increased the all-up weight — probably because of a deficient knowledge of physics!

Equally, many survivors still reckon those drawn-out, detailed briefings were, to a great extent, a case of the blind leading the blind, particularly where Met forecasts were concerned: no satellite weather intelligence in those days!

Were Met forecasts *really* largely guesswork they wonder? Surely not? More likely those self-same warriors remember with a shudder only the times the Met man *did* get it wrong. Move out from the briefing room and join the lads as they put their orders into practice, to bludgeon those who would subjugate and exterminate without conscience

EAST WITH THE NIGHT

Top left:
A Fiskerton strangely devoid of well-wishers as No 49 Sqn prepares to do battle, probably during the winter of 1943/44 with an early dusk fast descending — probably too cold for all but the hardiest of souls.
Imperial War Museum

Centre left:
No 625 Sqn's Sqn Ldr Cliff Day and his sixfold team of fellow veterans, aboard BI DV278 'CF:V', on her tiptoes, about to leave the moonscape that is Kelstern in winter, Berlin-bound 20 January 1944. It is the penultimate trip of their tour (begun with No 101 Sqn Holme-on-Spalding Moor back in late May 1943) and they will leave Kelstern with mixed feelings: exalted and relieved to have survived when so many worthy mortals have not; reluctant to be leaving the operational arena. DV278 led an equally charmed life, finally succumbing to the foe when raiding Falaise in daylight 14 August 1944, crewed by Poles (Skipper Flt Lt L. Rebinski) from No 300 'Masovian' Sqn, Faldingworth.
P. J. Slingsby/A. Stevens

Bottom left:
A last blush of sunset transforms the fenland into a wonderland of shadow, a vista of immeasurable beauty as a Lanc of No 149 'East India' Sqn tucks up her wheels and takes wing to wage war, leaving behind a Methwold soon to be hemmed in by darkness.
R. K. Frampton

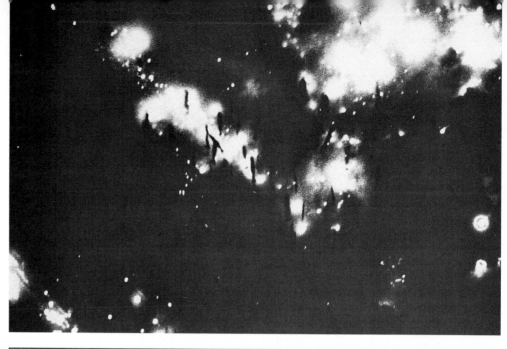

THE PAIN AND THE SORROW

Top, centre and bottom right:
'...The target, with growing pools of fire, is disappearing under the nose and the sky has turned crimson...'

Don't ask, don't expect those who took Lancs into battle, to apologise for the undoubted devastation they wreaked.

They won't.

Don't ask, don't expect they who supported those who took Lancs into battle, to apologise.

They won't.

That is all but a few who, as old age overtakes them, increasingly voice their shame, their regret that in youth they were willing participants in the execution of Bomber Command's policy. Such is their right.

But, was it really so wrong to bludgeon Germany in the way Bomber Command did? Why has so much vilification been levelled at the men — and women — who served their country, the allied cause, with such distinction?

Whilst, thankfully, not even their severest critics deny the courage, the determination of aircrews (the ground staff rarely, if ever, getting a mention), each attack on their still-revered, 'Butch' sees them bleed a little more, retreat further behind a cloak of increasing bitterness, a feeling of contemptible betrayal.

Were they able to speak from the grave — those who have one — what would the young bloods who died in their thousands on ops to Dortmund and Nuremberg and Berlin have to say on the subject?

Were they, or their spirits, looking on in disbelief, anger, utter dismay when controversy raged over the commissioning of a long-overdue statue to their boss? For that matter, was Sir Arthur himself 'in the wings' when HM the Queen Mother performed the unveiling?

Do not believe the pundits who say the massed bombings of Essen, or Politz or Kassel and their like had little effect, or were morally wrong. Had they spent just 10min with Albert Speer, Reichminister for Armaments and War Production, they would have been convinced otherwise.

H. Vikholt/M. F. Chandler Collection/ E. A. Eyres

Below:
Fortunate were Lanc crews who managed to take home with them the results of their labours...such as this token awarded to Rhodesian Bill Whamond and his No 106 Sqn crew for hitting the aiming point at Bremen on the night of 13/14 September 1942. W. N. Whamond

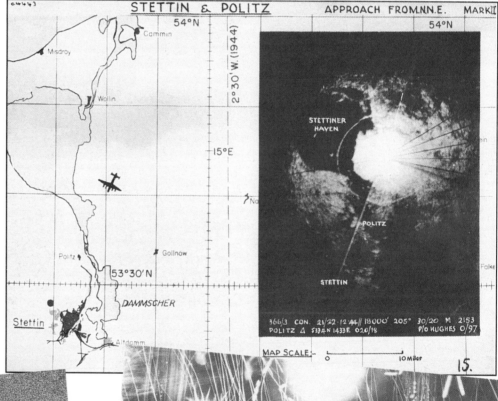

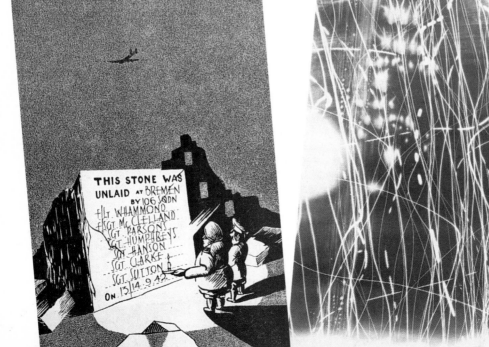

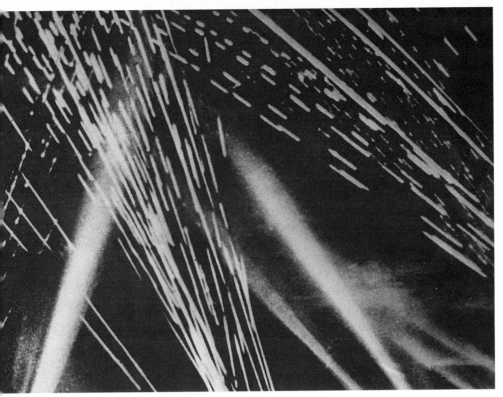

WHO'S TO DIE?

'...Above the flares and level with us, appears a thin wavering line of bright yellow lights. The lights twinkle like sparklers. The flak has started...'

No picture can convey how terrifying yet somehow wonderful a spectacle a target was when under attack.

It was at once a blaze of every kind of light...flares...searchlights...

roman candles...flaming onions...gun flashes...incendiaries bursting in clusters...everywhere great masses of smoke and fire.

It was searchlights appearing to leap out of the ground...their kniving, wavering beams suddenly converging on some luckless bods in a Lanc writhing and twisting, flak flashing and winking around her...at 20,000ft appearing tiny and silver, as does a moth appear tiny and silver when caught in the light from a torch or car headlights.

It was a blossoming of brightness that were fighter flares...the light from their hanging necklaces laying mistily on the flesh of the night.

It was flak-tongues flickering over the flames...appearing as a vast unbroken mass of cotton wool, perhaps grey, perhaps pink, with a golden glow beneath it...prickly with the scintillation of bursting shells.

It was a gut-churner...the stuff of nightmares.

The night skies over Wilhelmshaven (top left) and Mannheim (bottom left) snapped by unknown Germans apparently oblivious to danger.

D. H. Davis Collection/R. H. J. Rowe Collection

23

NIGHT BOMBERS

Slowly they climb thro' fast falling dusk
Over nodding English fields,
Theirs not the sudden glow of glory that
Their fighter brothers know,
Unerring they fly through cloud, through
Storm and darkness.
'Til — not turning — their dreadful duty done —
Climb to meet the dawning sun.

Anon

SETTING COURSE

We climbed above the flare-path, through the grey
Half-light which on that winter's evening lay
Cold on the fields, and as we climbed we met
The sun's last glory as it slowly set.
The dusk ran like a rim around the sky
And to the West we saw, how magically,
A golden bay, mountains and valleys bright,
All colour crushed there in a daze of light,
A fairyland that beckoned us to come,
Whom duty bade turn East towards the gloom.

Anon

HELL IS THE RHUR

The Ruhr the Ruhr, the burning Ruhr, we ride the hostile sky
'Let's get the bomb run over skip'. The Ruhr's a place to die!
There's .37s and .88s, the Flak goes whistling past,
There's Focke-Wulfs and Messerschmitts, so loud the Brownings blast.
Its aiming points and Marker flares, and see the Cookie blaze!
But Skip, the Reaper stalks about; amongst the searchlight rays!
There's time fused shells, and white-hot shards of shrapnel rake the air.
The bursting flak's not choosy — as long as someone's there!
There's Fighter flares, and cannon shells streak glowing through dark sky.
Its cordite fumes, bright muzzle flash — and who's the One to die.

John Roy Walsh (January 1986)

THE TOMMIES COME

In darkened skies massed Merlins hum
A tune that promises death to some
Who have taken freedom by the throat
And enslaved countries one by one.
To others that deep diapason
Gives hope and courage to carry on.
Endure they can — endure they will
While Merlins sing that people still
Do care — do fight — to bring

Them free to peace and light.
The throbbing roar that fills the night,
A music full of power and might,
A great nation's greatest chorale winging
Through the sky to set them singing
The fettered peoples' hopeful anthem
As high above massed Merlins hum,
Bright eyed they say,
'The Tommies come'.

Harry Brown DFM, No 50 Sqn
*c*1984

PRACTICE THEY MUST

It is arguably true to say that operational aircrew faced death in more ways than any other combatants; and more often. Apart from oblivion directly attributable to the enemy in the violent form of being shot down by flak or fighters, there was the dreaded prospect of death due to drowning or exposure in the event of a ditching at sea.

Such an eventuality was even more daunting if there was damage — definite or suspected — to the aircraft... if there was duff weather... if there was darkness.

If and when the inevitable became a stark reality each man found himself acting automatically, mentally running through every stage of the ditching drill so often practised in the hangar, at dispersal, wherever, back at base; a bit of a bore though not without the odd touch of banter, even outright humour.

There would be no banter, no humour as the Skipper concentrated on putting the Lanc down on the sea, his Sutton harness secured, intercom contact only with his engineer and rear gunner. There would be no jokes and little chatter among the crew as each member braced himself for the impact.

A strict procedure was laid down for the crew taking up ditching stations. The bomb aimer and mid-upper gunner took up their positions first. Next it was the flight engineer and rear gunner, followed by the navigator and, finally, wireless operator. Any extra man (such as a 'second dickey' pilot) moved to his allocated station 'as expedient'.

'Expediency' is an apt word when discussing ditching drill. The honed procedure as issued to Lancaster crews was drawn up as a result of input from survivors of numerous ditchings (not necessarily Lancaster related) and makes for thought-provoking study.

As is to be expected, pictures of ditchings are few and far between so here, as stand-ins, are Lancaster crews going through the motions in more leisurely circumstances.

Above right:
Dispersal practice for a No 106 Sqn Crew at Syerston, October/November 1942. About to jump from the rear door of Lanc 1 R5611 is squadron navigation leader Flt Lt Norman Scrivener, but does anyone know the identity of the ones in the dinghy? For the record, R5611 failed to return from Pilsen 13/14 May 1943 with Sgt F. J. Howell and crew.
N. H. Scrivener

Right:
Flg Off Eric Willis, RAAF, and his lads, who joined No 622 Sqn, Mildenhall in February 1945 and were still operating when war in Europe ceased, get to grips with an unruly dinghy at a location long forgotten. Note the car with roof-mounted loud-hailers on the opposite bank of the lake. H. E. Pam

A MEASURE OF PLEASURE

Privileged are you who, talking to any sometime Lancaster aviator, succeeds in drawing him out to discuss his thousand or more memories of forebodings and fears and tensions and uncertainties of life continuing... his brow becoming more furrowed, his stare more pronounced as faces of long-dead pals and colleagues file past in his mind's eye.

He will be anxious to move on to recall more pleasant aspects of squadron life: the sanity that was being with lively, fun-seeking companions at Mess parties; at dances; on pub crawls...wonderful memories of wonderful people, with him until life is snatched from him in old age.

And there was the indescribable thrill of flying on days, even nights, when the war did not call him and the weather was kind.

Like the freedom to fly low and fast, hugging the landscape or sea, having trees or fishing smacks flash beneath... until boredom set in.

Like the wonderland that was being among the stars (or so it seemed) on night 'Y' (H₂S) runs, or high-level bombing details... until boredom set in.

Like the challenge that was a daylight formation exercise... until boredom set in.

Like these memory-joggers:

Above:
No 15 Sqn's Flt Lt 'Lace' Lacey and crew from Mildenhall, on board BI HK799 'LS:D', complete with bulged bomb bay and G-H leader stripes on her fins, keep a watchful eye on BI NG357 'LS:G'. Flg Off Doug Hunt, RAAF and his clique (and whose bomb aimer 'Pat' Russell took this picture), keep station with them during the exhilarating near-wave-top flight to Wassenaar, near The Hague, 7 May 1945. This was one of a series of mercy sorties — code-named 'Operation Manna' by the RAF — mounted to relieve the plight of a starving Dutch population. D. A. Russell

Above:

The pathfinders of No 156 Sqn from Warboys enjoying themselves one fine late spring or early summer day in 1943, with the Lancs looking still virtually 'as new'. In view nearest is BIII ED842 'GT:W', then 'owned' by Plt Off A. R. MacLachlan and his clan, and a Lanc that would end her days as a test vehicle with the Royal Aircraft Establishment, Farnborough before being struck off charge in March 1951. By then she'd had a long career, having been delivered new to 156 Sqn nearly seven years previously. Far different was the fate of the MacLachlan seven on an op to Munich on the night of 6/7 September 1943 in BIII JB177. Their tour was violently terminated and seven dreaded telegrams were soon en route to their next of kin. Centre is BIII JA674 'GT:O', more often than not under the command of Plt Off (later Flt Lt) M. A. Sullivan from New Zealand and who, along with his squad, would fail to return from Frankfurt 20/21 December 1943 in her.

Top is BIII ED829 'GT:Z', then under the 'ownership' of Flt Lt G. L. Mandeno and company. She was fated to go down on Berlin 23/24 August 1943 with Plt Off A. R. W. Illius and crew, only their second op, whereas Mandeno and crew survived their tour. R. D. Newton

Right:

A slight touch of camera shake fails to rob us of an arresting oblique of Waddington as 'PO:G' of the Aussie-controlled No 467 Sqn prepares to begin circuit procedure following some long-forgotten foray or aerial assignment spent emulating the birds from on high, or down low, as ordered so to do.

Noteworthy is Waddo's bomb dump discernible in the foreground, an incongruity sprawling over acres of scrub and thicket, the home of wildlife long tolerant of man's intrusion into its domain. R. D. F. Brooker

"FIRST OP"

Dennis Dear

We spilled out of the crew truck stumbling in the thick blackness; a sudden beam of light flashed across the concrete apron outside the Ops room and remained for a few moments until the door was slammed again. It was enough to give us a direction and Smithy was able to fumble the door open and we trooped into the harsh brightness of the room we had left some eight hours ago.

The Padre came across, tired and ineffective, and asked us if we'd had a good trip. Smithy answering for the crew said "Yes" but how the hell could you tell on your first trip. You didn't know if you'd had a good trip or a bad one. I'd have said it was a bloody stinker, but then every trip might be like this, and sometimes you might get it worse. Our rear gunner was saying far too loudly, that next time he'd be a bloody Padre, and the Padre gave him a half embarrassed smile and a mug of sweet sticky tea. The Wingco came over then and nodded to all of us. "Well thats number one chaps — good show" and ushered us over to a corner of the room where a flight lieutenant intelligence type was sharpening pencils.

We were like a bunch of kids attending a new school for the first time. We gathered round the table in a group and the photographic sergeant had to come across and take my camera magazine. He jotted down details as I replied to his questions giving aircraft letter, bombing heading, height and time of bombing. To my "straight and level for the photograph" he smiled and with a "Good Show!" ambled away swinging the magazine in its brown canvas holder to greet another crew just coming through the door.

I came back to the table where the crew were now seated and squeezed onto the end of the bench by the gunners, only to be called up to the head of the table beside the navigator. The Intelligence Officer instructed the new boys again, "Skipper, navigator and bomb aimer always nearest to me."

And now the questions start. We speak with authority of three tenths cloud over target and settle for moderate heavy-flak. Hell we don't know if the flak was heavy or light — let him ask the old hands, we certainly shall — we want to know whether it can be worse than it was tonight. The flight lieutenant scribbles our answers on a sheet of foolscap and gradually draws out of us the details he requires. We keep referring to the navigator's log and are glad that Mac made so many entries of the incidents reported over the intercom. Christ: he could not have stopped writing over the target; still, perhaps it was his way of keeping his mind occupied during the bombing run.

The fighter attack is noted in detail. They go into it so thoroughly that you feel you ought to have noted the colour of the Hun's eyes. Christ, don't they realise that you don't care if you shot him down or not, as long as he left you alone! But the questions go on. Did I see the breakaway — did I hell, but I saw the ugly red and yellow tracers flash past the port side and I saw the wings vibrating as we swung into a tight turn to starboard. I thought the wings were going to shear off, even if the bastard didn't shoot them off; and my stomach seemed knotted into a tight ball which bounced about inside the framework of my body, and there was a hard dry lump in my throat as I heard the panic in the gunners' voice. But he didn't want to know about that; he wanted ranges and tactics and you detected the fact that he wasn't concerned about you but only wanted to know what the Hun had done.

And at last it was all over and we were on our way to the Mess feeling that we'd started to earn our keep and were now part of the squadron.

It was noisy in the Mess dining hall — everyone talking loudly of the night's experience. I'd finished my egg and bacon and was on my third cup of tea when I realised I was talking as loud as the others. We were arguing whether flak was nearer when you heard it above the engine noise or when you could smell the acrid stink of it. I suddenly tired of the conversation and pushed my chair back from the table, said cheerio and hurried out into the cold darkness.

Once in the night air I walked slowly back to the billet trying to recapture the pure stark beauty of the target area. Already the fear that had gripped me over there, was quickly fading and the memory of it was rather like a picture seen once for a few moments over somebody's mantel. This was a canvas of breadth and depth of bizarre color and remote horror. The foreground splashed with streaks of red and yellow of the fires in the city below, were, in the picture, no more than mere pointers to the central theme of reds and greens of the target markers. Brilliant cascading showers of silver bright colours, aiming points for the four thousand pounders which would stir the comparative pallid tones of the fires with occasional eruptions of deep red colour. The background was divided into black segments by the white fingers of searchlights, criss-crossing the sky beyond the burning city. And over the whole of this vast three dimensional canvas was splashed the apparent haphazard stabbing flashes of the flak, each splotch of red, wrapped in its own cotton wool was fading from my mind and I felt a desperate need to see it again, another night, so that I could fill in the gaps in my memory.

I was nearly at the billet now, which loomed black against the cumulous shrouded sky, hiding the friendliness of the stars. The relief of return was wearing off now, and sheer exhaustion was cracking the thin veneer of exhilaration. I suddenly thought again of the fighter attack a bare four hours ago; I stumbled quickly to the side of the concrete road and vomitted into the long dank grass.

THEY WHO DARED

'...And at last it was all over and we were on our way to the Mess feeling that we'd started to earn our keep and were now part of the squadron...'
For several of these lads — old enough to fight for their country, considered too young to vote — time is running out. Berlin — the Big City — is but a few hours away and if it does not claim them, prove to be their graveyard tonight, there is always tomorrow night, for this is the so-called Berlin season.

It is that period of the bomber war when the German capital must feel the weight of a Command steadily increasing in might and strength, despite the mauling it had taken during the Battle of the Ruhr and beyond. Until the opening of the inevitable second front, it was the *only* war possible for the Allies, despite what certain critics said and wrote at the time, and criticisms which are still being uttered 50 years on from the comfort of armchairs, with the infallibility of hindsight. How else could the war have been carried to the enemy at that period?

As before every op, the sense of apprehension (soon to dissolve once in the air), is still with them. To those who know the score — the wing commanders, flight commanders et al — the seasoned veterans stand out from those just beginning their tour.

An initial, apparent carefree attitude when they were full of expectation has, after five ops or so, hardened into experience. Optimism has been steadily blunted, yet they carry on determinedly, many becoming fatalistic. Too many friends are dead, or missing without trace, and it is not unknown for those who remain to see their faces beckoning them from the bottom of a beer glass in the Mess.

The following pictures show typical enactments before any operation, but in this case known to be before Berlin.

Right:

Witness No 101 Sqn aircrew handing in the likes of wallets and letters at Ludford Magna, 20 January 1944. Pockets must be emptied of everything which might provide any clues to the enemy — even down to seemingly insignificant items such as bus and train tickets. Despite such precautions, the enemy seems to be generally already informed when airmen do fall into their hands. On hand are WAAFs who will see that each man's personal belongings are placed in a blue bag for safe-keeping until his return (hopefully) next day. In exchange they will each soon sign for an escape kit and foreign money to the value of £10 (or thereabouts) to aid evasion if fortunate enough to bale out of their stricken Lancaster. This pre-op ritual will be observed before moving on to the locker room.

On this night 101 will lose only Flg Off S. W. W. Perry, RCAF, and his assembly, yet of the 19 crews who return to fight another night, the reaper will claim 10 of them in the months ahead. Even some of those who will leave Ludford tour-expired are destined to die — typified by Australian Norman Marsh (in our picture he is standing next to the two WAAFs). He will perish as an instructor. Popperfoto

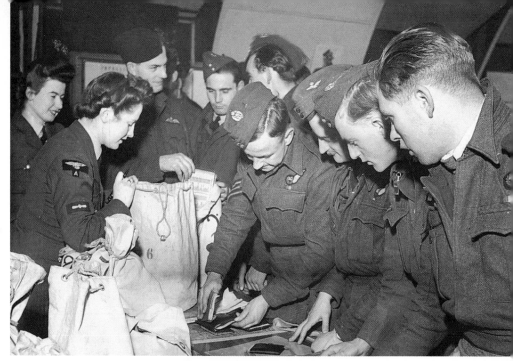

Below right:

All the jostling in the locker room is over, everyone hoping nothing has been forgotten, necessitating the irritation of rushing back for it later.

Outside in the damp air the whine of engines and screech of brakes which heralds arrival of transport that will take them to dispersals near and far, fails to disturb an overriding hush of expectancy brooding over a drome now filled with challenge...a compelling dread...a sense of destiny.

Were we not to know our sneaked snapshot was taken at Elsham Wolds — home for Nos 103 and 576 Sqns — during the winter of 1943/44, the scene could be staged at any of several dozen airfields the length and breadth of bomber country whenever ops were on.

Can we hope life was spared for these warriors? Are they, and the WAAFs here well in evidence, enjoying well-earned retirement?
G. S. Morgan

SEVEN TO A CREW

They laugh at Death, yet Death creeps quietly in,
Perching on young shoulders, unheeded,
And in the smoke-filled bar-room noise,
He beckons slowly with a foul mouthed grin,
And with the stench of graveyard breath
Breathes invitations to seven aged boys.

For by the time the moon has set again
Upon the dead of tomorrow's target,
He will order, and the seven will obey
And they will never more feel rain
Or sun, upon their upturned faces.
And the sea will close upon his chosen prey.

But for the moment; laugh while mine host
Calls time; for Death is laughing too
And he is patient. Unlike the landlord and his bell
He has no licence to protect. So here's a toast
To Death, who lets the seven saunter one more night
In ignorance, and so prepare themselves for Hell.

Dennis Dear DFM
Nos 207 and 9 Sqns

FLAME OF VALOUR

No amount of perusal of squadron records can tell us the full story of Bomber Command's contribution to victory. Page upon page of operational flights are presented in a no-frills, matter-of-fact manner and it does not take the reader long to wonder what tales of human endeavour remain untold... can never be told.

And time is running out, whereby more of a steadily decreasing clique can be persuaded to recount their stories before they depart on their final sortie.

It does not help that, despite an inevitable mellowing in old age, there still is a reluctance to 'line-shoot', as they see it. It does not help that time and time again their breed has been vilified beyond belief.

As but one example among hundreds of dramas acted out in hostile skies, yet given scant mention in the chronicles of a typical unit in the forefront of action, is a 'hairy-do' played out on the 12th day of July 1944.

Flt Lt R. G. Williams and his brotherhood of seasoned pathfinders from No 7 Sqn had come through many a trip full of incident since arriving at Oakington mid-March 1944. Thus the railway yards at Vaires on the outskirts of Paris presented no more of a tough target than had been the like of Mount Couple and Aachen, not forgetting Düsseldorf and Essen.

As it transpired, the evening raid mounted against Vaires — abandoned by the master bomber due to near-total cloud cover — all but proved to be their last.

A direct hit from flak tore out the starboard-inner engine of Lanc III PB118 'MG:F' and peppered the starboard-outer, resulting in it being feathered. A huge hole was rent in the starboard wing close to the fuselage, and one at the navigators' positions had to be stuffed with a Mae West to keep out the wind which would have added to their predicament.

The pilot's instrument panel was shattered, as was the cockpit Perspex behind his seat. The H₂S blister, along with aerials, disappeared; electrics and hydraulics were non-existent; the bomb doors and undercarriage dropped down and locked. And, as if that was not enough to contend with, a 500lb bomb complete with long-delay fuse had hung up! Amazingly, not one crew member was injured and Williams began to nurse his crippled kite homeward... with no instruments and no power on one side — a daunting prospect.

Mile after agonising mile they neared Oakington but then the port-inner lost power and it was time to put her down without delay, which Williams did in masterly manner on the edge of Rivenhall, near Braintree (Essex), then in the hands of the 9th USAAF in the presence of the 397th Bomb Group operating B-26 Marauders, and whose personnel were no strangers to kites coming back 'on a wing and a prayer'.

Following many more 'adventures' this illustrious crew finished an outstanding tour by leaving a visiting card at Cologne on the penultimate day of 1944.

What became of PB118? Repaired, she was later issued to No 1654 HCU and was shot down by a marauding intruder on the night of 3/4 March 1945, near home base Wigsley.

Bottom left:
A close-up of PB118 showing how neatly the starboard-inner Merlin has been torn from the bulkhead. Just visible forward of the fuselage roundel is No 7 Sqn's unique under-size 'MG' code presentation. J. F. Corrigan

Below:
Gauge the skill and nerve required by the Skipper of PB118 from study of this full view taken from beyond the Rivenhall perimeter. J. F. Corrigan

Bottom right:
The crew (left to right)
Back: Navigator II (Set operator): WO W. S. Baxter DFC, RAAF, Navigator I (plotter): Flt Lt J. F. Corrigan DFC & Bar RCAF, Wireless operator: Sgt E. Oldham DFC,
Pilot: Sqn Ldr R. G. Williams DSO, DFC
Front: Flight Engineer: Sgt S. Gibson DFM, Mid-upper gunner: Sgt J. H. Lenaghan DFC
Rear gunner: Flg Off H. P. Brundle DFC. J. F. Corrigan

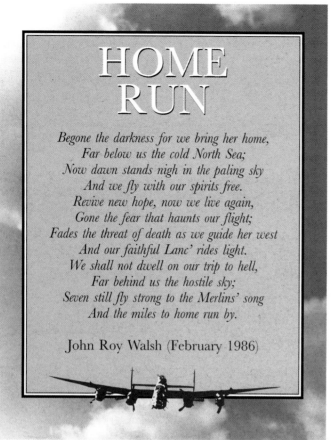

HOME RUN

Begone the darkness for we bring her home,
Far below us the cold North Sea;
Now dawn stands nigh in the paling sky
And we fly with our spirits free.
Revive new hope, now we live again,
Gone the fear that haunts our flight;
Fades the threat of death as we guide her west
And our faithful Lanc' rides light.
We shall not dwell on our trip to hell,
Far behind us the hostile sky;
Seven still fly strong to the Merlins' song
And the miles to home run by.

John Roy Walsh (February 1986)

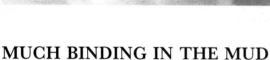

MUCH BINDING IN THE MUD

When the day dawned whereby, for those aircrew fortunate to have survived the war, they were able to hang up their helmets and return to civilian life, catching up on lost years, little did they realise that 30 or so years later a relaxing of the rules would allow 'Joe Public' to pore over what they did in the war.

For some — maybe most — there is no objection... knowing they cannot stop the practice anyway... knowing they performed of their best... can still stand tall and proud in this 50th anniversary year despite what may be written and presented about the campaign they took part in.

Even so, some may wince uncomfortably when calling to mind a half-forgotten episode when they 'put up a black' and incurred the wrath of their superiors for a careless action which put their station's effort for the night, or day, in jeopardy; even resulted in cancellation.

Rest assured worthy warriors, rarely are such incidents given more than a passing mention — if mentioned at all — in the once-secret records now public property.

Rest easy when you learn that Court of Inquiry and Court Martial reports are — perhaps rightly — locked away for goodness knows how many more years... for certain beyond your remaining lifespan.

Thus, we shall say little about what befell Flg Off Les Wareham and his flock before an evening attack on Caen, 7 July 1944, a less than successful effort as it turned out *(top right)*. Suffice to say that BI LL837 'BQ:Q' of No 550 Sqn became bogged at the edge of North Killingholme's northern perimeter track, but did not hold up proceedings for long. *A. R. Marsh*

An experienced, respected crew, the Wareham septet went on to complete a typical tour of the period some seven weeks later. No 550's commanding officer Wg Cdr P. E. G. G. Connolly, much in evidence before the Caen operation, was not so lucky, his life being extinguished when piloting LL837 on the abortive Revigny railway yards bombing raid, 14/15 July 1944.

Above:
For we who have never taxied a lumbering, overladen Lancaster out of her dispersal pan and down an aerodrome's 75ft-wide peri-track at night it is nigh on impossible to imagine the skill and dexterity required. Not surprisingly, no photograph of a night bogging 'as it happened' has come to light but this impression by acclaimed artist Ken Aitken conveys the urgency... the noise... the intense activity. K. C. Aitken

"LEAVE"

Dennis Dear

By the time you have had your second cup of tea at Kings Cross, the leave is fading into the useless pages of the scrapbook that is your life. Already the squadron is reaching out for you and your name will soon be chalked up on the battle order again. The train is hurtling towards the uncertain possibility of death at sixty miles an hour yet creeping slowly as Shakespeare's schoolboy; back to life.

It is the only life, the uncertainness, the strain which gets so bad that leave is the only drug. Yet leave begets that self-same strain and the ecstacy of fear overcome; is the only drug for leave. The train wheels drum this vicious circle of realisation into your impatience 'til the books and magazines, purchased for the journey, become mere words jumbled in pretty coloured covers. The well-meaning gent in the opposite corner seat says, "sorry to be going back?" and you answer "Yes" because he couldn't understand, and you curse again the slowness of the journey.

Twenty minutes before the train is due to arrive you are looking for the black-bellied green and brown shapes that are your life and when "A" flight's big black hangar looms into view, you sigh with relief. And then the emptiness is upon you again as you see propellers turning in the evening sun, and the squadron taxying round the perimeter track. Soon the airfield will be bare and you will be alone again.

You gather your suitcase and raincoat from the rack and say "Goodbye Sir" to the old gent in the corner. His "Good Luck" follows you out into the corridor where you are impatient for the Station.

The one taxi is free and you bundle into it calling "Officers Mess, hurry!" and the driver wonders why. At the mess you dump your kit in the cloakroom and rush out down the concrete road leading to the flights. You thumb a lift from the Padre on his way to the chequered caravan to see the take-off before he waits alone for their return. Sitting beside him you wonder if he prays for them or whether he thinks its no use.

You arrive as the first aircraft is turning onto the runway, you recognise the pilot and two-finger him and you know he's thinking "Lucky bastard, just had leave."

And some, you do not recognise and realise they are fresh crews, replacing someone you know and will know no more.

And finally they are all gone and the field is quiet against the drone of their engines overhead.

Back in the Mess, you drink alone at the bar and wish you had come back in the morning — afraid to go to bed in an empty hut, with empty beds that have no kit beside them. Seven days is a long time and the Reaper harvests quickly.

PERMISSION TO ENJOY THEMSELVES

'...By the time you have had your second cup of tea at King's Cross, the leave is fading...'

Leave! What a magic word that was! As much as it was essential for aircrew to have leave, so it was important for those who supported the boys with wings from the ground, to 'get away from it all', escape the pressures, the constraints, the relentless life centred totally on attacking the enemy. Armed with a precious leave pass each individual would head for the nearest railway station, there to begin the long journey home. The more remote bomber bases, often miles from a large town, were usually served by a small branch line station which, but for the war, may well have closed already — stations such as Firsby Junction, near Skegness, which became well known to thousands of airmen. Many of these tiny halts and the branch lines themselves have long since disappeared; but how invaluable they were during the war. Most airmen would, on posting, never even have heard of the RAF station to which they were to report, let alone know where it was and how to get there. RAF Spilsby produced a booklet for the benefit of arrivees entitled 'Journey's End'. It could have been just as appropriately titled 'World's End'. Journeys to such places in remote, rural East Anglia, or North and East Yorkshire would be tortuous and time-consuming, and tended to eat well into that precious '48-hour', unless you knew the ropes. Some preferred to hitch-hike, for in wartime Britain there was invariably a lift available, be it from a car-driving civilian engaged on war work, or a lorry-load of soldiers.

Then there were those who came from across the sea and could not count on seeing their families for goodness knows how long. For them there were numerous clubs and centres in the likes of York or London, with wherever and whatever called in the way of tastes, requirements, what-have-you. Many Commonwealth airmen took the opportunity to seek out relatives in the UK, most of whom they had never met before. Ground staff tended to take their leaves singly but aircrew frequently took theirs as a complete crew.

Here we look in on New Zealander Flg Off Lew Hooper and his boys, in happy mood, awaiting the train that will steam them a million miles from the war. The picture could have been taken at any one of dozens of small country stations, which might have averaged no more that two or three passengers a day in previous years, served by a wheezy tank locomotive pulling a couple of ancient non-corridor coaches. More likely, it looks to be a main line station such as Grantham, where it was 'all change here for London'; where they would hope for a reasonably quick journey (by wartime standards), albeit usually standing room only, with no refreshment bar, and blacked-out windows, every coach packed to capacity with journeying servicemen and women. Some of these could be *en route* from one end of the country to the other, eg from the far north of Scotland to a posting in westernmost Cornwall, a journey which could take two to three days under wartime conditions. The Hooper septet, typical of any mixed-nationality crew to be found throughout Bomber Command, had joined the conflict late on, and had some way to go before becoming tour-expired with No 619 Sqn, Strubby when Germany capitulated.

Left:
(left to right)
Mid-upper: Sgt Bill Bishop, Navigator: Flt Sgt George Mann, RCAF
Pilot: Flg Off Lew Hooper, RNZAF, Flight engineer: Flt Sgt Les Weaver
Rear gunner: Sgt Peter Brown, Bomb aimer: Flt Sgt Stan Mays. L. D. B. Hooper

NOT A CARROT IN SIGHT

Right:

'...*And some you do not recognise, and realise they are fresh crews, replacing someone you knew, and will know no more...*'

If leave was precious at any time it was perhaps more so at Christmas and, conscious of keeping up morale, Bomber Command ensured that those personnel on duty, or who must be on hand, at least had a hearty meal on Christmas Day. And, as study of this menu will reveal, the meal was worthy fare — more so when considering that Britain's civilian population was coping with rationing, the misery of queuing for the bare essentials of daily life.

Below right:

What would have been the reaction of the nation's populace had word reached them of such apparent extravagance? We have little doubt that dissenting voices would have been few in number. How many of the lads here seated in the Sergeants' Mess at Ludford Magna on Christmas Day 1943 are still around to rekindle a memory? How many of them spare a thought for times past when, yearly, they enjoy a yuletide safe in the knowledge that tomorrow, family and friends can again sit down to lunch together... not be blown apart in action with the enemy or be posted away never to be seen or heard of again. *J. W. Lawrence*

* *Early war-time propaganda had it that carrots improved aircrews' eyesight, particularly night vision!*

Menu

Cream of Tomato Soup
Bread Rolls

*

Fillet of Fish   Egg Sauce

*

Roast Turkey   Sage and Onion Stuffing
Roast Pork   Apple Sauce
Brown Gravy

*

Roast Potatoes, Creamed Potatoes
Garden Peas, Brussels Sprouts

*

Christmas Pudding
Brandy Sauce

*

Coffee, Cheese and Biscuits

*

Beer, Minerals, Cigarettes
Oranges, Apples

---

101 Squadron,
Ludford Magna.

Christmas 1943

*

Wishing you Health and Happiness
at Christmastide
and throughout the Coming Year

R.A.F. STATION
LUDFORD MAGNA

*

Sergeants' Mess

*

CHRISTMAS DINNER
1943

LEAVE (Abandon hope all ye who make out an application).

The griff is that 7 days leave can be taken with a 48 hours pass. (Accent on the " can "). This leave and 48 is only permitted once during any 3 months. 48 hours can be granted separately. Railway Warrants are issuable according to your entitlement, the leave year started on 15th August, 1944, so you've had last year's.

RAILWAY SERVICES.

Firsby (L.N.E.R.) is the nearest and best station from which to travel. This, being a main line junction, provides trains to take the wanderer to any place to which he desires to go. A nice thought, but opportunity is a fine thing. There is a late train from Skegness to Firsby at 22.45 hours.

However there is quite a good service to Boston and Skegness, and for those who have the necessary pass, the following is the time table of trains which run to London. Make sure that they still do run.

Up Trains.

Dept.	07.08	10.13	13.53	16.36	18.14	21.05
Arr. King's Cross	10.54	13.15	17.45	21.32	22.38	02.40

Sunday.

Dept.	10.52		19.01
Arr.	14.06		22.18

The times of arrival at King's Cross are purely hypothetical, and are only included to show that the trains do finish up somewhere.

Down Trains.

Dept. King's Cross	09.00		13.10	16.05	17.50E	17.50S
Arr. Firsby	12.46		16.25	19.13	21.41	21.44

E Except Saturday.   S Saturday only.

Sunday.

Dept. King's Cross	10.10	18.05
Arr. Firsby	17.35	21.23

The 16.05 train from King's Cross on week-day's is about the only that ever runs to even approximate time, and so it is the only one worth catching.

"OPS ON TONIGHT!"

The Docherty Crew

How many of us have winced in disbelief, maybe squirmed with not a little embarrassment when watching films wherein aircrew in their aircraft are portrayed using rather stilted, unreal language? Then again, how many of us have more than an inkling of how a bomber crew did communicate with each other during a bombing raid? To set the record straight, what follows is a complete operation undertaken by an experienced, disciplined Lancaster crew, through its intercom and radio telephone (R/T) communication. It is a remarkable reconstruction of a raid on Stuttgart on 28/29 July 1944 by Flg Off Eddie Docherty and his No 630 Sqn crew, and is the work of Eric Armstrong, Tom Bailey and Bill Horsman (flight engineer, navigator and bomb aimer respectively).

With all the crew again in contact over four decades after they last flew together, it was decided to produce a tape recording of the Stuttgart trip, each man speaking his 'own lines'. Read it... study it... absorb it: and we ask you to remember that it represents a time scale of no less than 8hr 5min... a long time to sit in darkness in the cramped claustrophobic confines of a noisy, vibrating Lancaster... a long time to be under tension, in apprehension, in fear.

THE STORY	– A raid carried out by a Lancaster of Bomber Command in World War Two.
THE PLACES	– From East Kirkby, Lincolnshire, home of 630 Squadron, 5 Group, RAF, to Stuttgart, Germany.
THE TIME	– The evening of July 28th, 1944.
THE AIRCRAFT	– Lancaster Mark 1 LL 966 'LE:P' ('Peter').

During the morning and afternoon, the aircraft has been checked by ground and air crews and flight-tested, with the bomb load put aboard by the armourers. The aircrew have had their flying supper of bacon and eggs and been to main briefing. Now, fully prepared, they have been driven to the aircraft dispersal and dressed in their flying gear and parachute harnesses, the crew are in the Lanc in position and about to start an intercom check.

Each crew member is a specialist in his particular field with his allotted tasks, but working, as always, in close cooperation, to form a formidable team.

EDDIE: Intercom check, Skipper to crew. Engineer?
ERIC: OK Skipper.
EDDIE: Bomb aimer?
BILL: OK Skip.
EDDIE: Navigator?
TOM: Loud and clear, Skip.
EDDIE: Wireless Op?
DICK: Reading you OK Skip.
EDDIE: Mid-upper?
MAC: OK Skip.
EDDIE: Rear gunner?
PADDY: Hearing you OK Skip.
EDDIE: Ready for starting engineer.
ERIC: Ready Skip. No 2 tanks ON, booster coil ON, pulsometer pumps ON, master cock ON, ignition ON, contact starboard-inner.
ERIC: Booster coil OFF, Ground/flight to flight, run up at 1200 RPM, Switch DR compass ON. PAUSE. Flaps checked, bomb doors closed Skip. Pulsometer pumps OFF, rad shutters OPEN, ready to run up Skip.

Countless checks are carried out between pilot and engineer to ensure that all is mechanically sound with the four Merlins.

TOM: Nav to Skipper, eight minutes to take-off Skip, runway is 030, wind 300/15, QFE 1009.
EDDIE: Roger nav, pilot to engineer, are we clear to taxi?
ERIC: All clear to taxy this side. we are following 'D:Dog' — that's old Steve Nunns. Checks OK Skip, flaps 20°, brakes ON, temperatures and pressures OK, green from the caravan.
EDDIE: Engine up to 0 boost and even, brakes OFF. We are on the

take-off run — gaining speed — easing off at 105mph, airborne NOW, brakes ON, U/C UP.
TOM: Airborne at 21.55 Skip.
EDDIE: Yes navigator, flaps 15° engineer.
ERIC: Wilco Skip
EDDIE: Flaps UP.
ERIC: Flaps UP Skipper, pulsometer pumps OFF.
EDDIE: OK engineer, 2650 + 7
ERIC: Watch that kite on your port bow Skip.
EDDIE: OK. I see him.
TOM: Navigator here, we should be setting course in a few minutes Skipper. 180°.
EDDIE: Roger nav, where are we bomb aimer?
BILL: Base is on our port beam. I'll give you the turn in a minute. PAUSE. 10° to port, over base NOW.
TOM: Thanks Bill, 180° and climbing at 160 airspeed. Set course 22.10.
ERIC: No 1 tanks OFF, oxygen regulator ON.
EDDIE: OK engineer, navigation lights OFF, oxygen ON. TIME PASSES.
BILL (personal thoughts): Here I am, lying in the bomb aimer's compartment up front and flying out over England. As I scan the earth beneath me, I watch the pale little pools of purple slowly coalesce into the black of night.
  A different surface below us now, barely visible, but broken up into a thousand ridges, troughs and peaks, constantly on the move, as I watch. Why, of course, it's the sea.
BILL: Enemy coast ahead navigator.
TOM: Thanks Bill, pinpoint on crossing please.
BILL: Crossing coast NOW navigator.
TOM: Roger bomb aimer. New course of 112° now Skip.
EDDIE: Skipper here, getting dark now, so eyes peeled everybody, still climbing. Now on course 112° navigator.
BILL: Flak up front. Navigator, river to port of our track — five miles. We are dead on track, good show. Flak now joined by searchlights.
  Skipper? all bombs fused and selected.
EDDIE: Roger bomb aimer.
MAC: Tracer on the port bow, obvious combat; one aircraft down in flames.
ERIC: Navigator, aircraft going down on our port bow, looks like a Lanc, 12,000ft.

33

DICK:	W op to Nav, Met wind from base, 310/35 mph.
TOM:	Nav to Skipper, wind has veered round a bit so turn 5° to starboard onto 117°.
EDDIE:	Wilco navigator, turning on to 117°, airspeed now 155.
ERIC:	Engineer to navigator, Lanc exploded, starboard bow up; going down in flames.
TOM:	OK engineer, I have that.
EDDIE:	Skipper to gunners, eyes peeled fellers. 14,000ft still climbing but power is falling off.
ERIC:	No more power Skip, over to S gear.
EDDIE:	Roger, starboard bow, another aircraft going down, bad luck.
ERIC:	That's three down so far, looks like being a rough trip Skipper.
MAC:	Mid-upper to Skipper, combat, starboard rear, two Lancs having a go at a fighter — he's hit, in flames going down, looks like an ME110.
EDDIE:	OK mid-upper, thank you, Keep your eyes peeled. Have you got that navigator?
TOM:	Nav to Skip, yes, here Skip, I got it down. Can you maintain 155 airspeed?
EDDIE:	We'll try nav, we'll try. Aircraft coned on starboard bow, getting some flak. Poor buggers.
TOM:	Nav to Skip, next turning point coming up in three minutes. Engineer, Window at one per minute please. New course will be 135° compass, Skipper.
EDDIE:	Roger nav.
ERIC:	Engineer speaking, port bow up — flames and explosion from a Lancaster — Lanc gone down navigator.
TOM:	OK engineer, I have that recorded. Nav to Skip, turn onto 135° now Skip.
EDDIE:	OK nav, turning onto 135.
PADDY:	Fighter, fighter, corkscrew starboard, Go, go, go. Down starboard, down port, both of us are firing. Up port, up starboard.
MAC:	We've got him, he's on fire, see him Paddy?
PADDY:	Skipper, I see him. Watch him bomb aimer, he's coming across under our port bow.
BILL:	Bomb aimer to Skip, I see him, he's going down, all fire and smoke. Some activity up front to port, would that be Ludwigshaven? Somebody well north of track.
EDDIE:	Good show gunners, let's get back on the job, cut the chatter. Back on course now navigator, 135, 17,000 feet.
DICK (personal thoughts):	Talking to myself again, if they could hear me they would really think me round the bend. Perhaps I am, this flipping Morse is enough to destroy one's sanity. I feel rather cold and peckish, perhaps a nibble at a sandwich would warm me up. Ah, here it is, unhook this mask for a moment. Cor lummy, it's as hard as a rock and ice-cold — of course, I'm forgetting, we're at 20,000 feet. Ah well, I'll have to go hungry for a bit.
EDDIE:	Get that mike off, somebody.
DICK:	Sorry skip, wireless op here, just received message from base. They're expecting fog on return, I'm listening out for diversions. It will be a pity to spend a night away from base.
EDDIE:	OK W op, thank you. Bloody met man wrong again — one of these nights he'll get it right for a change.
BILL:	Bomb aimer here, he drew some nice diagrams though Skip, warm fronts and cold backs.
EDDIE:	We'll meet that foggy problem when we come to it.
TOM:	I like your optimism. Engineer, increase window to two per minute please.
ERIC:	Roger, Wilco.
BILL:	Bomb aimer here Skip, there's several aircraft beneath us, could be Stirlings. They're getting some flak, poor sods — the best of luck to them. Bomb aimer to nav, there's a river up front Tom, with a sort of S-bend, right on track.
TOM:	Thank you bomb aimer, that's the Rhine. Skip, I reckon we're two minutes behind time, can you increase speed?
EDDIE:	Roger navigator, can we get anymore power engineer?
ERIC:	Can do, but we'll gollop fuel skipper, we're OK for petrol though. I've been on No 1 tanks for the last hour and have transferred No 3, so No 2 tanks are full.
EDDIE:	OK then, get some power on engineer. Navigator, if I reduce our rate of climb for a while, I can increase speed with this extra

	power. How long for, would you reckon?
TOM:	Not long Skip. I'll work it out quickly and let you know.
DICK:	Wop to Skipper, sighting on Fishpond, enemy intruder away on our tail a long way away yet though.
EDDIE:	Keep your eyes peeled gunners.
BILL:	Bomb aimer to nav, crossing river bend now.
TOM:	Thank you Bill.
ERIC:	Looks like a collision up front. Two lots of wreckage and red and green flares. One could be PFF. Did you get that navigator?
TOM:	OK engineer.
EDDIE:	Pilot to rear gunner, are you OK Paddy?
PADDY:	Bloody cold skip, but otherwise OK. All in one piece as far as I can judge.
EDDIE:	Pilot to mid-upper, how about you Mac?
MAC:	OK Skipper, busy night tonight though, lots of activity.
EDDIE:	You are all doing a great job. Keep on the ball, a long way to go yet. You OK bomb aimer?
BILL:	OK Skipper, I reckon that was 2 Lancs back there. First wave and PFF backer up kite.
EDDIE:	How are we doing engineer?
ERIC:	OK Skip, no problems; its a relief to get Window out of the way a bit. I can move around a bit now.
EDDIE:	Important though. Pilot to W op, are you with us Dick, you're pretty quiet back there, are you having a kip?
DICK:	Fat chance of that. No, I've just been viewing Fishpond, thought I had a contact, but he's gone off to port — thank God.
EDDIE:	Good show Dick, keep it up, keep looking for the buggers.
BILL:	Bomb aimer to nav, looks like a raid taking place up front, port bow. Fair bit of activity and explosions.
TOM:	Thank you bomb aimer, that will be the Mossy diversion on Karlsruhe. I reckon we are back on time skipper.
EDDIE:	OK nav. Engineer, leave the power on, we'll get up to bombing height first and then knock it back.
ERIC:	OK Skip.
BILL:	Bomb aimer here skipper. I think Jerry's putting on a spoof target up front. Reds and greens and some fires — they don't look right to me.
EDDIE:	OK bomb aimer, good show — they're cunning devils aren't they? Pilot to engineer, 2000 + 4. Navigator, we are at bombing height, airspeed 160, that do you?
TOM:	Roger and thanks skip, can you maintain that? New course coming up in about ten minutes. It will be 025° compass.
TOM (personal thoughts):	A pause in my calculations. Me and my thoughts. ON track, on course, all is well at the moment. Will we make it tonight? That wind should be OK. Why shouldn't we make it, we've done ten trips already, the crew are a highly competent bunch — a super team. We keep each other out of trouble. If we cop it one night, you couldn't go with a better bunch of fellers. I wonder if we will survive a tour? It would be nice to keep in touch when it's all over. Back to work Bailey.
EDDIE:	OK nav.

Opposite right and following pages:
It may not be widely known that every raid undertaken by Bomber Command was the subject of a detailed report prepared by staff of the Operational Research Section. Now available for scrutiny at the Public Record Office, Kew, these once highly secret documents make for fascinating, absorbing study — if not quite of the standard of reproduction we take for granted 50 years on. All Crown Copyright

[Top centre document - faded]

14. Foret de Nieppe. Photographs obtained on 30th August showed much damage to this target, affecting at least 16 buildings, 12 of which were virtually destroyed. The roadway and light rail line were cut in several places.

ENEMY RESPONSE

15. Against the Stuttgart force. About 200 fighters were active, two-thirds of them ... was too thin and low to give adequate cover. The Stuttgart force was at first intercepted near Orleans, and then continuously from Koublenz to the target. Little trouble was met on the return route. The Hamburg force, on the other hand, met comparatively few fighters on the way out or over the target - the enemy seems to have suspected another raid on Kiel - but were strongly pursued on the way home after crossing the Schleswig coast, especially E. of Heligoland. Single-engine fighters were active against the first ... on Foret de Nieppe; then they refuelled and were about ... intercept those returning from Stuttgart when they were distracted by the ... raid on Foret de Nieppe. They believed ... Flak at Stuttgart was at first mainly in the form of predicted control unseen, but this soon gave way to a moderate barrage to 16-18,000'. No searchlights exposed, and there was little light flak. Several aircraft were illuminated in the Orleans-Chateaudun area en route. Reports of the flak at Hamburg varied considerably; most of the barrage seemed to be between 17,000' and 18,000'. Searchlights could not penetrate the cloud base.

ENEMY AIRCRAFT DESTROYED

16. Our aircraft claimed more victories over fighters than on any previous night: 27 destroyed, 6 probably destroyed and 12 damaged (including 1: 1: 1: supporting fighters). ...

SUMMARY

17. 40/1142 aircraft (4.4%) were lost on this night: 39/496 (7.8%) on Stuttgart and 23/307 (7.5%) on Hamburg. So many fighters were destroyed that many observations of falling aircraft must have referred to British victories; but the following is an approximate estimate of how and where most of the losses occurred.

	Fighters	Flak	Unknown
Stuttgart	1 outward	4 outward	16
	2 at target	2 at target	
	2 homeward		
Hamburg	1 outward	1 outward	?
	2 at target	1 at target	
	3 homeward	3 homeward	

3 aircraft returning from Hamburg were wrecked beyond repair - one in combat, one due to a landing accident - and a third was destroyed in a taxying accident. No casualties were sustained on Foret de Nieppe.

TRANSPORT

18. 13/13 Mosquitoes carried out a diversionary attack on Frankfurt between 0015 and 0119. 3 aircraft dropped marker, and the rest bombed on them in cloudy weather. All returned safely.

MINELAYING

19. 4/5 Halifaxes laid 76 mines in the Elbe.

............/MAJOR EFFORT.

[Top right document]

SORTIES

6. No. of aircraft despatched .... 49? St. 307 H. ...
   " reporting attack on primary targets ... 461 298 ...
   abortive sorties .... 30 ?
   aircraft missing 39 23
                                        (7.8%) (7.6%)

WEATHER EXPERIENCED

7. Bases:- Mist became widespread in S. Yorkshire and E. Lincs. by 0400.
   Targets:- Stuttgart: 8-10/10ths. Patchy thin medium cloud. Tops 8-10,000'.
   Foret de Nieppe: cloudless. Hamburg: 7-9/10ths. thin St.-cu.
   9-10/10ths. St.-cu over the Continent en route. ... NW-WNW/25 m.p.h.
   breaks over the Zuyder Zee. Half moon, setting at 0100.

NIGHT PHOTOGRAPHIC STATISTICS

8. (Hamburg)

   No. of aircraft plotted within target area (ground detail...10).... 14
                          "   "   off "   (fire tracks....15)
                                            (ground detail... 1)....
                          "   "   off "   (fire tracks....15)
   "   estimated to have bombed in target area (max....270)... 17?
                                               (min...141)
   "   " within ½ miles .... (max....203)... 16?
                                            (min...151)

NARRATIVE OF ATTACKS

9. Stuttgart. The thick cloud quickly obscured both ground - and sky-markers, ... reporting to be scattered, with much undershooting. Open aircraft which went below the cloud later stated that bombing was ...

10. Hamburg. Both ground- and sky-markers were well grouped. The bombing was accurate and many fires were started in the dock area.

11. Foret de Nieppe. Both attacks on this target were accurate and concentrated in perfect weather.

DAY RECONNAISSANCE

12. Stuttgart. This attack, and those delivered earlier in the same week, ... city suffered most heavily, caused great devastation in Stuttgart. The old ... Many parts of this district were completely flattened. The V.K.F. Norma ball bearing factory, the Alfred Knecht petrol filter plant, and about 12 other factories were damaged. The main railway station, the main post and telegraph office, the large Reichsbank building, ... and many other public buildings were hit, some severely. 8 out-lying villages were seriously affected.

13. Hamburg. No such irreparable damage had been caused in Hamburg by the great 1943 raids, that fresh incidents were difficult to distinguish. There seemed, however, to have been surprisingly few in the built-up area, considering the accuracy of the attack. A few warehouses and about 6 factories were affected in varying degrees.

.........../14. Foret de Nieppe.

[Left document - Operational Order]

... NR OPS 21 O-P FORM B FORM B

5 GROUP 1820B
GROUP BASES AND STNS
QY BT

''B'' NO 333

JULY 1944

... A/C OF 5 GP AND 270 A/C OF OTHER GPS , ASSISTED BY P.F. GP ...
1 GP ABC A/C WILL ATTACK THE TARGET
... WAVE - 120 A/C 1 GP (EXCLUDING 30 SUPPORTERS AND 10 ABC A/   H + TO H +
... WAVE - 10 ABC A/C 1 GP + 120 A/C 3 GP   H + 6 TO H +
... WAVE - 100 A/C 1 GP   H + 6 TO H +
... WAVE - 100 A/C OF 5 GP

... DESTROY AN ENEMY INDUSTRIAL CENTRE

... T 28/29TH JULY 1944

... BASE 38 +
... BASE 80 +
... BASE 18 (106 SQUADRON)
... BASE 45

...BEL — AIMING POINT C CHARLIE

...MAL

...E - READING (A) - 4948N 0030E (B) - 4820N 0120E (C) -
...3N 0350E (D) - 4850N 0600E (E) - 4900N 0730E (F) - 4854N
...20E (G) - TARGET

...UTE A - TARGET - 4845N 0922E (H) - 4832N 0918E (J) - 4850 N
...0730E (K) - 4803N 0345E (L) - 4614N 0120E (M) - 4920N 0000 (N) -
...O - BASE
...UTE B - TARGET - (H) - 4823N 0916E (O) - 4750N 0700E (P) - 4803N
...525E (Q) - 4730N 0335E (R) - 4737N 0145E (S) - 4900N 0000 (T) -
...- BASE

...HR IS 0145 HRS
...RD WAVE 50% A/C - 0151 HRS TO 0155 HRS
...TH WAVE 50% A/C - 0153 HRS TO 0157 HRS

...PETROL :- CLUSTER LOAD 2154 GALLONS , NORMAL
...   LOAD 2050 GALLONS
...OMB LOAD - 53 BASE AND 106 SQUADRON
...X 2000 HC NOSE INST. AND 12 CLUSTERS TYPE J ,
...BOMBS - 52 AND 55 BASES : AS MANY AS POSSIBLE
...X 2000 HC NOSE INST. AND 12 CLUSTERS TYPE J BOMBS .
...THOSE A/C WHOSE LOAD CANNOT BE CHANGED IN TIME ARE TO CARRY
...NORMAL 10%
...DISTRIBUTORS TO BE SET TO GIVE STICK SPACING
...NIGHT PHOTOGRAPHY - ALL A/C TO CARRY NIGHT CAMERA AND PHOTOFLASH
...TO BE FUSED POINT FIVE OF A/C HEIGHT . 25% A/C TO CARRY COMPOSITE
...FILM . REMAINDER H.S. NIGHT FILM
...WINDOW IS TO BE DROPPED IN ACCORDANCE WITH THIS HQ LETTER 100/33/
...AIR OF 21/7/44
...MANDREL IS NOT TO BE SWITCHED ON UNTIL REACHING 0300 E ON
...OUTWARD JOURNEY
...BROADCAST WIND PROCEDURE AS LAID DOWN IN ASI NAV 15 IS IN FORCE
...TONIGHT
...REQUIREMENTS
...52 , 53 AND 55 BASE   10 CREWS EACH
...   54 BASE   4 CREWS
...NO WIND MESSAGES ARE TO BE TRANSMITTED FROM A/C BEFORE 0055 HRS
...THE FIRST TRANSMISSION FROM COMMAND WILL BE AT 0105 HRS , FOR
...THE FOLLOWING THREE HEIGHTS
...10,000 FT. , 15,000 FT. , 20,000 FT. .
...DATUM HEIGHT : 60,000 FEET
...1) METHOD FOR TONIGHT 28/29 JULY 44 ON B A R B E L WILL BE
...   NEWHAVEN/WANGANUI
...2) PATHFINDERS WILL OPEN THE ATTACK AT H-6 WITH LONG STICKS OF
...   ILLUMINATING FLARES , RED T.I.S AND WANGANUI FLARES
...   GREEN/YELLOW STARS
...3) IF WEATHER PERMITS THE EXACT AIMING POINT WILL BE MARKED
...   WITH MIXED SALVOES OF GREEN AND RED T.I.S
...4) THE AIMING POINT WILL BE KEPT MARKED THROUGHOUT THE ATTACK
...   WITH GREEN T.I.S
...5) IN ADDITION WANGANUI SKYMARKING WILL BE CARRIED OUT THROUGHOUT
...   THE ATTACK WITH FLARES GREEN/YELLOW STARS
...6) A MASTER BOMBER WILL BE PRESENT THROUGHOUT THE ATTACK AND
...   WILL GIVE AIMING DIRECTIONS USING THE FOLLOWING :
...   MASTERS CALL SIGN   BOXKITE
...   MAIN FORCE   TONNAGE
...   FREQUENCY   5145 AND 6440 KCS
...7) MAIN FORCE AIRCRAFT SHOULD AIM THEIR BOMBS IN THE FOLLOWING
...   ORDER OF PREFERENCE UNLESS OTHERWISE DIRECTED BY THE MASTER
...   BOMBER
...   (A) CENTRE OF MIXED RED AND GREEN T.I.S
...   (B) CENTRE OF GREEN T.I.S
...   (C) CENTRE OF RED T.I.S
...   (D) CENTRE OF WANGANUI FLARES ON A HEADING OF 112 MAGNETIC
...   WITH BOMBSIGHT SET FOR TRUE HEIGHT AND AIRSPEED AND
...   ZERO WIND . R.A.S. OF 165 M.P.H. OR AS NEAR THIS SPEED
...   AS POSSIBLE
...8) A SPOOF ATTACK ON SOLE WILL BE CARRIED OUT AT H-30 WITH RED
...   AND GREEN T.I.S

...O. ACKNOWLEDGE BY TELEPRINTER

...P. 281820B

...IY AS
...1 K WITH R
.../2047/28 AM AR

[Centre-right document]

SECRET

NIGHT A/C REPORT NO. 675

COPY NO. 21

BOMBER COMMAND REPORT ON NIGHT OPERATIONS

28/29th. JULY, 1944.

STUTTGART; HAMBURG; FORET DE NIEPPE; Frankfurt;

SUMMARY

1. Stuttgart was heavily attacked for the third time within a week, and Hamburg received its first heavy raid for a year. A launching site in France was twice visited in the night. Fighters were active in the moonlight, and 63 of the 1142 aircraft despatched were lost. Our crews, however, claimed an unprecedented number of victories, destroying 27 (probably 33) enemy aircraft.

WEATHER FORECAST

2. Bases:- Rain will spread N. of the Wash by 0400. Fit until then.
   Targets:- Doubtful weather at Stuttgart. Thundery activity may cause ... and leave 5-7/10ths. St.-cu. below 8,000', with patchy medium cloud above, ... much layer cloud en route. Large amounts at Hamburg, perhaps extending to 20,000'. Much St.-cu. with local breaks in Pas de Calais.

STUTTGART; HAMBURG; FORET DE NIEPPE;

PLANS OF ATTACK

3. Stuttgart. NEWHAVEN/WANGANUI marking. Blind marker illuminators were to drop red T.I. and white hooded flares, unless there was more than 6/10ths. cloud, in which case they would release skymarker flares (G/Y.stars) with their T.I. Primary visual markers were to drop mixed red and green T.I. after definite visual identification, using the reds as a guide. Secondary blind markers, ... bombing at intervals throughout the raid, were to drop skymarkers. But if T.I. were visible, they would drop no markers. Visual centrers, also distributed throughout the raid, would aim green T.I. at the centre of mixed reds and greens, or of greens, or of reds, in that order of priority. With 1-second overshoot. Main Force crews were to aim their bombs as the visual centrers were to aim their T.I., except that if no T.I. were visible they would aim at the skymarker flares. A Master Bomber would direct the attack. Marker aircraft unable to mark according to plan, would bomb with the main force. H = 0145.

4. Hamburg. Blind P.F.F.IFF. Primary blind markers were to drop red T.I. and skymarker flares (G/Y.stars). Visual centrers, attacking at intervals throughout the raid, were to keep the √2 marked with green T.I., aimed at the centre of all T.I. with a 1-second overshoot. Secondary blind markers, also ... spread throughout the raid, were to drop skymarker flares or WANGANUI flares. Main force crews were to aim at the centre of green T.I., red T.I. or WANGANUI flares, in that order of priority. Marker aircraft unable to mark according to plan were to bomb with the main force. H = 0115.

5. Foret de Nieppe. This target was to be attacked twice, but the same method was to be used both times. 5 OBOE Mosquitoes were to drop red T.I., and the main force were to aim at the centre of these markers. A.B.C. aircraft were to be present during the second attack. H = 2345 and 0400.

.........../SORTIES.

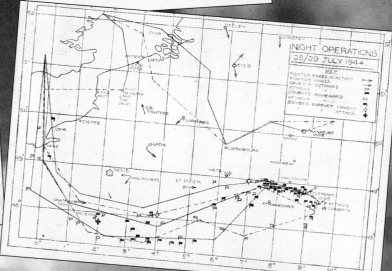

NIGHT OPERATIONS
28/29 JULY 1944.

KEY
FIGHTER BASES IN ACTION
FIGHTER MOVES
ATTACKS OUTWARD
COMBATS OUTWARD
ATTACKS HOMEWARD
COMBATS HOMEWARD
BOMBER SUPPORT COMBAT

TOM: Nav to Skipper. Turn to new course of 025° compass now, 20 minutes to target.

EDDIE: OK nav, turning on to 025, we seem to be going through a flak belt, shouldn't be many fighters around, but keep your eyes peeled everybody.

MAC: Mid-upper here Skip, you spoke too soon, a 109 just passed from starboard to port, like a bat out of hell.

EDDIE: OK Mac, I reckon he's gone now, but it proves a point. Keep on your toes gunners. Bloody hell, that flak was close. Everybody alright?

BILL: OK skip. bomb aimer here. PFF markers going down right on time and dead ahead, but no flak or lights anywhere. They're kidding, must be.
First bombs going down and Jerry's woken up at last. Flak looks nasty, good bombing, right in the markers; big explosion just off centre.

TOM: Navigator here, could be a gas works, they're slightly port of the main aiming point. Hello Skipper, navigator, turn on to 043 at 0233hrs for bombing run. 043 at 0233 over.

EDDIE: Navigator, OK 043 at 0233.

TOM: Nav here. Bomb aimer, wind is now 337/43.

BILL: OK Tom, 337/43 set. Over.

EDDIE: Hello bomb aimer, Skipper, turning on, turning on.

BILL: OK Skipper, turning on, all bombs fused and selected, master switch is ON.

EDDIE: Master switch is ON, bomb aimer.

BILL: Skipper, running up, bomb doors open.

EDDIE: Bomb doors open, bomb aimer.

MASTER BOMBER: Hello all Steel Gray aircraft — bomb the greens, bomb the greens.

BILL: Hello Skipper, left, left, steady, steady.

DICK: W op to Skip, there's a Lanc just above us, bomb doors open.

EDDIE: Bomb aimer, did you hear that.

BILL: OK Skipper, right, steady.

EDDIE: Skipper to W op, where is he now?

DICK: OK Skipper, we've lost him.

BILL (voice lowering in cadence): Left, left, steady. Steady. Steady. Steady. Right, steady. Steady. Steady. BOMBS GONE. PAUSE. Jettison bars across. Wait for the camera lights. PAUSE. Hello Skipper, camera lights, bomb doors closed.

Below:
Double-page spread from navigator Tom Bailey's log book showing the entry for Stuttgart 28/29 July 1944. To Tom (and most aircrew) a log book was a 'bind' to keep up to date and he entered as little information as he needed to in order to have it signed at the end of each month. Note that he did not even enter times of take-off. A neat, well-kept log book even so. F. T. Bailey

EDDIE: Bomb doors closed, bomb aimer.

BILL: Checked, no hang-ups Skipper.

EDDIE: OK boys, let's go home and get the hell out of here.

TOM: Nav to Skip, next course, 273°, speed 175.

EDDIE: OK navigator, 273°, speed 175. Bomb aimer, how did it go?

BILL: Hello Skipper, looked very good, wind seemed OK, bombing looked concentrated on the reds, there's two really big fires.

EDDIE: Bomb aimer, will you say again, there's two what?

BILL: Two big fires, Skipper.

EDDIE: Yes, the night is bursting around us — it is like bloody hell let loose. Hold tight everybody, I'M still struggling to get control, hang on, she's responding. Everything seems to be OK, no warning lights, we're back to level flight. Skipper to crew, everybody OK? Let's hear from you, intercom check.

BILL: Bomb aimer OK Skip.

DICK: Wireless op OK Skip.

TOM: Nav OK Skip, but I lost all my pencils — trying to sharpen one now. What the hell was all that?

MAC: Mid-upper here, they had our number that time and I reckon we got about six shell bursts. That's what the hell it was. Skipper, I must nip back for a pee.

EDDIE: OK as quick as you can. Wireless op, keep an eye on him and tell me when he gets back please.

PADDY: Rear gunner OK Skipper, that was a warm spell, I think we got hit this end.

DICK: He's coming back now Skip, just getting into his turret.

EDDIE: Skipper to mid-upper, are you there?

MAC: Yes, sorry Skip, had to go for that pee — I was getting desperate.

MAC (personal thoughts): What a beautiful night. What are we doing away up here anyway? 20,000ft. Boy, I dunno, I wish I was home. How many thousands of miles is it? I see old Paddy's guns are still moving around a bit, he hasn't fallen asleep yet.
Well, there's a Lanc over there, hope they are all OK.
I wonder what those poor people on the ground are thinking, listening to all this roar and bombs dropping on 'em. Hmm, funny world this. Boy, I wish I could have a smoke; can hardly wait to get on the ground to have one.
Yep, I am sure getting tired of this. Third night running, Kiel one night, Stuttgart the next two nights, what are things coming to. Gees, I hope we get back safe. Ah, I guess we've been pretty lucky.
Never thought two years ago when I was in Prince Rupert, BC area, that I'd be up over Germany, the only Canadian in an RAF crew.

						Day	Night
Date	Hour	Aircraft Type and No.	Pilot	Duty	REMARKS (including results of bombing, gunnery, exercises, etc.)		
					Time carried forward :—	199.25	171.15
1/7/44		LANCASTER I 'P' LL846 P/O DOCHERTY		1ST NAVIGATOR	N.F.T. AIR SEA FIRING	00.55	
4/7/44		" "	"	"	N.F.T. FIGHTER AFFIL. BOMBING.	01.05	
4/5/7/44		LANCASTER I 'P'		"	6 OPERATIONS : ST-LEU-DESSERENT.		04.25
6/7/44		LANCASTER I 'P'		"	AIR TEST.	00.20	
7/8/7/44		LANCASTER I 'P'		"	7. OPERATIONS ST-LEU-DESSERENT.		04.35
9/7/44		LANCASTER I 'Q' ME 845		"	HIGH LEVEL BOMBING.	01.50	
22/7/44		LANCASTER I 'P'		"	N.F.T.	00.30	
23/24/7/44		LANCASTER I 'P'		"	8 OPERATIONS : KIEL.		04.55
24-25/7/44				"	9 OPERATIONS : STUTTGART.		08.10
25-26/7/44				"	10 OPERATIONS STUTTGART.		08.25
28/7/44		LANCASTER I 'P'		"	N.F.T	00.30	
28-29/7/44		LANCASTER I 'P'		"	11. OPERATIONS : STUTTGART.		08.05
30/7/44		LANCASTER I 'S' ME 796		"	12 OPERATIONS : CAHAGNES	05.05	
31/7/44		LANCASTER I 'S'		"	13 OPERATIONS : JOIGNY-LA-ROCHE	05.50	

SUMMARY FOR JULY 1944 1. LANCASTER I
No. 630 SQUADRON R.A.F. 2.
DATE 3rd AUGUST 1944 3.
SIGNATURE G. Bailey F/o 4.

SQUADRON LEADER O.C. B FLT.
No. 630 SQUADRON R.A.F. 16.05 | 38.35

W/Cdr .... O.C. 630 SQDN.
TOTAL TIME ... 215.30 | 209.50

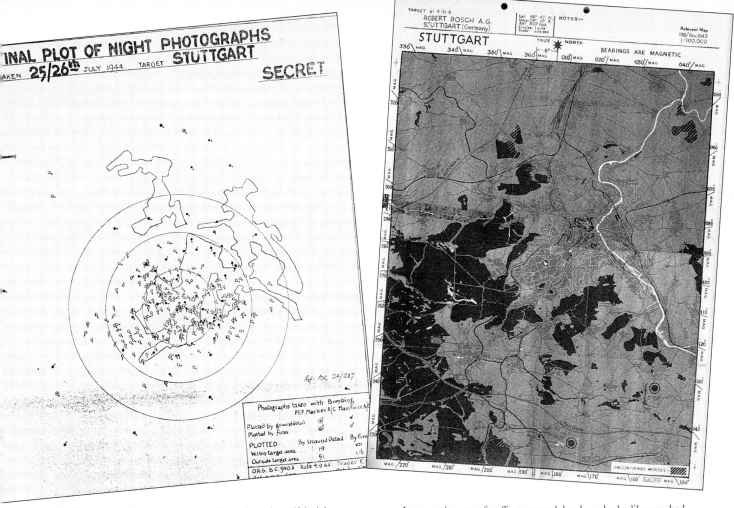

TARGET № 4/616
ROBERT BOSCH A.G.
STUTTGART
STUTTGART (Germany)

STUTTGART

TRUE NORTH

Relevant Map
138/Rev.1943
1:100,000

BEARINGS ARE MAGNETIC

UNCONFIRMED WOODS

Oh! I bet they... I can't fathom that. Boy, what a beautiful night.

EDDIE: Pilot to crew, controls OK and responsive, she flies OK. Anybody notice anything at all — report. Engineer, let's have some power on, we're climbing up out of this, got that nav

ERIC: Do you want me to check down the back, Skip?

EDDIE: No, hang on and see how things go, watch for signs of leaks or temperatures going up.

ERIC: OK Skip.

PADDY: Rear gunner here Skip, it's a bloody good prang back there, very concentrated, looks like a Lanc blown up over the target though. Br...r. it's mighty cold back here.

PADDY (personal thoughts): What a wonderful sight just to see the good old shores of England when dawn is breaking. We were the lucky ones!

Night after night as I looked down upon the holocaust we were creating I would think about the innocent victims of our actions and offer up a prayer for them.

I would ask God to help me and my crew to survive the night and for our safe return to England.

There were times when I wondered why God allowed all this death and destruction to happen on both sides, but I really didn't understand then. NOCTURNA MORS.

EDDIE: OK Paddy, we are still climbing and it'll get a bit colder yet, but keep your eyes peeled, we mustn't miss a thing.

DICK: W op to Skip, have signalled base — target bombed on time and just had a reply.

EDDIE: Thank you Dick, 23,000ft now and it certainly feels colder up front here.

ERIC: Shall I nip down the back now Skip? No problems with pressures and temps.

EDDIE: OK engineer, but be careful with your oxygen bottle and give me a call on the way.

ERIC: Wilco. PAUSE. I am over the spar and down to the mid-upper turret. No sign of holes or damage — all in one piece Skipper.

EDDIE: OK engineer, get back up here. 26,000 ft and it's like daylight up here.

BILL: Bomb aimer here Skip, a few bursts of fighter activity below and

Jerry setting spoofs off at ground level — looks like crashed aircraft. A long string of fighter flares starboard of our track and below.

TOM: Nav to Skipper, new course in two minutes, 290°.

EDDIE: OK nav.

DICK: W op to Skip, a contact on Fishpond. Dead astern and below, good distance away yet though.

EDDIE: OK Dick, keep a sharp eye on it. We are at 28,000ft.

TOM: Nav to Skipper, turn onto 290° now.

DICK: W op here, contact closing and changing course, range 3 miles.

EDDIE: Keep your eyes peeled gunners.

DICK: Range two miles and closing fast Skipper.

EDDIE: Thank you w op. Any sign of it gunners?

PADDY: Rear gunner here Skip, can't see it but be prepared to corkscrew.

EDDIE: Roger.

DICK: Range 1,000 yards Skipper and closing... contact broken off, aircraft diving away to starboard.

TOM: Nav here, could that have been one of our Mossie intruders, they do filter into the stream looking for Jerry night-fighters? No IFF though, strange?

EDDIE: Could be Tom, but everybody keep on the ball, let's not slip up now we've got this far. Good work Dick, keep looking.

BILL (personal thoughts): Looking down into the depths below, I can see tiny flashes, like sparks from a cigarette lighter, then, seconds later, the twinkling peppering of flak, bursting across the dark sky. Reminds me of firework displays when I was a kid — great fun in those days, but deadly now.

BILL: Bomb aimer here, river below and searchlights on our port beam.

TOM: Thank you Bill, that should be Mannheim, we're pretty well on track but getting in front of time with the help of a tail wind.

ERIC: All quiet again now, we seem to be doing OK, I think I'll risk a drink of coffee. Want some Skipper?

EDDIE: Ah, yes, half a cup. That's better, must put this mask back on though.

ERIC: I am changing to No 2 tanks, Skip, let's run these down for an hour, we don't want all the eggs in one basket, do we?

Jerry is having a little rest with his FWs, haven't seen any for some time. All quiet on the intercom. Tom tells us we are heading for the Belgium border, so some way to go yet. Hope we don't get spotted up here.

Pilot to gunners, OK back there?

PADDY: OK Skip, but bloody frozen, I've never felt so cold, I can't feel a thing.

MAC: You don't need to, just think of that nice warm bed waiting for you back at base. OK Skip, cold but not so cold as Paddy, it must be his Irish circulation.

TOM: Nav here Skip, should be crossing Belgium border in five minutes.

EDDIE: Thank you Nav, how's the engineering department?

ERIC: OK Skip, no signs of trouble engine-wise, all is well.

EDDIE: Roger, how are we for time nav?

TOM: About four minutes early, closing up on the first wave.

EDDIE: Well, no complaints about that. Dick, any sign of diversions yet?

DICK: No Skip, no diversions on the air yet, roll on EK.

EDDIE: Pilot to engineer, did you get rid of all that Window?

ERIC: Yes Skip, there's room to dance around now if you are in the mood.

EDDIE: How far to the coast navigator?

TOM: 15 minutes Skipper.

EDDIE: Roger, I'm going to let down, 1800 revs, 0 boost, engineer.

ERIC: OK Skipper, now for a chance to thaw out as we get lower.

TOM: Nav to Skip, coast in two minutes.

EDDIE: Thank you, have signs of flak up front, Jerry's final effort, we should be OK at this height though.

BILL: Crossing coast now navigator.

TOM: Thank you bomb aimer, don't forget the trailing aerial Dick. Navigator to Skipper, last course now Skip, 330°. ETA base 0605. We've been airborne over eight hours.

EDDIE: OK turning on to 330° now. Light flak up front and down below, somebody's crossing a convoy, bloody trigger-happy these navy blokes.

EDDIE: Have you got the color in Dick, there's a convoy coming up.

DICK: Yes, already to go Skip.

BILL: Bomb aimer here Nav, English coast coming up.

TOM: OK Bill.

EDDIE: Just heard a couple of aircraft calling SILKSHEEN. They took off before us. At last we are down below 10,000 ft, it will be a relief to get this oxygen mask off. Any coffee left engineer.

ERIC: Yes, hang on Skip we'll finish it off between us.

ERIC (personal thought): We'll deserve a rest after this one. Stuttgart three times running — you could have knocked me down when he said Stuttgart again at briefing tonight. What's old 'Butch' Harris up to?

Still I'm glad we are on Lancs and not Halifaxes. We've had this kite 'P:Peter' for eight trips now and she's a good 'un and the lads look after her really well, with a kind of pride you might say. Funny, how you can get attached to one kite — we must have a few photos done standing in front of her — ground crew as well as us.

EDDIE: OK engineer, let's go through the check list, auto pilot out.

ERIC: M gear, air intakes cold, break pressure OK.

EDDIE: Aerial in Dick.

DICK: Roger Skipper, home and dry, 'Q:Queenie' and 'D:Dog' calling for landing, nearly there.

EDDIE: Hello Silksheen, Gauntley 'P:Peter', landing instructions please.

R/T OP: Silksheen to Gauntley 'P:Peter', join circuit at 2,000ft upwind. You are No 3 to land. Runway 130, QFE 1010, wind 205° 10 mph. Call on the downwind leg.

EDDIE: Gauntley, 'P:Peter', Roger Wilco. Did you check the bomb bay Bill?

BILL: All clear Skip, I was just doing it when we copped all that flak.

EDDIE: That's OK Bill. Right engineer, flaps 20°

ERIC: Flaps 20° Skip.

EDDIE: Red in pistol Dick.

DICK: OK Skip, it's in.

EDDIE: Speed 160, turning downwind. Hello Silksheen, Gauntley 'P:Peter' downwind.

R/T OP: Silksheen to Gauntley 'P:Peter,' you are clear to land, reduce to 1,000ft.

EDDIE: Roger out. Undercarriage down.

ERIC: OK Skip, undercarriage down, brake off, undercarriage locked down.

EDDIE: Roger, flap 30°, IAS 140, cross-wind coming in to finals. Hello Silksheen, Gauntley 'P:Peter' funnels.

R/T OP: Roger Peter, pancake, OUT.

EDDIE: OK engineer, full flap, airspeeds please, navigator.

TOM: Roger, 120, 120, 115, 115, 115 112, 115, 112, 112, 110, 110, fence, 100, 98, CUT… and we're down. Nice landing Skip.

MAC: Bloody good show Skipper.

EDDIE: Gauntley 'Peter', landed and clear.

R/T OP: Roger Peter

ERIC: Flaps UP, rad shutters open, pumps off, itot head heater off.

EDDIE: OK engineer, both outers OFF, watch the brake pressures. Taxying to dispersal… here we are at last. Both inners OFF.

EDDIE (personal thoughts): With the Merlins silent once more, we ad another operation to our tour. I'm getting to know the lads now and they have proved again tonight what a competent crew they are — every one of them. I have every confidence in them and consider myself dead lucky to crew up with them and mighty proud of the way they call me Skip.

DICK: Cheer up lands, only another 19 to do. A few more and we'll be veterans.

DICK'S PERSONAL THOUGHTS

Another sortie over, well, the flying part that is. After a wait for the crewtruck to take them back to the debriefing room and a welcome hot cuppa, all crews will be quizzed by the intelligence officers, in order to determine the degree of success of the operation.

The village of East Kirkby is awakening even at this early hour, with the villagers going about their business as the aircrews slowly wend their ways back to their Nissen huts, to catch up on some well earned daytime sleep. They need it, could be OPS ON again tonight!…

…Frustrating, terrifying at times, a great feel of achievement, quietly exciting. Bloody Met forecast wrong again, ten tenths cloud around target. A storm, icing up, one engine overheating, flak on outward trip, fighters, flak around target, flak coming home, searchlights picking you up, red tracer like action replay, creeping up and fortunately curling away all around you.

Navigator breaks his pencils — fighters — then over the North Sea — more cloud — dropping down below cloud — then a bloody British merchantman opens up. Is there no let up?

Just a routine trip eh! After interrogation, walking through the village back to our billets, not talking, in the early hours. Complete silence, such peace and quiet after four, droning Merlin engines. Smell of cordite and 100 octane fuel. A few birds starting up the dawn patrol. Thank God we're back and unscathed, I wonder what it's all about sometimes. What the hell are we doing here?

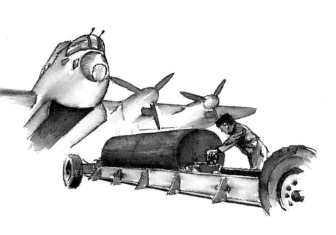

UP FRONT

'...During the morning and afternoon the aircraft has been checked by ground and aircrews and flight-tested...'
Almost 'before and after' nose close-ups.

Above right:
Newly allocated to the Docherty septet, B1 LL966 'LE:P' as yet shows little sign of wear and tear. By the time the crew finish their tour she will have her fair share of chipped paint, oil and exhaust stains, despite the loving care of her ground crew. Here, two erks apply plenty of elbow grease, knowing how important it is to have Perspex clean and gleaming. Smudges, dirt and scratches can all present problems for gunners on night ops. Just as they can hide a fighter, so can they cause a gunner to believe they are a Hun, the latter possibly resulting in wasted precious petrol and time due to violent evasion maneouvres, as well as needlessly scaring the crew out of their wits.
   Still to do an operation when photographed late in June 1944, she is devoid of any nose adornment other than a framed 'P', a semi-official marking to denote a 630 Sqn kite. The Docherty Crew

Right:
Now a veteran, she has a goodly number of painted-on bomb symbols, together with the name 'Prune's Pride'. Barely visible directly under the cockpit window is the large outline of a Plt Off Prune caricature, drawn by navigator Tom Bailey but never finish-painted. Flight engineer Sgt Eric Armitage is seen posing and relaxed in his Skipper's cockpit seat. The Docherty Crew

Left:
TOP-NOTCH

'...We've had this kite 'P-Peter' for eight trips now and she's a good 'un...'

Were it not for the code letters LE this could be any Lancaster on any hardstand at any of three dozen or so aerodromes spread the length and breadth of Bomber Command from Tees to Thames in eastern England. The codes identify it as 630 Sqn in standard dull 'brick red' outlined in yellow as per No 5 group practice from the late summer of 1944. The black horizontal band on the dull red fin and rudder was a tactical marking to aid grouping of squadrons and identity of gaggle leaders in the air during daylight ops, adopted in varying forms by Nos 1 and 5 groups.

She is in fact LL966, pride and joy of Eddie Docherty and his flock, and which carried them through 16 ops, opening their account with a 3hr 45min night attack on Pommeraval 24/25 June 1944, ending Mönchen Gladbach 19/20 September 1944, a night effort lasting 4hr 20min and which saw them tour-expired save for a practice bombing flight in daylight, 23 September.

A B1 built by Sir W. G. Armstrong Whitworth Ltd at Coventry, and fitted with Merlin 24s and paddle-blade props, she represented the peak of standard Lancaster development and production.

By the end of September 1944 LL966 was a seasoned veteran and soldiered on until the second month of 1945, taking off for Rositz on the evening of 14/15 February with South African Lt G. R. Lacey as Captain, and fated to be among four of her kind listed as missing from a force of 224 raiding an oil refinery.
The Docherty Crew

Far left and right:
LIFE-BLOOD

'...Petrol: cluster load 2,154gal. Normal load 2,050gal...'

Another 'pair', this time of 'Prune's Pride' being refuelled, a slow business even allowing for the fact that two tanks will be topped up at a time. With two squadrons to service (East Kirkby's other resident squadron being No 57) the station fleet of AEC bowsers and drivers will be kept busy for many hours. A long haul to Stuttgart means around eight hours in the air (it can vary due to routeing) and tanks will be filled to near-overflowing until the Lanc's standard maximum capacity of 2,154gal registers on gauges and dipsticks.

A full fuel load means a lighter bomb load — 7,000lb, the two needing to be balanced out within the Lanc's normal mid-war AUW of 63,000lb (in round figures), gradually increased to 65,000lb by the war's end. The Lanc would do on average about one 'air-mile' per gal which could be stretched to as much as 1.13ampg with very careful handling of engines on long flights (eg the Tirpitz raids). The bowsers held 2,500gal of fuel, and pumped at 40gpm, thus it could take an hour or more to fill up a near-empty Lanc, though on average the topping-up process would take less. AEC built 1,514 of these excellent machines to cater for the four-engined bomber force.
Clearly, on this occasion, the bowser is on hand early in the day judging from a lack of clutter and blue-clad humanity. On another day refuelling will be in progress concurrently with a dozen or so preparatory activities (including bombing-up) necessary prior to any operation. Note that wheel/tyre protective cover has yet to be removed. The Docherty Crew

ATKEN —

HEMSWELL HORRORS

'Full load tonight,' the rumour starts
'Orders are out —— we're on.'
It brightens the eyes and quickens the heart
Any doubts we had are gone.

We wonder where the target is
What it is and why.
But all that gen a secret is
Till just before we fly.

Out to the flights in a watery sun
to 'Baker', menacing and crouching there.
We 'daily' and clean and check each gun
And more than often we swear.

DIs over, our conscience clear
And assured, for we're the ones
Who depend upon a vision clear
And no oil upon our guns.

Back in the billets we squat and stand
And smoke and laugh alike
Then off for grub, a happy band
On somebody else's bike.

We eat as much as normal
The 'sprogs' a little bit flushed
But manners appear to be formal
And no one likes to be rushed.

Then off again to briefing
In a dingy Nissen hut.
Wallets are handed for keeping
Which means another link cut.

The Wing Co talks to the silent rows
Of pilots, gunners; all's quiet when
In answer to unspoken 'hows'
He gives out the target gen.

'Navigators, synchronise watches.'
Then, with a final 'good luck'
The ears of each of us catches
We head for the waiting truck.

But first of all our dressing
Is done with deliberate care
For nothing is more distressing
Than the cold of the upper air.

Then each with fag and cup of tea
We talk and wait for the lorries
When up we get, harnesses free
It's crowded but nobody worries.

The wagon stops at every kite
Off jumps each crew of seven
And walks into the fading light
Just one stage nearer heaven.

Into the dull black monster 'plane
The crew climbs one by one
We stow and test and check again
To ensure that all is done.

We stack the 'window' load the guns
Then out again to the clean fresh air
For NAAFI tea, a couple of buns
And a joke that we all can share.

Harness on then back inside
To a roar that our voices drown
As the skipper opens the throttles wide
Then he slowly closes them down.

We taxy out with a wave and grin
To a hard worked ground crew who
We depend upon, our confidence to win
For their work will see us through.

At last we reach the caravan
Past a group of girls and men.
The Aldis flashes from an unseen man
Blinks green and we're off again.

'Baker' lumbers forward, gathers speed
Tail comes up with a steady care
Then like a captive swallow freed
She leaps into the air.

We climb and circle above the drome
Until that time when all 'planes turn
And head due south nearly touching home
Where the lights of Reading burn.

The reds and greens of nav lights
Are the only touch we hold
With dozens of other squadron kites
Flying out there in the cold.

The crew is silent as they scan
The approaching dusk with eyes
That guard each crew, each man
From collision and death in the skies.

Far below now is Reading's gleam
The aircraft wheel to port
But we've no time to sit and dream
As we head for gleams of a different sort.

Over France now, going east
Staggering in the slipstream's blast
Hoping to shatter the German beast
Who over our lives a shadow cast.

Soon we begin that awful climb
Up through the cold dank sombre clouds;
Grey clouds full of ice and rime
That cover us with freezing shrouds.

Still we climb, the engines' beat
Continues loud and mightily
Until, at 20,000 feet,
We're far from home and Blighty.

The flak bursts wink, the searchlights weave
The blackness of the winter night.
A gunner with a frozen sleeve
Clears his eyes for keener sight.

Suddenly a blinding flash
Splits the darkness — it's a Lanc
In flames going down to crash,
With octane blazing in every tank.

Bomb aimer reports the target way ahead
I swing my turret and I see
The flares fall slowly, dripping red
Also flak and searchlights swinging free.

The beams cease swinging, instead they hold
A tiny silver fish, diving, turning
Until at last that crew so bold
Dive to the ground with aircraft burning.

Our run-in starts, the bomb doors wide
Into unnatural light we steer
Unable to duck, nowhere to hide
As the flak gets closer, ever near.

The seconds pass like endless days
On that bombing run that we're now upon
Till at last old Wilkie says
'Left ... left ... steady ... "Cookie" gone.'

'Eight, nine, ten' ... there's more to follow;
'Clusters are going, hold her steady.'
God I wish it were tomorrow
All gone now we're through already.

Below and behind the ground is churned
With bombs and flares belching smoke
To the skies; but we have turned,
Leaving the 'pleasures' to another bloke.

A 'plane goes down, another and another.
Each flaming coffin carrying dead
That was somebody's son or brother
And the fighter zooms overhead.

We're lucky though remain unseen
As we press on fast for home.
But we have to keep our eyesight keen
Till we're safe over the channel's foam.

The journey home seems very long:
Full of flak and fighters galore.
And still the engines sing their song
Of triumph that we seven share.

At long last we reach the Island;
Another hour and we see our base.
Circuits done, wheels down, we land
On England's pleasant face.

Welcome back we tell our story
Of the trip 'bang on', a wizard prang,
Not forgetting the death and glory
Of the crews whose death knell rang.

Our story over, we are free
To walk into the dawn and say
Well, that's the end of another spree,
We're safe for another day.

Maybe we'll die tomorrow
For someone always goes
On a one-way trip to sorrow
To be buried among our foes.

Who will return tomorrow?
For someone always dies,
Leaving a mother to sorrow
For the end of a son in the skies.

Les Buckell (No 150 Sqn —— 1945)

Above:

THE SKY THEIR AMPHITHEATRE

'...Navigator here. We should be setting course in a few minutes, Skipper. One eight zero...'

Already the roar of the motors will be taking the edge off the crew's minds, wearing away the nervous excitement, the foreboding — any of a dozen emotions — with them since seeing their names on the battle order and brought to a climax on learning the target at briefing. Already, below them, darkness is steadily settling over the earth. It is near-formless now, dissolved in a haze of mauve. As do the last gleams go from the sunset, so does an arena of deepening colour drain away, leaving sediments of red and gold, a hint of violet. How huge and tranquil is the sky, sprinkled with insect-like aircraft by the hundred and whose navigation lights of red, green and white will soon fade from view. Aboard each and every Lanc all the confusions of rumour and counter-rumour, hopes and fears will be burned away or realised within the hours ahead...

J. F. Clark

Right:

THE RIGHT STUFF

'...Fighter! Fighter! Corkscrew starboard, go, go, go!...'

Picture yourself at the controls of a crippled Lancaster... descending rapidly... in pitch blackness, a mere 500ft above Germany. Add to this scenario that you have no parachute... that you are alone... committed to attempting a landing... and a fate unknown.

Such was the terrifying prospect facing Flt Sgt Tom Fogaty DFM, Skipper of BII LL704 'KO:H' from No 115 Sqn, Witchford, in the early hours of 31 March 1944.

The target that bleak, cold, clear night of 30/31 March 1944 was Nuremberg and it would prove to be a night of disaster for Bomber Command and much debated for aeons to come.

Early on it became apparent that losses would be high, Fogaty's navigator Flg Off Peter Paddon logging at least 50 combat sightings, kites going down in flames. And, just when such combats seemed to be less frequent, all hell broke loose aboard LL704. When about 50 miles northeast of Mannheim, height 22,000ft, time around 01.00hrs, a fighter's cannon fire thudded into the Lanc with deafening, deadly effect. Despite executing a corkscrew manoeuvre the kite was badly mauled and on attempting to trim for straight and level flight the skipper found it impossible to hold height. With the starboard-inner already feathered, they were losing height at 500ft a minute, still an hour from the target. Down in no time to 17,000ft, there was no alternative but to dump the bomb load. Thus relieved, the Lanc's rate of descent dropped to 200ft a minute but they were being steadily left behind by the bomber stream.

Pilot and navigator decided to turn to port about 50 miles northwest of Nuremberg and rejoin the stream on its outward track southwest of the target. They were on this southerly heading, down to 15,000ft, feeling vulnerable, when flak opened up, tossing them about violently.

Then, when some 30/35 miles southwest of Stuttgart, height 2,500ft, time about 02.35hrs, something seemed to 'give' in the controls and LL704 went into an alarming shallow dive to starboard. Unable to correct, baling out was inevitable. However, the engineer's chute was jammed under the pilot's seat, and with the Lanc at no more than 1,000ft by now, Sgt Johnny Dams was instructed to take his Skipper's and bale out. This left Fogaty on his own. Somehow he managed to straighten the doomed aircraft, now less than 500ft above the ground. Applying full flap and with landing lights on, he peered into the gloom, espying an orchard passing 20ft beneath with, beyond, what looked like a field. Then, bracing himself (he had loosened his safety straps sometime earlier), he prayed...

When he came-to he was lying on the snow-covered ground about 50yd from the wrecked Lanc. He had a bump on his forehead, a grazed leg, and was minus a flying boot. Truly miraculous! Understandably confused, he was later informed by his interrogation officer that when found by local farmers he was shouting 'Voici, voici', thereby indicating he thought he was in France. The farmers took him to a farmhouse nearby and thus began 14 months as a prisoner of war. All his crew likewise survived, each amazed to learn how he had put the Lancaster down.

Two decades after the war, Tom still ran through that last trip in his mind. Although it cannot be confirmed, it seems certain his Lancaster was hit by cannon fire from underneath, doubtless a victim of schrage musik. Newspix via P. W. Moore

DEATH COMETH SOON OR LATE

'...Engineer to navigator... Lanc exploded, starboard bow up... going down in flames...'

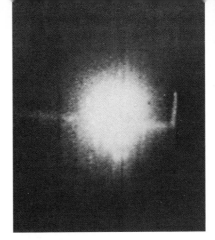
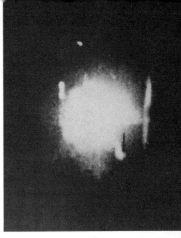

Above right:
This is the death of a Lancaster in the night skies high over Germany. A remarkable two-frame still from a film taken by a special camera fitted to the Fw190 flown on Wild Boar/Wild Sau sorties by Hauptmann Friedrich-Karl (Felix) Mueller, who finished the war with at least 23 allied bombers to his credit and a chestful of awards to match.

When it came, death was all too frequently violent. Slim were the chances of survival when a night-fighter in experienced hands 'locked on' to a lumbering, droning Lancaster. True, a Lanc could survive, but so much depended on the vigilance of the crew... how experienced it was... how well it worked as a team.

The crews unhesitatingly went into battle accepting that the chances of finishing a tour were odds against. If, as complete crews, or as individuals, there were any misgivings, they were suppressed, left unsaid. Their minds did not dwell on such undoubted facts as the lack of armour-plating on the Lancaster, or the relative ineffectiveness of 0.303in Brownings beyond 400yd.

Later serving crews had other worries. How many were lost before it was realised that the enemy 'homed' on to the H₂S radar and instructions were given to use it sparingly? And how many crews were lost because of schrage musik? There can be little doubt that higher authority knew of its existence. After all, enough crews who survived and/or witnessed such attacks had filed their reports. It seems inconceivable that steps — albeit limited — were not taken to counter it or to promulgate its likelihood as a method of attack to the squadrons. Many aircrew today will claim they were told nothing of upward firing guns in fighters. Certainly on many squadrons new crews were still actively discouraged from weaving (which surely reduced the risk of attack) even in the final months of the war. Perhaps too much faith was put in the famed 'corkscrew' manoeuvre? We shall never know. Friedrich-Karl Mueller (Audrey Taylor)

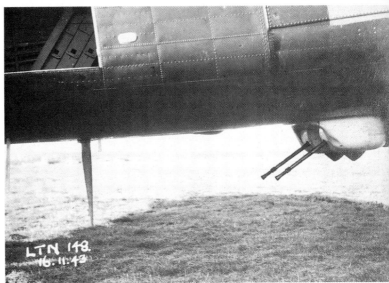

LTN 148.
16·11·43

Centre right:
Throughout the war, there were experiments with fitting of ventral guns to Lancasters, but none proved satisfactory. Some early Manchesters and Lancasters were fitted with them, but sighting problems at night proved insuperable and in any case the advent of H₂S cupolas virtually ruled them out. Some 3 Group squadrons with bulged bomb bay, non-H₂S Lancs tried out ventral guns from time to time, particularly when daylight ops were resumed in 1944, not with any reportedly marked success; and 6 Group also, as shown in the photo of a Lanc BII of No 408 'Goose' Sqn, Linton-on-Ouse, taken in November 1943. For the inquisitive, the aerial below the fuselage is for 'Mandrel' (see footnote).

It is surprising, perhaps, that the front turret was retained throughout, apart from a few isolated cases such as the BI 'Specials' of 617 Sqn, and some 'local mod' removals (probably unofficial) by certain PFF Squadrons (such as No 7). Other than a few notable low-level raids, how often were the front guns fired or the turret even manned for that matter? In night air-to-air combat, head-on attacks were nigh impossible at closing speeds of 400mph or more. Yet the penalty imposed by the front turret in weight and drag might well have justified its complete removal, certainly when Bomber Command was operating almost wholly at night. S. T. Hall

Footnote:
'Mandrel' was a method of 'noise jamming' the Germans' 'Freya' early-warning radar chain by unsuppressed transmissions. It was first used in action late 1942, installed in Boulton Paul Defiants operating off the enemy coasts, but later extended to the more inland radar chains by fitment to bombers operating with the main force. Some were fitted with a second noise jammer to interfere with German air/ground radio transmissions, thereby affecting the night-fighters. 'Mandrel' was not commonly fitted to Lancasters, becoming more the speciality of No 100 Group, formed in November 1943 specifically for Radio Counter Measures, with squadrons of Wellingtons, Stirlings, Halifaxes, B-17s, etc, for this purpose. Their aircraft usually infiltrated the bomber streams, but sometimes operated in larger units sent ahead of the main force to put out a 'Mandrel' 'screen', which, at times, greatly reduced the effectiveness of enemy defences, creating a 'wall' of radar/radio jamming.

In his book Instruments of Darkness (William Kimber, 1967), Alfred Price estimates that 'Mandrel' effectively saved 1,000 bombers and their crews in its 2½ years of operation. No 6 Group carried out trials with 'Mandrel', as it did with G-H, though neither was fully adopted by it, probably because, by that stage of the war, 100 Group, plus the specialist Lancaster RCM Squadron (No 101), had adequate capacity to meet the Command's requirements.

Bottom right:
LOOKING BACK I SEE THEM STILL
'...If we cop it one night, you couldn't go with a better bunch of fellers...'
If ever a picture carries a powerful message this is it!
Shoulder to shoulder in death, just as they stood shoulder to shoulder in life, are three members of a No 103 Sqn Lancaster crew, killed on the Stuttgart attack mounted on the night of 28/29 July 1944. A villager risked much by sneaking into the church at Glonville, Eastern France, to take this poignant snapshot of pilot Flg Off Bob Armstrong (nearest camera), rear gunner Sgt Keith Kibbey (far left), and wireless operator Sgt Doug Thomas (centre), lovingly, respectfully, laid out before the funeral service.

Shot down by a night-fighter en route to the target, the fate of those aboard Lanc I ME799 'PM:K' from Elsham Wolds bespeaks well the agonies, the mixed fortunes typical of so many crews. A seasoned septet, with 28 ops behind them, within sight of becoming tour-expired, the list of targets in their log books read like a gazetteer of Europe. Beginning Essen 26/27 April 1944, they had taken part in raids both memorable for their success, and some best forgotten...had had their share of 'hairy-do' raids as well as others notable for a lack of incident... until their luck ran out.

Surviving the fighter attack and subsequent bale-out, navigator Flt Sgt Cyril Shaw and flight

engineer Sgt Malcolm Macrae joined forces within 48hr, having made contact with the Maquis. They remained with the Maquis for three months before reaching American army lines in October 1944. Bomb aimer Flt Sgt Terry Holmwood and mid-upper Sgt Bert Cutting quickly found themselves prisoners of war, if entering captivity by different routes. Whilst Terry was unhurt, Bert had a broken leg and the villagers of Glonville who had befriended him, had no option but to deliver him to the German hospital at nearby Baccarat.

Back in the UK the two evaders lost no time in advising relatives of their less fortunate crew members, providing answers to searching questions. The survivors themselves gradually lost sight of one another as each got to grips with the fresh challenges, the uncertainties and problems stretching ahead. It is thought that Bert Cutting is now the sole survivor, two known to have died of the dreaded 'Big C'. We thought long and hard before publishing this photograph and to which Bert Cutting kindly gave his consent, feeling, as we do, that such things convey a vital message about the horrors and vagaries of war. A. M. P. Cutting

43

THE EYES HAVE IT

'...OK engineer, full flap... airspeeds please, navigator... 110... fence ...100... 98... cut!...'

As any one-time pilot or flight engineer will tell you, who could ever forget the pictures their Lanc windscreens framed? The dark woolly puffs among the sunlit clouds... the deadly sparkles in the dark among the weaving searchlights... or the finest picture of all, the black line of the English coast taking shape ahead, with pale, still, vertical fingers of light pointing skywards from the home bases... the red pundits flashing their ident letters. Then the familiar warming voice of the WAAF in flying control cutting in on the R/T, confirming the stacking height, QFE, wind, or any change thereto.

And there was the welcoming runway, the caravan, the empty dispersals slowly filling up as the kites returned, all pallid in the morning light, the strange washed emptiness of the drome in the dawn looming up to meet them. Then, easing back on the throttles over the boundary fence... holding her off... back a bit, back a bit. Tired as all aboard would be, there would be the added satisfaction of a hoped-for good landing. If they were fortunate there would be little wind about, so she would float some.

Cut!... soon followed by the motors crackling and popping in distinctive Merlin fashion. And so another trip was over... one more step towards the magic 30, or whatever signified 'tour-completed' at their time on the squadron.

Right:
To illustrate such word-pictures here is an evocative twosome with a glimpse of Mildenhall, 1944, seen from the engineer's seat of a Lanc on 'short finals', flown by Oliver Brooks. Strangely, a signpost still stands at the road junction immediately below, probably having survived because the once-public highway had been annexed within the airfield boundary as a perimeter road. And is that an old bus shelter alongside it? Whatever, it looks a potential hazard for landing aircraft! Mildenhall is the last Lancaster base known to have been in an 'at war' situation, when, in April 1986, it was directly involved in the launch by the USAF of bombing attacks on Libya. O. V. Brooks

Below:
...And the moment of touchdown for a pathfinder Lanc of No 35 'Madras Presidency' Sqn as its mainwheels kiss the runway at Graveley during the closing months of the war. H. W. Lees

Summary of Events

SECRET.

References to Appendices

Place	Date	Time	Summary of Events	References to Appendices

EAST KIRKBY.

1944.
25/26.July.

21 Lancs dropped 21 x 2000 HC. and 252 x 500lb. 'J' type incendiary bombs on the primary target. There was some broken cloud at 18,000ft. with some low stratus at 2000/3000ft. All crews saw the markers and heard the master bombers instructions. There was a fair concentration of marking with a few rather wide scattered fires which were seen over an area of several square miles with a fair concentration near the centre of the markers. Some incendiary sticks were very wide. The glow of fires could be seen 100 miles away on return. Ground defences were only moderate at the target. There was some fighter activity on route but no combats took place.

26/27 July.

Target - GIVORS Marshalling Yards.
57 Squadron. Off 10. Primary 10.
630 Squadron. Off 8. Primary 7. Missing 1.
17 Lancs dropped 119 x 1000 ANM and 68 x 500 GP bombs on the primary target. Severe electrical storms were encountered in cloud and heavy rain 150 miles before reaching target and on return, but the target area was clear of cloud with some ground haze. There was a long delay in marking the target and crews were ordered to stand by. Finally orders were received to bomb the green markers and some good bombing was reported. There were no defences at the target but a little fighter activity on the outward route. No combats took place.

27th July.

Stand down.

28/29 July.

Target - STUTTGART.
57 Squadron. Off 15. Primary 12. Abortive 1. Missing 2.
630 Squadron. Off 11. Primary 10. Missing 1.
22 Lancs. dropped 12 x 2000lb., 100 x 1000lb., 20 x 500lb and 144 x 500 'J' type incendiary bombs on the primary target. The marking was punctual and accurate and most feet with good visibility above. The main concentration of bombed these or the glow reflected on cloud. The marking was punctual and accurate and most of the markers but a number of scattered fires were

---

R.A.F. Form 540
See instructions for use of this form in K.R. and A.C.I.,
para. 2349 and War Manual Pt. II., chapter XX., and
note in R.A.F. Pocket Book.

OPERATIONS RECORD BOOK
of (Unit or Formation) R.A.F. STATION, EAST KIRKBY.

Summary of Events

SECRET.

Place	Date	Time	Summary of Events	References to Appendices

EAST KIRKBY.

1944.
28/29 July.cont'd.

seen over a wide area. Defences over the target were moderate, but fighter activity was intense over Germany. A number of combats took place, but no claims are made.

29th July.

Stand by for night operations - stood down, but stand by for daylight operations on 30th July.

30th July. Daylight.

Target - CANADIAN Army Support.
57 Squadron. Off 13.
630 Squadron. Off 12.
All aircraft brought back their bombs in accordance with instructions received from the master bomber to abandon mission. This was due to the target being covered by low cloud.

30th July. 31st July. Daylight.

Stand by for night attack - cancelled.
Target - RILLY LA MONTAGNE Supply Dump.
57 Squadron. Off 3. Primary 3.
630 Squadron. Off 3. Primary 3.
6 Lancs dropped 60 x 1000lb. and 24 x 500lb. bombs on the primary target. Weather was clear with slight ground haze. The target was clearly seen and crews bombed visually with good results, bursts being seen on and around the railway lines. Defences were moderate, but no fighters were seen.
Target - JOIGNY LAROCHE Railway Centre.
57 Squadron. Off 7. Primary 6. Missing 1.
630 Squadron. Off 9. Primary 9.
15 Lancs. dropped 150 x 1000lb. and 60 x 500lb. bombs on the primary target. The weather was clear with good visibility and slight ground haze. The target was clearly seen and the red markers accurately placed. The bombing was very concentrated around the engine round houses and the crews considered the attack very successful. There were no defences over the target and no fighters were seen.

W.M.Kavanagh
Group Captain, Commanding,
R.A.F.Station, East Kirkby.

Above:
Pages from the East Kirkby Operations Record Book revealing coverage of the Stuttgart 28/29 July 1944 attack in mere summary form. Crown Copyright

630 SQDN

DATE	AIRCRAFT TYPE & NUMBER	CREW	DUTY	TIME UP	DOWN	DETAILS OF SORTIE OR FLIGHT	REFERENCES
28/29th	Lancaster III PB.345	S/L.R.CALVERT. NZ.404890	PILOT	21.51	05.34	NIGHT BOMBING ATTACK ON STUTTGART 13 aircraft were detailed to attack Stuttgart. Eleven actually took off at which 10 attacked the Target whilst one 'V' Captain Flight Lieutenant, Joblin is missing. The bomb load for all aircraft was 1 x 2000 lb H.C. 4 12 x 500 lb J Type Clusters and all carried H.2.S. A.P.I. and F/F. P.P.F. marking was punctual and the majority	
		P/O.W.MOONERY.	F/ENG.				
		F/O.M.HEADON. J21913	NAVR.				
		W/S.HONG.R.	A/BMR.				
		P/O.J.DAWSON.	W/OPR.				
		F/S.G.GANSELL.	M/UPPER.				
		F/S.FREEMAN.D.	R/GUNNER.				
28/29th	Lancaster III MD.797	F/L.G.JOBLIN. NZ424362	PILOT	21.53		NIGHT BOMBING ATTACK ON STUTTGART of Green T.I.'s were accurate according to the H'2S. The Master Bomber ordered the Green T.I.'s to be attacked and most crews bombed them, or the glow reflected cloud but the results MISSING NO TRACE. were largely unobserved owing to cloud. The main concentration of fires appeared to be around the Green T.I's but there were a number of	
		F/S.BUTCHER.W.	F/ENG.				
		F/O.D.LAMBON.	NAVR.				
		P/O.M.PETSCH.	A/BMR.				
		F/S.STEINER.G.	W/OPR.				
		SGT.COUSIN.R.	M/UPPER.				
		SGT.SHENFELLOW.J.	R/GUNNER.				
28/29th	Lancaster III PB.214	F/O.D.MALLINSON.	PILOT	21.57	05.50	NIGHT BOMBING ATTACK ON STUTTGART scattered fires over a wide area. The anticipated cloud cover was not met with on the outward route and Fighter activity was intense from about 0500 E. to the Target. Moderate heavy flak was experienced at the Target. Weather: 8/10ths – 10/10ths S.C. tops 9,000/10,000 feet. Visibility good above.	
		SGT.GARDNER.J.	F/ENG.				
		F/S.NASSAU.C.	NAVR.				
		F/S.POMEROY.F.	A/BMR.				
		F/O.LYTTLE.H.	W/OPR.				
		SGT.MCCARTON.J.	M/UPPER.				
		SGT.CROSS.D.	R/GUNNER.				
28/29th	Lancaster I LL.966	F/O.C.E.DOCHERTY	PILOT	21.58	06.04	NIGHT BOMBING ATTACK ON STUTTGART.	
		SGT.ARMITAGE.R.	F/ENG.				
		F/O.F.BAILEY.	NAVR.				
		F/O.W.HORSMAN.	A/BMR.				
		F/S.RYON.S.	W/OPR.				
		F/S.MCLEOD. R197751	M/UPPER. R/GUNNER.				
		SGT.BOW.W.					

R.A.F. Form 540

OPERATIONS RECORD BOOK

Page No.

Place	Date 1944	Time	Summary of Events	Ref. Appx.
	JULY 28/29th		STUTTGART. 180 Lancasters were detailed, 4 were cancelled and 176 took off. 5 returned early, 157 were successful and 14 are missing. CASUALTIES. 50 Sqn. – P/O Carphey. 61 Sqn. – F/Sgt. McPherson. 467 Sqn – F/O Fotheringham, P/O Jebem. 460 Sqn. – F/O Wilkinson. 106 Sqn – F/Sgt Pemberton. 57 Sqn – F/O Wardle, P/O Nicholls. 630 Sqn. – F/Lt. Joblin. 207 Sqn. – F/O Marshall. 49 Sqn. – F/Lt Powell 619 Sqn. – F/O Patterson. 44 Sqn. – F/Sgt. Duncan, F/O Salt. RESULTS. There was much medium cloud and crews were forced to bomb the glow of T.I's through it, results again being impossible to assess. Moderate heavy flak was encountered at the target and fighter activity throughout the route. However, photographs taken some time after the last attack disclose severe and widespread damage to this target which has so often eluded us in the past.	A 8.. B 8..
	30th (DAY)		CAHAGNES (Near Caen) 186 Lancasters and 1 Mosquito were detailed, 2 were cancelled and 185 took off. 1 returned early, 6 were successful, 176 failed and 2 are missing. CASUALTIES. 106 Sqn. – F/Lt.Lines F/Lt. Baker. 97 Sqn./RESULTS. Apart from a few scattered sticks, this target was abandoned before bombing, owing to much low cloud over the target area.	A894 B894
	31st (DAY)		RILLY LA MONTAGNE. 97 Lancasters and 3 Mosquitos were detailed and took off, 3 returned early, 90 were successful, 5 failed and 2 are missing. CASUALTIES. 617 Sqn. – F/Lt. Reide. 9 Sqn. – F/O Worner. RESULTS. The weather was clear with slight cloud haze and the target could be visually identified. Smoke and dust on the Northern Aiming Point and delay fuse bombs on the Southern rendered assessment of results difficult but subsequent photographic cover discloses moderate damage.	A895 B895
	31st. (NIGHT)		JOIGNY LAROCHE. 107 Lancasters and 4 Mosquitos were detailed and took off, 108 were successful, 2 failed and 1 is missing. CASUALTIES. 57 Sqn – F/Lt. Spencer. RESULTS. This target was bombed visually. There was no cloud with good visibility and some ground haze. Clouds of smoke rising to approximately 4000 feet and a number of fires were reported. Neither flak nor fighter defences were encountered.	A896 B896

Air Marshal,
Commanding, No. 5 Group.

Officers' Personnel Occurrence Reports, F.478-F.486.
'V' GROUP NEWS FOR JUNE — Appendix 'A'
5 Group Operational Instruction No.33, and letter — Appendix 'B'

Top:
Page from No 630 Sqn Operations Record Book (ORB) recording participation in the Stuttgart 28/29 July 1944 raid by the Docherty crew. Observe how basic the information is. Spelling mistakes — usually mens' names and initials — not uncommon.
Crown Copyright

Right:
How the No 5 Group Headquarters Operations Record Book summarised the Stuttgart assault mounted on the night of 28/29 July 1944. Crown Copyright

REUNITED AT LAST

Tom Bailey

Where the crew of 'LE:P' went after their tour of ops:

Eddie Docherty (Pilot) — No 17 OTU. Instructor.

Tom Bailey (Navigator) — Transport Command. Base Navigation Officer.

Bill Horsman (Bomb aimer) — No 405 PFF Sqn.

Dick Ryan (Wireless operator/AG) — Hospitalised.

Eric Armitage (Flight engineer) — No 617 Sqn.

Jarvis McLeod RCAF (Mid-upper gunner) — Re-enlisted in RCAF and became a pilot.

Walter Row (Rear gunner) — Short service commission in RAF Gunnery Administration.

The crew went their separate ways in 1945/46 after operations; five eventually demobbed, with infrequent contact for many years.

I remember accompanying Bill on a Thames canoeing trip from Oxford to London in 1947 because a pal of his had withdrawn at the last minute, but for the most part the friendships between crew members lapsed.

It was not until 1980 that Bill Horsman was motivated to start tracing his old crew. Dick and Eric proved to be easy to trace via old addresses; Mac our mid-upper was found by a friend of Bill's at a RCAF reunion in Canada.

Tom's whereabouts needed some research which Bill handled with great determination after remembering our canoeing conversations back in 1947. I had mentioned teaching as a career so he set out in person, to the Department of Science and Education, County Durham, to get a letter forwarded to my home address. 1982: contact eventually made.

In July 1982 Bill arranged a mini-crew reunion in Northampton for Dick, Eric and Mac. Unfortunately Tom was heavily booked for a holiday with relatives and friends and could not make it, but this was the start of a renewed effort to track down the missing two — the pilot and the tail-ender. Tracing Eddie and Walter was more difficult after many years of no contact, but the RAFA in Glasgow helped Bill to establish Eddie's whereabouts in 1984. This discovery led to a crew conference which decided to arrange a visit to Peebles, Scotland, May 1984, to surprise our old Skipper with a 'This is your Life' enactment, aided and abetted by his wife, Violet, and hotel staff. Tom supplied the script and photos for the red book. Violet was undergoing hospital treatment and could not travel very far.

Even Mac and his wife, Helen, came over from Canada for the great occasion and came on the scene towards the end of proceedings. A surprise for most of the crew as well! So, six crew found and one to go. Tom volunteered to start searching for Walter (Paddy to us), ably assisted with suggestions from the lads. The three-and-a-half-year search for Walter is best explained by the following letter sent to crew members in April 1986:

Dear Crewmember,

THE IRISHMAN HAS LANDED:

He has come out of hiding from his turret and is alive and well.

The quest for finding Walter, started in late 1982, has been accomplished at long last after 3½ years of letters, phone calls, searches, researches and detective work, not surpassed by even Sherlock Holmes himself.

I met him on Thursday 17 April, at his home at Hampton, near Hampton Court, West London, a mere 50 miles away, where I spent a very happy and interesting day in his company. We talked, each listening with rapt attention to the other's news, spanning 40-plus years. The crew of 'LE:P' (Peter) figured largely and, of course, he sends his regards to his old crew mates. He does not mind the nickname 'Paddy'.

But to start at the beginning. The details of the trace are in a file over one-inch thick, so at the present time, I will spare you news of the leads and misleads followed up and dropped, and give you the barest outline.

RAF records doubted that an airman named Walter B. Rowe existed (the flourishing handwriting on an old photograph led us to believe that his name was spelt Rowe when in fact it was Row) and requested his service number. PRO Kew (RAF Squadron Records) — Flt Sgt and Plt Off numbers — RAF records Gloucester — next of kin — interview with sister-in-law — trace for brother in London — results negative — service organisations — Salvation Army — radio — TV — electoral rolls — Somerset House, marriages, deaths — Dublin — Irish Embassy —

Commonwealth Secretariat — PRO Dublin — Sunday Mirror — Sunday People.

Both Bill and I wrote to Dublin for a copy of Paddy's birth certificate; Bill received his first, then letters to birthplace — relatives and friends — priests — RAFA Dublin — DHSS Newcastle (Paddy 65 and due for pension?) — personal letters — no replies but no return of letters to DHSS — TV and radio for second time — Sunday Mirror — Sunday People (article appeared) — Paddy tipped off by a friend — letter from him giving short message and his phone number — meeting arranged almost immediately.

Paddy's news revealed a varied career both in the RAF and in Civvy Street, and retirement in Devon was being planned as he was keen to move away from London. He sent his regards to all the crew and would like to meet everyone; arrangements to be made after his trip to Devon.

I cannot say 'the same old Paddy'; I tried to call him Walter but found it difficult; he is greying now, of course, with not so much on top. Well groomed, as of old, and immaculately dressed, with his soft, cultured tones often followed with that gentle Irish chuckle. It was the Paddy of old when he smiled. Let us keep him smiling.

Thought you would like to be informed of member No 7 back with his crew!

Sincere regards to you all,

Tom.

The Magnificent Seven all alive and kicking. A full reunion had to be planned and October 1986 was chosen with Denford (Bill's home) as the main venue. We met on a Friday evening, having travelled far and wide from our homes in England and Scotland. After dining well, with conversation flowing until the early hours, there was a lull in the nostalgic reminiscences to enable us to listen to the tape made by the crew. Called 'Ops on Tonight!' it was a reminder of an operation we experienced together so many years ago, when each member of the crew played his part in the team effort.

After bed and breakfast at a nearby guest house, we all met later that morning for a ploughman's lunch at a nearby inn, where lively banter and repartee was the order of the day. Fortunately, Bill has a very large garden and this gave us plenty of room to relax in during the lovely sunny afternoon of the Saturday. A team effort of tree pruning and fruit picking went well, with no complaints, and the task was rewarded with an evening meal of Canadian salmon salad. Despite the long journey it was delicious.

Returning to our guest house that evening reminded me of making our way back to the old Nissen huts of wartime RAF aerodromes.

It was to our very own airfield that we made our way on the Sunday with an early take-off to arrive mid-morning in the small village of East Kirkby. Here we were greeted by the village host, Edna Ely, relatives and friendly helpers, who made us completely at home, with a welcoming fire and warming coffee. The VIP visitors' book was inspected and signed and many black and white wartime photo albums were passed around showing the crew as they were when boys in blue.

After this generous hospitality we really went back in time, by touring the old drome. Part of it has been purchased by two local farmers, Fred and Harold Panton, who have already renovated the wartime watch tower and allowed a handsome memorial to be erected on the site of the old guard room. Here we paid silent homage to fallen comrades. Already a wide range of exhibits are accumulating in the area, for what is to be the new home of the Lincolnshire Air Museum. Sometime in the future the Lancaster guarding the gate at RAF Scampton will be transferred here and housed in a hangar where its life should be lengthened considerably (*See Footnote).

Lunch at the local pub 'The Jolly Sailor' (that name should be changed) proved to be an opportunity for meeting many local people who were eager for photos and autographs. A full Lancaster crew had not been seen for many a long year.

Soon we were flying off in search of peri-tracks, dispersals, runways, and what is more, found some of them. The gymnasium, the chapel, the concrete bases of our Nissen huts, the old loos, and you'll never guess, the CO's private residence, still inhabited and looking spick and span.

With a sad farewell to our temporary wartime home, we motored back through the Bomber County to Thrapston, Northamptonshire, for supper at Bill's, prepared by his wife, Helen, ably assisted by Mac's wife, another Helen.

We talked over the highlights of the weekend and all agreed that the get-together was a terrific morale booster and immensely worthwhile.

Monday morning and a hearty breakfast, more photos taken, cheery farewells, the take-off was complete. What had it all proved? That the *esprit de corps* learned of friends during the war years had not died, but had been recaptured and renewed by seven men — no — seven comrades, in a weekend over 42 years later.

I am sure that Mac, as the lone Canadian, did not regret having been drafted into an otherwise all-RAF crew. We were proud to have him as one of the team. He played his part with cheerfulness and complete co-operation. We thank him and his wife for undertaking the long journey from British Columbia and making the reunion for the crew of 'LE:P' (Peter) a complete success.

Today, although Eddie and Bill have completed their earthly ops, five of us remain, four scattered throughout England: Dick — Bognor, Eric — Sheffield, Walter — Devon, Tom — Oxford; and way out west, Mac — Vancouver Island.

We continue to correspond and to meet occasionally to sample the *esprit de corps* fostered during that time 50 years ago and cherished to this day.

* Footnote:
The Lancaster has since been moved to East Kirkby. See under 'Survivors'.

OURSELVES WHEN YOUNG

'...It would be nice to keep in touch when it's all over...'

The Docherty seven — a typically competent Bomber Command crew.

The usual mixture of officers and NCOs, they were perhaps slightly 'non-standard' in having but one Commonwealth member, an irrepressible Canadian mid-upper gunner by the name of Jarvis ('Mac') McLeod.

However, in the beginning there *was* another cousin from the Commonwealth. He was Ron Culliford, a friendly, able Australian pilot who had steered his team through the rigours of OTU, HCU and LFS, only to die within days of arrival at East Kirkby.

Posted to No 57 Sqn, he was detailed to fly as second dickey with a seasoned crew (Captain: Plt Off A. E. Oberg, RAAF), in the event raiding Juvissy on the night of 18/19 April 1944. As so often happened during the Command's relentless offensive, fate stepped in, Lancaster III ND475 coming down two miles southeast of Whittlesey, Cambs, on return, cause unknown.

And so, without undue ceremony a shaken, subdued headless crew soon found itself shunted back to another conversion unit, this time No 1661 HCU, Winthorpe, there to link up with a replacement pilot. Thus it was that Scot Eddie Docherty took over the mantle of command — no easy task — steadily gaining his adopted brood's confidence and trust.

Leaving Winthorpe and its Stirlings with a further 37hr 55min entered in their log books, and an 'average' rating, they graduated to Lancs at No 5 LFS, Syerston, totting up another 16hr 10min (their final exercise being a cross-country on the night of the invasion of mainland Europe). Then, with no chance of a hoped-for leave, it was off again to East Kirkby, but this time to No 630 Sqn, the 'junior' outfit there (in terms of length of service only, of course!), to begin a tour which would not be without incident, not without variety, targets ranging from Aunay-sur-Odon, 14/15 June 1944, in support of the allied invasion (their baptism of action), to Mönchen Gladbach 19/20 September 1944 (their final operation). Total operational hours amounted to 164 (45hr 50min day, 118hr 10min night), a relatively quick tour completed in three months, due to a proportion of shorter daylight ops in support of the allied forces' advance across Europe during the summer months. On a tour of night ops, flying hours would normally touch, or exceed, the 200 mark (such as in 1942/43).

Left:
Incredibly, 42 years separate these two pictures of the 'Magnificent Seven'. Compare an August 1944 dispersal snapshot of them in uniform (hats and all) with one taken outside former bomb aimer Bill Horsman's summer house one fine October day in 1986. Some waistlines may be a little thicker, hair somewhat greyer and receding, but their inner spirit has not changed one jot.

Identities, both studies, are left to right: Back: Mid-upper gunner: Sgt 'Mac' McLeod; Bomb aimer: Flg Off Bill Horsman; Flight engineer: Sgt Eric Armitage; Navigator: Flg Off Tom Bailey; Wireless operator: Flt Sgt Dick Ryon. Front: Pilot: Flg Off Eddie Docherty; Rear gunner: Sgt 'Paddy' Row. (Ranks as at August 1944.) R. S. Ryan/The Docherty Crew

CREW REUNION

Now here, we talk of many things,
Of joys and hopes, and soaring wings,
Seven men of differing kind,
Within the ramparts of each mind.

Shadows of the past we see,
The youthful crew we used to be,
The sands of time still trickle, slow,
For seven friends of long ago.

Fellow creatures of the night,
There as one, in roaring flight,
Togetherness, the golden spear,
To turn aside the sword of fear.

Suspended now in time and space,
Pleasure on each young-old face,
Voices, laughter, from the past,
Are reunited here at last.

For photographs, those ghosts of time,
With smiling wives, we pose in line,
Mirrored people, who will be,
Unageing to eternity.

Muted farewells, eyes that smart,
As we met, so must we part,
The earnest faces we all see,
Return to vaults of memory.

Walter Scott, Ex-No 630 Sqn, RAF, East Kirkby (1986)

RIGHT PLACE — RIGHT TIME

East Kirkby housed not only two full squadrons of Lancs, Nos 57 and 630, each with 25–28 aircraft, but also No 55 Base, which, from its establishment in April 1944, was responsible for a certain degree of centralised organisation and servicing within No 5 Group. It encompassed East Kirkby's, Spilsby's and Strubby's squadrons, with an Air Commodore in charge. Likewise, a few miles down the road, No 54 Base was established at Coningsby, to look after the squadrons at Coningsby itself, Woodhall Spa and Metheringham. Each base had its own test crew, the 'base' system eventually spreading through the other bomber groups.

The job at 54 Base came up at just the right time for Flt Lt Frank Thomas DFC and his fellow veterans (average age about 22), who transferred *en bloc* to Coningsby on completing their tour at East Kirkby on 57 Sqn in mid-May 1944. For them, several of whom had become involved with local girls, it was an ideal posting, and certainly better than instructing.

They were to spend a very interesting year at Coningsby, doing not only routine post-modification and servicing test flights, but also numerous trials and experiments, including:

June 1944	Former Dams raid aircraft ferried from storage at Metheringham to 617 Sqn at Woodhall: ED909, ED929, ED915.
August 1944	Same type, flight tested for 617 Sqn: ED932, ED924, ED921. (Could this have been preparatory to possible use on the *Tirpitz* raids, either with Tallboys, or perhaps even the bouncing bomb? Why else would they have been reactivated at this particular juncture? The test crew were told only that they were being adapted for daylight raids.)
September 1944	PB359 'ZN:T' of 106 Sqn: drogue towing for gunnery practice; accepted by 5 Group, making its squadrons independent of outside drogue units.
October 1944	ED933 'N' of 617 Sqn (another BIII specially modified for, but not used on, the actual Dams raid): use of coloured smoke puffs fired from formation leader's aircraft as a guide to other aircraft forming up. Demonstrated to AOC 5 Group and adopted. (Probably superseded by coloured fin markings.)
November 1944	NE165 'OL:Y' of 83 Sqn. New mod: engine synchronisation lights after fitment and testing by Rolls-Royce.
December 1944	Mk Is PB801, PB803, PB809, PB810. Testing of new aircraft for Air/Sea Warfare Development Unit (Coastal Command).
January 1945	ND858: Further smoke and drogue tests.
February 1945	ED906 another former 'Dams' Lanc, still in its special form, now fitted with dual controls, flight-tested. (Possible Grand Slam use?) ND692 — Bomb bay heating tests for 83 Sqn.

These facts noted from flying log books of Syd Bradley (navigator) and 'Buck' Buckley (rear gunner).

It was a busy job at Coningsby, with sometimes four test flights per day, but a pleasant and rewarding one in which they had considerable freedom of operation as to where they flew on tests. In their detachment of 50 weeks, they logged exactly the same number of hours as they had on ops — 208, though all daylight. In mid-May 1945 the crew returned to No 57 Sqn at East Kirkby to fly Exodus trips (POW repatriation), then resumed test flying briefly at 'EK' itself, but by then things were rapidly tailing off. In late June the job was discontinued and the crew split up and went their various ways.

'Buck' Buckley (rear gunner), by then a WO, joined the crew of 'B' Flight Commander, Sqn Ldr Mike Beetham DFC (later to become MRAF Sir Michael), and with whom he moved to Graveley in December 1945 to join 35 Sqn. Flying hours had been much reduced after VE-Day, but in April 1946 there was an upsurge as formation flying practices began for the planned visit by No 35 Sqn to the USA to 'show the flag', and for which it was re-equipped with shiny Lancs in the black and white 'Far East' livery. Buck transferred to the crew of Flt Lt 'Pete' Stockwell in May 1946, formation flying on most days, on two occasions carrying newsreel and press cameramen to record the formations over London etc in a series of well-published pictures. In June there followed long astro navigation training flights over the Bay of Biscay in preparation for the transatlantic trip. When Buck was interviewed by the CO of No 35 (Wg Cdr Alan J. Laird Craig DSO, DFC) about going on the tour, he hesitated a few vital seconds before committing himself, having only recently married, and that was that — he wasn't selected, and he was 'finished', demobbed, very soon afterwards.

Buck is still married to that same girl, Kath, from Boston, which is where they settled, and where he is still an active member of the local Air Crew Association branch.

As he says: 'I was naturally disappointed not to go to the USA, but I couldn't really complain, as I'd already had my quota of luck in surviving the war. Even before I'd started aircrew training, I'd asked for my gunnery school posting to be changed from Morpeth to Stormy Down (S. Wales), as my sister was a WAAF at St Athan. The adj's first response was 'no chance', but three days later he surprised me by saying he'd fixed it. The chap who went to Morpeth in my place was killed only a couple of weeks later in a Botha crash. Then, at 1660 CU, Swinderby, I'd crewed-up with Flg Off D. E. Reay and we were posted to Spilsby (207 Sqn). Came our first op, and I had a bad cold. Reay said he didn't want to put the crew at any risk, ordered me to report sick, and he took a spare gunner. The whole crew was lost that night, 23/24 November 1943, returning from Berlin in Lanc

49

W4959 'EM:S', shot down over the sea. I returned to Swinderby, sick and demoralised at seeing the crew's names on the 'missing' board there. Full of apprehension I was posted to No 57 Sqn, Flg Off Thomas and crew. I caught the train to Boston and walked to the Market Place. It was then 10pm and I asked a group of RAF lads about buses to East Kirkby. They turned out to be none other than Frank Thomas and his boys, so it was straight into the nearest pub to get acquainted. I was never to regret joining them. On arrival at East Kirkby, I was guided to the Nissen hut and shown my bed. Asked which aircraft the crew had been allotted, I told them 'L-Love'. All went quiet in the hut. 'My' bed had been previously occupied by a succession of crew members of 'L-Loves', none of whom, men or machines, had lasted long. It was suggested I move the bed and my belongings to the other side of a certain join in the lino. I did. It worked; our 'L-Love', JB723 got us through and I'm still here today 'three times lucky', if not the fourth.'

Frank Thomas DFC, AFC, left the RAF for a few months, but then rejoined. He became involved in the introduction of the Canberra into service, and later had an exchange posting to Australia. He retired as a Group Captain in 1976 to live in his native Wales. He married Barbara, a flight engineer in the ATA, who had more types and hours in her log book than Frank. Syd Bradley, the nav, retired some years ago from school-teaching. Six of the crew held a reunion a few years back, but all attempts to trace the missing seventh — Walter Adams, flight engineer (who was known to have become an executive in the film industry), have so far failed.

Re-introductions would be welcomed.

Below:
Flt Lt Frank Thomas and his brood, looking an extraordinarily happy bunch. Were they celebrating the award of their Skipper's DFC, perhaps, around 24 April 1944. One obvious thought, with late evening shadows apparent, was that they might have been about to leave for, or had returned from, the final op of their tour; but that was done not in their faithful 'L-Love' (JB723) but in ND977 'DX:R', to Bourg Leopold, 11/12 May 1944, their last op in 'Love' being 26–27 April 1944, a long, nine-hour 'do' to Schweinfurt... Or had they, perhaps, just been told of their 'plum' posting to Coningsby as 54 Base Test Crew — enough to raise a smile on the faces of any newly tour-expired veterans... whatever.
Left–right (ranks as at end of tour): Navigator: Plt Off Syd Bradley; Bomb aimer: Plt Off Charles Paton DFC; Pilot: Flt Lt Frank Thomas, DFC; Flight engineer: Sgt Walter Adams Mid-upper: WO Robby Young; Rear gunner: Sgt Alan G 'Buck' Buckley; Wireless operator: Plt Off Mike Kingsley
All of the crew except Mike Kingsley are thought to survive (April 1995), the only unknown quantity being Walter Adams, news of whom would be welcomed by his former colleagues.
A. G. Buckley and fellow crew members

Below left:
'L-Love's' band of loving carers — it's ground crew, with 'Chiefy' in the cockpit. Inevitably, names are long forgotten. Any identities welcomed. We wonder who was responsible for the cupid-like figure on the side. The bomb score is 23, and the picture must therefore have been taken towards the end of the Thomas troupe's tour, by when JB723 had brought them safely through 24 out of their 27 ops — a remarkable serviceability record.

However, not all 'Loves' ops had been flown by Frank Thomas, as she'd been taken for two trips in January 1944 by Flt Lt K. R. Waugh and his crew on their first two ops on No 57 Sqn, while the Thomas crew were apparently on leave. 'Buck', the rear gunner had actually, by the end, done 29 ops, having been coerced, if not really quite ordered, at less than one hour's notice, to substitute for Flt Lt Waugh's rear gunner on a night op to Leipzig, 19–20 February 1944. Much against his wishes, and those of Thomas and crew, he went, full of trepidation, having even missed the briefing. The next night he was pressed to go again, and couldn't really refuse, he felt. It was another difficult target — Stuttgart, 20–21 February, again in ND468 'DX:M'; another long flog of over seven hours, losses on those two nights being 78 and 73 respectively. Waugh and his crew were all Geordies. Buck, a Londoner, understood neither their language nor their operational procedures, and he was very relieved to return to the Thomas fold when Waugh got a replacement gunner, as all the omens seemed against him. Not long after Buck had done his two ops with them Waugh and his crew transferred to No 97 Sqn (pathfinders) at nearby Coningsby, and were lost on the raid to Munich, 24–25 April 1944, on which Buck and the Thomas crew were also operating, and were lucky to escape after being coned by searchlights over the target area for 10min. Two nights later, 26–27 April, they were on another tough one — Schweinfurt, and on which they lost their very popular and well-respected flight commander, Sqn Ldr Mick Boyle DFC, the man who had eventually gently persuaded Buck to operate with Waugh on those two trips. Too many coincidences for comfort.
ND468, in which he'd done the two ops with Waugh was shot down on 3–4 May 1944, Mailly-le-Camp, flown by Flg Off R. A. F. Scrivener. JB723 'Love' didn't last long either after the Thomas crew had left her for pastures new, FTR from St Leu d'Esserant, 4–5 July 1944, Plt Off R. R. Smith, RAAF, and crew. A replacement 'Love', NG126, was also lost, on a raid to Bremerhaven, 18–19 September 1944, flown by yet another pilot by the name of Waugh (R. J.). In fact, virtually all the aircraft in which Buck flew during his days on No 57 Sqn were lost, the exception being ND977 'DX:R', in which the crew had done their final op. It survived the war to be SOC December 1946.

How lucky Buck counts himself having, on so many occasions, been 'Right Place: Right Time'. So easily could it have been the other way. The circle of fate never quite closed.
A. G. Buckley and fellow crew members

SENSE OF OCCASION

'...When we took off loaded for the first operational trip no one had any idea how they would react...'

We must not forget that to No 44 'Rhodesia' Sqn at Waddington went the honour of becoming the first operational unit to equip with Lancasters. Ever since being detached to the Aircraft and Armament Experimental Establishment at Boscombe Down for the purpose of familiarising themselves with the two prototypes (BT308 and DG595), aircrew and key ground staff personnel could hardly wait to get to grips with the new generation heavyweight. Close liaison with A. V. Roe at Woodford further convinced them what a thoroughbred was coming their way, a big advance on the ageing Hampden equipping the squadron since before the outbreak of war. Never before had a manufacturer and a squadron enjoyed such intimate contact.

The great day arrived. Whether by accident or design is uncertain, but ironically it turned out to be Christmas Eve 1941 when the first machines (L7537, L7538 and L7541) flew in from Woodford and Ringway. In no time an enthusiastic crowd gathered and there would be feverish activity during the days to follow, the pressure on to work up to full operational status without delay. In the event it would be 3 March 1942 before the squadron was cleared for taking the Lanc into action. That night four aircraft were detailed for a gardening foray to the Heligoland Bight; the 44 Sqn Operation Record Book shows them to have been as follows:

Mining: 'Yams' and 'Rosemary' areas of Heligoland, to carry 2 x assembly 22s, 1 x ordinary, 1 x PDM.

Take-off   18.15 L7549 'KM:Q' WO Crum (landed 23.10)
          18.15 L7546 'KM:J' Sqn Ldr Nettleton
          18.15 L7547 'KM:D' WO Lamb
          18.20 L7568 'KM:W' Flt Lt Sandford

Some historians have quoted Sqn Ldr Nettleton as having been first off, but Bert Crum has always claimed to have been 'the first operational Lancaster Pilot', a claim firmly upheld by his crew, and in particular one of the air gunners in it, Bert Dowty, who recalls the occasion quite clearly. He assures us that Nettleton's take-off was delayed slightly due to a mag drop. The ORB quotes the times of take-offs as the same for the first three (ie 18.15), as it was no doubt planned that all three should go off together as a 'vic' across Waddington's grass. (How incredible to think these days of such large aircraft operating off grass fields!) There could have been only minutes in it in any case. The historic take-off was witnessed by the AOC of 5 Group at that time, Air Vice-Marshal John Slessor.

In 1965 Bert Crum wrote to us thus:

'I still have my log book, though there is not much Lanc information to be gained from it as I was shot down after my third trip. Altogether I only flew 18 hours on this type. Of course they were 18 significant hours. When we took off loaded for the first operational trip no one had any idea how they would react; no bombed-up take-off had been attempted before. Secondly, there was the case of the weak wingtips with a full petrol load. Thirdly, I claim to have been the first operational plane (Lanc) from Waddington.'

As it was, that first op was uneventful, and the sea frozen, all four Lancs returning safely.

However, such were the fortunes of war that within a mere seven weeks, three of the four crews were either dead, or potential prisoners, Bert Crum's included.

Above:
Even before that first op on 3/4 March, there had been some casualties during the 'work-up' to operational status: L7542 of 44 Sqn pranged on overshoot at Skellingthorpe on 7 February 1942, and L7538 of 97 Sqn (the second unit to receive Lancs) in a similar incident at Waddington, 20 February 1942, both aircraft being listed as write-offs, though with no crew fatalities. However, the first Lanc to go missing on ops was R5493, 'KM:M' also of 44 Sqn, on the night of 24/25 March 1942, on a gardening sortie to the Lorient area, Flt Sgt L. Warren-Smith, a South African, and his crew of four British, two Rhodesians and an Australian, all lost. She is seen here at Woodford shortly after roll-out following assembly, probably being prepared for her initial test flight or engine runs, there being no exhaust stains or oil slicks. How many hours flying would she achieve, we wonder, before being lost? The records say a mere six hours prior to take-off on the night of her demise. Avro

Left:
Our picture of L7533 (the seventh production aircraft) newly delivered to Waddington in January 1942, still without squadron markings, serves to remind us how little the basic design changed during almost three and a half years of war. Collected from Woodford by Flt Lt Peter Barlow and crew, she was to be a relatively early loss, failing to return from Warnemünde on the night of 8/9 May 1942 with veteran WO Peter Lamb and his lads aboard — another of the crews on that first Lanc op. The Barlow septet went on to leave Waddington an emeritus crew — one of barely a handful of the original Lanc aircrew so to do. B. A. Gill

51

A BIG DECISION
Augsburg: the first daylight —
17 April 1942

Much has been written about this raid, but we felt it appropriate to include here Bert Crum's own account, written in the early 60s, and the comments of his front gunner on the raid, Bert Dowty, whose recollection of the events remains crystal clear.

The crew of seven joined up at No 44 Sqn on 17 January 1942, Crum having completed a tour of ops on Hampdens with 50 Sqn, winning a DFM in the process. The 'core' of the new septet was, in fact, a 44 Sqn Hampden crew: Sgt A. D. E. ('Dicky') Dedman, a Rhodesian (and who was to be second pilot to Crum), his navigator Sgt Norman Birkett and wireless operator/air gunner Sgt John Miller. Flt Sgt J. ('Sandy') Saunderson joined them as first wireless operator, and fresh from OTU, with no previous ops experience, came Sgts Bert Dowty and A. ('Frankey') Cobb as front and rear gunners respectively. They converted to Lancasters via the Manchester. Apart from that very first Lanc op on 3/4 March 1942, Crum and his crew did only one more operation before Augsburg — to Essen, though without Bert Dowty, another gunner being 'blooded' on that occasion.

Practice low-level formations had begun on 12 April, and it is from the final full dress rehearsal that Bert Crum takes up the story:

A BIG DECISION

'That trip with six of us in tight formation, at nought feet, had been a very enjoyable affair. Sqn Ldr Nettleton with Flg Off Garwell and WO Wright led the one flight, whilst our flight was led by Flt Lt Sandford with WO

Beckett and myself in attendance. We had left our base at Waddington, flown south to Selsey Bill, done a smart about-turn, proceeded to the north of Scotland, done another about-turn, and finally did a shoot up of the hangars back at Waddington. We all suspected that this was a prelude to something more sinister. Thus it was, for at the briefing next day it was revealed that our target was to be the MAN Diesel factory at Augsburg. So it all tied in for we were to travel the whole distance in formation, at low level, and the target was to be this particular factory to deny the Germans these engines for their convoy-sinking submarines. To do this we each carried 4 x 1,000lb 11-second delay bombs and our full complement of 2,154gal of petrol.

'Came the day, a nice one, and for me 17 April was to be my day of a big decision. There was one change in the team; 'Lucky' Wright had cycled to the village to collect his shoes from the repairer and in his place Flt Sgt Rhodes deputised.

'The take-off was uneventful as was the trip to Selsey Bill. Right there stood the Royal Navy and one of the things one never did was to fly within firing range of their guns. Therefore, we did a quick turn which at nought feet and flying a 30-ton bomber in close formation causes some apprehension. The English Channel came and went, the French cliffs came and went, and nothing — yes nothing — was fired at us. Onwards over their countryside we flew. There in the distance we could see 97 Sqn heading for the same target as ourselves.

'Then it started — for we were flying alongside a German aerodrome where fighters were taking off to intercept us. We kept very close as cannon and tracer shells from the rear were passing through the squadron ricocheting off the land or hitting and firing ricks of hay and houses. Some confusion started to set in as aircraft were being hit. Flames were coming from Joe Beckett's aircraft and smoke from that of 'Dusty' Rhodes. My own outer port engine became useless and I went even lower to the ground and flew up one of the forest firebreaks, having to go under HT cables in the process. Soon my port-inner went and also part of the fuselage at my side. The shells rattled on the steel plate at the back of my seat. Because the squadron was maintaining a fast rate of knots and because my port engines were useless I was having to race my starboard engines more than I would normally have done. This was carrying me over to the other side of the squadron where I was having to shut off and allow myself to drift back to my proper position. Because of this I was being left behind and having to

fend for myself. So the fighters picked on me, and like a punch-drunk boxer, we had to absorb a lot of punishment and the end came when half of the tail went missing, the R/T went dead, and smoke was coming from one of the dead engines. There we were wallowing through the air, speed decreasing, and not daring to use the engine. I had to come to that big decision mentioned before — force-land. The bombs had to be dropped safe, secret equipment had to be destroyed and a landing had to be made. We succeeded, wheels up, and finished up 20yd from the edge of a wood.

'Poor Bert Dowty was trapped in his front turret. He had been in there during the whole of the trip including the landing and now he was unable to get out of it. No wonder he screamed as I, with my face smeared in blood, attacked the turret with a hatchet to release him. Dicky Dedman my co-pilot was still holding on beside me. Jock Miller my mid-upper gunner suffered a cut face and a spent German bullet fell out of his flying boot. The others, Norman Birkett (navigator), Sandy Saunderson (radio operator), and Frankey Cobb (rear gunner) came out unscathed.

'Leaving the aircraft for me is worth a mention. I was able to get out directly from the pilot's seat. My side of the the plane had disappeared as also had the screen in front of me.

'The Lanc lay there bent but proud, but being still on the secret list she would have been a valuable asset to the Germans. Picture the scene as six British aircrew stood around trying to set fire to the aircraft. With petrol flowing from her there we were lighting matches, cigarette lighters, until finally we attacked it with a Very pistol and *slowly* she started to burn. As the blaze increased, so ammunition started to explode and we departed in haste.

'Remembering that Joe Beckett and Dusty Rhodes had come down nearby, I took it upon myself to go over and see what I could do to help. Thus it was that the crew split up. The rest of the crew headed south and I to the other crashed Lancs. It was like looking for the end of the rainbow; those clouds of smoke never seemed to get any nearer. Eventually I gave up my search when I heard the noise of engines from motor cycles and other vehicles. The German fighters were also milling around, no doubt gloating over the fallen Lancs below them.

'Remembering the RAF rule to put 15 miles between yourself and your stricken aircraft I set off and joined a party of French folk working in a field. I was eventually taken home by one of them to his very substandard cottage, where I changed my uniform for civvies, had some food, and went on my way. I walked into the night and after passing a military barracks I decided not to push my luck any further, so the rest of the night was spent in a copse. To acclimatise myself I advanced slowly, and after another near escapade with a German car I spent that night in a barn. I was awakened next morning when a woman came in with her pike to get hay, I surmise for her cattle. I don't know why she decided to take this hay from just where I was lying underneath but I did not relish this pike being pushed into my anatomy, so I stood up. I feigned to be Belgian; her husband came in and they offered me breakfast. As I was eating and conversing with them in my basic French a party of Germans came in. This coincidence does not leave much to the imagination.

'So my trip finally landed me in German hands. Then via Chartres, Paris, Frankfurt-on-Main, Dulag Luft, I finished up in Stalag Luft III. The rest of the crew had kept free from capture until they crossed into southern France of Pétain. To complete the circle, one night as I was being marched into a Polish POW camp I heard a voice shout 'Crummy', and — believe it or not — most of us had met together once more. But that is another story.'

(Authors' Note: It was later learned that the Frenchman who alerted the Germans about Bert Crum was eventually 'dealt with' by the French Resistance.)

For the Augsburg raid, Bert Dowty, just short of his 20th birthday, was in the front turret from shortly after take-off. In the past 10 years he has done

Above left:
WO Hubert V. Crum DFM, RAF
'Pilot of the first Lanc to take off on ops.' H. V. Crum

a great deal of research into the raid, and still regularly visits the crash sites and graves in France on its anniversary, in the process meeting, and still keeping closely in touch with, eye witnesses of theirs and the other nearby crashes. He confirms Bert Crum's description of the event and that it was 'Hughie' (as Dowty called Crum, to avoid confusion, them both being 'Berts') who helped him out of his turret. He was shocked to see his bloody-faced, axe-wielding Skipper alongside him so soon after the Lanc had come to rest in what he describes as a 'most marvellous belly-landing — absolutely copybook'. Crum had just stepped out of his seat straight on to the ground, his cockpit side having just disintegrated.

As soon as Bert was freed, the rest of the crew were accounted for, including Miller with his bad scalp wound. That they had all survived was truly remarkable, as none too many full Lanc crews got away with being shot down.

Crum quickly organised them in setting about the destruction of the still largely intact Lanc, he himself starting under the starboard wing with his axe, hacking at the leading edge trying to expose and sever the fuel pipes. It took the combined efforts of several of them to achieve this, with German fighters still about. Eventually they got the fuel to start dripping out, but even firing Very cartridges failed to ignite it. So, Bert Dowty went back to

his front turret where he had, as always, stowed a small tobacco tin containing matches and a precious ten cigarettes. By striking the matches two at a time, he eventually succeeded in setting the fuel on fire with a huge 'whoosh', badly singeing his face and losing his eyebrows in the process.

The 4 x 1000lb bombs had been jettisoned on 'safe' some way back, when their Lanc had become doomed, but there were still incendiary devices to activate in order to destroy internal equipment and which eventually helped the fire to spread. By then the ammo belts were starting to pop off and it was time to leave the scene as quickly as possible.

Crum was concerned about his close pal WO Joe Beckett. He thought it was Joe's Lanc, L7565 'KM:V' burning on the ground behind some farm buildings only a few hundred yards away in this quiet location, near Folleville, Le Bois Normand, some 75 miles ESE of Caen. Off he went alone in that direction, hoping he could help, and it was the last they were to see of him until the reunion in a POW camp over two years later. The rest of the crew split up into three pairs to go their own ways. As he watched Dedman disappear, Bert Dowty thought, 'Damn, he's taken my tin with the Woodbines in!' but it was too late to go after him.

Bert Dowty has since established beyond doubt that it was, in fact, Flt Lt Sandford's R5506 'KM:P' which had gone down almost alongside them, hitting the gable end of a low farm building, killing all the crew in the disintegration caused by the impact. Joe Beckett's L7565 'KM:V' had fallen to the fighters about 1½ miles back, cartwheeling into a cider apple orchard between St Leger and Lambert, giving its crew no chance. Dusty Rhodes and crew perished a few miles further on, downed by one of the same pack of 109s.

That night, the crack German Fighter Squadron JG2 — of the Richthofen Group, whose base at Evreux the Lancs had inadvertently flown over, celebrated the shooting down of Sandford's Lancaster as its 1,000th victory since formation in World War 1 (including a number in the Spanish Civil War). It is at Beaumont-le-Roger cemetery that Sandford, Beckett and their comrades are buried.

And so, in a trice, Nos 2 to 5 in the sequence of Lancs

lost to enemy action had gone down, with but one of the crews escaping with their lives. 44 had lost four of its starting strength of six. It was to lose another, R5510 'KM:A', flown by Flg Off Garwell, his Lanc mortally wounded by flak over the target, but skilfully put down soon after bombing, with the loss of three crew members. To Garwell and his remaining crew, therefore, probably went the doubtful distinction of being the first Lanc crew actually to be taken into captivity. It left Nettleton and crew as the sole No 44 Sqn representatives to make it back.

Of Bert Crum's crew, four had struck off westwards, the other two southeastwards, but all six of them were caught two weeks later, on 30 April 1942, by then in Vichy France, and not far from each other, still in two groups. They were reunited at Châteauroux, some 120 miles from their start point. From there they were interned at Fort De La Revere, on a mountain top, inland from Nice.

Their escapades as POWs would qualify for a book in its own right. From Nice, the six went to PG73 in Italy, where in September 1943 they passed under German control after Italy's capitulation. Dedman, being a Rhodesian, was moved to another camp north of Rome, and his inseparable pal Birkett (a Scot) opted to go with him, claiming to be South African. The other four were eventually transferred to POW camps firstly in Germany, then in Poland where Bert Crum later joined them, as already related. As the Russians advanced westwards, they were to take part in long enforced marches from Poland back into Germany, fortunately surviving a rocket attack by RAF Typhoons when heading for Lübeck, though many in the column were killed. Finally meeting with a one-man British patrol, they were eventually liberated on 2 May, just before VE-Day, and flown back to England in Lancs from Osnabrück.

Bert Dowty came back in one from 97 Sqn — appropriate perhaps, as 97 had been their partners on the Augsburg raid, (though faring rather better, losing only two of their six Lancasters). It was flown by the CO of Coningsby, landing at 'an airfield in Surrey near Cranleigh' (most likely Dunsfold).

Bert Crum took off on his 'final trip' in the late 1980s, and of the crew only Bert Dowty and Jock Miller are known to survive, letters to Dicky Dedman in Durban having been returned ominously marked 'gone away' eight years since.

Bert Dowty remains very active in his retirement, living almost within sight of Lincoln Cathedral, and researching numerous aspects of Bomber Command's raids and losses, tracing former aircrew for friends and relatives, and being a keen supporter of the various RAF associations, including No 44 Sqn, whose reunions he has helped to organise. He is one of nine known survivors of the Augsburg raid (at the time of writing, Spring 1995), eight of whom held a reunion at Waddington on its 50th anniversary in 1992, the other seven present all being from 97 Sqn.

Top left:
The Crum crew (minus Bert Crum himself) looking a somewhat motley bunch after two weeks on the run in France before being caught, seen shortly after internment at Fort De La Revere, near Nice, May/June 1942.
Left to right, back row:
Second Pilot: Sgt Dicky Dedman, Navigator: Sgt Norman Birkett,
Second wireless operator/Mid-upper gunner: Sgt 'Jock' Miller
Front gunner: Sgt Bert Dowty,
Left to right, front row:
First wireless operator: Sgt 'Sandy' Saunderson, Rear gunner: Sgt 'Frankey' Cobb. via H. V. Crum

Centre left:
The two Berts — Dowty (left), Crum (right) at RAF Waddington under the nose of PA474 in September 1971 for the launch of the first volume of Lancaster at War, the first time they had met since their release in 1945. Lincs Echo

Below left:
Another Augsburg casualty: R5510 seen at Woodford (or possibly Ringway) when absolutely brand-new with spinners still apparently in primer. Delivered to 44 Sqn early in March 1942, she was to become 'KM:A' 'Apple', Flg Off Garwell's mount on the raid, and in which he crash-landed after bombing the target, with the loss of three of his crew. The remaining four were to become the first Lancaster crew to fall into German hands, to spend the rest of the war as POWs. After the war 'Ginger' Garwell DFC, DFM, became a senior customs officer at Nairobi Airport. (His DFC was awarded June 1942 when he was a POW.) AVRO

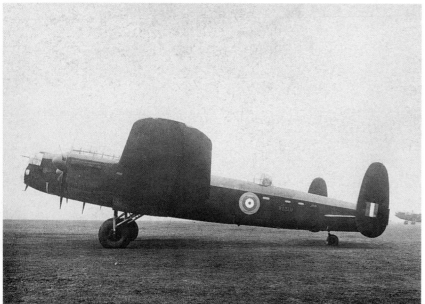

SIX OF THE BEST

Aircrew and ground staff alike needed little excuse for escaping the restrictions and intensity of life on a Lancaster station, be it in the front line or operating in a support role. In a Britain totally geared for war... rationing, the 'black-out', and all that. Mind you, even the beer was on ration and too frequently it was a case of travelling from pub to pub, hotel to hotel, the progress of each cycle rider or car driver becoming more erratic (though never life threatening), the mood more hilarious as the evening wore on. It is probably true to say that, in general, those with wings and those without went their separate ways. There tended to be aircrew pubs and hotels and ground staff pubs, though, naturally, some intermixing was inevitable.

Many (perhaps most?) crews, during their tour of operations, looked after the erks responsible for keeping their Lancs airworthy and in top-notch condition, frequently inviting them to an evening's session of free ale or beer and a meal at a hostelry close to the drome. Whatever the gathering, there might be a game of darts, shove-ha'penny, even skittles, and the landlord and his spouse could usually be relied upon to provide some tasty sandwiches of ham and pickle, maybe a plate of bacon and egg — no questions asked! Being well out in the country, with farmers as neighbours, did have its advantages. Such conversation as there was might later give way to a sing-song, joining the locals at the inevitable ancient piano (no one conscious of how out of tune it was); and when 'time gentlemen please' was called there could be an invitation to repair to a back room until the early hours, sometimes with the local constable being treated to the odd tot. It was useful to 'keep in with him' anyway in case, one night, your bike lamp wasn't working, or your navigation back to base was a bit wayward. ETA back at the station depended on what the squadron had planned for them. When finally they did emerge from the bowels of the dimly-lit, fuggy atmosphere of the pub they would be feeling no pain!

Our sixfold scenario show:

Above:
With inclement weather forcing a brief halt to the intensive flying programme at No 1654 HCU, Wigsley, December 1944, Kiwi Flg Off Lew Hooper and his crew sample the local brew. Left to right are: wireless operator, Kiwi Flt Sgt 'Andy' Andrews; mid-upper gunner, Sgt Bill Bishop; rear gunner, Sgt Peter Brown. Note the 'issue' bikes. Crew posted to No 619 Sqn at Strubby and still operating when Germany capitulated. L. D. B. Hooper

Centre left:
Erks from a No 6 Group Station regaling the throng in a Yorkshire pub, and soon to become somewhat animated. E. D. Whillans

Bottom left:
No 101 Sqn pilot Flg Off W. A. McLenaghan, RCAF, as yet unwilling to discard his greatcoat, sits close to the open fire inside a Ludford Magna public house (older readers will recognise the wall adornment). He and his crew would fail to return from a night raid on Pforzheim, 23/24 February 1945, but Mac would survive as a prisoner of war. And thereby hangs a tale, for it seems that during interrogation he was first asked why he was not flying his regular Lancaster 'H-HOW' (BI DV302 'SR:H') when shot down! Additionally, just before the interrogation ended the German officer thought he might like to know that the wife of his flight commander (Sqn Ldr Peter Sleight) had given birth to a son within hours of the take-off on that fateful night! A snapshot taken by fellow Canadian Flg Off Jim Cooke, also a Skipper with No 101 Sqn and destined to complete his tour. J. G. R. Cooke

Bottom right:
Evidently, on No 156 Sqn, a PFF Unit based at Upwood from March 1944, the ground crews of 'A' flight held their own get-together, extending invitations to their peers, such as 'B' flight commander Sqn Ldr Peter Clayton, a veteran held in high esteem, and who saw the war out with two tours behind him (his first tour had been with No 97 [Straits Settlements] Sqn). P. F. Clayton

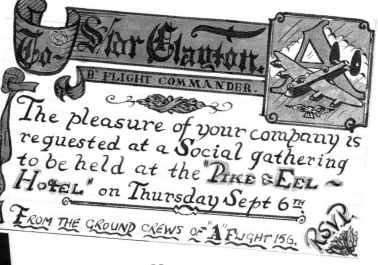

"I'LL GO ROUND AGAIN"

Dennis Dear

Everyone is talking and the bright early morning sun streams in through the Mess window picking highlights on the cups and saucers standing on the bare wooden tables. The sun has no warmth but its very brightness assures it of a welcome after the lonely darkness of the night sky. This is the moment of return from hopelessness and fear. The relief only lasts for a short time and must be savoured to the full whilst the turmoil that is your mind resolves itself into a calmness which is all too short-lived.

The chatter around you is loud and dominant and is the prerogative of those who come back, the safety valve which helps the return to what you know as normal. The talk is of searchlight cones and flak and fighters and the fires over the target and it seems unnatural in the bright daylight which sparkles the frost-filled grass outside.

And when the talk gets too loud and has gone on too long, you finish your fourth cup of tea and walk out into the sharp light. Out into the chill of the morning which beats cold upon your throat and you tuck the silk scarf into the open neck of your shirt, and head towards your billet. Heavy flying boots, scuff against the concrete of the road and for the first time you are conscious of the weight of the holster strapped against your leg and you remember the revolver is still loaded.

Back in the hut, the sun spotlights the dust on the drab lino and the coke and ashes spill out of the pot-bellied stove at the end of the room. Yesterday you left your clean laundry on the bed and now stuff your clean shirt and underclothes into the gaping neck of one of the kitbags by the bed. You strip completely and crawl between the sheets which have the faintly damp and clammy touch of the grave. Your body is overwarm, and prickly-tired and dirty, but you are too exhausted to wash, content only to stretch at full length and close your hot bloodshot eyes.

Sleep will not come yet, for the caffeine pills taken out there last night are still proving their efficiency. Now is the time to savour the sour tang of fear now that fear has been pushed aside for a few hours, by the ecstacy of safe return. Now the night's horrors are unreal in the safe morning light and you tell yourself that you were not really afraid.

And the two crews who did not come back — two fresh crews, new to the squadron last week; and you cannot remember their faces or their personalities and you wonder if they did really exist at all. Yesterday you spoke to one of the bomb aimers — wished him good luck as he got out of the crew truck — and now you cannot remember what he looked like.

The adjutant will be writing the letters now — "only on the squadron a short time but already his personality and cheerfulness had impressed itself on everyone — we shall all miss him."

"Fourteen letters, sergeant — all in the same vein."

And the sergeant will go back into the orderly room to draft out the letters before passing them on to a clerk who will tap out the same cant of condolence on the Olivetti typewriter. And the fourteen letters will be put into the fourteen manilla envelopes already addressed to the next of kin to follow fast up on the telegrams that were sent earlier this morning.

And after a week they may ask in the crew room if anybody has an old brevet to spare — a grief-stricken parent wants his son's wing or wings and his kit has already been packed and stored away. So bring out your old brevets you lucky bastards — your own folk may want one another day.

Gradually the caffeine is working out of your system and the interruptions of your own crew coming back into the billet are beginning to annoy you, as does the sound of engines running up on the dispersals. And at last the hot ache of your body no longer hurts and you drift into the unconsciousness of exhaustion.

You are conscious of your Skipper's unshaven face above you, his bleary bloodshot eyes are empty of emotion or interest as he swears down at you, "Wake up you lazy bastard, its one o'clock, briefing in twenty minutes."

And you know the roundabout has started again and you are booked for the shilling double ride.

A little later as you walk down to the briefing room in the company of your crew you remember your last waking thoughts and realise that the fourteen telegrams will have already been delivered while you slept.

TO SEE ANOTHER DAWN

'...This is the moment of return from hopelessness and fear... the prerogative of those who come back...'

At first glance merely any Lanc cutting through the air, Merlins growling, anywhere above wartime Britain or the hostile skies of Continental Europe... even performing for the benefit of an appreciative crowd at some postwar display. Think again! This is, in fact, an enactment — a 'beat up' of their home aerodrome by a crew who have just returned from their final operation — performed not infrequently... yet witnessed by a privileged few from the ground.

And it was not always a crew known for their boisterous behaviour in the mess or pub who threw all caution to the wind and let off steam. With such a release of tension, of fear, of foreboding... these and other emotions... with them ever since arriving on the squadron months before... seeing too many of their colleagues disappear never to be heard of again... it was not surprising that the temptation to let go was too much. And when they did have their fling there was a tendency for their peers to turn a blind eye, nod knowingly, for they understood. Certainly Wg Cdr Gareth ('Tubby') Clayton, boss of No 576 Sqn, along with others of the hierarchy at Elsham Wolds did.

The one uncertainty all these years later is not knowing which crew, which Lanc it was that tried the already stretched patience of local farmers, long tolerant of their noisy air force neighbours, panicking livestock, cracking the odd window pane, that day in 1944. Does anyone remember?

Is it asking the impossible whereby seven youngsters who had shared so much together, and who, within hours, left Elsham never to return as a group, saw the war out... reached three score years and ten... can tell us?
M. T. Boyne

ALL PRESENT AND CORRECT

On occasions it was necessary to stop the war, as it were, and line up both aircraft and crews for inspection. Real binds they were, too, for it meant a good deal of washing, ironing and pressing (naturally interlaced with many an Anglo-Saxon expletive!)

Such events might be because a new Commanding Officer wished to meet his air and ground crews as a group, or it could be due to an unwelcome visit by the Air Officer commanding the Group. Such inspections would be tolerated with reluctant resignation but, for a chosen few, one review which would send a buzz of excitement round the whole station was an opportunity to see, perhaps meet, 'Butch' himself. Only now and again did he venture from his lair at High Wycombe, and none too many of his devoted disciples could tell their folks at home they had actually seen him in the flesh; an even smaller number would he have spoken to.

Very occasionally too, a station would be chosen for a visit by Their Majesties King George VI and Queen Elizabeth, when it really would be a full turn-out in best blues, though emphasis was always made that the day-to-day operational requirements must in no way be compromised. Perhaps it did no harm to have a 'smarten up' anyway.

Of course, lining up the kites presented an inviting target for a marauding Hun, though no incidents are on record that we know of.

Below:
No 49 Sqn CO Wg Cdr Alex Adams (third left, with peaked cap) discusses a point or two with Plt Off 'Jock' Simpson before meeting his crew, and the ground crew who service his allotted Lanc 'EA:E' (identity uncertain). Far left is OC 'A' flight Sqn Ldr Jimmy Evans, a veteran who had come through the earliest Lancaster operations with No 44 'Rhodesia' Sqn in 1942. Most unusually, he was a navigator. Picture taken at Fiskerton during the winter of 1943/44. J. H. Simpson

Above:
Spotlighting the inspection theme are: No 156 Sqn Lancs being aired at Warboys one unrecorded, long forgotten day in May 1943. Among the original squadrons forming the pathfinding No 8 Group, No 156, led by their inspiring CO Wg Cdr Tommy Rivett-Carnac, had discarded its durable Wimpeys for Lancs in January 1943, blooding them on Lorient 26/27 January. For the purist, nearest machine in our picture — BIII ED734 'GT:H' — survived until Essen 25/26 July 1943, taking the Flg Off J. M. Hudson assemblage to their doom.
T. S. Rivett-Carnac

Left:
On two occasions at least, No 514 Sqn evidently did not feel exposed to intruder attack, lining up its wares at Waterbeach.

These contrasting studies in perspective show us:

The unit's original equipment — the Hercules-motored BII — line abreast on 26 January 1944. The only squadron to form with the BII (Foulsham, 1 September 1943), No 514 acquitted itself well before converting to the Merlin-engined BI and BIII in June 1944.

Nearest the camera is DS813 'JI:H', fated to go missing on Stuttgart 28/29 July 1944 with Flg Off A. F. Fowke, RCAF, and crew. Next in line is LL624 'JI:B' which would ultimately be struck off charge 29 September 1944 following battle damage received earlier. G. A. Henry

Bottom left:
Five months later the BIIs had been supplanted by BIs and BIIIs. Note how quickly engine cowlings became oil- and grime-stained. Keen eyes will also spot tape on the mainwheel tyre assemblies, a simple yet effective method of detecting tyre creep. BI LM181 'JI:E' did not return from Homberg 20/21 July 1944 with a septet skippered by New Zealander Flg Off L. W. McLean. IWM

PAY.

We mention this first because for some un reason Pay-Day seems to be the hub of the universe. It is expected that shortly the Treasu so increase the Family allowances that attenda Pay Parade will be superfluous for at least the m types. Until that day arrives reference to S Routine Orders will tell you that like " Alice " was a Parade last Wednesday, and there will be an next Wednesday, but never one this Wednesday. only thing that occurs on this Wednesday, called B Wednesday, owing to the blank look of amazeme the face of the Accountant Officer when you query account, are Pay-Queries and supplementary Parades. These are held in the N.A.A.F.I. betw 17.00 and 18.00.

NOTE (heavily underlined).—Before the comer can draw any Pay, he must fill in an ARRIV CERTIFICATE, most important this, because u this is done the Accounts Section at Base do not k that you have arrived. (Sloppy things).

So hurry along to the Orderly Room and fill in said ARRIVAL-CERTIFICATE. It won't take lo as the powers to be do not want to know your p history before the Conqueror arrived, at least not true

"FLAK IS BLACK"

Charles Cuthill

The November air is smooth and clear. We are flying at 155mph (indicated), at 18,000 feet, in a stream of lumbering Lancasters, on yet another 3 Group daylight. This is our third trip in a week.

I can see my breath as I lean forward, against the pull of my shoulder straps, to read the magnetic compass. The reading agrees with the gently twitching needle of the DRC repeater. Good.

"Pilot to navigator. Compasses synchronised," I tell him.

I do this check only to keep well in with the navigator, who periodically has to log it. But what pilot needs a compass (or a navigator) unless he's leading the stream. We are just playing follow-the-leader.

The navigator has complained of being frozen — he's an Aussie; and, now, with the cabin heating turned up, my feet are starting to roast. No one else has complained of the cold, not even the gunners.

We are lying about halfway back in the stream — though we would sooner be nearer the front. But this is not the loneliness of a night raid (then, you rarely see other aircraft); because, without turning my head, I can see a hundred Lancasters flying in small formations — mostly in vics of three. They are directly ahead of me, and out to my left and right; and some are level with me, and others are a little above or below. Motionless at a glance, like strung-up models, they fly with their noses each inclined towards my windscreen's centre. Far below us, a continuous layer of strato-cumulus is making our Lancasters, in their dark night-camouflage, stand out like flies on a white ceiling.

The vic-formations appear to have found their spacing by chance; yet, despite this apparent disorder, the stream at the moment is well-grouped. Each vic is led by a GH Leader aircraft, which is equipped with a blind-bombing radar device — and is identified by two yellow horizontal bars painted on the tail-fins. Our crew is a GH Leader crew, and our two wing-men — called followers — are strangers from another squadron…

I watch our followers wallowing gently as they strive to maintain station, a wingspan's distance behind and beyond our wingtips… and movement between the formations is continuous but, usually, unobtrusive, for we need to maintain the stream's compactness.

There's a formation to starboard closing in on us. I look to my left, there is space for us. The formation continues to close so I will have to move. Trying to judge where the churning slipstreams and vortices from the aircraft ahead will be spent, I turn the wheel left; feeling the air as we go — and checking that our wing men come with us but keep their distance (because swirling air can toss us together, and BANG!).

Our nose swings into the space and I straighten up. The air remains smooth: we have been lucky.

I wonder if the Fortresses will be coming our way? They take such a long time forming up. When we had started out they were high above us in the dawn sky, climbing and turning, with their wings glinting silver — and each engine, underneath, glowing with a burning-white pin-point of light. On one of our raids I saw them high to the south, flying through a massive flak-barrage — but they still had held their precision-formations. We had gone our way, unmolested…

Revs, 2200; boost, +3lbs — set. Our progress makes a veritable continuity of sound, whether or not you choose to listen. The roar of propeller and exhaust; the whine of the superchargers and the valve-gear clatter; and the rushing-thrum of slip-streams and airflow, around and through the airframe. All this, and the vibrations with it! Set, after a time (with your ears cupped beneath a leather helmet) you no longer notice… but you do notice change — without listening; because even a change in revs will startle a crew, unless, first, you tell them. Usually, I tell them.

The engineer is seated beside me, and we look to the engines. He, the starboard pair and I, the port. The long black oil-laced cowlings dance in the sun: and my anxious glance catches the silvery-spin of the blades, and the propeller-hubs' smooth rotation. I check for lengthening streaks of oil and coolant-leaks, and any loose panels; then examine the exhausts for changes in efflux. Everything's OK!…

The engineer gives me the thumbs-up, then goes to check his panel and make up his log.

Huh! I've forgotten the name of the target already. It's an oil plant in the Ruhr, somewhere. What did they say about it at briefing?: "…expect plenty

of flak; and prang the target good and hard!" (But THEY weren't coming!… and oil-targets always have plenty of flak.) Also: "Knock out the oil, then their fighters can't fly!" Now that sounded good, at the time…

Today as we crossed the Channel, I saw a Cookie falling. When it hit the sea, it blew a mountain of water into the air… a crew in trouble, perhaps — getting the weight of their plane down, for the landing, before returning home: or, maybe a crew not wanting to take their Cookie to the target! Crews don't like the thin-cased Cookie. Its weight is 4,000lbs, and some say that a flak-splinter will set it off. (We've got 13,000lbs of bombs under the cabin floor, and the Cookie's in the middle.)

I check my watch. Barely a minute has passed since last I looked. Resuming my scan; ever alert, but for ever wondering — my thoughts creep down to my stomach, then grip it tight… now the gum I was chewing has stuck to the roof of my mouth. Hell!

I unhook my oxygen mask and, with difficulty, prod out the gum. The engineer seeing my predicament, passes me a barley-sugar. I attempt a smile. Then replacing the mask, I hold my breath: the oxygen comes through in long cool puffs against my cheeks. Satisfied that the flow is correct, I tighten the mask to my face and breath more freely.

"Pilot to crew. Oxygen Check!"…

I begin to feel hot and cramped: the base of my spine is starting to ache. What am I doing here? I shift around. The continual scanning is making my neck red-sore. My scarf has slipped down — and my Mae-West, with the parachute harness atop, is forcing my battledress-collar against my neck. Attempting to re-adjust these encumbrances, I feel an increasing resistance as I turn my head — which forces an 'eyes-front' on me. I find, with a growing agitation, that the corrugated rubber tube leading to my oxygen mask has caught up in one of the clips of my parachute harness.

As I angrily go to reposition the tube, three white flak-bursts appear out to port. I watch the puffs drifting harmlessly by, like dandeline seeds caught in the wind.

It's our ack-ack that's white? German flak is black!

I ask the navigator if we have crossed the bomb line. He confirms that we have. "Then log white flak," I tell him… and now I remember: Those Forts! They were flying through white flak-bursts — and over Germany.

Next time, white flak will surprise me no more than black flak does.

The cloud below us is starting to break; we will soon be at its edge. I had not realised the comfort it gave, despite the German radars who must have pictured our track and reported us coming. All too quickly the grey-green country with its great dark forests is fully in view. It is the largest expanse of Germany I have seen in daylight. As we roar above, I sense a million pairs of eyes upon us and feel their cold hostility.

Occasionally I catch the glitter of silver under the aircraft ahead. It's Window. Thousands of tinfoil strips, cascading down — each the size of a paper-chain link; and our counter to the German radars. We carry bundles of the stuff, held together by elastic bands; and packed in brown-paper parcels which have to be opened. It can cramp a cockpit… every minute or so, the bomb aimer (and sometimes the WOP or the engineer) slips a bundle of Window down the window-chute: all the crews are doing it. When the bundle hits the airflow, the elastic band breaks; and the tinfoil strips scatter and go fluttering down… but I get little satisfaction from seeing Window falling, in this cloudless sky.

Look there, high above us!

Feathery-white fingers, each with a diamond at its tip, are beginning to trace criss-cross patterns in the sky. Fighters!… Our top-cover?

Banking, they turn to sweep the stream… They must be ours, they don't come down. Their's is the grandstand seat to the great arena.

"Navigator to pilot. Turning-point in five minutes. Next course, zero-eight eight."

We never make straight for the target, we dogleg, it keeps the enemy guessing. For us; though turning points make a trip longer, they split the journey and help relieve tension — and, with good planning and a little luck on the way, they keep us clear of defences. A leg to the next turning-point means time, not distance: the navigator excepted.

I am conscious of a periodic drumming. The beat gets louder and faster, even though the rev-counters are holding alignment. Unless the noise is abated soon, there will be cries of derision from the crew led by the navigator...

I tune the inboard engines by ear, varying the revolutions of the port-inner slightly, until the drumming sounds least. The engineer is looking across at the starboard engines. I do the same to the port: moving my head, until I have both the propellers sighted in line. Within the merging discs I watch the shadowy-outline of a single blade, rotating... and feeling for the port-outer's pitch lever, I give it a nudge. The blade shadow slows. A further two nudges and the shadow is halted. When the engineer has finished doing the same with the starboard propellers, we should be rid of the beat.

For some time, we have been gradually converging on a line of cumulus clouds out to starboard. When we have turned to our new course (088°), we will be flying directly towards them...

The stream leader and his formation are turning to starboard, and the rest of us prepare to follow. The clouds — still distant and higher than I thought – pile one against the other, with their domes shining white against the sky... there's an anvil-top, and another. Thunderstorms! (They didn't say anything about this at briefing!)

Dwarfed by the clouds, the leading Lancasters are approaching them three-quarters of the way to the summits... clouds: too high to fly over, too low to fly under; and if we try to fly round them, we'll either be shot down or run short of fuel.

The stream leader must be getting close... he should turn back: otherwise we are going to lose one another and collide in that fog. Hell — he's going to try to fly through it!

"Pilot to crew. Prepare for turbulence!"

Banking to port, the leading formation has already become hidden by cloud; and the formation behind them cuts out of sight as they turn to follow. Soon it will be us... There must be a gap!

Already, towering cloud banks each side are forcing vics to close in on one another. Our wings begin to rock, then we are riding the churning air... Steady now! I work the wheel full left, hard right — forward, as the nose rides high — no time for though... until, sweating, we come to smoother air. There have been some near collisions.

Against the grey-white clouds, I've never seen Lancs so near us looking so small... a glance down the cloudside brings on a frightening dizziness and I'm force to look up: just in time — to turn and stay out of cloud. Then I follow the others into the darkening chasm.

Wing-tip to wing-tip, then closer still. Close enough to see the masked-faces of other crews in their cabins and turrets — and there are no rude signs passing between us.

Suddenly, pulsing air catches the wings and snatches the wheel — and I'm fighting to keep following and stay out of cloud; while the stream keeps turning again and again... Our path is not the one they had planned at Group HQ.

Curtained within his 'magic-box,' and irritable, the navigator calls me: he'll be in a sweat, watching his compass repeater-needle going wild as we twist and turn.

"Skip, we're miles south of track," he says: "Keep on like this, and we'll fly straight into a flak area!"

"OK, we'll soon be in the clear," I tell him: because up front I can see vics out in the sunshine... The stream is opening out, as GH leaders edge their formations out into the clear, much smoother air. Leaving the cloud, I look up. Its whiteness is blinding.

I call up the crew, re-set the revs, and trim. Then, with the navigator continuing his grumbles, I try to relax. Our followers are still with us, thank goodness.

My face is beginning to feel hot in my mask; but my sweat is cooling the back of my neck, and my three pairs of gloves (silk, wool, leather) have the wet showing through. I hate to think of the two pairs of socks and my fur-lined boots... Ahead of us, Germany again! It stretches to the horizon in a cloudless sky. Tussling in the cloud, I had forgotten what country lay below us... the land is covered by a thin haze-layer, and the towns lie in great bubbles of smoke which hug the ground.

The stream leader — showing no sign of altering course — is heading straight for the nearest bubble...

No one is speaking, but over the intercom comes the sound of heavy irregular breathing. I am becoming irritated.

"Microphone — someone!" I yell.
Click!

The breathing-sound stops. The navigator has switched off his mike. I knew it was him: because the breathing varied as he leaned and moved about, while plotting at his table... the leader is starting to turn, Thank God!

The stream has changed course thirty-degrees port. Now we'll skirt the town instead of flying over it. But if our navigator had had his way, we would have struck out on our own, to regain track, five minutes ago.

Suddenly, in front of the stream, four bursts of flak punch at the sky.

The tight rolling balls of jet-black smoke drift through the formations towards us, thinning out and changing shape as they come. One changes into an Oliver Hardy shadow, until a slipstream blasts it.

"Pilot to crew. Flak, up ahead!" I say it belatedly, half-hoping it mightn't have happened. The navigator — thinking more of the accuracy of his plot than his safety, simply murmers: "Good." But I notice that he doesn't draw his curtain back, to confirm it.

Up front, bursting flak dirties the sky and unsettles the crews. The stream opens out; formation widen — and some have started to weave... the bomb aimer says that Windowing's a waste of time because the flak-gunners can see us. I tell him to step up the Windowing-rate: though I'm not sure what good that will do — but our orders are to do it.

The sporadic firing comes closer: close enough to see the flash and flame in the bursts. I feel very alone (awaiting the chop!...) — because, right now, some damn gun-crew will have its sights on us, personally.

"Revs twenty-six fifty, engineer!"

I begin to weave: gently, because of our followers. A climbing-turn, left... a descending-turn, right. Now the spitting black blobs are everywhere...

BANG!... the sound is like a heavy door, hard-slammed.

"Jesus, that was close!" someone say... but the engines all seem to be running well and the control-pressures still feel normal.

"Pilot to crew. Intercom check!"

Everyone's OK. The engineer slips from his seat to read his panel...

"Can anyone see any damage; or smoke, trailing?" I yell, looking across at the engines.

"No, Skip," calls the rear gunner.

"No me," adds the mid-upper: "It burst underneath, somewhere... our followers are still with us!"

"Temps and pressures, normal, and the fuel looks good," says the engineer. "I'll check them again when I've looked down the back."

"OK — don't forget the oxygen bottle," I tell him.

"Mid-upper to pilot. The tail-enders are catching the flak now, but they'll soon be clear of it. I haven't seen any go down..."

"Navigator to pilot: when I can get a word in! We should be back on track, and at the turning point, in five minutes."

For the moment, how quiet it is. I reduce the revs and re-trim... then I'm having to grip the wheel hard, to stop my arms trembling.

"I can't see any damage, Skip," says the engineer climbing back into his seat. "The port-outer was overheating, so I've set the shutter to manual — she's OK. I'll keep an eye on it."

...on one of our daylights, approaching a target, we had feathered the port-outer because it was overheating and starting to stream white glycol-smoke. I guiltily presumed that the trouble was caused by my over-revving the engines in the target area. (Coming home, unable to keep up with the stream, the mid-upper thought we were about to be attacked by a Focke Wulf. But it was a grubby-looking Thunderbolt, nosing-in to look us over. The Thunderbolt had stayed with us until we re-crossed the bomb line. We enjoyed this company.)

On our return to base, I filed a report expressing my guilt. Next day, our ground crew happily told us that they had found a small splinter of flak in the offending engine's radiator — and it was the flak-splinter which caused the engine to smoke, not the over-revving. And the splinter had to pass between the propeller blades, first.

Soon we will be starting the run-in to the target. Then, our navigator (operating the GH set) will direct me to the target and tell the bomb aimer when to release the bombs. Our followers will drop their bombs visually with us.

"We are nearly at the turning-point," says the navigator, confidently. "After that, we start the run-in. Next course, zero-one-nine, Skip."

Even as I go to set the repeater-needle, nature calls. Every trip it's the same: Tell me we are about to start a run-in, and I need a pee. I hope there'll be time. With only one set of flying controls, it's an awkward situation: You can't just rush back to the Elsan, in the tail! I'm about to ask the bomb aimer to pass me the can, but he's here — holding it ready.

The plane's in good trim. So after peeling off my gloves, I loosen off my seat-straps and parachute-harness; then, bracing my feet against the rudder pedals, I push myself up. Thus, propped, half standing against the back of my seat; I search, find, and take aim...

It is a rush — getting back down and all-tight into my seat again, because the stream leader has already turned and started his run-in... now the vic in front of me is turning; and I follow them — varying my bank, to keep properly spaced behind. We don't want to be at the bomb-release-point above or below another formation; nor to be pushed aside by one... a GH attack is a delicate affair.

It requires a long run-in to the target, with each GH aircraft (and its formation) following the same pre-determined line of approach. On a 'normal' raid (using a visual bombsight), aircraft in the stream attack the target individually; and, usually, the run-in is comparatively much shorter, with the direction of approach being made within an allowably wide arc. These differences in attack often mean that a GH raid will come under more accurate and concentrated fire from the flak defences, and for a longer time, than does a 'normal' bombing raid.

I roll carefully out of the turn, and adjust: watching for the repeater-needle to settle on 019° — but, characteristically, it continues to hunt a degree or so either side.

"Pilot to navigator — steady on zero-one-nine!"... this should please him: It's the first time this trip that he's got an asked for course. The run-in to the target has started.

We are getting to know the GH routine well. The engineer is Windowing. The WOP, having shut down his equipment, is standing at the astrodome, acting as an extra lookout in the target area. The bomb aimer is lying prone in the nose, having made a final check to his bombsight and gear. Since the ground is in view, he is following the run-in on his map; and should the GH fail, he will guide me on to the target and drop the bombs, visually, using the bombsight. The two gunners have increased their vigilence. I know — because I am having to counter a stronger-yawing as they swing their turrets with a greater fervour... and the navigator, always the hardest-worked, is harder at it at the moment — as (behind the drawn curtain) he interprets the pulsing green GH-strobes, to direct me along the tracking-line.

I try to fly accurately as I follow the navigator's instructions, but our followers are closing in. I want to tell them: "Open out the formation!" — but we have a strict R/T silence. What if one of us gets hit in the bomb bay!

Each vic runs in behind the other; though some climb or descend a little, to find smoother air. No flak, yet... the leader must be nearly at the target.

Now he's through it, turning left and diving away — with his followers, breaking formation, after him. Then, instantly, above the target and level with us appears a thin broken line of smoke.

The smoke rapidly thickens into a black cloud as dozens of shells, bursting together, leave dead-prints in the sky. But the procession of Lancasters continues on to the target as if nothing is happening; and once through it, they are turning left and diving away in single file. On the ground, slipping from sight under the nose, great brown-grey wave of smoke and dust are starting to rise. The bombs are doing their work... only the bomb aimer will see our own bombs fall.

We may need instant power. The revs rise in crescendo as I bring them up to 2850; and I pull back on the throttles to maintain speed.

"Steer, zero-two-five," the navigator calls.

"Zero-two-five," I confirm. Now, the path to the target is stamped with bursting flak. A large explosion erupts into a grey smoke-ball, scattering silver objects which tumble down. A Scarecrow: to frighten us into believing that one of our planes has been shot down (but the explosion looks dry, and our planes aren't silver!).

"Navigator to pilot. Bomb-doors open." I move down the lever on my left... the doors are opening: I know, because of a change in the sound-pattern; and the pitch-up, which I check with the wheel.

"Zero-three-zero, Skip. No, zero-three-two!"

"Zero-three-two." I inch on more power to maintain the speed.

We are into the drifting smoke from the barrage-flak. The target-sky looks impenetrable... But there must be space, because Lancs keep going in and coming out. (Always I tell myself this!) The Lancs coming out are down there now — to our left, not far away. They are streaking for home, lucky blighters... it would only need a diving-turn to join them!

But concentrate, we must! The navigator and I. It needs our whole being.

He with his 'magic-box,' guiding; and me to do his bidding with the instruments, rudder, and wheel. The rest of the crew have to wait in fear... Christ, I need this yawing to stop.

"Lock your turrets, gunners!"...

"Course out of the target, two-five-zero. Don't forget, Skip!" reminds the bomb aimer.

I look up from my instruments as we shudder and bounce. The formation ahead is close. Opening the throttles, I go to pull into smoother air... too late to turn, there's a bubbling fire-ball in front of us. It mushrooms into a tight swirling grey cloud; then spews out a Lancaster, whole(!), blazing from wingtip to wingtip. The Lanc — I can't take my eyes off it. She falls slowly away, nose down: rolling to the right — spinning beneath us in a cartwheel of flame, out of my sight... moments ago, its crew was thinking and working just like us!

We thump through the top of the explosion, trailing the smoke and the stench of it with us. In front, surrounded by flak-burst and with its bomb-doors open, is a solitary Lanc of that formation of three; apparently unconcerned. I check my chute-pack, to know it is there; whilst our navigator, imperturbably, continues to call out corrections to the course. I try my best...

Unheard spits of flame erupt into rolling clouds of oily-black smoke: the evil blobs are surrounding us. I glimpse the engineer's masked-face, and our eyes meet (has he seen my fear?)... through the smoke, the bombs of the lone Lancaster are falling slowly away, spaced out like ladder-rungs. I pray for ours to be gone. It's a long time home...

"Bombs away!" As they leave — the thumps in quick succession... each is carrying a portion of my fear.

Look, three white mushrooms floating among the black! Parachutes drifting down. The upturned faces, so close: yet we can only pass by them (poor sods!).

"Bombs gone!" calls the bomb aimer: and the Lanc feels crisp and buoyant... she's ready for home. But wait, we must. A thirty-five second wait, the bomb aimer said... and with accurate flying: the photograph is needed... shit!

"Bomb-bays clear, close the doors."

"Doors, closing."

"Our followers bombed with us," cries the mid-upper: "Let's go!"... but we need the photo to say that we've bombed, and where: and our bomb haven't arrived, yet!

The smoke from the target-flak is thinning. Christ, if we were to get hit now!... I've noticed an area below us where shells are bursting together — a dozen at a time. There's a second lot... and thirty-five seconds: That's a lifetime!

"Photo's taken! That's it, Skip."

Filled with joy, I'm ready to leave. But still we must wait...

"Followers clear!" yells the mid-upper.

Now the wheel hard-left, and rudder with it: until the right wing-tip is high over our heads. Then down, high-tailing for home after the others, with the repeater-needle vaguely near 250°... the odd poop of flak is marking our path. But oh how the diving helps us unwind...

Speed 180mph (indicated). The engineer has pulled back the throttles and reduced the revs, and we are now in a gentle descent... the stream is becoming strung out in its race for home. I glance back at the target, and the last of the Lancs are running in. My arms are shaking as I go to re-trim.

The crew have begun chattering over the intercom as if we're at cocktails. I shut them up. The bomb aimer is standing behind me with his mask hanging down, looking tipsy — and we're still at 15,000 feet! He starts to smile. The pimples stand out on his pale face; and one of them — freshly-picked — is bleeding. Wanting to add emphasis to his need for oxygen, I playfully push the wheel forward then pull some 'g' — and my goggles slip down off my forehead. I cannot see... then pushing my goggles back up, I cannot see for laughing.

"When we get back, remind me to get my goggle-elastic changed," I tell him.

Soon we will turn due west, and hold 10,000 feet to the coast. Then down we will go again; down, to taste the salt in the spray. And after we have crossed the surf into Breckland (I can smell the fry of the eggs and bacon, already!), we will lift our wings over the trees and steeples until the airfield is, once again, in sight.

And tonight, by the fifth pint, we will have drowned our fear.

GOOD COMPANIONS

'...Wingtip to wingtip, then closer still. Close enough to see the masked faces of other crews in their cabins and turrets...'

Above, below, and on either side there are aircraft — Lancs, maybe Hallies too — not seeming to be moving forward at all, but continually rising and falling, just as toy boats do when floating on the gentle swell of a lake in an urban park.

It is a comforting sight sharing this wonderland high above the cloud tops with friends. It is so unreal... almost mesmerising... but eyes must keep searching, all minds must be alert for this is the Kingdom of the Hun. Soon the dreaded, expected flak puffs will rudely interrupt the serenity, and aboard each kite the knots inside already-tight stomachs will tighten more. As always, each man will be wondering how *his* crew, *his* kite can possibly get through unscathed. How much can each man stand before something within snaps and breaks?

Then there is no more time left for wondering. Mouths will feel to be stuffed with cotton wool... heads will be pounding... ears roaring...

For those who think of the Lanc only as a night bomber, here are a few reminders that the boys of Bomber Command could hold their own when it came to keeping it tight during their ventures in daylight after D-Day.

Top right:
Hitherto drawing comfort from hearing the RAF near nightly passing four miles high, the people of occupied Europe could witness Bomber Command's aerial might as it assisted land forces in pounding the common foe once the second front opened.

Lancs and a lone Hally from No 6 Group on the loose, as snapped from a No 433 'Porcupine' Sqn RCAF Lanc X operating out of Skipton-on-Swale. W. R. Weir

Right:
Cockpit views of 'IL:F', B1 NN754, from No 115 Sqn's 'C' flight, aloft from Witchford. J. R. Dowling

Below:
And Lancs from No 582 Sqn, a PFF unit established at Little Staughton.
J. L. Duffy

Opposite and inset:
The Kiwis of No 75 (NZ) Sqn, Mepal heading for hostile skies, present a spectacle to behold. (From the rear) P. N. Howarth and (from above) A. G. Benest

FLAK RIDE

'...Motionless at a glance, like strung-up models...'

They drone on, climbing steadily... boring out over the North Sea, which always seems to take a surprising time to cross, minutes crawling by as slowly as the shrouded, crinkle-like water glimpsed through cloud-gaps thousands of feet below.

Each crew peer out, ever watchful for the Luftwaffe, drawing comfort from the vapour trails high above — their fighter umbrella. Comfort, too, being with big friends, each appearing as graceful as a soaring eagle, held aloft by broad, competent wings supporting lean, underslung Merlins emitting barely visible plumes of exhaust fire.

In the near-rarified air each kite gently shivers as if alive... metal her flesh...the roar of her motors her heartbeat.

Boring on, still climbing... as yet unhindered... as comfortable as if out on a cross-country stooge.

Boring on, now at bombing height... the clock creeping nearer zero hour... already-racing pulses racing even more as alien territory lies but minutes ahead.

Boring on... the sky ahead black with flak puffs, each scattering lethal shards of metal in all directions.

Boring on... trying not be where the next burst punches the sky.

No picture can truly capture the drama being acted out, but try to use your imagination when studying a foursome thus:

Centre right:
Vapour trails stream back like signposts to the watchers far below. Another vivid shot taken from a No 550 Sqn Lanc during the Dortmund Operation mounted on 20 February 1945.
R. H. Whitehead

Right:
As yet in clear, friendly air, a Lanc from No 550 Sqn, North Killingholme, snapped from a sister machine. L. Dale

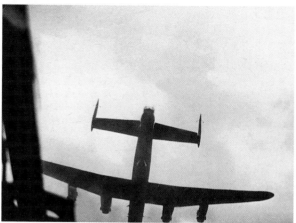

Inset below:
AS HE SAW IT

'...I go to pull into smoother air... too late to turn, there's a bubbling fireball in front of us...'

With so few Lanc aircrew (or any aircrew flying with the RAF for that matter) possessing a camera, or film, or willing to defy authority — the taking of photographs being strictly forbidden — too many of the dramas played out in the skies above Germany and occupied Europe are lost to posterity. Thankfully, there were men of talent who felt moved, for whatever reason, to sketch, even paint their impressions while memories were fresh. Inevitably, more than a few of such portrayals were discarded in the postwar years, when survivors of the air battles hung up their helmets and began to carve out a career, take on the responsibilities of a family, a home, put service life behind them.

Here, however, is one such example that has survived the passing years: a vivid mind-picture in pen and ink by No 576 Sqn Skipper Laurie Arthur, drawn within hours of return from the massive daylight assault on Duisburg, 14 October 1944. An awesome demonstration of allied air superiority, the daylight was followed by a night attack of comparable strength. All told, Bomber Command despatched a total of 2,018 aircraft within 24hr, for the loss of 21 crews (18 of them in Lancasters). B. E. Smith

Below:
THROUGH THE PEEKHOLE

'...As they leave — the thumps in quick succession... each is carrying a portion of my fear...'

This is what a belly full of bombs looked like as viewed from a circular inspection hole cut into the front bomb bay bulkhead. In this case it is a Lanc from the Kiwi-controlled No 75 'New Zealand' Sqn, Mepal, supporting the allied army in the field soon after D-Day 1944, carpet-bombing German troops and armour in the Falaise Gap.

Mild conditions on such a day would not cause undue problems in the event of a malfunction, but on bitterly cold winter nights at heights around 20,000ft, temperatures as low as -40°C, it was a different story. Despite there being slip heaters provided to prevent bomb hooks and such freezing to carriers and release mechanisms, it was sometimes necessary to use the axe to hack off the complete contraption — a most unpleasant task to say the least. As a result it was not always easy to placate the armament officer, who had to write off an expensive item of equipment!

There were the hang-ups to contend with, for it was not unknown for a bomb (or incendiary container) to stay attached to its carrier for some reason, defying all attempts to dislodge it. More often than not the jettison bar provided did the trick, thereby dumping the ordnance into the sea, wherever, but on other occasions a bomb or SBC would drop on to the bomb-doors. Many a Lanc landed with a bomb or incendiaries hung-up, a particularly nerve-wracking task for the armourers to deal with if the weapon was fitted with a long delay, not to mention the trepidation of the crew landing the Lanc still with 'stores' aboard. J. K. Aitken

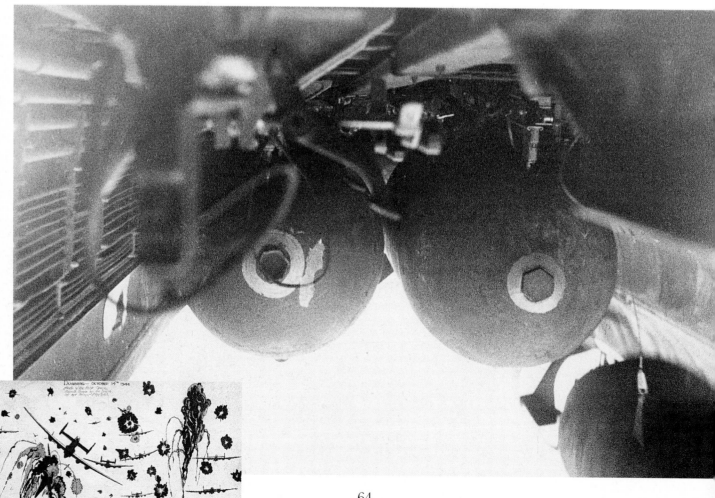

DEATH WAS WHERE YOUR SKY WAS

'...She falls slowly away, nose down: rolling to the right — spinning beneath us in a cartwheel of flame...'

Why is it that so many ill-informed pundits dismiss Bomber Command's daylight ops as a 'piece of cake'? True, by comparison with the mind-sapping 8/9hr night grinds to the likes of Magdeburg, Leipzig and the Big City — Berlin — itself, crews did, by mid-1944, have a more than even chance of completing a tour; but, make no mistake, the Reaper still called for too many lads — among the cream of their generation — during those hectic months following D-Day. Again it is true that with the Luftwaffe steadily getting short of fuel and oil, coupled with a lack of experienced pilots for its Fw190s and Bf109s, and with increasing numbers of allied fighters able to provide escorts, attacks by fighters thankfully decreased; but right to the day the Hun collapsed, the flak was murderous.

To each and every crew a sky full of flak puffs ahead of the gaggle was a real stomach-churner. Every crewman in every kite would be quiet... thinking... pulse racing... secretly praying for a recall even at that late stage.

Then the smoke puffs from the flak bursts would be careering past by the dozen... oily and black... wind-torn and tattered... each man feeling alone, naked. Each Lanc would be recoiling and shuddering her entire length as the flak polka-dotted the sky around with cotton puffs of death. And there was the noise... the sound... the fury of confusion to contend with. It was a hell impossible to describe... a hell endured time and time again if luck held.

Suspended in time for evermore, but three Lancs the victims of flak.

Top right:
Wrong place, wrong time for seven good men during the Cologne daylight of 2 March 1945. The end was almost in sight yet still they fell. It was the last raid on the city before it fell to American troops four days later. Whilst six Lancs (and three Hallies) were lost that day, we shall never know which one Aussie rear gunner Flg Off 'Joe' Pascoe captured on film as an everlasting image of war's grim reality. Joe, from No 550 Sqn, was one of relatively few Bomber Command aircrew who flouted the rules by taking his camera with him on ops. So busy was he, constantly rotating his turret, searching the sky for fighters, he had few opportunites for taking pictures. L. Brooks

Centre right:
Very occasionally, quite by chance, the demise of a Lancaster would be recorded by the fixed camera mounted in a sister machine. Here is one such, reckoned to be BIII PB303 'ZN:R' from No 106 Sqn, Metheringham, downed during the Homberg daylight mounted on 1 November 1944. With her port-outer ripped out, fuel still streaming back from the severed pipes, fuselage damage apparent, she was observed falling away from the gaggle in the target area (the Meerbeck oil plant) and disappearing into cloud. Could that be a pair of legs under the fuselage below the mid-upper? Flg Off G. J. Symes, RCAF, and his brood were the only crew lost on what proved to be a disappointing attack, due in no small measure to scattered marking by Mossies.
The full story of what befell PB303 will never be known. She finally came down in Holland.
L. Horne via J. L. Armitage

Bottom right:
Trailing smoke, a Lanc drops away from the stream to a fate unknown.
A thousand or more eyes will be looking on...fellow travellers willing the blossoming of parachutes before she is lost to view...before heads turn away, necks become stiffer as the endless search for fighters continues.
L. Dale

LETHAL

'...Jesus, that was close..!'

Be truthful: how many of you think of the Lancaster in combat with jet fighters? Not many we'll be bound. But encounter them, do battle with them, they did during the final phase of the war in Europe. And not without giving a good account of themselves either!

Take a morning raid on the Blohm and Voss shipyards at Hamburg on the last day of March 1945 as an example of what good crew co-ordination, good discipline... plus a measure of good fortune... could do in the face of determined attacks by a pack of around 30 of the formidable Me262s. Having come through 13 daylight operations over Germany during the month of March 1945 and not been molested by enemy fighters, the Canadian-controlled No 6 Group Lancaster squadrons had every reason to believe that Hamburg would be no different. Flak they would expect as always.

And, right on time the flak came up. Initially heavy, it lessened as the force of 100 Hallies, followed by a near enough equal number of Lancs began discharging their loads above solid cloud smothering the city and beyond. With good fighter cover the Hallies passed through without seeing too much of the foe, but, due to unnecessary (as it turned out) doglegs, the Lanc gaggle was some nine minutes late, by which time the Mustang cover had departed, and the Me262s were soon all over them and a mêlée lasting seven minutes or so — and which seemed more like 27min! — ensued.

All told, 28 crews were to report one or more combats out of some 78 encounters with the jets... and five Lancs went down. It might have been more had not some of the Mustangs returned to give assistance.

On the plus side the Lanc gunners downed four of the 262s, along with three probables and at least four more damaged.

In the space available to us here we can but outline what befell one of the units involved and we have chosen No 429 'Bison' Sqn RCAF from Leeming as, newly re-equipped with Lancs, it was their baptism of action flying their new mounts.

Some baptism!

In brief, Lanc RA571 'AL:D', skippered by WO K. L. Weld, RCAF, and crew, was attacked twice. PD209 'AL:K', flown by Canadian Flg Off R. P. Pike and his brood, came under attack once and the fighter was claimed as probably destroyed. RF207 'AL:S', with Flt Lt R. K. Mitchell, RCAF, as captain, came under fire once.

ME536 'AL:Q' (Flg Off H. A. M. Humphries, RCAF, and his crew) came through one attack, and another Me262 was claimed as a probable.

And PA226 'AL:H', with Flg Off S. F. Avis, RCAF, and his band within, was attacked no less than four times and sustained severe damage.

With no personal accounts upon which we can draw we are indebted to

the diarist who bluntly, yet somehow graphically, recorded for future generations a summary of their ordeal... 'Hamburg: attacked primary at 09.05hrs from 19,000ft heading 029 deg true at 165 TAS. 10/10th cloud, tops 10–12,000ft, fair visibility above. Bombed one red smoke puff which still remained. M/B had left before arrival — nothing could be seen of the target. A very uncertain effort which could not have been good. 1 x 500lb bomb was hung-up and jettisoned safe at 5405N 0430E at 10.39hrs from 12,000ft. Aircraft was attacked four times in the target area by enemy fighters. Three Me262's attacked at 09.03hrs. Corkscrew was ordered and both gunners opened fire. Two E/A/C broke away but one followed through and fired, damaging the m/u turret. At 09.04hrs another Me262 attacked. Both gunners opened fire, as did the Me262. It then broke away at

150yd. At 09.08hrs still another Me262 attacked at 800yd, opened fire, and gunners gave 'corkscrew port'. At 600yd both gunners fired until the Me262 broke away to port, up. Another attack ensued at 09.10hrs when a Me262 came in from astern below. Corkscrew was ordered and the fighter opened fire. Both gunners fired at 600yd and the fighter broke away at 75yd. It destroyed the starboard aileron and left a large hole in the starboard wing. No one was injured. No claims are made from any of these attacks...'

A subdued group of combatants — it was their first taste of action with their outfit since being posted-in earlier in the month — made it back to Leeming to fight another day.

Less fortunate were Flg Off R. R. Jones and his crew of five like-Canucks and their British flight engineer who, in NG345 'AL:V', failed to return.

IN CHALK FOR ALL TO SEE

'...And tonight, by the fifth pint, we will have drowned our fear...'
Too frequently forgotten by historians and students of the air war are the countless men and women who laboured behind the scenes preparing for each operation. With security paramount, perhaps, not unnaturally, few pictures were taken of such stalwarts and their handiwork. Thankfully, isolated individuals *were* determined to see that odd glimpses of their graft reached a wider audience — if having to wait half a century!

Here are three examples:

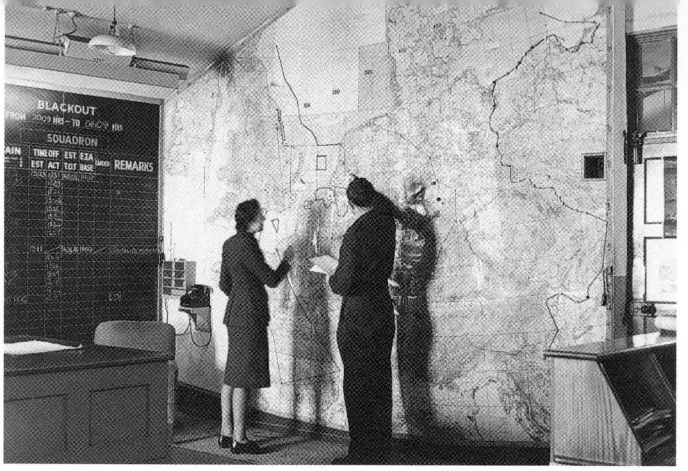

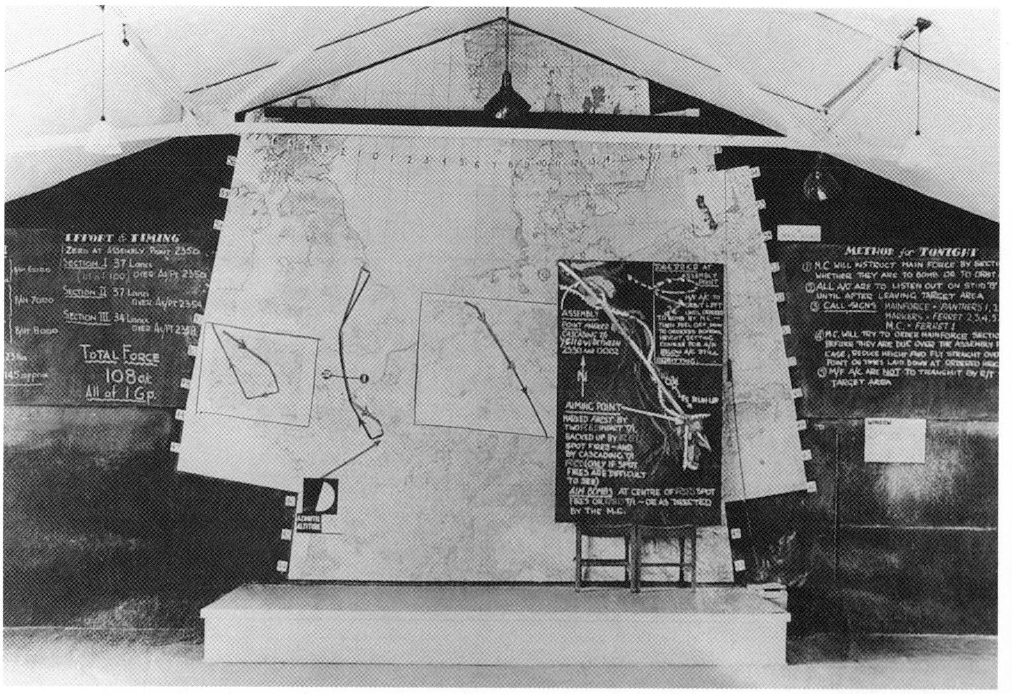

Top right:
How many of those stalwarts, who laboured long and hard and often, have felt the call, a compelling urge to retrace their steps... expecting, yet not expecting to walk into the intelligence section, the briefing room, and finding them as they were when last they saw them? Like Flt Off Peggy Burnside and Sqn Ldr Bruce Dermer, here working their way, through the many stages of preparation before a daylight effort laid on against Nordhausen 3 April 1945. Was it enterprise, or foresight, a sense of history which resulted in the call for a camera that day at North Killingholme?

Are you out there Peggy, Bruce? What have you kept to remind you of your accomplishments, your commitment? R. V. McIntyre

Centre right:
A complete briefing display at Waltham (a No 1 Group airfield housing No 100 Sqn) and drawn up for a daylight mounted against the bomb and ammunition store at Maintenon, 30 April 1944. Despite what armchair critics would have us believe, Bomber Command had become truly professional by this stage of the war. Meticulous planning went into each and every operation, in particular every effort being made to prevent unnecessary civilian casualties in occupied Europe. On the Maintenon raid No 1 Group's own marking force — The Special Duty Flight (otherwise known as No 13 Base Flight) from Binbrook — pin-pointed the target for the 116 Lancasters taking part. Results were spectacular. Much of the site was destroyed, whilst civilian homes nearby were untouched. One Lancaster and crew failed to return. R. S. Blucke

Bottom right:
By way of comparison is the operations board at Kelstern (another No 1 Group Station), recording in summary form No 625 Sqn's participation in the massive, only partially successful, evening raid on Caen on 7 July 1944 and well documented in recent years. Points to note are the low heights at which each aircraft bombed; that only one second dickey pilot was carried; that 625's 1,000th sortie was completed during the attack. Overall that hectic day the Command despatched a total of 467 aircraft (of which 283 were Lancasters) and files extant tell us losses were light, being one Mosquito in addition to three Lancs and their crews.
G. R. Ross

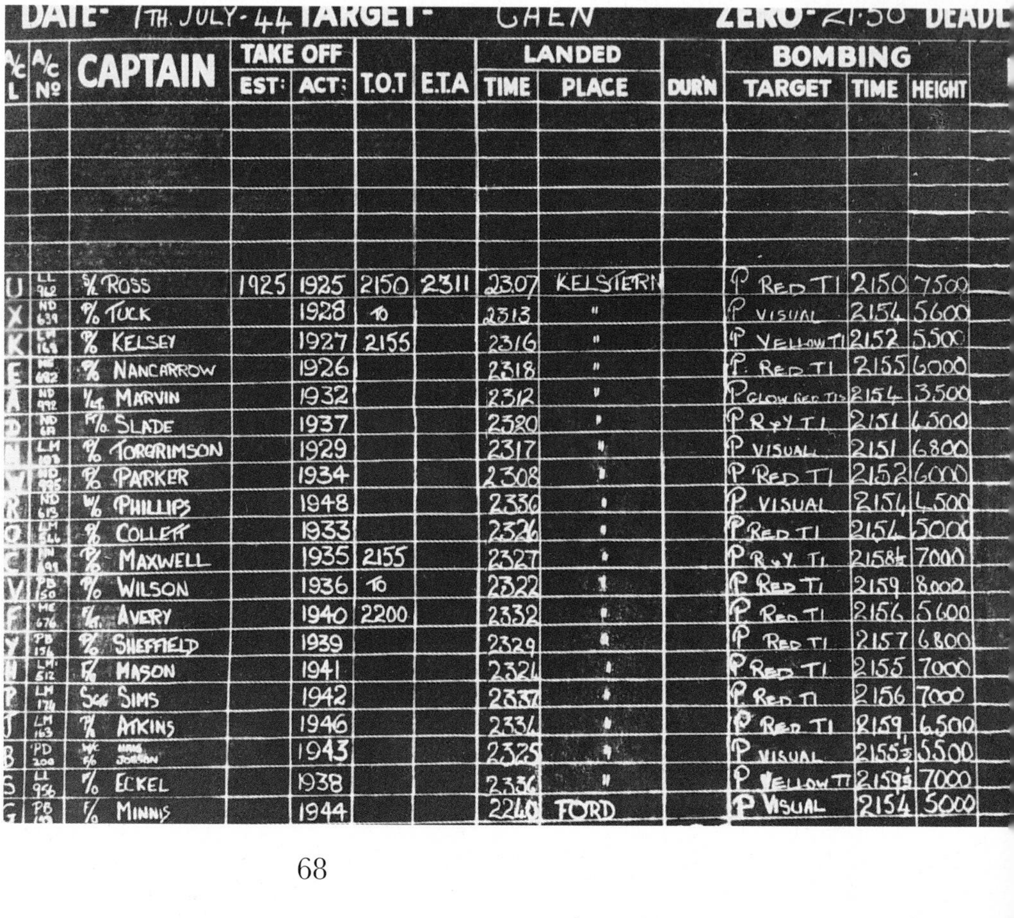

DATE- 7TH. JULY-44 TARGET- CAEN ZERO-21.50 DEADL

A/C L	A/C No	CAPTAIN	TAKE OFF EST:	TAKE OFF ACT:	T.O.T	E.T.A	LANDED TIME	LANDED PLACE	DUR'N	BOMBING TARGET	BOMBING TIME	BOMBING HEIGHT
U	LL 962	S/L ROSS	1925	1925	2150	2311	2307	KELSTERN		P RED TI	2150	7500
X	ND 639	P/O TUCK		1928	TO		2313	"		P VISUAL	2154	5600
K	LM 169	P/O KELSEY		1927	2155		2316	"		P YELLOW TI	2152	5500
E	ME 682	P/O NANCARROW		1926			2318	"		P RED TI	2155	6000
A	ND 992	1/Lt MARVIN		1932			2312	"		P GLOW RED TIs	2154	3500
D	ND 6[illegible]	F/O SLADE		1937			2320	"		P R+Y TI	2151	6500
N	LM [illegible]	P/O TORGRIMSON		1929			2317	"		P VISUAL	2151	6800
W	ND 995	P/O PARKER		1934			2308	"		P RED TI	2152	6000
R	ND 613	W/O PHILLIPS		1948			2330	"		P VISUAL	2154	4500
O	LM 566	P/O COLLETT		1933			2326	"		P RED TI	2154	5000
C	[illegible]	P/O MAXWELL		1935	2155		2327	"		P R+Y TI	2158½	7000
V	PB 150	P/O WILSON		1936	TO		2322	"		P RED TI	2159	8000
F	ME 676	F/Lt AVERY		1940	2200		2332	"		P RED TI	2156	5600
Y	PB 154	P/O SHEFFIELD		1939			2329	"		P RED TI	2157	6800
H	LM 512	F/O MASON		1941			2324	"		P RED TI	2155	7000
P	LM 174	Sgt SIMS		1942			2337	"		P RED TI	2156	7000
J	LM 163	P/O ATKINS		1946			2334	"		P RED TI	2159	6500
B	PD 200	W/C [illegible]		1943			2325	"		P VISUAL	2155½	5500
S	LL 956	F/O ECKEL		1938			2336	"		P YELLOW TI	2159½	7000
G	PB [illegible]	F/O MINNIS		1944			2240	FORD		P VISUAL	2154	5000

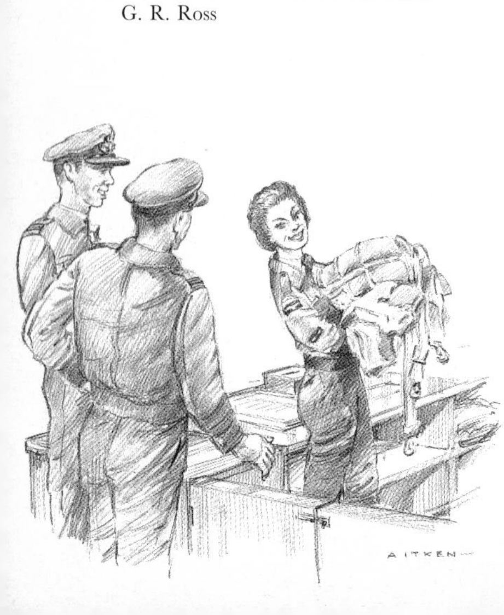

BETTER HIM THAN ME

There is no hope, they were too low,
Too low for parachutes to show,
And he is gone, he's met his end,
He who was my special friend
Who laughed with me and did share
All my happiness and despair,
Shared all my fears and all my plans.
He was my friend, I loved that man
And yet inside, insidiously,
A whispering voice,
'Better him than me'.

Harry Brown DFM, No 50 Sqn, 1944

DUISBURG DIRGE

We started in the early dawn
Headed for Happy Valley
And thought as we stifled a great big yawn
We're up before Reveille.

The Wing/Co had said: 'It's a piece of cake
No flak, no fighters, don't worry
You're flying at 18,000 feet
So there's no bloody cause for hurry.'

We got bashed about in the slipstream
And my forehead creased in a frown
When at last the target came in sight
And the Lancs started going down.

One, two, three — all dead ahead
They went an awful cropper
I began to wish I'd stayed in bed
As I thought:' We're next for the chopper.'

'At 18,000,' the Wing/Co said
'The flak's a piece of duff'
But as I viewed the TIs red
I knew I'd had enough.

The downward vis was smashing
In fact too good for me
For another kite was crashing
So long and RIP.

A parachute went floating by
With harness hanging loose
The flak still covered the clear blue sky
As it tried to cook our goose.

And far below no eye could miss
The shining silver river
'Come on to hell outa' this'
Said a voice with a bit of a quiver.

At last the job was finished
Bombs gone from every rack
But our fear was undiminished
As we started our journey back.

But when we reached our base at last
We received another fright
They said: 'It's better to forget the past
For you're going again tonight.'

'Tonight,' the 'Gen Man' told us
'You can have a special treat
Although no need for all this fuss
We're giving an extra 2,000 feet.'

'The time has come,' the Walrus said
You've heard that tale before
But those few bright words the Wing/Co said
Were the duffest gen of the war.

L.G.Buckell, No 150 Sqn, 1945

"CHARLIE"

The day he was gonged, he had money to burn,
We had one with Charlie, the best of our bunch.
We made a few speeches and talked out of turn
And drank too much beer before having lunch

A Section Officer in Ops Intelligence
Had sewed on the ribbon below his brevet,
This white and purple diagonal elegance
Would cost him a fortune, in beer and sherry.

At lunch, the wingco, ex-solicitor
Called him to the bar, to buy the beer
'I'll have a sherry. Now yours? Is it a
Gin and Bitters? — Oh! Two more here!'

Twenty odd calls for the steward to serve
And he signed the chit for a couple o'quid

Acknowledged 'Congrats!' with his usual verve
And managed to keep his happiness hid.

But Ops came up, and put a late show on
And he was selected to go to the war,
He wasn't too happy at having to go on
A trip to the City, he'd done six before.

They were late on the target and shot up by flak
And an eighty-eight caught them near Bremen,
They bought it — a flamer — and didn't come back
For the Reaper was handy to claim 'em.

Next day when we heard, he had failed to return
We had one for Charlie — the best of our bunch
We didn't make speeches, or talk out of turn
But drank it up quietly and went in to lunch.

Dennis Dear DFM

Right:
PULLING OUT THE STOPS
'...The stream is becoming strung out in its race for home...'

Every squadron had a crew which managed to get back first, no matter now long, how tough a trip was. Even on nights when the heavens opened and violent thunderstorms or high winds scattered the stream all over Germany, still that same crew invariably would be down and through interrogation, its post-ops meal, by the time others from the squadron landed.

That is until the daylights began. The disciplined gaggles did not usually present the necessary freedom whereby crews accustomed to landing first could forge ahead of their colleagues. And so it was not unknown for a little 'ganging up' to come about...occasions when the taps would be opened (to blazes with fuel consumption figures!)... the race on to be down first.

As on 7 February 1945, returning from Wanne Eickel. Zoom in on No 15 Sqn as the kites, at little more than tree-top height, jostle for pole position, scurrying for Mildenhall. Filling bomb aimer Pat Russell's blister as he lies prone with his camera in the nose of BI NF953 'LS:A' (Skipper: Flg Off Doug Hunt, RAAF), is BI NG357 'LS:G', holding within Canadian Flg Off Jim Cowie and his comrades (despite what the squadron's ORB records).

Two nights later Jim Cowie and his whole entourage were dead...on only their second op... brought down during an attack on the Hohenbudberg railway yards, Krefeld, (flying 'B' Flight Lanc I HK620 'LS:W'). D. A. Russell

PASSING ON THE SKILLS

For most Lancaster aircrew, completion of a tour of ops was such a distinct mathematical uncertainty, that few would actively or consciously admit to even contemplating it. You lived for the day, the hour, the moment, the job in hand, and did not risk thinking far ahead. The minority who did survive a tour (as they will modestly claim, due to a large degree of luck, aided by a little skill), knew only too well what awaited them: a posting as an instructor, a prospect which — for most — was far from inviting. Sure, a rest from ops, and the sheer relief of having completed a tour would be welcomed; but instructing! Well, it had a far from attractive reputation, and within weeks most would be yearning for a return to the ops scene.

As pupils when learning their respective trades at gunnery, navigation, engineer, wireless and bombing schools, trainee aircrew would cast their minds no further ahead than to wonder which of the RAF Commands they might be posted to: Bomber, Coastal, Transport. Even when the nucleus crew got together at OTU, then progressed to become a septet at HCU, the realistic limit of their horizons would be what type they might fly, and to which group or squadron they might be posted. That was about the furthest they could realistically look ahead. Any thoughts of completing a tour, and what may lie beyond that, was too far off, too unreal, to even comtemplate.

By the time they reached HCU stage they would be hanging on to every word from their 'screens' (as instructors were known), men who had somehow made it through a tour, and who, if the circumstances were right (a few beers could help), would perhaps open up and pass on some of their own operational experiences, taking care not to line-shoot, generally avoiding scaring the you-know-what out of the fledgling crews. Green as they might have been, each rookie crew could not fail to respond to a screen who had a good patter, inspired confidence, did not show fear or hesitation when flying with them; showed infinite patience.

Trainees were not to know that their tutors had largely learned to instruct as they went along, relatively little tuition in the art of instructing, of teaching, being given. Typically, an instructors' course, if any, would usually come about after doing the job for some months, certainly until later in the war.

A vital element of instructing was time spent in classroom and hangar, and to illustrate this we have purposely chosen two facets of the training of a flight engineer, a most important, but often unsung member of the bomber crew. In the early days of the four-engined bomber force, most flight engineers were fitters who had been 'invited' to volunteer for aircrew duty, as by mid-1942, second pilots had become a luxury the RAF could no longer afford, due to losses and the rapid expansion of the bomber force. Many had been prewar entrants, Halton apprentices, with first-class background experience and technical training. Some would never have flown before joining a crew, other than, perhaps a short air experience flight in a Magister. There were many who, in the mid-1942 period, had their first

ever flights after joining their squadrons, finding themselves on ops almost immediately, such was the pressure.

No 4 School of Technical Training was set up at St Athan in 1941 to meet the demand for F/Es, and was to remain the sole establishment of its type until its closure in 1951, by when 22,599 had been trained in its 10-year existence.

See the story which follows by Walter Faraday.

Below:
No one doodles, no one dozes, as the mysteries of hydraulics are unfolded. You had to get to know the systems, backward and blindfolded, as you'd be working mostly on dark nights, with no lights; under 'G' loads, being shot at, etc. Picture taken at a No 1 Group training base — Lindholme, Sandtoft or Hemswell. Also uncertain are the identities of the lecturers. Would that we knew. T. A. Pearce

Bottom:
At No 4 S of TT St Athan aspiring flight engineers, complete with headsets, learn the intricacies of controls and systems, August 1944. Respectively right to left, are Lancasters' Mk III, II and I nose sections, each mark requiring slightly different engine-handling techniques.
Crown Copyright via M. Stringman

'NEVER VOLUNTEER FOR ANYTHING'
(Or How I Became A Flight Engineer)

Walter Faraday

Walter, a Lancashire lad, son of a Hoover salesman from Burnley, had left school at 15 with no special skills, eventually joining the RAF on 2 May 1938 at the age of 17 years 9 months. He did his initial training at No 1 Depot, Uxbridge, then fitters' courses at Manston and Halton before a posting to Sealand (5 FTS) as a flight mechanic on Harts and Oxfords. It was while at Sealand, on 3 September 1939, in a barrack block, that he listened to the Prime Minister's (Neville Chamberlain) dramatic broadcast telling the nation we were at war with Germany.

From mid-1940 to December '41, Walter served as engineer (fitter II E) on high-speed launches, ASR Base, Lerwick (Shetlands). It is from there that he takes up his story:

'After the Shetlands I returned to Sealand for a short time and then to a small station, RAF Cleave near Bude, Cornwall, with a flight lieutenant CO. It was just like any other RAF station but on a smaller scale. It was the home of an Army Co-operation Unit which operated six Henley target-towing aircraft. They carried a crew of two: pilot and winch operator. The winch operator streamed the drogue (looked like a windsock) for the army gunners to pot at with their 4.7in guns. It also had three or four Queen Bees, radio-controlled Tiger Moths (I forget what they were used for), plus the CO's Tiger Moth, plus visiting aircraft. There were only five engine fitters and myself. I was a corporal by this time and probably the least qualified of all. The weather was always perfect; we were on double British Summer Time (two hours forward instead of one) and the army were calling for three sorties a day, sometimes more.

'It was hard going and we very seldom, if ever, left the station, so when a chap with a clipboard and a pencil at the ready arrived to call for volunteers for flight engineers it seemed a good opportunity for me to get out, so I volunteered. I was 21 at the time. This would be about the beginning of May '42. There were no formalities, no interviews, no aptitude tests, no selection boards and no aircrew medical. The station MO gave me the once over and that was that. Very shortly afterwards I was posted to St Athan to join a 10-week flight engineers' course. There were no Lancasters at St Athan at that time although the course did include a week at Woodford where they were being built. I passed the course in the same way I passed my other courses — only just on the right side of the borderline. We were then posted out to various bomber stations, myself and one or two others to Syerston by August 1942.

'The first time I ever flew was to St Eval, Cornwall, in a Manchester with the Station Commander, Gp Capt Walker ('Gus' Walker, later to become Air Chief Marshal Sir Augustus). I was supposed to be engineer but all I did was sit next to the pilot. I missed the aircraft altogether on the return trip. I was just in time to see it belting down the runway as it took off. No 61 Sqn had been doing anti-sub patrols over the Atlantic and were

then just starting to return to their base at Syerston. I returned to Syerston either that day or the following day in one of the squadron aircraft.

'I did another trip to Boscombe Down. This time the pilot was a squadron leader. All I did was stand next to him and help him to smoke his cigarettes. He had 20 Players standing on the throttle box and invited me to help myself. He flew fairly low and we had a good view of Stonehenge. I don't know what this trip was about and we didn't stay long at Boscombe. I didn't log either of these trips. It was the first time I'd seen a Lanc or a Manchester at close quarters. I don't remember the name of the pilot. Soon after this I was posted to Swinderby with the others who had come from St Athan.

'There seemed to be a lot of people at Swinderby, all doing nothing in particular. The weather was fine and pleasant, I remember. I think I'd been there for about a week or 10 days when a volunteer flight engineer was called for to go to Waddington for a fortnight. I volunteered. I didn't ask any questions. I just got myself and my things into a Hillman pick-up and went over to Waddo. On arrival I found I was a member of No 44 Sqn with a blank log book in my hand. The next day I went over to the crew room and found a number of officers and sergeants playing shove-ha'penny and reading the papers, none looking very fresh and all looked a bit desultory. They were all aircrew on ops. All at once in strode Warrant Officer 'Lucky' Wright calling for Sgt Faraday (I'd received my other tape on completing the course at St Athan). He didn't seem very tall, but he was stocky, full of energy and confidence, and quite smartly turned out in contrast to some of the others. He didn't waste any time. "I'm going to do an NFT". (What was an NFT?) "You're on ops with me tonight" were his next words after I'd said who I was. I think I'd been provided with flying boots and a helmet at Syerston, so I drew myself a parachute and joined Lucky and his aircraft W4110:'K'. This was on 2 September 1942. The air test lasted 30min. I don't think Lucky was very impressed with me as a flight engineer but he didn't chuck me out of the crew. I should have told him I had no flying experience. Perhaps he knew; I don't know.

'The trip that night was to Karlsruhe, six hours. I didn't enter the take-off time. We didn't get hit thankfully. I don't know what I could have done if we had. Over the target with the searchlights, fires on the ground, flak and everything, I noticed the fuel pressure dropping. Red lights on the engineer's panel. I think this Lanc had stack pipes. I didn't trouble Lucky with it. The engines were still turning satisfactorily. He had quite enough with me in the cockpit, never mind anything else. His only instructions to me before the take-off were pointing at the forward escape hatch in the bomb aimer's floor.

Above:
IN SPITE OF, NOT BECAUSE OF
Walter Faraday, 1661 HCU, Winthorpe, December 1943.
'...I remember the Medical Section at Winthorpe. They'd been looking high and low for my aircrew medical documents and couldn't find them. So they sent for me. I said I hadn't got any such documents, as I hadn't had an aircrew medical. They seemed surprised at that, but when I said I'd done a tour of ops, they said I must be fit for aircrew. I never heard any more about it.' via W. Faraday

Right:
With a ground crew bod apparently 'giving it the gun' at full throttle is BI W4110 'KM:K' in which Walter Faraday did his first op with WO 'Lucky' Wright. Plt Off H. J. Barley, RNZAF, flew her for seven ops, September/November 1942, during the first half of his tour. She then became the regular steed of Sgt C. W. Baldwin and crew, who did 17 of their tour of ops in her through to mid-March 1943. At the time of this photo, thought to be early March, her nose shows a tally of 45 sorties, seven of them ice-cream cones for Italian targets. The 'Digger' on the front turret vent would suggest an Australian connection in the crew at some stage, but what does the harp signify we wonder? Was one of her skippers Welsh? We'd be glad to know the answer.
Having first operated with No 44 Sqn in early August 1942, the old girl led a charmed life on ops for nine months before being lost on the night of 13/14 May 1943, Flg Off W. D. Rail and crew failing to return from Pilsen. via Walter Faraday

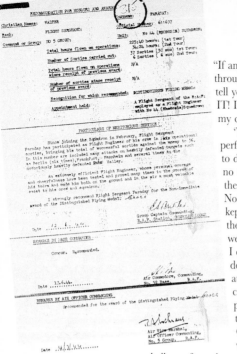

"If anything happens — straight through that bloody hole and if I tell you to do something — DO IT! I get all the useless B–s on my crew."

'The take-off was a performance. He had everything to do himself. Waddington had no runways at that time and the field wasn't altogether even. Not used to this sort of thing I kept slipping backwards from the throttle box. Perhaps as well at this stage of my career. I didn't know what I was doing in daylight never mind at night. Comments from the crew were ribald and to the point, and Lucky's remarks turned the cockpit blue. Crossing the coast on the way out we received a challenge from the ground. Perhaps an army post, I don't know. Lucky told me to tap out a letter H on the key in front of me. I didn't know any Morse. More expletives to put it politely. I'll just say I never have forgotten, nor ever will forget, that four dots make a letter H in Morse code.

'Over the target Lucky called up another pilot (Frankie Stott) on the R/T and said he would see him at breakfast. Safely back at Waddington Lucky calls out, "Hello 'Jetty', Hello 'Jetty', this is 'Onlooker King'! Are you receiving me?" After that we were soon on the ground again and the trip was over. I remember Lucky calling out eighteen grand to the navigator when he reached his operational height. I did another four trips with Lucky: Bremen, Duisburg, Frankfurt, Düsseldorf. He was then at the end of his tour. I remember the call signs "Jetty" and "Onlooker", the only ones I can recall out of dozens I must have heard later.

'After those few trips with Lucky I then awarded myself a brevet. I sewed a letter E into an old AG badge and tacked that on to my tunic. And that's how I came to be a flight engineer.

'So, after less than two weeks on No 44 Sqn, I then returned to Swinderby (61 Con Flight) and joined Fred Dashper, a Canadian pilot. 25 trips with him on No 61 Sqn, from Syerston, and then to 1661 HCU, Winthorpe to be an instructor on a course I'd never done myself.

'I never regretted my decision to be a flight engineer, except perhaps if we were over a particularly warmish target when my mouth used to go dry.

Once back at base it was all forgotten until the next trip.'
Authors' Note: After completing his own tour of 30 ops on 20 April 1943 (ie the five with Lucky Wright on No 44 Sqn, and 25 with Fred Dashper on No 61) Walter instructed at 1661 HCU, Winthorpe from May to September 1943, flying Lancs and Manchesters, with a brief spell also at No 5 Group TU, Fulbeck, on 1485 Bombing and Gunnery Flt, in July/August 1943 (Manchesters, Lancs, Wellingtons). He returned to No 44 Sqn (by then at Dunholme Lodge) end of December 1943, and crewed-up with a pilot he'd met at Winthorpe, Steve Cockbain (who was by now a Squadron Leader and OC of B Flt 44 Sqn). They were to resume their operational careers on 15 February 1944, with a seven-hour trip to Berlin, followed by ops to Stuttgart, Frankfurt, Essen, Maisy (France), Caen (early hours of D-Day), Pont-au-Bault, and Caen again in the early hours of 12 June 1944. It was on this trip that their Lanc NE138, 'KM:Z', was hit by flak; the starboard-inner caught fire and they returned on three engines. Perhaps it was a portent of things to come.

Nine days later, again in NE138, they took part in the Wesseling raid, on the night of 21/22 June 1944, on which their Lanc was badly damaged by an enemy fighter, and four of the crew baled out as it seemed the Lanc was a 'goner'. The remaining crew, however, got her back — an epic story in itself, and it was at this juncture they decided to call it a day. As Walter has said, 'It was perhaps the right time to do so, as by then I'd developed a bit of a nervous twitch'.

Both Steve Cockbain and Walter Faraday returned to Winthorpe to instruct again, in July 1944, and the HCU had the dreaded Stirlings. Only two weeks into their new job, Steve and Walter survived a take-off crash in one. Walter's last flight at Winthorpe was in a Stirling on 3 December 1944. He went to Swinderby instructing on Lancs May/June 1945, took the Bomber Command Instructors School Staff Engineer Course in July 1945, returning to 1660 HCU, Swinderby instructing on Lancs until November 1946, then returning to another of his old squadrons — No 61, this time at Waddington, and by now flying Lincolns. He was to continue on the Lincoln until eventual retirement from the RAF, serving with No 100 Sqn, 230 OCU, Scampton (again as an instructor/staff engineer), No 115 Sqn, Mildenhall, No 90 Sqn, Wyton, and finally No 58 Sqn, Benson, his last flight in an RAF aircraft being in Lincoln RF331 on 28 June 1951. He retired from the RAF in 1952, a Flight Lieutenant, with a total of 972hr, of which 449 were at night (260 of those on ops). He counts himself lucky to have survived. So many of the pilots and crew with whom he flew didn't survive, including Steve Cockbain, who was killed in a Stirling crash. Lucky Wright came through the war and took a pub in Nottingham, but died in 1967. Fred Dashper, too, survived, and he and Walter have met several times in recent years.

Walter is living happily in retirement in Lancashire, and takes an active part in squadron reunions etc. 'A real character' in every way.

TRAINING CONTINUES —
WITH A SURPRISE

'Let's give that lot down the back a surprise...'
Advanced training, too, had to be continued, as new techniques, new equipment, came into use. Not too widely known is that No 627 Sqn, which flew Mosquitos on low-level marking, and master bomber missions for 5 Group from April 1944, also used a Lancaster for training of Mossie navigators on H₂S.

Whereas, due to the confines of the Mosquito cockpit, no airborne dual instruction could be given to the navs, a Lancaster, suitably equipped, had the capacity and endurance to carry several, who could take their turns at the H₂S with the instructor. For this purpose, initially in March 1945, a Lanc was borrowed from No 97 Sqn at nearby Coningsby, and a pilot transferred in to fly it. He was Flt Lt W. J. K. (Bill) Endean DFC, RNZAF, who had just completed a tour of ops on No 50 Sqn at Skellingthorpe. He was not wishing to go as a flying instructor, but was known to be able to handle a Lanc 'pretty well', so this job seemed a reasonable compromise.

He'd started his tour with No 50 Sqn in early September 1944, and even at that relatively late stage of the war, of his 37 ops, 30 were at night, some of the latter on long flogs into eastern Europe of 9½/2/10½/2hr, such as Politz (three times), Munich and Gdynia (Poland) to sink the *Lützow*. Another long night trip was to Bergen (submarine pens), on 28/29 October

1944, 7hr 10min, of which 4hr 30min was spent on instruments in cloud. Bill claimed this was the only op which caused him any real problems, as he relates:

'It seemed to me that most blokes who were shot down bought it just after the target, having relaxed after the fiasco, and fatigue setting in. Men went to sleep and Huns came in. My solution was a thick slice of good Lincolnshire bread, with a layer of Mr Heinz's sandwich spread — good for the digestive system which in turn reacted on the nervous system, and kept the brain alert. It rather overworked — at the wrong end on that particular night! I'd never had any bowel trouble throughout the tour, but on this occasion I had it good and proper. The ceiling was down and we were at only about 1,000ft. Rather than soil the trousers, I put 'George' in, and after instructing 'Silas' Hall, my flight engineer to correct the trim, I went aft to the Elsan, having notified the crew of my intention. The rear gunner, Ginger Lee, was so excited at having his Skipper down the back with him that he opened the bulkhead door to say 'goodday'. Due to the fuselage vacuum effect, he copped the lot.'

The New Zealander became a great believer in dropping down virtually 'on the deck' during the homeward journey if the opposition got a bit hot, his theory being that the Hun fighter pilots didn't like flying much below

100ft in the dark. He'd studied another former 50 Sqn pilot's theories on that strategy — Mick Martin, who'd survived.

As Tom Hall, his engineer, confirms: 'He'd tell the nav to "shut-up", then spread his small pilot's map across the throttle quadrant, and together we'd negotiate our way across Germany and out over Holland at *very* low level in the dark, weather permitting, of course. We always made it back without any undue stress or strain. The crew weren't too enamoured with the tactic at times, but it got us through.'

It was due to such escapades that he'd earned the nickname 'Mad' on the squadron.

Bill Endean rarely did anything 'by the book', it seems, other than to deliver his bombs on the target — right place, right time. His take-off technique for a fully-laden Lanc was certainly not in accordance with Pilots' Notes, again as Tom Hall explains:

'On the take-off run, at the merest suggestion of the wheels beginning to lift off, he'd call for 'gear-up', and up they came, with the nose held down, and the Lanc flying a few feet above the runway until speed built up, which it did surprisingly quickly, enabling the aircraft to then climb away quite easily. He reckoned that if you were going to stall, better to do it from 10ft rather than 50 or 100ft; also that even if an engine had failed at the critical moment, the quicker speed build-up would have probably saved us. As it was, they were always tense moments, and I was ready to pull the override lever and push the throttles 'through the gate' to +18 emergency boost if ordered. One evening, awaiting our turn to line up, a Lanc taking off ahead of us was obviously struggling to get airborne before the end of the runway. It's pilot pulled if off, but at too steep an angle, and it stalled and crashed into the fields beyond the runway's end, bomb load, aircraft, crew disappearing into oblivion. Bill commented there and then, "If only they'd taken off as we do!..." '

The crew's last op was to Sassnitz, a Baltic port, on the night of 6/7 March 1945, a 9hr trip, as part of a 191-strong Lancaster force, plus five Mosquitos, from which one Lancaster FTR. This brought their operational hours total to 250, of which 221 were at night, and they were declared 'tour-expired'. Endean wanted to continue on ops until the war's end, but most of the crew felt they'd done their bit after 37 trips, and probably didn't want to tempt fate too far. So they went their own ways, Bill Endean to No 627 Sqn at Woodhall Spa. Not long after his arrival there, he

was incensed to learn that his engineer, Tom Hall, had been posted to the Bomber Command Film Flight Unit at Syerston, where he was to continue on ops. He roared over to Syerston on his motor bike, stormed into the flight office and played 'merry hell' with Tom and everyone in authority, but all to no avail, and returned to Woodhall, where at least he'd be flying a Lancaster.

His first trip on his new unit was in a Lanc borrowed from No 97 Sqn at nearby Coningsby, and which was used for a month until a specially-modified Lanc was ready. This was to be ND823, fitted out as a flying classroom, with three of the latest H_2S sets on board, and collected from Boscombe Down by Endean himself. (It may have been joined later by another Lanc.)

From 5 April 1945 to mid-September 1945, Bill flew ND823 exclusively. Regular training flights of one-to-two hours were the norm, on H_2S cross-countries mainly, sometimes dropping TIs at Wainfleet, or occasional bombing practice, operating as 627's 'H_2S Flight'. This somewhat monotonous routine must have bored Bill at times, to put it mildly, after the adventures of operational flying. He had, as he described it, 'a roving commission with 'AZ:Z', to go where I pleased, so as not to let the Mossie bods on the new H_2S sets know where they were. One day, I went up to have a look at the Derwent Dam at low level. Those Mossie boys knew where we were right enough that time, and were changing the colour of their pants.'

Over the years, odd stories had filtered through to us from navigators who had flown on these training trips from Woodhall Spa, and on which something unusual had obviously happened, though most seemed reluctant to spill the beans. One such former nav, however, (Arthur Turner) asked if we'd ever come across a pilot named Endean, a New Zealander. 'Mad Endean' he was known as, we were told. Arthur described in detail how, on return from one somewhat sedate H_2S cross-country, he was to get the fright of his life.

Bill Endean was flying the Lanc as normal. He'd long dispensed with the full Lanc crew, carrying only the trainee navs (usually four of them) and an instructor. When not under instruction the navs would be free to man the turrets and visit the cockpit. On this day, Arthur was sitting in the flight engineer's seat, admiring the cloudscape from about 10,000ft, when Bill shouted to him... 'Let's give that lot down the back a surprise — hang on' (or words to that effect), whereupon he shoved the throttles and pitch levers fully forward, pushed the nose down hard, until the Lanc was screaming (at over the 300 mark, Arthur thinks), put his right foot on the throttle quadrant, virtually stood up in his seat and hauled back on the wheel.

The Lanc performed a perfect loop.

It had, in fact, become something of a speciality to Bill, hence the nickname 'Mad'. The impact on the unsuspecting souls in the fuselage can be imagined, though no doubt the instructor may have had an inkling of what to expect by then.

Bill Endean, still 'large as life' — a 'Rumpole-like' character, visited the UK for a reunion with his 50 Sqn crew in 1984, and they confirmed publicly to a man in the press and on radio, that he'd looped their Lanc 'VN:U' on training flights and air tests to prove it could be done, lightly loaded.

The H_2S Flight was disbanded in September 1945. ND823 was flown out to Tempsford, and eventually struck off charge in 1947. Bill returned to his native New Zealand and continued to fly light aircraft until shortly before he, too, was 'SOC Mangonui, 1993, aged 69'.

Tom Hall retired from the RAF a Wing Commander (Ground Engineer) in 1977. After leaving 50 Sqn he went on to do another three ops with the Bomber Command Film Flight Unit at Syerston, in Lanc 'G7:Y', flown by former 50 Sqn colleague Flt Lt Joe North. They were all daylights, the last one being on the huge finale of 25 April 1945 to Berchtesgaden (Hitler's 'Eagle's Nest') near Salzburg, their Lancaster orbiting the target for half an hour to film the raid. Three years of his early postwar service were spent with the Missing Research and Enquiry Service, a unit formed to find, and identify, bodies of downed RAF airmen in Europe. This organisation as a whole accounted for 53,000 airmen who had been posted 'missing believed killed'. After leaving the RAF, Tom served for two years with the Royal Saudi Air Force, then with the Save The Children Fund until his 'third' retirement in 1987. After the encounter with his former Skipper at Syerston in April 1945, he was not to see or hear of him again until the crew reunion nearly 40 years later.

Top:
The Endean crew, 50 Sqn, Skellingthorpe, after an air test, 18 January 1945, on which they took two of their ground crew, whose names, regrettably, are not recorded. The Lanc is BI NF922 'VN:U' 'UNCLE', in which the crew did most of their tour of operations.
The line-up is (left to right):
Bomb aimer: Ken Franklyn, Flight engineer: Tom Hall, Rear gunner: 'Ginger' Lee, Mid-upper gunner: Frank Turner, Pilot: Bill Endean, RNZAF, Navigator: Bob Baber
Wireless operator: Geoff Carslake
Ground crew — Who are you? Where are you?
Official via W. J. K. Endean

Above:
The photo shows ND823 at Woodhall Spa, with its 627 Sqn code 'AZ-Z' (probably unique on a Lancaster), the bar above the Z being to distinguish its call-sign from that of the squadron's Mossie of the same letter. A pilot and several trainee navs are either about to board, or have just de-planed. There look to be some knowing smiles. Bill Endean is almost out of view, just below the roundel, talking to what would appear to be a Royal Navy Officer. via W. J. K. Endean

UNRIVALLED

Throughout history this land of ours has produced 'men of the hour': men of genius, vision, determination.

Such a man was Roy Chadwick, designer of the mighty Lancaster, and it says much for the soundness of his creation that, to quote Sir Arthur Harris, 'It could be saddled with ever-increasing loads without breaking the camel's back'.

Whilst it is beyond the scope of this book to cover the development of a legend, let us sneak into Ringway and Woodford and share the enterprise of Alex Jack, the Avro Group Chief Inspector, through whose camera lens we can study early moments in the Lancaster's introduction. An avid photographer, Sandy (as he was invariably known) was ideally placed to record on film the type's production and development, though he was to express regret in later years that his weighty responsibilities did not allow him time and opportunity to photograph more vivid slices of the life and times of a remarkable thoroughbred, all the more historically significant in view of a disastrous fire destroying much of the A. V. Roe extensive archive in October 1959.

Presented here are some of Sandy's historic pictures:

Top right:
Roy Chadwick: from a painting by Geoffrey E. Lea, and which hangs at the Lincolnshire Aviation Heritage Centre, East Kirkby.
Courtesy Fred and Harold Panton/C. S. Waterfall

Centre right:
L7527, the first Lancaster off the production line and which made her maiden flight on the final day of October 1941. Observe lack of dorsal fairing to mid-upper turret (the fairing a production feature introduced in March 1942) and rear turret complete with full Perspex panels (which squadrons began modifying in 1943 but never incorporated at the factories). Also evident are the early type roundel, and the distinctive fuselage windows, deleted by the end of 1943 yet, unaccountably, forever featured in paintings by artists regardless!

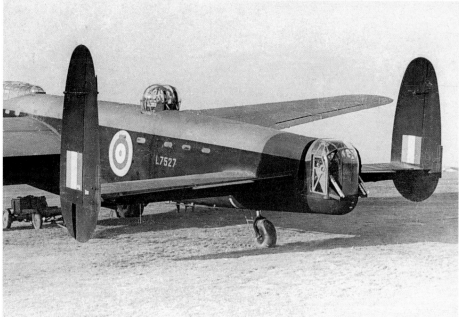

Following extensive use as a test and development vehicle, L7527 was finally 'called to the colours', being issued to No 1654 HCU, Wigsley, where her work-worn appearance, coupled with old and new modification standard, was not out of place. However, such was the shortage of Lancasters as 1943 drew to a close — losses at times outstripping production as the Ruhr hammering gave way to the pounding of Berlin — that L7527 passed to No 15 Sqn at Mildenhall, a unit in No 3 Group re-equipping with Lancs. Despite her limitations — rather sloppy controls, poor climbing ability and ceiling, plus a troublesome petrol thirst — she survived until Essen, 26/27 March 1944, failing to return with a crew captained by Plt Off T. G. Marsh.
A. C. Jack

Bottom right:
A seemingly tranquil setting at Woodford: a pastorale, the airfield nestling up to the foothills of the Peak District, yet with industrial Stockport and the city of Manchester but a few miles distant. The scene belies activity aplenty during the early months of production, as a new Lanc flies low over another probably receiving final adjustments to trim and rigging before its first flight. It was a busy time for the company test pilots, Messrs Thorne, Gleave, Orrell and Brown, later joined, in 1944, by Sqn Ldr Ken Cook DFC, a tour-expired veteran, and Sqn Ldr Peter Field-Richards at Langar, with other RAF pilots being seconded to the companies as necessary to assist with flight testing. When Lancaster production peaked in the summer of 1944 it was not unusual for a test pilot to do eight flights in a day, some on 'initials', others 're-tests' — Jimmy Orrell alone flew more than 900 different Lancasters during the 1942/45 period. It was dawn-to-dusk without pause. Ken Cook related that he would don his parachute harness as a matter of course as part of his dressing routine at home each morning, not removing it until retiring to bed at night. It would no doubt be much the same for test pilots at the other manufacturing plants, such as Alex Henshaw at Vickers, Castle Bromwich, to whom the delight of flying Lancs and Spitfires the same day became the norm. How he must 'sigh for a Merlin' now. A. C. Jack

Top left and centre left:

The AVRO production line had been established at a new factory at Chadderton in 1939, just as war was looming. There was no airfield nearby, but the company had acquired Woodford, some 18 miles away, in the mid-1920s, and it was there that large assembly sheds had been built, and later enlarged to accommodate the main Lancaster final assembly lines. Pending their full readiness, the prototype Lancasters and a few early production ones were taken to nearby Ringway for assembly, but Woodford soon got under way. It is a routine which continues to this day under the British Aerospace Company's name. Lancaster sections were transported by road from Chadderton to Woodford, always at night (just as were the Lincolns, Shackletons, Vulcans, 748s, ATPs in later years). These two pictures taken around March 1942, show a Lancaster nose, and a fuselage/tail section outside the Chadderton works, awaiting the journey to Woodford behind one of the specially modified fleet of 'artics', this one being an Albion. Whilst apparently snapped at the same time, there is no saying whether the two sections would be married together within the same aeroplane at Woodford. A. V. Roe

Bottom left:

All in a day's work at Woodford — a single day's production of seven or eight Lancasters on average, July/August 1944, awaiting collection by the ATA pilots for delivery direct to squadrons, or perhaps in some cases to maintenance units for fitting of additional equipment. Day in, day out...night in, night out, with few weekend breaks or holidays for Woodford's 3,000 employees, or throughout the 'Lancaster Group' for that matter. August 1944 appears to have been the month of peak production, with over 300 rolled-out across the whole group, a truly remarkable achievement of organisation and efficiency. On the left of these waiting warriors is PD279, which went to No 218 'Gold Coast' Sqn and survived the war. A. V. Roe

Below:

R5667 was delivered to No 83 Sqn at Scampton late May/early June 1942, and, coded 'OL·F', she was the subject of a series of 'round the clock' air-to-air photographs which appeared in the Recognition Journals, and on the MOS Aircraft Identification cards issued to many service units such as army and navy gunners (some of whom still continued to fire on any aircraft, it seems, until almost the war's end!). This picture is reproduced from MOS card 'Lancaster I, Issue I, 14(A)', showing 5667 still without fairing to mid-upper and with masking tape between centre — and main-fuselage sections still visible. She was to survive on ops for six months, then passed to No 1656 CU at Lindholme, where, on 19 August 1943, flown by Sgt D. W. H. Butterfield, a tyre burst on take-off causing a violent swing off the runway and a crash in which the Lanc caught fire. Fortunately, the crew escaped, the only casualty being 5667 itself, which was written off. Crown Copyright

STORY OF A LANC

If ever you are fortunate to eavesdrop on the lively talk filling the corner of a pub or hotel or club, wherever and whenever one-time veterans gather, you are in for a treat, an enlightening experience you will never forget.

Be they men or women, ground staff bods or aircrew types who can still tell you their service number with not a moment's hesitation (but who probably cannot recall what they did last week), the conversation will inevitably centre more on people they knew, units and stations they served on, rather than about the Lancs themselves.

But be patient, listen well, for mention them they will. As their heads again ring to the sound of Merlins or Hercules, the distinctive, slightly nauseating tang of dope and rubber, the stink of 100 octane petrol and burnt oil seems to pervade the atmosphere as incidents aplenty are recalled.

Take a gathering of like-minds who 'did their bit' at Waltham (rarely referred to by its official title of RAF Grimsby) as being typical. Voices will be raised or reduced to a whisper at recollections of kites which endured for months on end, be they paint-worn and oil-streaked, until, it seemed, just about every part had been patched or replaced; or memories of kites which disappeared without trace on ops, or met an untimely end in crashes for one reason or another within days of arrival.

And with each flash of memory comes to mind their crews... remembered, yet not remembered; for once-familiar faces have, too frequently, become misty, their names long-gone as the passing years take their toll. And among those remembered, yet not remembered, will be Frank Wadge and his band of hopefuls whose ordeal in Lanc I ED749 'HW;J' is worth the telling.

Posted to No 100 Sqn, they were surprised to be allocated their very own Lancaster within days of arrival, albeit ED749, by then being rather long in

the tooth, as it were. They opened their account with a visit to the German capital on 15/16 February 1944 and settled down to squadron life and an undoubted meat-grinder of a tour stretching ahead.

Leipzig 19/20 February, their second outing, proved to be a non-event due to faulty oxygen supply in ED749, and knowing glances, knowing comments first cast their way before their baptism of action, made them just a little uneasy. Was 'J-Jig' really jinxed?

Next came Stuttgart 20/21 February... almost their undoing. Taking off at five minutes past midnight they arrived over the target at 03.58hrs, only to find all in darkness, so they proceeded to do a dogleg. Immediately the PFF indicators went down and they began a second run-in, height 22,000ft and at 04.02hrs added their bombs to the concentrated attack developing. Then, five minutes after leaving the target area, the intercom went dead and clearly the trip home was going to be difficult.

Pressing on, they had reached a point 65 miles NW of Saarbrücken by 04.50hrs when, at a height of 23,000ft a fast-moving twin-engined aircraft collided with their Lanc. The violent impact caused 'J-Jig' to lurch and dive uncontrollably for 3,000ft and Wadge ordered his crew to 'prepare to abandon aircraft'. However, at around 19,000/20,000ft the Skipper regained control and once more headed homewards, aware their kite had been badly damaged, but not knowing the full extent. Finally, they were homed by searchlight to Ford on the South Coast and landed safely — and with relief — at 06.45hrs.

Before flying back to Waltham in another 100 Sqn Lanc sent down to collect them, they had a last look at ED749, no doubt marvelling at their escape, and wondering what must have happened to the German fighter which hit them. They then posed for a photograph with the Lanc which had

brought them home. But they were never to receive that picture, nor Frank Wadge receive his DFM. With only two of his crew available due to injuries, and forced to take spare bods, he set out for Schweinfurt on the night of 24/25 February 1944 (Lanc III ND593)... and vanished in mysterious circumstances. Wadge reported over the R/T that he was unwell and set course for base at 21.11hrs. Told to 'cross coast and jettison petrol', he called again at 21.45hrs and reported that 'jettison release will not function'. Ordered to go out to sea and dump his bombs, no further news was forthcoming and another batch of telegrams were soon on their way to loved ones...

Opposite:
Close-ups showing damage caused by the collision with the enemy fighter. Consider how lucky mid-upper gunner Ron Girton was to survive.
Crown Copyright

Above:
ED749 'HW:J' pictured at Ford on 21 February 1944 along with the Wadge septet (left to right):
Pilot: Flt Sgt Frank Wadge
Flight engineer: Sgt White
Bomb aimer: Sgt Johnny Hughes
Navigator: Sgt Lyons
Rear gunner: Sgt Jim Taylor
Wireless operator: Sgt Pete Armstrong
Mid-upper gunner: Sgt Ron Girton
Crown Copyright

Left:
Repaired, ED749 was later issued to the Polish-manned No 300 ('Masovian') Sqn at Faldingworth, before serving out her time with several training units. She was finally struck off charge in October 1945. Polish Sources

Bottom left:
It was only right that the City of Manchester should have a Lancaster on display for its 'Wings for Victory' campaign in March 1943 — a brand-new one too, fresh off the A. V. Roe production line at Chadderton, the self-same ED749. She is seen here in final stages of assembly in the city centre's Spring Gardens, already a great attraction, and no doubt provoking a sense of immense pride in its admiring onlookers. Foreground is the fuselage of another 'ED' Lancaster, also obviously straight off the assembly line, sans outer skin so as to show structure and internal equipment. In the background, some of Manchester's distinctively styled and liveried buses — Crossleys and Leylands, the one on the far left appearing to have had a coat of grey camouflage applied over its normal red and cream.
Daily Express

FIRST OF THE BREED

As rewarding a spectacle as it was when we sat back to watch such war-winning aircraft as the Lancaster and Spitfire, Hurricane and Mosquito droning over London to mark the 50th Anniversary of the end of war in Europe, how many of us bemoaned the lack of a Halifax and Stirling, Wellington and Whitley? These and other worthy types played no small part in carrying the war to the enemy.

And what about those less successful like the Albemarle, Botha and Manchester? Is it too much to hope that persistent rumours of an Albemarle in a Russian forest will become fact... that a Botha may yet emerge from the depths of Wigtown Bay? We have only to pick up any one of the specialist aviation magazines reaching the bookstalls each month to read about amazing restoration projects... enthusiasts taking on tasks mind-boggling in terms of dedication, time and effort, not to mention money! Such buffs think nothing of taking years to rebuild aircraft hauled out of jungles and lakes as rusting hulks, among them some types not seen for half a century or more.

And here's a thought. Is there a case for building more full-size replicas? Certainly such is possible, if only made of fibreglass or plastic, whatever, for static display only. Is anyone, any group interested in creating that Stirling and Whitley and Manchester? The museum at Elvington has shown the way and the day cannot be far off when their part-replica Halifax is complete.

Top:
For those of us who have never set eyes on one, here is a real Manchester to study, ponder over, albeit through the medium of a snapshot taken by Canadian engine mechanic Trevor Kovasco way back in late 1941. Join him on the grass at Coningsby as pilot, Plt Off David Maltby from No 97 'Straits Settlements' Sqn gives two Vultures the 'gun'. What did a Vulture sound like, we wonder? Trevor Kovasco knew. He also knew the never-to-be-forgotten sound of a Vulture disintegrating in mid-air...was, on another occasion, airborne when a Vulture simply seized up. Twice he had reason to pray to the Almighty when Manchesters in which he was a passenger, monitoring engine behaviour, went down like a lift, to spread themselves over the landscape. In common with most of the men who flew in Manchesters, David Maltby first went to war in Hampdens. His initial Manchester ops (four) were done as second pilot to Flt Lt 'Mo' Coton before achieving captain status and leading his own crew to and from Hamburg, 15/16 January 1942. He then graduated to the Lanc, his Squadron (97) being the second to re-equip with the Manchester's replacement, successor. By mid-March 1943 a seasoned veteran, he (along with his crew) was selected to join the special Squadron (No 617) forming at Scampton under Wg Cdr Guy Gibson for the express purpose of attacking the Ruhr Dams, successfully dropping their spinning war load at the Möhne Dam, 16/17 May 1943. He was to become a flight commander on No 617 Sqn, but Sqn Ldr David Maltby DSO, DFC and his crew sadly perished when their Lanc, JA981, a new breed with bulged bomb doors, cartwheeled into the sea on recall from the abortive Dortmund-Ems Canal raid mounted on the night of 14/15 September 1943.

So many of those intrepid Manchester aircrew failed to survive the war. If they did not die in those Manchesters which were shot down, or 'fell down' as a result of engine trouble when on operations, they died in crashes around the UK. At best, a surprising number saw the war out as POWs. J. T. Kovasco

Below:
Just one of the Manchesters which never made it back to home base is L7316 'EM:U' from No 207 Sqn, Waddington, downed off the Frisian Islands during a venture to Cologne 31 August/1 September 1941 with Plt Off Tom Gilderthorpe and his colleagues, the pilot and one other crew member surviving to become POWs. No 207 Sqn was the first to be equipped with the Manchester, re-forming at Waddington, 1 November 1940 for the purpose of so doing. German Sources

THE INSEPARABLES

It was said by some that bomber crews became closer than relatives. They invariably described the loss of one or more of their number as 'like losing a brother'. Certainly, the bond was strong; strongly protective, too, if any one man was in trouble, or having difficulty making it through a tour. For many, it was the bond, the camaraderie, which kept them going. The two gunners, in particular, established their own special relationship — strictly within the seven, not outside it. They needed a special mutual trust and understanding which fostered the instant 'no questions' reactions to either one's orders, co-ordination being vital when split seconds made the difference between life and death, survival and oblivion. There were no set orders for gunners — guidance, yes, but they had to get it right between themselves from the start; decide and agree who was to be mid-upper, who was to be tail-end charlie. Gunners needed to be unflinching, with an agressive streak. Many had taken the job because it got them (or kept them) out of the mines, Jocks, Taffs, Geordies aplenty, mostly tough blokes who knew how to look after themselves — and their fellow crew mates when needed — both on the ground and in the air.

A good pair of gunners was highly valued by the crews. None would know, of course, how they would fare in battle, so achievements at gunnery school were not always the best guide. It is said 'a man does not know himself until he has come under fire'. Until a crew had come under fire itself, no one really knew themselves, individually or collectively, or how they would react. Action would be the ultimate test. The seven-man team could only hope they had not made any mistakes when crewing-up at OTU, HCU, etc. Whatever their non-combat level of proficiency, would they stand the ultimate test in the battles ahead?

Was there any such thing as a typical crew? Before being let loose into enemy skies, all seven would have been tried and tested to the furthest possible degree over many months of training (two years in the case of some pilots), individually and, gradually, collectively. Their final weeks of training as a self-contained unit should have weeded out the less competent, shown-up any unacceptable personality clashes (and there were numerous such cases), etc, before the crews progressed to the squadrons. Even there, they would undergo more training, more scrutiny, more tests in as near combat conditions as could be simulated, before being declared 'Ready For Ops'.

How *do* you select a crew to feature in a book? It is no easy task. Most crews claiming to be 'typical' would arrive on a squadron, get on with their job efficiently and unobtrusively, though by no means anonymously as their operational tally mounted, when interest would inevitably start to focus on them as paragons of hope. Their main aims: to do their best over the target, complete their tour, and — quite simply — to survive. Some would get through a tour within three months, largely without incident, unscathed. Others were posted in and lost without trace within days, before they'd got to know themselves properly, let alone their squadron colleagues. There were crews who seemed to be accident-prone, others who would attract incidents from the start, surviving numerous brushes with fighters, flak damage, mechanical failures, equipment malfunction, lightning strikes, even a prang or two. They would either survive or succumb, depending on which way fate was slanted on a particular night, as much as on their own skills. Perhaps there is no such thing as a 'typical' crew.

For the large majority, completing a tour of 30 or 35 ops or so (depending on time of war), enough was enough — you'd done your bit. Some opted to carry straight on, individually or as part of complete crews, either with PFF for a second tour of 15 ops (and more if one chose), or perhaps on a main force squadron after a spell instructing. It was up to the individual or the crew as a whole. Another alternative was to volunteer for No 617 Sqn. Some even went on for third tours, achieving quite phenomenal tallies of ops — men like Cheshire, Tait, Gerry Witherick, David Hamilton, Tubby Baker, Tony Davies, Danny Everett, Ken Letford, 'Chan' Chandler, to name but a few, most of whom had started on ops in the Hampden, Whitley and Wellington days of 1940.

We have chosen a crew whose operational experiences ranged from the 'typical' or 'normal' in their earlier days, through to what can only be described as 'somewhat exceptional' as time went on, and for which they needed to possess in good measure the qualities of skill, camaraderie and determination which were so vital to survival in Bomber Command. In particular, we focus on the two air gunners within the crew, who carved parallel paths through their RAF careers over three years of war and beyond, illustrating that extra-strong bond which helped them and their crews to get through it all.

Summer 1942 marked the formative period of the Lancaster force as it began to expand rapidly, the production lines of both aircraft and crews becoming established. They were still difficult days (and nights) with indifferent bombing results and high losses, even though the advent of the Lancaster had reduced the percentage loss rate. Two young air gunners were being processed through the system, both volunteers who had signed

Left:
AIRING THEIR WARES
A rare vintage: early spring 1943, certainly from a photographic point of view, there not being too many pictures about of Lancasters of that period — a most intensive and demanding one for Bomber Command. Here, on a seemingly sedate 'stooge' over friendly Lincolnshire is ED702, March 1943, still looking pristine, probably not long after delivery to No 49 Sqn at Fiskerton. She could be described as a typical 'Phase 2' machine, which had started to replace the earlier L, R, W-serialled Lancs in late 1942, still with fuselage windows, but now a Mk III with Packard-built Merlins. Claimed by No 49 Sqn's CO, Wg Cdr Leonard C. Slee almost from new, he was to fly her on only two ops before handing over command of the squadron to Wg Cdr Peter W Johnson, who was to take her on her next eight ops, April/June 1943, in his first two months of command, all tough targets.

Then, on the night of 20/21 June, Leonard Slee returned to claim her back for one more op, and for which, by now a Gp Capt, he'd been specially called back to lead a 5 Group attack on a factory making radar parts at Friedrichshafen, as 'Master Bomber'. In the event, 702 let him down near the target with engine trouble, and he had to hand over to his deputy. Surprisingly, however, she was back on ops the next night to Krefeld in the hands of Plt Off C. T. Anderson, giving no problems. Wg Cdr Johnson took her again for his next five ops, late June/early September, by now operating less frequently as had become more usual for squadron commanders, for whom one or two ops per month was becoming the norm. They included the historic raid on Peenemünde, 17/18 August 1943.

On her 34th trip, 23/24 September 1943, again with Plt Off Anderson, she went missing on a raid to Mannheim, after an operational life of six months almost to the day from when Leonard Slee first 'blooded' her. It will be noticed that in this picture she carries no nose art or bomb tally — not surprising perhaps, as she was new at the time. But did any 49 Sqn Lancs carry any form of nose adornment — even bomb tallies? We have certainly not come across a picture of one that did, it being considered unlucky. Following a run of losses by the squadron in its earlier days of aircraft with nose adornments, its then-CO banned the practice, this rule being passed down to successive COs, and strictly enforced through the war's end. L. C. Slee

Left:
THE INSEPARABLES

Buckingham Palace, 22 June 1943. Bill Townsend and his happy band after the Dams Raid awards ceremony. Next to Wg Cdr Gibson's crew (all of whom were decorated), Townsend's was numerically the most highly rewarded, with six out of the seven receiving medals, Bill himself, still only 22, the CGM. He'd been promoted to Pilot Officer shortly after the raid; Lance Howard, his Aussie navigator (far right) had been commissioned just prior to the raid, though it had not been gazetted. He was initially recommended for the DFM, but it was changed for the DFC. Third left is bomb aimer Charles Franklin, who got a Bar to his DFM (quite rare); far left and second left, Ray Wilkinson and Douglas Webb, the 'gunner twins', both of whom got DFMs. It seemed appropriate that, so close had the two become, even their recommendation for the award was a joint one, commenting on 'their teamwork, complete understanding with their pilot, and skilful handling of their guns', signed by Gp Capt J. N. Whitworth, OC of Scampton, endorsed by AVM Ralph Cochrane, AOC, No 5 Group. Absent from the line-up is wireless operator George Chalmers, who also got the DFM. Next to right is the crew's former wireless operator on No 49 Sqn, Jack Grain, who had taken leave to attend the ceremony with his old chums, and who spent several other leaves with them. Also missing is flight engineer 'Sandy' Powell, who didn't get a medal, which seemed somewhat iniquitous; but then, perhaps, the same could be said for all the undecorated ones who had put their lives 'on the line' that night. But couldn't that also be said for so many in Bomber Command throughout the whole war? It was reported in the Press in December 1994 that Charles Franklin's medals (DFM and Bar included) had been sold at auction for £8,250. Let us hope they went to an appreciative home. Charles's health failed him in the postwar years, and he died in rather sad circumstances in 1975. Jack Grain eventually went back on ops and was killed on almost the last day of the war when the Stirling in which he was flying crashed into the sea off Cromer.

No photo is known to exist of the crew posing with their aircraft, Bill Townsend considering it unlucky to do so. Douglas Webb

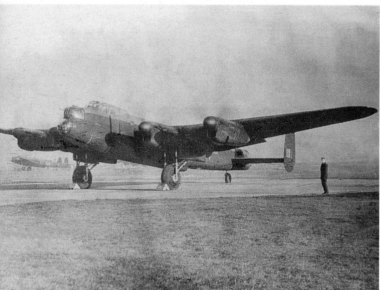

Centre:
SHINING STEED

Photographs of Lancasters at Woodhall Spa, other than with crews posed in front of them, are somewhat rare, but here, looking pristine and obviously quite new, is BI NG181 'KC:M', Armstrong Whitworth-built, one of several new machines delivered to No 617 Sqn in time for the second Tirpitz raid of 28/29 October 1944, for which it was allotted to Flt Lt Arthur Kell, RAAF. It has no exhaust shrouds (thus improving performance on the 13hr-plus endurance required to get to the Tirpitz), and was probably also delivered minus a mid-upper turret. It has a bulged bomb bay for carrying 12,000lb Tallboys, which it would do almost exclusively during its relatively short operational career. Including the second and third Tirpitz raids, it was to be Arthur Kell's 'regular' for five ops, though for the final op of his tour, Kell switched to LM695 'KC:N', seeing the New Year in during a night attack on the cruisers Köln and Emden in Olso Fjord. After three more training flights on NG181 during the first week in January 1945, Kell was tour-expired, but had not actually left the squadron when it was detailed for yet another long distance trip to Norway, to attack targets in Bergen on 12 January 1945. For this, Sqn Ldr Tony Iveson and crew took NG181 instead of their usual ME554 'KC:F'. They had done all but their previous ops in 'Freddie', including the three Tirpitz raids, this being their 17th op with 617. Their experiences in NG181 on the Bergen raid are graphically told in Tom Bennett's book 617 Squadron, The Dam Busters at War (Patrick Stephens Ltd, 1986). Suffice it to say NG181 was virtually shot to pieces by fighters and flak, three of its crew baling out over enemy-held territory due to a misunderstanding on loss of intercom. The remaining four somehow nursed her back to Sumburgh, where, with the whole tail section hanging on by a thread, they had to overshoot on final approach and go round again when a Spitfire very stupidly cut-in on them. Iveson got her down safely, but she was a lame duck, and there was no question of flying 181 back to Woodhall. So, the next day Arthur Kell flew up to collect them (ironically, in their own Lanc ME554), and to have a last look at his prized 'M-Mother'. The return flight to Woodhall was to be Arthur's swansong on No 617 Sqn.

This photo of NG181 at Woodhall is copied from a print in the flying log book of Ray Wilkinson, a keen photographer. He was rear gunner to Kell on the latter's last six ops; including the second and third Tirpitz attacks.

'M-Mother' was eventually repaired in situ at Sumburgh, returning briefly to No 617 Sqn in May 1945, and scrapped five months later. Rarely did any of 617's Lancasters pass to another squadron after overhaul or repair, as the SABS (bombsights) with which they were fitted necessitated extensive modifications, with additional wiring and 'plumbing'. Ray Wilkinson

Bottom left:
WELL-WISHERS AT WOODHALL

Scene from the flight engineer's seat of Lanc flown by Flt Lt John E. R. Williams and crew, awaiting their turn to line up, as the one ahead 'opens its taps' and moves off. For where, we ask? Somewhere special judging by the number of spectators. It could not be for the D-Day 'spoof', night of 5/6 June ('Operation Taxable'), as the first aircraft for that did not leave until nearly midnight. It could not be Tirpitz-bound, as John Williams was tour-expired by mid-August 1944. So, when and what? Possibly one of the squadron's first daylights following D-Day, to Wizernes (VI 'sites'), 22 June, from which they were recalled due to cloud obscuring the target, that day in their 'regular' EE131 'KC:B', which was later to be written off in a crash landing in Russia on the first Tirpitz raid, 11/12 September 1944, manned by Ian Ross and crew. By then she'd been with No 617 Sqn for more than a year.

John Williams and his men had done 19 ops with No 61 Sqn (plus two early returns, one due to an engine fire), September 1943 to February 1944, when posted to No 617 Sqn, with whom they did another 23.

Like quite a number of former wartime aircrew, John Williams DFC and Bar, was ordained postwar, and was for many years before his death the vicar of Rye (Sussex). J. E. R. Williams

n at 18, both still only 19 when posted to Lancasters on completion of gunnery training.

The first of them to arrive at Scampton, mid-1942 was Douglas Webb from Leytonstone, who had been a trainee newspaper photographer in London before signing on in the RAF. He was assigned to the all-NCO crew of Sgt W. C. (Bill) Townsend, who had reported to No 49 Sqn's Conversion Flight on 10 June 1942, having converted to multi-engined aircraft at 16 OTU, initially on the Anson at Wroughton, then the Hampden at Upper Heyford. He'd done two ops from the OTU in Hampden L4070, taking part in the first ever 1,000-bomber raids on Cologne, on the night of 30/31 May 1942; then two nights later, 1/2 June, Essen, only to have to return early with the master gyro U/S. However, he got the posting that all budding bomber boys wanted — Lancasters.

At that stage, the Lanc conversion units had not been established, Lancasters and experienced instructors on the type being in very short supply, so it was very much a case of learn-as-you-go, with each of the early squadrons having its own con flight. Conversion was via the Manchester initially, with the odd taste of Lanc flying to whet the appetite. One of the first tasks at the con flight was to bring the crew up to the complement of seven (from, for example, the four in a Hampden), by addition of either a second pilot or flight engineer (the latter in short supply in mid-1942) and two specialist air gunners. At the same time, it was usually sorted out between 'observers' who was to be nav or bomb aimer. Bill Townsend had not arrived at Scampton with any crew from 16 OTU, so he was starting from scratch. Sgt C. Lance Howard, RAAF, (nav) joined him from the start, together with Sgt Jack Grain (wireless operator), Sgt Douglas Webb (mid-upper) and Sgt E. Pittard (bomb aimer).

It appears Bill Townsend was given a captaincy from the outset, though some pilots were still, at that time, doing the best part of a tour as second dickies. Conversion to full operational status on the Lancaster was to take almost three months, with the odd change in crew make-up during the shake-down period. It was in the later stages of training that the crew experienced their first real incident. On the night of 1 September 1942, they were returning from a long cross-country down to Land's End under simulated full war load conditions, with dummy bombs aboard, under the watchful eye of the Station Navigation Officer, Sqn Ldr Alabaster. On return after 6¾ hours flying it was to find Scampton and much of central and eastern England fogbound. However, the pilot did a good beam approach, saw the flarepath ahead, and was about to touch down (may, in fact, have actually 'greased' it on), when the Squadron Leader ordered him to overshoot, insisting that he opened up and went round again. Who was Townsend, a mere sergeant pilot, to argue with such authority? He did as ordered, with the prospect of a long flight back to the West Country, the only area known to be in the clear.

They turned southward from Scampton, but only 10min later through the murk spotted a flarepath below and decided to try to land. In they went, not knowing it was only a short grass field — Harlaxton, just south of Grantham, used by Oxfords and Ansons for night flying practice. Bill got the Lanc down well enough initially, but was unaware of a misleading uphill slope, which caused the Lanc to bounce. The grass was wet, they overran the end of the short field, and collided with a concrete pill box. The rear gunner got a bit knocked about — nothing really serious but enough to get him grounded for a while, otherwise the crew got out safely. Their Lancaster W4140 was quite extensively damaged, but was later repaired and went to No 156 Sqn, going missing on Duisburg 26/27 April 1943. Bill Townsend's log book was endorsed by the CO of Scampton, Gp Capt Whitworth, 'Carelessness and error in Captaincy-in-Flight'. However, after only two more training sorties, the crew were signed off by the Con Flight OC, Sqn Ldr Peter Ward-Hunt. They were ready for ops and after the usual couple of weeks 'graduation' leave, joined 'B' Flight of No 49 Sqn. On 18/19 September 1942 came their first taste of ops — mining, E Coast of Denmark, 7hr 35min, in Lanc W4113. This was followed by another mining sortie, in W4761, 24/25 September off Bornholm Island, 8½hr, from which they had to divert to Marston Moor. Then came their first bombing operations: 1/2 October, Wismar, 6½hr, from which they again had to divert (Acklington); and 6/7 October Osnabrück, 4hr. On each of these four trips Douglas Webb had been in the mid-upper with 'spare' gunners occupying the rear turret in place of their allotted original, who had been injured in the Harlaxton episode. It was decided the time had come to choose a permanent replacement.

There was a choice of three air gunners, newly posted-in from gunnery

schools, and it was left to Douglas Webb to make the selection, as it was he who would be working most closely with whoever was decided upon. After flying with each candidate on air-firing exercises, he had no hesitation in picking out Sgt Raymond Wilkinson — a choice neither he, his Skipper nor the rest of the crew ever regretted.

Ray Wilkinson had been a joiners' apprentice in his native South Shields when, like Douglas Webb, he'd volunteered at 18, and progressed to No 49 Sqn via No 9 (O) AFU, Llandwrog, with 24hr flown in Whitleys and Blenheims, a pass mark of 72%, and an 'average' rating; then 1485 Target Towing and Gunnery Flight, Dunholme Lodge, 11½hr in Manchesters.

Douglas and Ray agreed between them that Ray should man the rear turret and Doug continue as mid-upper. And so it was to be — the Townsend gunnery team was complete; the bond was formed. Their first op with their new comrade in his place was to Wismar (again!) in Lanc W4181 12/13 October, 6hr 20min. It was just before take-off they discovered that Ray had never flown at night! However, they were on their way, soon beyond the novice stage, and by the end of 1942 had done seven more night ops, including Cologne, Hamburg, Genoa (three times), Turin (twice), all the Italian raids being 8½–9¾hr. All their ops to then had been in the early 'W' and 'R' series Lancs, four of them in W4113, which survived the war and became much photographed as 'GP:J' of No 1661 HCU, Winthorpe.

Above:
'ASTERS' LAST FAREWELL
Arthur Kell (centre) and crew at Woodhall Spa, thought to have been snapped after the third and decisive Tirpitz attack of 12 November 1944, before former Squadron Bombing Leader Keith Astbury (third from left) was finally banished back to the repatriation centre at Brighton. He'd gone 'AWOL' in response to fellow-Aussie Kell's telephoned appeal, there being no other qualified bomb aimer available to operate the special bomb-sight (SABS). The squadron CO, Willie Tait, had turned a blind eye, though Astbury's re-appearance was strictly contrary to Group orders. For several weeks after his actual final departure, the aircrew regularly kidded the station commander that 'Asters' was in the Mess, waiting for them to join him for a drink, reputedly causing the unsuspecting senior officer to develop a nervous twitch every time the name was mentioned. Identities of all the group are not known, but far left is WO Douglas Webb (air gunner), who joined the crew for Arthur Kell's last four ops on the squadron, done in December 1944, thus linking up again with his great pal Ray Wilkinson (far right) — The Inseparables. Although, by then, most of 617's Lancs had no mid-upper turrets, it was found useful to carry two gunners, not only as an extra pair of eyes on the very long ops, such as they did on 21 December 1944 to Politz (Stettin — oil refinery), a 10hr night job, on which the two gunners were able to share the vigil from the rear turret; but also on daylights on which the front turret could come in useful — the Webb/Wilkinson combination having already experienced that, of course! Identities of the other three crew members are uncertain. The picture is thought to have been taken before an air test, not an op, so could perhaps be a mixture of Arthur Kell's 'Tirpitz' and 'post-Tirpitz' crew posing with Keith Astbury before the latter's positively final departure, in which case, second left could be Flt Sgt W. Robind, RAAF (navigator), third from right Flg Off D. E. Freeman (wireless operator), and next-to-right Plt Off J. Soilleux (engineer). The Lanc is more than likely NG181 'KC:M-Mother'. Any positive identifications would be welcomed.

Arthur Kell DFC and Bar, was to continue flying on his return to Australia, for a time with Qantas, but he came back to Britain to join the RAF on a short service commission, and actually flew Lincolns with No 617 Sqn. He eventually returned to Australia again, and became CFI at the Bankstown (Sydney) Flying Club. Having come safely through 50 wartime ops, he was then to lose his life in a most tragic flying accident in January 1968. While doing aerobatics in a Chipmunk, some loose coins fell from his pocket, jamming the base of the joystick and causing the aircraft to crash, killing Arthur and his student. Is there any justice? Ray Wilkinson

Above:
REMARKABLE QUINTET
How many ops does this crew have between them we wonder? Photographed at Woodhall on 9 April 1945 after return from a daylight on the U-boat pens at Hamburg, is Flt Lt Ian M. 'Jock' Marshall and his crew, with two ground crew, both almost certainly armourers, who had also looked after the Townsend crew's 'O-Orange' (ED886) during its days on No 617 Sqn,

from April to December 1943. The smiles suggest they are sharing the delight of the crew of 'Jock' Marshall, and in particular, his rear gunner on that occasion, Douglas Webb (second from right, standing), who had just claimed an Me262 jet fighter. With only a rear turret on their BI 'Special' PD134 'YZ:Y' of 'C' Flight, the crew was reduced to a basic five, dispensing with a second gunner and the wireless operator, as, by now VHF was in wide use. In the exposed bomb bay they had carried a 12,000lb Tallboy. Are those two armourers still around? Does anyone know their names or whereabouts?

(Left to right) Bomb aimer, Flg Off Len Sumpter DFC, DFM: Had been bomb aimer to David Shannon on the Dams Raid and for 14 months thereafter on Lancs and Mosquitos, doing 30 ops in all. Prior to that he'd done a part tour with 57 Sqn, 13 ops, so his tally by the war's end would be 52. At 32, well over average age. He had been in the army (guardsman) before joining the RAF.

Pilot, Flt Lt Ian M. 'Jock' Marshall DFM: Had done a half-tour as co-pilot on 49 Sqn from May to October 1942, Manchesters and Lancs, then transferred to 9 Sqn as a captain, completing his first tour of 31 ops, late March 1943. Instructed at 1654 HCU, Wigsley, on Lancs, Hallies and Stirlings, July 1943/September 1944. Posted to 617 Sqn October 1944, his first two ops being against Tirpitz; ops total 50 by the war's end.

Navigator, Flt Lt Ken Newby: Completed first tour of 30 ops with Nos 106, 207 and 44 Sqns. Instructed at 1660 CU, Swinderby for nine months, joined 617 Sqn at the same time as Marshall, with whom he became an ever-present, 49 ops total. Like Len Sumpter, born 1911, he was operating at age 32 — 10 years over the average for aircrew.

Rear gunner, Flg Off Douglas Webb, DFM: As related in this chapter, 24 ops with 49 Sqn, 3 with 617 (including the Dams), at least 12 with 617 on second tour; total calculated to be 41 by the war's end. Log book regrettably parted with.

Flight engineer, Flt Sgt Frank Cholerton: Tour of 27 ops with 49 Sqn July 1943/February 1944, with Flt Lt R. E. (Eric) Hidderley, including 11 to Berlin. Met up with 'Jock' Marshall on the 'Academy Flight' at 1654 HCU while instructing; they joined 617 Sqn together and Frank did another 20 ops; total 47. Did not go with some of the crew to Mildenhall; instead volunteered for 'Tiger Force' and stayed with 617 until April 1946, including a four-month detachment to India in Lancs January/April 1946, then to 97 Sqn on Lincolns. Detached to No 617 Sqn for its tour of the USA in Lincolns, July/September 1947. Went on operation 'Red Lion II', 97 Sqn Lincoln detachment to Singapore, April/May 1947, then to 9 Sqn (Lincolns) September 1948/May 1952, including a four-week detachment to Pakistan, October 1949. A year on Washingtons (B-29s) 1952/1953, then back on Lincolns, No 230 OCU, No 7 Sqn, No 214 Sqn, including two detachments to Eastleigh for Mau Mau operations, during 1954. Continued on Lincolns with Radar Recce Flight (Wyton) and 199 Sqn (Hemswell) until January 1957, when he went to Transport Command, Hastings, Britannias, Belfasts, until retirement from the RAF as a warrant officer in December 1976, with 12,750hr in his log book. Some record, with no medal to show for it!

Ken Newby, Douglas Webb, Frank Cholerton are still going strong 50 years on. Len Sumpter died shortly after attending the Dam Busters' '50th' events, 'Jock' Marshall in the mid-80s. Surprising, perhaps, that with such a wealth of flying experience, 'Jock' did not follow others into airline flying, but, like Len Sumpter and Ken Newby, returned to business-life almost straight after the war. Frank Cholerton

Left and below:
Unique Log Book entries — of Sgt Ray Wilkinson, the only man to have flown on the Dams raid, and against the Tirpitz with No 617 Sqn. The entries for May 1943 are signed by Sqn Ldr George Holden, who later succeeded Guy Gibson as CO of the squadron.

MAY. 1943. "617" SQD. SCAMPTON.

Time carried forward :— 141·35 160·00

Date	Hour	Aircraft Type and No.	Pilot	Duty	REMARKS (including results of bombing, gunnery, exercises, etc.)	Flying Times	
						Day	Night
13·5·43		LANC. ED 886	F/SGT. TOWNSEND	REAR GUNNER	X COUNTRY AND TACTICAL RUNS		1·45
16·5·43		LANC. ED 886	F/SGT. TOWNSEND	REAR GUNNER	OPS. LOW LEVEL ATTACK ON THE RHUR DAMS.		6·15
30·5·43		LANC. ED 886	F/SGT. TOWNSEND	REAR GUNNER	LOW LEVEL CROSS COUNTRY	1·40	
31·5·43		LANC. ED 886	F/SGT. TOWNSEND	REAR GUNNER	LOW LEVEL CROSS COUNTRY	1·35	
31·5·43		LANC. ED 886	F/SGT. TOWNSEND	REAR GUNNER	LOW LEVEL CROSS COUNTRY	1·35	
					LANCASTER HRS DAY	19·00	
					LANCASTER HRS NIGHT		12·10
					TOTAL FLYING HRS '617' SQUADRON FOR MAY.	31·10	

W/Cdr O/C '617' SQUADRON. LANC. ED. — L

28·10·44	09·43	LANC. NG.181	F/O KELL	REAR GUNNER	FROM BASE TO LOSSIEMOUTH	2·05	
	07·43	LANC. NG.181	F/O KELL	REAR GUNNER	OPS. TIRPITZ BATTLESHIP - TROMSO LANDED SHETLAND ISLANDS.	4·00	6·00
29·10·44	02·02	LANC. NG.181	F/O KELL	REAR GUNNER	FROM SUMBURGH (SHETLAND) TO LOSSIEMOUTH	1·00	
30·10·44	17·54	LANC. NG.181	F/O KELL	REAR GUNNER	FROM LOSSIEMOUTH TO BASE	2·00	
31·10·44	12·37	LANC. NG.181	F/O KELL	REAR GUNNER			167·55

NOVEMBER 617 SQUADRON WOODHALL SPA. 1944.

258·25 201·35

1,200 died in Tirpitz
BREAKING up of the German battleship Tirpitz, sunk by the R.A.F. in Tromso Fjord, Norway, in November 1944, disclosed the remains of 1,200 of her crew.

Date	Hour	Aircraft Type and No.	Pilot	Duty	REMARKS (including results of bombing, gunnery, exercises, etc.)	Flying Times	
						Day	Night
4·11·44		LANC. M^c NG181	F/O KELL	REAR GUNNER	TO LOSSIEMOUTH	1·60	
5·11·44		LANC. M^c NG181	F/O KELL	REAR GUNNER	LOSSIEMOUTH TO BASE	1·50	
6·11·44		LANC. M^c NG181	F/O KELL	REAR GUNNER	STRETTON & RETURN	1·20	
7·11·44		LANC. M^c NG181	F/O KELL	REAR GUNNER	TEST AUTO CONTROLS	·45	
8·11·44		LANC. M^c NG181	F/O KELL	REAR GUNNER	KINLOSS & RETURN	3·50	
9·11·44		LANC. M^c NG181	F/O KELL	REAR GUNNER	WREXHAM & RETURN	1·20	
		LANC. M^c NG181	F/O KELL	REAR GUNNER	AIR TEST	·30	
10·11·44		LANC. M^c NG181	F/O KELL	REAR GUNNER	TO ADVANCED BASE - LOSSIEMOUTH	2·00	
11·11·44		LANC. M^c NG181	F/O KELL	REAR GUNNER	OPS. - TIRPITZ BATTLESHIP - TROMSO SUNK - LANDED PETERHEAD	4·20	6·00
12·11·44		LANC. M^c NG181	F/O KELL	REAR GUNNER	PETERHEAD TO LOSSIEMOUTH	·35	
13·11·44		LANC. M^c NG181	F/O KELL	REAR GUNNER	LOSSIEMOUTH TO BASE	2·05	
14·11·44		LANC. M^c NG181	F/O KELL	REAR GUNNER		TOTAL TIME	281·65	207

By the year end the new 'ED'-serialled Mk IIIs were starting to appear, and the crew were soon flying ED432, 'EA:R', as their 'regular'.

The two gunners went off to 1485 TT & G Flight (then at Fulbeck) for a week's refresher course on Manchesters over the New Year, then on 13 January 1943 the crew flew ED432 out of Scampton to No 49 Sqn's new home at Fiskerton, from where they resumed operations on 21 January 1943 — a night trip to Essen, their first in ED432, after which some of the crew were due for two weeks' leave. During that break, they were to lose two of their number — Sgt T. Armstrong (flight engineer) and Sgt E. Pittard (bomb aimer), both going missing operating with other crews. For the next op, 11 February (an 'abort') to Wilhelmshaven in ED426 — rear turret U/S) Sgts A. Sutherland and J. Gibson filled in as flight engineer and bomb aimer, but were then replaced on a permanent basis by Sgts D. J. D. 'Sandy' Powell and Charles E. Franklin, who were to become almost ever-presents. The 'originals' had reached the half-way stage of their tour. The 'new' crew's first op together was on 13/14 February in ED432 to Lorient, a long trip, 6½hr. No rest, however, as they had barely got their heads down when their names were on the board for another long trip that night (14/15 February) to Milan, again in '432', over 9hr.

Over the next five weeks, there followed more coastal targets — Lorient (again), Wilhelmshaven, St Nazaire; a real 'nasty' to Nuremberg (7½hr), Cologne, Stuttgart, Essen (twice); and another 'early return', this time Bremen 21/22 February, W/T failure, in ED437. Neither of their aborts had been in ED432, which had brought them safely through 10 of their 12 ops since becoming her 'owners'. On 22/23 March, they took ED584 to St Nazaire, having to divert to Turweston. By now, since joining No 49 Sqn, Townsend, Howard and Grain had done 25 ops together, Webb 24, Wilkinson 21. Since the changes in February, they had become a good crew, working extremely well together, Townsend and Franklin having won DFMs for aiming point successes. They seemed to have settled down well and had become an efficient team.

As Douglas Webb recalls:

'We always maintained strict intercom silence at all times when not in action, with members speaking only 'on business'. Whilst we didn't have any running combats as such with fighters, we had our moments, spotting the enemy on occasions, and we both received and returned the odd burst, though nothing serious. The Skipper followed our instructions instantly and implicitly, and I think German night-fighter pilots somehow sensed when a bomber crew was alert, and which aircraft to stay away from. We were all very close on the ground, as well as in the air, and always stuck together.'

It was on return to Fiskerton from Turweston that they were asked, or 'invited', to accept a posting to Scampton, to a new squadron merely known as 'X'. Strangely enough, in the preceding two/three weeks they had done several formation flying exercises, one at night, which raises the question: were they being secretly tested for what was to come? The crew opted for the new posting, with the exception of the wireless operator, Jack Grain, a very superstitious chap, who had by then completed a full tour, and felt he shouldn't tempt fate; also, there was a possibility he might get married, (though in the event didn't). He elected to go instructing. The crew, therefore, needed a new wireless operator.

Flt Sgt George Chalmers was one of an influx of aircrew to the new squadron, many of whom were unattached. A big, quiet-spoken Scotsman, he had joined the RAF in January 1938, and in May 1939 was posted to No 10 Sqn at Dishforth, flying Whitleys, completing 29 ops before joining No 35 Sqn on Halifaxes, October 1940. He'd done seven ops when, on 24 July 1941, his crew's aircraft was badly shot-up on a daylight raid on the *Scharnhorst* lying off La Rochelle, and in which all the crew except George sustained injuries. He was considered tour-expired and posted to 1501 BAT Flight at Abingdon, but found the work boring and was glad to be posted back to a squadron following a minor disagreement with the unit's CO. He comments on how he came to join the Townsend crew:

'I was approached by Flt Lt Micky Martin and he asked me if I had any preference as to who I'd like to crew up with. Being a flight sergeant at the time, I said I would prefer to fly with an NCO crew. Later Bill Townsend made himself known to me, explaining he was without a wireless operator, his having left to get married. He introduced me to the rest of the crew and I found them to be a very pleasant lot, and later to be very professional in the air. We got on well together.'

So the crew complement on what was, of course, to be No 617 Sqn was: Pilot — Flt Sgt W. C. Townsend DFM; flight engineer — Sgt D. J. D. 'Sandy' Powell; navigator — Flt Sgt C. Lance Howard, RAAF; wireless operator — Flt Sgt George A. Chalmers; bomb aimer — Sgt Charles E. Franklin DFM; mid-upper — Flt Sgt Douglas E. Webb; rear gunner — Sgt Raymond Wilkinson.

They duly took their place on 'B' Flight under Sqn Ldr Henry Maudslay, and from 4 April were hard at it on low-level cross-countries, day and night, in various 'begged and borrowed' Lancs, clocking up over 56hr in the month, of which 16 were at night. On 29 April they flew for the first time their brand new Lanc III ED886, 'AJ:O' 'Orange', specially modified to carry the bouncing bomb. The intensive low-level training continued, culminating in the Dams Raid itself on the night of 16/17 May 1943.

For this they were the penultimate aircraft to depart from Scampton as part of the final reserve wave, take-off time 14min past midnight. ED886 barely made it off Scampton's grass runway, on a warm night with almost no wind, probably a bit in excess of stated AUW, as both gunners had decided to double-up on ammo, for which they were later to be grateful. With enemy ack-ack posts already well alerted by preceding Lancasters all along the route, out and back, the gunners were in almost constant action, Ray Wilkinson in the rear turret, Douglas Webb in the front (mid-uppers having been removed). If their rehearsal flying had been at low level, this was ultra-low, sometimes below tree-top height, passing under power lines as they battled their way as a 'singleton' to their target. Their Skipper's handling of the Lanc was described as quite exceptional.

Their orders were to attack the Ennepe Dam, some 25 miles south of Dortmund, but it appears they may have actually dropped their bouncing mine on the Bever, five miles to the south of Ennepe. Take it from one who has flown over these dams at lowish level, that identifying them from a light aircraft on a clear day proved far from easy, let alone in a fully-laden Lanc on a moonlit, but often misty, night, with all the attendant stresses involved. A full and very well-reasoned account of the attacks on the dams appears in *Operation Chastise* (Janes 1982), by John Sweetman (the book later republished as *The Attack on the Dams*). As Bill Townsend was later to comment to George Chalmers — 'Well, there were a lot of dams there'.

'O-Orange' was the last aircraft into Germany and the last out, its crew having to fight its way back to the enemy coast as their cover of darkness faded; then heading out over the North Sea, having to shut down one engine (in the event, a faulty oil gauge), finally landing back at Scampton on three, at 06.15 in bright sunshine, after 6hr 15min of the most demanding low-level flying any bomber crew was likely to encounter. Bill must still have been intoxicated by a mixture of relief, excitement and stress as he mistakenly landed downwind, the Lanc floating a long way, and only just pulling up in time to avoid embarrassment in front of a large gathering of senior officers, including the C-in-C himself, Air Chief Marshal Sir Arthur Harris. They were an hour overdue, and had put out a 'Mayday' when shutting down the engine over the sea. Douglas Webb recalls very clearly that the 'missing' telegrams were already there on the table at Scampton, ready to be sent out!

Their next assignments were to assemble firstly at Scampton on 27 May for the visit of the King and Queen, then at Buckingham Palace on 22 June for the awards ceremonies. For the few weeks following the Dams raid, there were no ops, though low-level flying training continued day and night for the crews, still exclusively in ED886 for Townsend and co. It was to be mid-July before they flew in anger again, this being on one of the 'shuttle raid' jobs, for which they were allotted a standard Lanc III, DV178, 'EA:N', borrowed from their old squadron, No 49, No 617 still being equipped almost wholly with the cut-away bomb bay 'specials' which were not suitable for normal bombing ops. Leaving Scampton on the night of 15 July 1943 they carried out a low-level attack on a power station at Aquata Scriva, near Milan (Italy), landing at Blida (Algeria) after a flight of 8hr 25min.

There was a scare back at Scampton, as their aircraft was erroneously reported as having gone down. As they went in to bomb, the power station erupted in a mass of flame, sparks and huge electric flashes, which gave the impression of an aircraft exploding, and which one of the preceding Lancasters obviously reported as such. George Chalmers' wife somehow got a message to this effect, and Wg Cdr Guy Gibson himself, who was still at Scampton then, personally sent her a telegram to reassure her that her husband and his crew were safe.

After a week's rest in the North African sun, they departed Blida on the night of 24 July, bombing another Italian target — Leghorn harbour — on the 8hr flight back to Scampton. It was Bill Townsend's 30th op, Douglas Webb's 27th, Ray Wilkinson's 24th, and was to be their last together as a crew.

They continued to fly on training trips, including low-levels and formations, on 28 July even taking AVM Cochrane 'bombing' in ED886, still their regular. On 30 August they flew her out of Scampton to No 617 Sqn's new base at Coningsby, which had hard runways, and from where on the night of 8 September they were to fly 'Orange' for the last time, on yet another low-level exercise, this time at night, 1¾ hours.

The next day they were detailed to take an almost-new Lanc, JA894, to Boscombe Down for some tests. It was fitted with new type bulged bomb doors for carrying 12,000lb high-capacity bombs, and which seemed to have affected airspeed indicator readings at low speeds. Some wing loading tests were also to be conducted. The crew had expected to be flying on these tests, but Sqn Ldr Blackmore, an A&AEE resident test pilot, opted to do the initial tests at minimum weight with just a flight engineer aboard. So, the Townsend seven were spectators that afternoon as the squadron leader did a series of low runs for the calibration team, stalling the Lanc as low as only 150ft or so, with special cameras on the ground recording results. Tests completed, Sqn Ldr Blackmore climbed away after the final run to join the circuit, and the Lanc passed out of view, with the crew all watching and waiting for it to reappear downwind. It never did, but a huge pall of black smoke appeared just over the horizon. JA894 had collided head-on with an Oxford which was climbing out from a neighbouring airfield with nine Air Training Corps cadets aboard, the Oxford coming up right under the Lanc's blind spot below the nose. All aboard both aircraft were lost, and the wreckage killed a civilian in a field below. It was a tragedy, and one in which Bill and his men could so easily have perished. It was a very shaken crew who were collected next day by Flt Lt Joe McCarthy. It was on the flight back to Coningsby on 11 September that they were to clock up their 200th flying hour on 617 Sqn; and it was to be their last ever flight together as a complete crew, as some were given a 'tour-expired option', which five accepted, including Webb and Wilkinson. The latter's log book was signed off by Les Munro as OC 'B' Flight, and Mick Martin 'for' OC 617 Sqn.

They then, in effect, split up and some took a few days' leave pending their new postings. One of those who was to stay behind on the squadron was their flight engineer, Sandy Powell, who had still not completed a tour. Neither had Ray Wilkinson, quite. Sandy was persuaded (or ordered?) to fill in for the newly-appointed CO of No 617 Sqn, Acting Wg Cdr George Holden, who had taken over Gibson's crew, but the engineer (Pulford) had gone sick. It was Powell who went in Pulford's place on the night of 15/16 September 1943, an ill-fated attack on the Dortmund–Ems Canal in which not only Holden went down, but also three others of the eight-strong force. It was pure chance that Bill Townsend and his crew had not been on the raid, their postings taking effect from the very next day, the 17th, and it was a relieved yet very saddened group who said their goodbyes. Lance Howard was to return home to his native Australia; Bill Townsend, Charles Franklin, Douglas Webb and Ray Wilkinson went to Balderton (1668 HCU) to commence their instructional careers.

George Chalmers, the wireless operator, had elected to stay on the squadron, and like Powell, on the day of the Dortmund–Ems op had been asked by Holden if he'd join his crew. Fortunately for him, the next day he was due to attend a commissioning course at Scampton, and told Holden he'd like to get it over with, but would be glad to crew with him after it. Holden accepted this, reluctantly, to George's everlasting relief. As it was, he continued to fly on ops until June 1944, in the crews of Leonard Cheshire, Joe McCarthy and Bunny Clayton, bringing his total of ops on 617 Sqn to 23 (66 in all), winning a DFC to add to his DFM. He was to become an instructor and would stay in the RAF postwar, eventually becoming an air traffic control supervisor, jobs including the Berlin Air Lift, and postings to Egypt, Italy and Malta, before retiring as a flight lieutenant in 1955. He then spent 30 years as a civil servant with the MOD at Harrogate on purchase of aircraft spares. He is now happily retired.

After a short spell at Balderton, Douglas Webb and Ray Wilkinson went on gunnery instructors' courses at Manby, then to 5 LFS at Syerston, where they did very little flying, Ray only a couple of trips in Lancs during his nine months there. Douglas had a separate niche at 5 LFS in the night vision trainer, but by the autumn of 1944, instructing had started to pall and both yearned to get back to a squadron. Douglas (by then a WO) persuaded the 617 Sqn Adjutant, Harry Humphries, to pull a few strings, which he did, and in early October, Doug was posted back to No 617 (now at Woodhall Spa) as 'Night Vision Instructor', on a strictly non-operational basis, with Ray following as his 'assistant'. Both titles were somewhat spurious as by then the squadron was starting to operate predominantly in daylight.

No 617 Sqn was still gathering itself after 'Operation Paravane' (the first of the *Tirpitz* attacks in mid-September via Russia), following which, many of the old stalwarts had become tour-expired, and a number of crews had split up. One such was that of Aussie skipper Flt Lt Arthur Kell, who had been on that first *Tirpitz* raid — his 24th trip with No 617 Sqn. He'd joined 617 in February 1944 when part-way through his first tour in which he'd done 10 ops with No 467 Sqn (RAAF) and nine with sister unit No 463.

All of his crew except the flight engineer had become tour-expired following 'Paravane', and with a second attack obviously in the wind, he needed replacements quickly. So, he 'borrowed' Len Gosling as his navigator (from Jack Cockshott's crew), recruited Freeman as wireless operator, Keith Astbury as bomb aimer, and Ray Wilkinson offered his services as rear gunner. Despite the latter's recent 'non-operational' posting-in, Wg Cdr J. B. 'Willie' Tait raised no objection. He'd already turned a blind eye to Astbury's nomination, as he'd been declared tour-expired, so why not Ray? His theory was that if a man wanted to operate, let him. So within days of rejoining his old squadron, Ray was back on ops, in time for the second attack on the *Tirpitz* on 28/29 October 1944. For this, the Kell crew flew a new Lanc, NG181, 'KC:M', on a flight lasting 13hr (six at night). The Lanc had no mid-upper fitted, otherwise no doubt Douglas Webb would also have gone along. Because of cloud, the Kell crew did not bomb, and brought their 12,000lb Tallboy all the way back to Woodhall, landing at Sumburgh *en route* to refuel. Thus Ray Wilkinson achieved the unique distinction of being the only man to have operated on the Dams raid and against the *Tirpitz*.

Two weeks later, 12/13 November, the same crew took NG181 again on the third, final and conclusive *Tirpitz* attack, this time positioning first to Lossiemouth for a 13hr 20min round trip to Tromso (again 6hr in daylight) to land back this time at Peterhead with an empty bomb bay, their Tallboy having been dropped to good effect.

It wasn't long before Douglas Webb, too, engineered his way back on ops, also with Arthur Kell's crew, joining up with Ray again for four trips in December 1944. Thus the 'gunnery twins' were back in action together! Three of their December ops were in NG181 which had no mid-upper turret, so Douglas again became front gunner with Ray in the rear, as they'd been on the Dams raid, an ideal combination for the two relatively short daylights they did against E-Boat pens at Ijmuiden (15 December) and Rotterdam (29 December). On the long night trips, however — to Pölitz near Stettin to bomb an oil refinery (21 December — 10hr), and Oslo Fjord in LM695 to attack the cruisers *Köln* and *Emden* (31 December, 7³/₄hr), they shared the vigil in the rear turret to provide a degree of relief. Anyone who has spent time in a rear turret would no doubt endorse that as a good idea. It was the coldest, most cramped position, with only a tiny, hard seat, and little leg room. The view from it was dreadfully cluttered, and how any gunners achieved any successes against enemy fighters from it is today almost beyond comprehension and belief.

The Oslo trip was Arthur Kell's 50th, and signalled the end of his tour, of which 31 had been done on 617 Sqn. The crew continued on training flights together for a week or so into the New Year, but then Douglas and Ray had to split up again after their few weeks' reunion. Ray went (for the first time on ops) as mid-upper with Flt Lt Bernard Gumbley, with whom he was to do four ops, 3-14 February 1945, all in DV405, 'KC:J', all daylights with Tallboys. Douglas continued to fly wherever he could find a spare slot, but mid-upper turrets were getting scarce, with numerous changes taking place, including the selection of 'C' Flight to take in the new Lanc BI 'Specials' with cut-away bomb bays and only one turret, ie the rear. It was those which would carry the 22,000-pounder Grand Slams which were on the way.

Both gunners were transferred to 'C' Flight, and joined the crew of Flt Lt Ian M. ('Jock') Marshall DFM, a former colleague from their 49 Sqn 'B' Flight days. His flight engineer, Frank Cholerton, was also from 49 Sqn, though of later vintage, and the bomb aimer was none other than Len Sumpter, another founder member of No 617 Sqn and fellow-participant on the Dams raid (in David Shannon's crew). So these were the only three 'originals' on the squadron, now operating in the same crew — a real 'old boys' reunion.

Jock Marshall had arrived on No 617 at the same time as the two gunners; he, Frank Cholerton and their nav, Ken Newby, having flown together on the last two *Tirpitz* raids. For Ray Wilkinson, the move to Jock's crew was indeed fortunate, as Bernard Gumbley and his men were to be lost only a month later on a raid on Dreys in BI 'Special' PD117, 'YZ:L',

21 March 1945, one on which Ray could have been with him but for the reorganisation. Such were the fortunes of war, even at this relatively late stage of the conflict. Douglas Webb was the first of the pair to fly with the new crew on ops — as rear gunner to Bielefeld viaduct on 22 February 1945, in DV391, 'KC:Y', and two days later as mid-upper against the always dreaded Dortmund–Ems, from which they were recalled. All ops were now daylight.

Then on 9 March, they were flying together for yet another 'abort' on Bielefeld, with Douggie mid-upper, Ray in the rear, again in DV391. For Marshall's next op, 27 March, in BI 'Special' PD115, 'YZ:K', it was Douglas's turn in the rear turret as the crew dropped its only 22,000lb Grand Slam on the Farge U-Boat pens with Len Sumpter doing the aiming. The Grand Slams were still in short supply, and dropping one was a great event for any crew. How Len and Douglas must have wished they'd had those monsters available some two years earlier! Ray and Doug continued to alternate as rear gunner in the 'Specials', and it was on one such trip that Douglas Webb had his moments of excitement (perhaps even glory!) when, on 9 April, in BI 'Special' PD134, 'YZ:Y', they had attacked the U-Boat pens at Hamburg in daylight with a 12,000lb Tallboy. After leaving the target, and giving the Skipper a course for home, Ken Newby, the nav, as usual took his place in the astrodome to keep watch for fighters, as he always had done, day or night.

As Ken relates:

'Escorting us were several Mustangs with drop tanks. Suddenly, about a mile off to our port appeared a twin-engined fighter, of a type I'd never seen before, moving very fast, closing behind a Lanc from another squadron. The Lanc just exploded in a big black and red ball. The Mustangs shed their drop tanks and sped off in pursuit, but the fighter was too fast for them and was soon away out of sight. Five minutes later, looking astern, I saw another of the same type (it might even have been the same one perhaps) 5-600yd behind us, closing fast, its guns flashing. I called Doug Webb, who'd already seen it. At about 2–300yd he gave it a burst, and as it sped past us, black smoke was coming from its right engine. It went into a wide, flat descent — almost a spin, trailing black smoke from the engine until, way below — still spinning — it disappeared into some low stratus, almost certainly a 'goner', but because we hadn't actually seen it hit the ground, it couldn't be claimed as 'destroyed', only 'damaged'. It was all over in seconds. We'd never been told about these new jet fighters (Me262s).'

Douglas Webb thought, at first, it was a Mosquito coming up behind, but then noticed their marker/master bomber's Mossie still up above and behind them. His instinct told him there shouldn't be two Mossies, and a Mossie wouldn't have four nose cannons firing either, so he opened up and saw the smoke start to pour from the fighter's starboard engine as it passed beneath his turret and out of view. He was surprised the master bomber (not their own CO on that day) had not forewarned them of the attackers. It was a very close call.

On 13 April, the two gunners were to join forces again, with Marshall and crew, in standard Lanc DV246, taking up their usual positions, Doug as mid-upper, Ray in the tail turret, for what was to be their last op of the war together as a team. It was to be a long but abortive 6¾ hour trip to bomb the battleships *Prinz Eugen* and *Lützow* at Swinemünde on the Baltic. For once they carried 12 x 1,000-pounders instead of the now almost-standard Tallboy, but cloud obscured the target, so they brought the load back.

When Marshall went again two days later — 15 April — it was in 'Special' PD134, 'YZ:Y' with Ray taking his turn in the rear turret. However, Douglas was not far away, flying on the raid as a stand-in rear gunner aboard 'Special' PB997, 'YZ:E' flown by Flt Lt Mark Flatman. In the event, both aircraft returned early as the fighter escort failed to turn up (a not unusual occurrence it seems).

The next day, neither was flying when the squadron finally clobbered the *Lützow*, though their flight engineer, Frank Cholerton, went along as a stand-in for Flt Lt Alan Quinton!

The war was drawing to a close. Douglas Webb took a few days' leave, and missed out on the squadron's last two ops. It fell to Ray Wilkinson to man the tail turret for Jock Marshall and crew, both in 'Special' PD134, 'YZ:Y', against Heligoland (naval gun batteries) on 19 April, then, on 25 April, the grand finale, a massed daylight on Berchtesgaden. They were one of three crews from 617 Sqn's contingent detailed to bomb Hitler's actual 'Eagle's Nest', but were unable to identify it in the morning mist and mayhem, so dropped their final Tallboy instead on the local railway station, returning safely, elatedly, relievedly, from a most spectacular 8hr round trip,

Ray in the back, Len Sumpter up front, now both indelibly 'The First and the Last' of No 617 Sqn's operational history. Pity Douggie wasn't there, too.

Thus ended Ray's and Doug's war; each, it appears, with 41 ops. Their tallies were not records by any means... but what ops! Surely few gunners can have experienced such a wide spectrum of historic events. Both were to continue flying, sometimes together, depending on it being a 'Standard' or 'Special', on Cooks Tours, bombing trials, etc and transferred, along with Marshall, with 'C' Flight to Mildenhall on 1 June 1945, to become part of No 15 Sqn, conducting Grand Slam trials ('Operation Ruby'). From July to September 1945, more low-level tours of Germany ('Baedekers') and trips to Italy to repatriate troops — some of those in 'Specials', too ('Operation Dodge'). Marshall left the RAF around August 1945, Ray transferring to Bob Horsley's crew, Douglas to Arthur Fearn's. In September 1945, Douglas was posted briefly to their old squadron, No 49 at Mepal, and finished his RAF career with a round trip to Gatow, Berlin, of all places ('Operation Spasm') in Lanc 'EA:X', piloted by the grandly-named Flt Lt Phillipson-Stow. Ray soldiered on with No 15 Sqn for a while longer, his final flight being in Lanc 'Special' 'LS:T', with Flt Lt Bob Horsley, finishing with total hours of 712, of which 242 had been at night. By the time of their demob, the duo were both flight lieutenants, with gunnery leader qualifications; but the days of the air gunner in the RAF were numbered.

Douglas resumed his work as a photographer, and still practises his skills in the Isle of Wight. Most regrettably, he found it necessary to part with his flying log book some years ago, but is still blessed with a very sharp memory, which has been invaluable to us.

Ray went back to the building trade as a joiner. He'd married a WAAF (Iris) in January 1944, and they settled in Great Yarmouth. He was a friendly, unassuming type who rarely mentioned his RAF career, the first his boss knew of it being when he asked for leave to attend the two premières of *The Dam Busters* film in May 1955. Soon after that he and Iris emigrated to Australia (Melbourne), where they were able to link up again with the likes of Lance Howard, 'Chesh' and Willie Tait at the 617 Reunion Tour held 'Down Under' in 1980. Sadly, Ray died of a heart attack not long after, but his widow, Iris, came over for the 617 Sqn '50th' celebrations in May 1993, in which Douglas Webb and George Chalmers also participated, now being the only two survivors of the crew on the Dams raid (May 1995).

Bill, after a few weeks at Balderton, went to a succession of OTUs instructing on Wellingtons until, in March 1945, after a 'disagreement' with a flight commander who had no ops experience, was sent out to India, where he instructed on Liberators until demob. He went to university and got two degrees, worked for Bristol Aeroplane Co for a while, then became an early computer training specialist. He eventually moved to a job with the Social Security Department, through the good offices of a senior official whom he'd met at Charles Franklin's funeral.

He and Douglas Webb were to fly together in a Lancaster again on the 25th anniversary of the Dams raid, in May 1968, when preserved NX611 made the round trip from Biggin Hill to Scampton. Douglas took his place in the rear turret, as he did for most of the flights NX611 was to make following its return from Australia in 1965. (Now back to taxying status again at East Kirkby; who knows, Douglas could be flying in it again one day!) It must have evoked memories of their epic trips in ED886 'Orange' a quarter century previously.

Following the Dams raid it appears 'Orange' did only two more ops, the first being on 11/12 November 1943, flown by WO G. Bull, on the Anthéor Viaduct in southern France, for which several of the 'Specials' used on the

85

Dams raid were reactivated, carrying 12,000lb HC bombs, including ED932. Then in December 1943/January 1944 No 617 Sqn was called upon to provide a detachment of three aircraft to Tempsford, for the 'Special Operations Executive', for dropping of supplies to the French Resistance or Maquis, and again three of the 'Specials' were chosen, their open bomb bays suitable for bulky loads, probably canisters. ED886 was one of the three, the others being ED906 (Maltby's) and ED932 (Gibson's). On the night of 10/11 December, the detachment's first op from Tempsford, ED886 'Orange', again, piloted by WO Bull, dropping supplies near Doullens, north of Amiens, was lost. Apparently, Bill Townsend all but wept on learning of the loss of their beloved 'Orange'. Bill passed away in the late 1980s, his widow Eileen, and their son Michael proudly representing him at the '50th' events.

There is no doubt about that extra-special bond which existed within the crew, and to Douglas Webb must go the last word:

'Just to give you an idea of Bill Townsend's crew, I can only tell you that it was quite unlike any other that I flew with. Bill had a great deal of personality and to my mind was outstanding in leadership, and also would never under any circumstances waste a bomb. The number of times that we would 'go round again', whatever the target, was sometimes unnerving to any new crew member. To explain that I must tell you that we lost our original bomb aimer (flying with another crew) and our original flight engineer, again with another crew. Our original rear gunner was replaced by Ray, so we had a few changes along the way. Although most crews that I knew were very close, ours was more like a family, and has remained that way, except of course for the interference of the old man with the scythe. However, you can see that it was no ordinary crew, and Bill kept us all together till he died.'

One day in the far distant future, may they all fly together again; and may 'Orange' be there running-up awaiting them.

FOOTNOTES:
Joe Kmiecik, AFM, was Polish, and had flown Spitfires in the war. He continued to fly with the RAF right up until his retirement (as a flight lieutenant) in 1981. He died at his home in Spain 1993. A truly exceptional pilot. Michael Cawsey, with many hours on Lincolns, Comets, VC10s and Tri-Stars retired from the RAF (as a squadron leader) in the mid-1980s.

Of the 133 aircrew who took part in Dams raids, 48 survived the war. Nineteen are still alive at the time of writing (May/June 1995), of whom three are pilots (Canada, New Zealand, USA), one f/eng (UK), three navs (two in the UK, one in Canada) five are B/As (four in the UK, one in Canada, one w/op (George Chalmers, UK), and six air gunners (one UK, two Australia, three in Canada).

Below left:
GRAND SLAMMER
BI 'Special' PD119 from a somewhat unusual angle, sleek and slightly sinister-looking, showing its 'daylight' camouflage to good effect, and its red/yellow codes on its tailplane (repeated on the undersides); only one turret, and faired-over nose. The very bulky SABS (bombsight) is seen protruding well into the nose blister. The 'Specials' were developed specifically to carry the 22,000lb 10-ton Grand Slam, first deliveries being in late January/early February 1945. However, the big bombs were in such short supply initially, they carried many 12,000lb Tallboys, too. When either type of bomb was released, the upward lunge of the aircraft was considerable, and resulted almost inevitably in a black eye or other facial damage for the bomb aimers, who needed to keep their eyes to the sight until after actual release. No exhaust shrouds were fitted, as most ops were by then in daylight. Unladen, there was nothing comparable which could catch them. PD119 dropped at least three Grand Slams, piloted by the CO of No 617 Sqn, Gp Capt J. E. Fauquier, RCAF. When the war ended she, like most of the other 'Specials', passed with 617 Sqn's 'C' Flight to 15 Sqn, Mildenhall, for continued bomb trials. She was eventually SOC while at Farnborough in September 1950. J. Barr

AS CLOSE AS YOU'LL GET...
To our knowledge, apart from one of an aircraft said to be taking off for it, no pictures exist of the Dams raid in progress, en route, or landing back — not surprising really, as apart from a dusk take-off, the operation took place at night, and the security surrounding it was so intense that not even crew pictures were allowed on the run-up to it. So, we have to thank the film-makers for a highly acclaimed simulation made in the mid-1950s, and which has stood the tests of time and the armchair critics. We have been fortunate to meet a number of aircrew who were detached from their Lincoln squadrons at Hemswell to fly the Lancasters which were brought out of storage for the film, and we were able to show in the first volume of Lancaster at War a unique collection of pictures taken during the filming. We have selected here two more images which we hope capture to some degree the atmosphere and drama of the event.

Bottom left:
It could almost be the Townsend crew's 'O-Orange' over the Ennepe (or Bever?) lake doing a 'sighting' run at less than 100ft in the early light of dawn, with Douglas Webb's front guns poised for action. In reality, Mk7 RT686, Austin Motors-built, banking away past the Langdale Chase Hotel after a very low-level run up Lake Windermere, more than likely flown by Flt Sgt Joe Kmiecik with flight engineer Mike Cawsey alongside July/August 1954.
Sanderson & Dixon

Below:
It could be the first or second 'wave' over the North Sea en route to the dams in moonlight. What atmosphere! Taken from a small print supplied by Joe Kmiecik, who was flying one of the trio of Lancs. The 'enemy coast ahead' will probably be Gibraltar Point, near Skegness, or near Southwold, Suffolk. Via J. K. S. Kmiecik

THEY WHO ALL-BUT KNEW, YET COULD NOT KNOW

THE MEN – AND WOMEN – SUPPORTING THE AIRCREWS WHO PROSECUTED THE WAR IN LANCS

On those unflagging,
steadfast individuals through
whose efforts the Lancs
and their crews waged
war on Germany:

'Few people realise that whereas
some 50,000 aircrew, before
and during the period of my
Command, were killed in action
against the enemy, some
8,000 men and women were
killed at home in training, in
handling vast quantities of
bombs under the most
dangerous conditions, in driving
and despatch riding in the
blackout on urgent duty and by
deaths from what were called
natural causes.

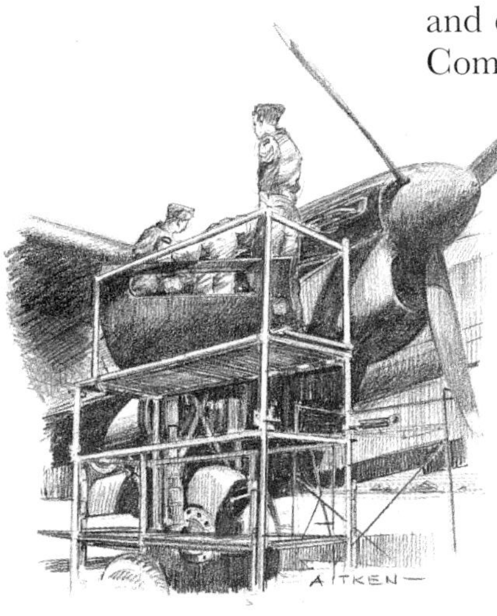

'These deaths from natural causes included the death of many fit young people who to all intents and purposes died from the effect of extraordinary exposure, since many contracted illnesses by working all hours of the day and night in a state of exhaustion in the bitter wet, cold and miseries of six war winters. It may be imagined what it is like to work in the open, rain, blow or snow, in daylight and through darkness, hour after hour, 20ft up in the air on the aircraft engines and airframes, at all the intricate and multifarious tasks which have to be undertaken to keep a bomber serviceable. And this was on wartime aerodromes, where such accommodation as could be provided offered every kind of discomfort and where, at any rate during the first years of the war, it was often impossible even to get dry clothes to change into between shifts. We never had more than 250,000 men and women at any one time in Bomber Command, so that the total of some 60,000 casualties among aircrew and ground staff should give some idea of what the Command had to face in maintaining an offensive for which the great majority were awarded the 'Defence' Medal. I know that among the people concerned the award was, and is, the subject of much bitter comment, with which I was and am in entire agreement...'

More heartfelt words from Sir Arthur Harris. What he did not say in his book *Bomber Offensive* but which he spoke of at some length, seated by the fireside at his home one Sunday afternoon four years before his death in 1984, was his admiration for the way families who lost loved ones bore their loss with quiet dignity, and without bitterness. He went on to say how heartened he had been, receiving letters from mothers, widows and fiancées, in particular, sent to him during his postwar years spent 'in the wilderness'.

In the pages that follow we present a selection of impressions and vignettes centred on the men — and women — who were, in truth, as much a part of the Lancaster story as were the crews who carried the war to the foe... yet who could never know what it meant to be a member of a unique brotherhood.

"THANK GOD"

Dennis Dear

She'd been trying to phone the Mess since ten in the hope that he might be there — but there had been no reply.

And then, at eleven a Lancaster had come from the airfield in a rush of sound, its wheels disappearing slowly and deliberately into the engine nacelles until only the tail wheel was left to spoil the graceful lines.

The Lancaster banked to port, turning over the village and she saw its letters on the side of the fuselage and the four oil streaks on the mainplane behind each engine. The turrets, turning, flashed in the sun and it had gone behind the large oaks by the churchyard, its engine noise beating back down the main street. Ten more aircraft followed at odd intervals and she knew the signs too well to try to phone again.

After half an hour they began to return, their night flying tests completed. They circled the airfield lowering their wheels and flaps as they approached the 'funnel' at the opposite end of the runway.

She could just hear the crackling sound of engines throttled back as the great planes dropped down; and occasionally the screech of scorching tyres as someone made a bad landing, bouncing up again before eventually coming to rest in a series of rumbling bumps.

He would not be home for lunch — would even now be hurrying back to the Mess to have a quick meal before the rush back to the ops room for briefing.

Her own meal was burnt but she did not notice.

She felt isolated from him now and yet somehow still part of his team. From now until he took off she knew each single item of the routine. He'd told her many times, of the quietness of the crews, each clustered round their own pair of cheap deal tables in the briefing room; the navigator's large green canvas bag spilling its contents across the whole surface.

The hushed speculation as to the target and the sign and sudden babble of sound when the large screen covering the map was rolled up to reveal it. A thin red cord snaked its way across Holland and into the centre of the Ruhr Valley where it finally embraced a large flat-headed pin which was the target. The cord changed colour for the return journey, green now, zig-zagging its way into Belgium before, suddenly veering North, it shot unerringly back to base. How simple it looked. Nothing on the map to indicate the natural hazards of wind and cloud and ice. Nothing to indicate the strain of coaxing an overloaded aircraft up to the last foot of height to get above the barrage; cursing the cold because it froze the intercom and cursing because it wasn't cold enough to get above twenty thousand feet. And there was nothing on the map to show the great barrier of searchlights, the fighters, and finally the flak over the target, seeming to fill every inch of sky.

Now the Wing Commander was up on the dais in front of the map, reciting his usual monologue: "Do a good job chaps, and then you won't have to go tomorrow."

But what he really meant was, do a good job so you can go somewhere else tomorrow. When the old man had finished all the section leaders followed on in the same old familiar order — Met, Intelligence, Navigation, Bombing, Wireless, Engineering, Gunnery — and finally it was all over and he was back in the Mess eating the familiar operational supper of bacon and eggs, and pondering over the chances of getting back tonight — yes — he thought — we've all got a chance of reprieve, all we've got to do is to eat thirty operational suppers and the full complement of thirty operational breakfasts and we can stay in bed every night for six months and, if we're smart, maybe for the rest of the war.

And now he was scrambling into a crew truck to go down to the locker room, jostling and swearing with the others. Then, rushing into the warm room where the parachutes were stored and yelling 'til one of the men heard his number and came back with his chute clutched in his arms, his helmet on top of the chute. Into the locker room, searching in the scratched dowdy wooden cupboard for his long woollen underclothes, cursing the button that came off and rolled away on the dusty concrete floor. Now struggling into the chocolate-coloured electrical suit with its long trailing lead and plug which had to be kept from dragging on the ground. His parachute harness was loosely clipped under his crutch now, the heavy seat-type parachute, swinging against his rump with each step he took. Then once again the scramble into the crew truck, hands full with helmet, Mae West, flying rations and maps, breast pockets under his flying suit bulging with his escape kit and foreign money in its waterproof protecting cover. And the weight of his revolver strapped to his right leg and bulging into the top of his flying boot, causing him to walk with a slight limp.

The truck rumbles around the perimeter track dropping crews at each dispersal point, and then "E:Easy", the WAAF driver pokes her head through the open window at the back of her driver's cabin and he curses while they struggle with the rear door. And finally they are all out and filing across to the huge hulk with its black-painted belly and sides and the drab brown and green on the upper surface of the mainplane.

Beneath the pilot's cockpit twenty yellow bombs had been stencilled showing up sharply on the black background. Twenty trips in the logbook, two thirds of a tour.

The ground crew sergeant salutes him with quiet respect, no parade ground bull here, and starts to talk of revs and boost and oil pressure on the starboard-outer engine. The ground crew know enough not to ask the target but ask instead, what time they'll be back.

His crew climb into the aircraft and settle in their respective stations, putting their equipment and flying rations in handy places. He follows them up the metal aircraft ladder and through the long fuselage, past ammunition runners for the rear turret, up the deep step over the bomb bay, clambering over the main spar which runs at right angles across the fuselage. The pear drop smell of aircraft dope is mixed with oil and grease smells now. Past the wireless operator putting signal cartridges in the racks, sorting out his signal codes, past the navigator with the ever-present green bag which is again spilling its contents. The engineer steps aside to allow him to clamber in his seat with the high armour plate painted green at the back with its bright yellow spot in the centre. One by one, the engines are started, run for a while, taken up to full power and then cut into sudden silence. Intercom, oxygen, turrets, everything is tested while there is still time to get it put right.

He checks the time again with the navigator then, "O.K. blokes, nearly an hour to take-off; let's get out and smoke ourselves to death."

Well clear of the aircraft they sit down on old tins and oil drums near the ground crew's dispersal hut. They're ragging each other and the ground crew join in. He sits a little apart now in silence waiting for the slow hands of his watch to take away the last forty minutes, while he keeps glancing at the watch tower across the airfield in case the arcing light of a red rocket should grant them a reprieve for another twenty four hours. Hoping that bad weather over the target would cause Met to scrub it, yet hoping that now they'd gone through the ritual of briefing they'd let them go.

Another fifteen minutes and the worst would be over, then there will be something to do, instead of sitting here in front of the crew trying to appear calm and steady. The Skipper, who takes everything in his stride, the skipper who does not care that in another fifteen minutes he will be fighting thirty tons of aircraft to prevent it swinging off the runway, before it has sufficient speed to get airborne. The skipper who has to choke down the nagging fear of airlocks in the petrol system which would deny the engines their power when it was most needed. And when it was airborne there would be five more lonely hours, hours made lonely by the responsibility of captaincy, the need to keep his voice calm over the intercom, the need to choose correctly whenever there were two choices of action, or there was no twenty first yellow bomb to be painted beneath his cockpit tomorrow. And after all that when he got back, if he got back, he could think of himself and his own life and of the one who waited so patiently in the village.

But it was time now for the final ritual. He turned the release buckle on his harness and banged it sharply with his fist. Suddenly released, the metal ends of the harness tinkled on the concrete of the dispersal point. He made his way under the engine nacelles of the starboard wing, ducked beneath the gaping bomb doors, refusing to look at the great dirty green dust-bin that was the four thousand pound bomb, and came to a halt beside the port landing wheel. The ground crew and his own crew were laughing as he fumbled with his flies; jeers and coarse jokes of encouragement filled the air now and a WAAF driver lent over her steering wheel to get a better view. His urine trickled down the great rubber balloon and formed a dirty puddle where the tyre flattened against the concrete under the weight of the aircraft.

"Okay blokes, let's go — twenty one today!"

They clambered in, the ground crew sergeant pushing the metal ladder in after them, slamming the aircraft door.

Once again he checked each crew member over the intercom and once again the engines were started.

"Navigator to Skipper — time we weren't here Skip! That's number eight Skipper, we're next." He opened up the two outboard motors leaving the other two just idling over. The ground crew gave him the chocks away acknowledgement and to the thumbs-up sign from the sergeant they trundled out on to the perimeter and took the ninth position in the long crocodile of aircraft making their way to the runway.

He slowed down as the long line stopped, finally coming to a standstill within a few feet of the rear turret of the aircraft in front. The rear gunner in front stuck his tongue out at them and grinned. As the green light winked

its permission to take-off, the first aircraft turned on to the runway and the line in front moved forward. He had let his mind wander and did not notice them move off again. The engineer tapped his shoulder and pointed; with a start he pushed forward the throttles, his hand slipped and the starboard motor roared into sudden life and swung the nose round to port. He corrected quickly — overcorrected and the brute swung across the other way. The starboard landing wheel bumped off the concrete track and he was swearing and praying now: "God don't let us bog, keep that bloody wheel from sinking in the soft grass; Get back you bastard, get back". He was overcautious now, giving the starboard engine little bursts of power which only brought the aircraft back slowly, slowly, 'til at last, another bump and she was back on the perimeter track. They edged forward slowly and already the sweat was pouring off him and trickling cold down his back. Apart from the strain and effort of the last few moments the warmth of his flying suit and the retained heat of the June sun inside the aircraft made him sweat more until his woollen underclothes were sticking to his back.

He'd seen lots of pilots, many experienced, bog an aircraft, and the panic that followed while they brought up the big tractor to pull it out — and how it made you and everyone behind you late. You had to use up precious fuel then to gain height quickly and push up the airspeed to catch up with the main stream. Not as though there wasn't enough petrol to do that in normal circumstances, but if the fog was down on base when you returned and you were diverted; or if you ran into trouble over the other side, or into intruders over your own coast; that's when petrol mattered, that's when you regretted your own or someone else's carelessness.

He was by the runway now, and he quickly ran over his cockpit drill; the Lancaster in front was half way down the runway now. He turned into the wind, rolling the aircraft well over to the right to allow for its tendency to swing to the left. The other Lancaster was not yet airborne and he had time to look out of the port window at the black and white chequered caravan with the small group of people, gathered there to see the squadron off. They were always there, the Group Captain with the Adjutant and the Padre, one or two other Officers, some ground staff and a crowd of WAAFs. He'd always appreciated these send-offs, especially those ground staff people — men and girls who'd probably walked a mile and a half from their billets and had got to walk all the way back. His engineer gave them the thumbs-up sign and he knew that his wireless operator was putting up two fingers in the astrodome. Sparks always said that it was the only time he could put two fingers up at Groupy and get away with it. He gave them his left thumb up, waved carelessly, and now the voice from the astrodome: "There's your green Skipper."

He wriggled in his seat, grasped the stick firmly, applied the brakes full on, and slowly pushed the four throttle levers up their arced housing. As the vibration increased with the engines pulling against the brakes he released them and the aircraft started slowly forward.

"OK blokes, hold tight."

They gathered speed past the first runway intersection and he wrestled to keep the swing in check.

"Airspeed navigator?"

And over the intercom came the tinny voice of the navigator calling the airspeed from the indicator over his table.

"Fifty, fifty, fifty five, sixty —

"Full power."

"Full power."

This from the engineer acknowledging the order, bracing his feet, both hands holding the throttles fully forward, anxiously scanning the instrument panel to check that everything was OK.

"Sixty five, sixty five, seventy, seventy five, eighty" — past the second intersection now, the rudders playing their part in checking the swing.

"Eighty five, ninety, ninety five, one hundred, hundred-n-five—hundred-n-ten" –

"Wheels."

"Wheels."

Again from the engineer as he pulled on the undercarriage lever and the red warning light went out.

"Wheels locked Skipper."

"Flaps five."

"Flaps five."

And the engineer took off five degrees of flap — five degrees at a time — gently does it — to save them falling out of the sky!

"– Hundred-n-ten, hundred-n-fifteen, hundred-n-twenty, hundred-n-twenty five, hundred-n –"

"OK navigator. Course please — flaps five."

"Flaps five."

"Zero-one-zero magnetic, airspeed one-six-five."

"Zero-one-zero magnetic, one-six-five airspeed — flaps right off."

"Flaps right off Skipper."

He swung her round slowly, fighting the slipstream of the aircraft in front, searching the sky all the time, to avoid collision with other aircraft.

"Twenty eight fifty, plus nine."

The engineer adjusted the engine revs and throttles.

"Twenty eight fifty, plus nine."

The sun was sinking below the horizon as they took off, but he knew they would see it set again as they gained height.

———

She had read a little after lunch and then her landlady, knowing the signs herself, had come upstairs for a chat. In her Lincolnshire dialect she had talked of the crops, the fine hot summer and had offered the spicier village gossip. And then, realising perhaps, the futility of her efforts in the face of desultory answers, she had gone downstairs again to prepare her husband's tea.

The airfield was quiet now except for a few moments when a doubtful engine was being tested. Then the sudden burst of engine noise stirred the birds in the trees. Once, a machine-gun was fired in short bursts and the sound echoed back from the range on the far side of the aerodrome.

She made herself a pot of tea and tried to read her book again. Tiring of this, she resumed her knitting, seated by the window where she could hear the occasional airfield sounds. The warm evening was still and quiet with only the 'click, click keep him safe', 'click click click, bring him back' of her needles to comfort her.

It was about half past eight when she heard the first of the aircraft warming up, followed quickly by others as their crews got out to their aircraft. By nine o'clock all was quiet again except for an occasional servicing vehicle on the perimeter track and the clicking praying of her needles. Half an hour later and the engine noises started again, but this time they didn't die down and one by one she heard the planes straining against their brakes and the gradual crescendo of sound as they rumbled down the runway. Each time she picked the moment the pilot called for full power and each time the engine roar reached its climax as the planes lumbered over the house — lower than they were this morning and seeming to take longer to disappear over the churchyard trees.

There was a box of matches on the table beside her and as each aircraft struggled over the house, she put a match on one side until finally there were fourteen with the open box beside them. She stayed by the open window knitting still, while the sound of engines filled the air above the village. The sky was still blue with streaks of white golden-tipped clouds and up there the full strength of the Group were flying their triangular course, gaining their operational height before setting course off the Lincolnshire coast. The whole sky was filled with aircraft, like mechanical goldfish in a bowl that was three miles high and all Lincolnshire wide.

A little later on they were very hard to pick out and the engine roar was like a distant waterfall, continuous and impressive and she was glad to be hearing it here and not 'over the other side'. The roar gradually faded out to sea and finally there was only the sound of a single plane coming back — probably with engine trouble preventing it from gaining height and returning on three engines. It passed over, heading toward Lincoln, to Bardney or Waddington or one of the many dromes nestling round the city.

She would try to get some sleep for a few hours; the fact that they had climbed for height before setting course, showed that it was in all probability a short trip somewhere in the Ruhr Valley. When they were going further, they climbed to operational height on the long journey over the North Sea — or over England on their way down to the South Coast. Anyway she'd try to rest for a few hours before the sound of their return woke her. She fell asleep thinking of the lone aircraft she had heard on its way back — that crew would soon be asleep too.

———

Over the target he was pulling the stick back into his stomach to gain a few more precious feet of height before the bastard began his second attack. His engineer was rolling on the floor with each movement of the aircraft and the navigator, trying to drag him along the floor, kept slipping in the blood. He could see his instruments clearly in the glare of the fighter flares and was surprised to find them all intact. The voice of the rear gunner came

— again over the intercom: "200 hundred yards, turn port, go! — harder", to a scream now, "harder."

He pulled the stick down, his left foot pushing the rudder pedal to its full extent and the ugly red and yellow tracer was flashing past, just high on the starboard side. He could hear his own gunners firing now, and the smell of burnt cordite came back to him from the front turret where the bomb aimer was firing as the Ju88 broke away, up, on the starboard bow.

———

The illuminated hands of the alarm clock pointed to two o'clock. She lay on her back, her arms outside the bedclothes pillowing her head.

It was about twenty minutes later that she heard the first beat of engines, swiftly followed by many more. Already the night air would be crackling with R/T messages calling strange and sometimes humourous code names of airfields, requesting permission to land. Her dressing gown was on the chair beside her; she reached out and pulled it round her shoulders, slowly stretching out of the bed and easing her feet into her sleepers. Over at the table by the window, the first light of the moon showed up the fourteen matchsticks and she sat down at the window looking out into the warm summer night.

The neighbouring buildings stood out as dark silhouettes against the yellow orange glow of the landing lights, the sharp flash of the airfield beacon sending out its identifying code letters, reflected in the windows of "The Bell" opposite. Overhead the sky filled with the engine noise of aircraft circling the aerodrome while others passed on further inland. She could not pick out their shape but could clearly see their red and green wingtip lights. And then the first one came into the "funnel" and once again she heard the spluttering cough of engines throttled back and the squeal of tyres as they touched the runway.

She lifted one of the matchsticks from the table and placed it back in the box. Half an hour passed and finally the fourteenth match was back with the others; a little sigh escaped her and her lips moved silently as she said her thanks. It would be nearly morning before he got back to her — interrogation and a meal, and then the relief of talking about it in the Mess. She could rest properly now and she slipped off her dressing gown kicking her slippers under the bed.

A little later she sighed in her sleep and an arm crept out round the pillow clutching it to her while a slow smile played across her lips.

———

Back in the operations room the Group Captain and the Wing Commander smoked in silence beside the central table with its batch of coloured telephones. They kept glancing at the night's battle order chalked on the large blackboard which completely covered one wall. Aircraft letter, number, captain, take-off time, together with the schedule for each aircraft's time on target. The last column showed the time of landing. Thirteen spaces were neatly filled; the fourteenth empty and staring, was opposite the line which began with the letter 'E'.

A fifteenth entry had appeared as the squadron had returned; a Halifax from No 4 Group which had been the first to land, with near empty fuel tanks and a gaping hole in the starboard wing.

It was over two hours since the last aircraft had touched down and no phone call had come through to say that 'E:Easy' was safely down on another airfield.

The door opened and the Padre came in looking across at the battle order – his glance carried on to the Group Captain who shook his head. The Wing Commander stubbed out his cigarette — "Better call it a day, Sir."

The Group Captain nodded. He glanced again at the board. "His wife's staying in the village, isn't she?"

"Yes."

They both looked at the Padre. He looked as tired as the crews they had talked to a little time ago. He picked up his gloves and buttoned his raincoat. He'd had no sleep for nearly twenty hours, and now this other duty had come upon him.

The Wing Commander put his hand on the older man's shoulder.

"Take my car old chap."

And the Padre walked listlessly out of the room past a clerk who was still putting away the night's target maps.

The Group Captain nodded to a Sergeant WAAF who walked over to the large blackboard and picked up a piece of chalk from the dusty ledge. Slowly she printed the one word "MISSING." It was a narrow column and she had to squeeze the last three letters to get them on the board.

LIKE FLUTTERING LEAVES
THEY FELL

'...Thirteen spaces were neatly filled;... the fourteenth empty and staring...'
Allies and Axis alike made widespread use of propaganda during the conflict.
In Germany as well as in Britain the populace was continually bombarded
with carefully worded, adroitly presented dissemination of information
through word and picture. Half a century on, events local and global are
available to the masses through 'instant' television. It is difficult to imagine
the impact wireless and newspapers, posters and leaflets had all those years
ago. Whilst Lord Haw-Haw (alias William Joyce) nightly transmitted his
diatribe, courtesy of the airwaves, Germany's newspapers and magazines
presented graphic studies of allied aircraft brought down over the
Fatherland, frequently accompanied by gruesome close-ups of bodies or
shots of captured, dejected aircrew, injured or otherwise.

Top right:
*Typical of hundreds published in Germany during the war is this photograph, dated 19 October
1942, and it is worth quoting the accompanying caption verbatim:*
*'The destruction of this big four-engined English Lancaster — a success of our intensified defence
effort. Only the population in the west of Germany, who are exposed to the first line of terror
attacks by British bombers, know what is understood in the words of the Reichmarschal's last big
speech, which established that our defence effort has steadily increased. The rising number of shot-
down planes during attacks by the Tommies on defenceless women and children, evidence of which
can be found all over the place in the wrecked remains. Our picture shows the tailplane of a four-
engined British Lancaster in one of the gorges of the Eifel area.'*
Atlantic-Ahreus Press Agency

Left:
AN OP TOO FAR
*'...She'd been trying to phone the Mess since ten in the hope that
he might be there — but there had been no reply...'*
   *Whilst Britain's Ministry of Information was not slow in
seeing the propaganda value of distributing newsreels and still
pictures of captured Luftwaffe personnel — in particular during
the so-called Battle of Britain — it was Dr Goebbels and his
Propaganda Ministry who raised the practice to a virtual art
form. Barely a week went by without German cinemas screening
newsreels featuring captured allied aircrew being paraded through
the streets of towns and cities. German cameramen seemingly took
an unnatural (to us) delight in shooting close-ups of injured
airmen. Audiences booed and hissed and were notably vocal
whenever an injured man came into view: the more bloodstained
and bedraggled he was, the more vociferous were the watchers.*
   *Our study here — a still apparently published in German
newspapers and magazines — purportedly shows survivors of a
Lancaster. Doubtless, with expected Teutonic thoroughness, prints
were distributed the length and breadth of occupied Europe, and*
*known captions ranged from describing the men as 'RAF terrorfliegers' to 'survivors of a four-
motor RAF Lancaster'. Regrettably, despite extensive enquiries, their identities elude us, as do
location and date, other than being somewhere in Denmark. Did they return to their families in
1945? Does anyone recognise himself? Are they still in our midst, enjoying well-earned retirement
half a century on? Here's hoping...?* Unknown German Source

Centre right and right:
DUTCH COURAGE
*'...Slowly she printed the one word 'missing'. It was a narrow column and she had to squeeze the
last three letters to get them on the board...'*
   *When, to mark the 50th anniversary of the D-Day landings in Normandy, Lancaster 'City of
Lincoln' from the RAF Battle of Britain Memorial Flight dropped a drifting cloud of poppies,
many tears were unashamedly shed.*
   *Prominent among the huge crowd visibly moved were no small number of people, young and
old alike, who had good reason to thank the veterans on parade for liberating their country.
Millions more across the length and breadth of a much changed continental Europe watched on
television, and maybe among them was he who, as a young man, risked much to take a series of
graphic snapshots both from ground level and an upstairs open window of a farmhouse at Pont-a-
Vert in the Département of Aisne, France, 17 April 1943.*
   *That Dutch teenager (forced by the Germans to be a farm labourer in a foreign country) did
not forget the episode and soon after the war made contact with the RAF in an effort to trace
Canadian rear gunner Charlie Hobbs and pass on copies of the photos he took. This he did.*
   *Was a fellow Dutch slave farm labourer, who helped Charlie remove one of his flying boots,
also watching the proceedings on television all those years later? We wonder.*
   *Ageing Lanc I R5484 'OL·V' from No 83 Sqn manned by a veteran crew, headed by
Canadian Plt Off Glen McNichol (whose commission had just come through) had taken off from
Wyton at 21.17hrs on 16 April 1943, bound for Pilsen, Czechoslovakia.*
   *As Charlie later related, their outward journey was without incident but, heading home, they got
too close to Mannheim, also receiving attention from the RAF that night.*

   *Electing to 'roof-top' so as to vacate the area without delay, they had two engines knocked out
by flak, which also wounded Scots mid-upper gunner Alex Willis.*
   *By the time Glen McNichol had nursed his battered mount to the French border another
engine went out (and with it all power to the rear turret)... and they were doomed, no longer able
to maintain height.*
   *And then, with the crew going through the added trauma of baling out, a fighter struck,
raking the stricken Lanc with cannon, wounding bomb aimer Bill Lewis (an American in the
RCAF) descending on his parachute.*
   *Unable to return fire with his turret a blazing inferno, Charlie went forward to the cockpit, a
shambles of broken Perspex, whereupon his Skipper asked him to unlatch his chest-type 'chute, it
now being too low to bale out.*
   *Then, with his arm on the back of his pilot's seat, Charlie stood helplessly looking on as the
fighter came boring in again, blasting the controls out of Glen's hands.*
   *So died as worthy a warrior as you could meet. Charlie somehow crawled from the wreckage
(from which McNichol and Willis did not escape), which had hit a stone farmhouse, and soon
found himself surrounded by Germans.* C. E. Hobbs

91

STAND DOWN

JOHNNY BOY

Warm gold this day, so blue the sky;
And proud the blue you wore;
A pilot's brevet on your breast
Through hostile days of war.
May the times we had be ever bright,
Your laughter quells my tears;
Now here you stand at Runnymede,
My vigil through the years.

Your name among the thousands
Etched clear into the stone;
'Twixt other names and many lives,
Though I know but yours alone.
Your memorial stands in tribute,
And I lament with saddened heart;
Do echo grief of other souls,
Who were, like us, to part.

John Roy Walsh (January 1986)

'No ops tonight' — routine to a clerk
Who could not know
The joy of reprieve for another day
Now for the letter home, the chance to say
'All's well, quiet trip, the crew's OK.'
No need to write the truth, they could not know.

Time to forget the death of 'Mac'
Who could not know
Again the day's quick passing, to the slow night's
fear
The glad surprise of friendly coastline, clear
In the sudden dawn — or exhausted sleep, near
A wife who knew — yet could not know.

Walk in the frost-filled air past villagers
Who could not know
The so short time, the ur
gent haste
To live before time's hands have chased
Another day into the empty waste
Of memories of those who could not know.

Drink in the hotel bar with countrymen
Who could not know
How the floating dust, lit by the wintry beams
Of the cold sun, powerhouse for what seems
To be up-ended searchlights, jogs your waking
dreams
Of nights away from them who could not know.

Loud empty laughter of yourself and crew
Who could not know
The cruel jealous stab our laughter brought
To the white drawn girl, who upstairs, fought
To check her tears — Mac's widow — who
thought
'He's dead and yet, they could not know.'

Dennis Dear

FACES

Faces that were with us, but have gone —
Faces that have travelled on.
Faces that we loved, and knew;
Giving place to others, new —
Faces of the men who flew.

Faces, young and keen, with shining eyes;
Faces bright and gay, lifted to the skies;
Faces gleaming in the sunset's light,
Ready for the coming flight,
Faces — fading in the growing night.

Faces — tired and weary, pale and drawn,
Dazzled by the light of dawn —
Faces that had suffered well,
Their red-rimmed eyes the tale to tell —
Faces that had flown through Hell.

Faces — that, in memory, live again;
Faces not forgotten, but beyond our ken —
We'll never know just where they fell,
For them no flowers, no tolling bell —
Just a comrade's prayer, to wish them well.

Anon, via R. R. (Bob) Smith

GREAT COATS

Hurriedly, carelessly, flung on to pegs
In the hall where the noise from the mess filters through
Of the jokes of the crews over bacon and eggs
With no hint of the dangerous task they must do,
Like faithful old hounds with an eye to the door
The coats hang there quietly awaiting their men;
And twice must the airfield resound to the roar
Of engines, before they are wanted again.

The sound of the last planes has died from the air
And the mess is alive once again to the din
Of cold, hungry youngsters, yet warmly aware
Of another job done that is helping to win.
There is no lack of laughs, but a tiredness must creep
Into eyes that have gazed on a City enflamed
So they eat and are off to their billets to sleep
But two or three coats hang there mutely — unclaimed.

R.J.Blurton
(Killed in action 23 October 1943; No103 Sqn)

THE PAST IS FOREVER

'...It was over two hours since the last aircraft had touched down...'
As survivors of shot down crews ease their way through the twilight years of their lives, how many, we wonder, wish they had a crew picture to muse over? A goodly number we'll be bound.

Other than the threat of swingeing action by their superiors if caught taking photographs (given that cameras, and film, were thin on the ground) there was a widespread belief that it was tempting fate.

Of course, in truth, for every instance of a crew going missing after posing for a group picture we can tell you of another who defied superstition and lived to tell the tale, be they shot down or tour-expired.

And, as can be imagined, when some of the stories behind those photos do emerge, they frequently beggar belief.

Take the case of Flg Off Harry Ross and his troupe who began their crusade with No 625 Sqn at Kelstern, then found themselves nucleus members of the fledgling No 170 Sqn which settled in at Hemswell following brief spells at Kelstern (where it formed on 15 October 1944) and Dunholme Lodge. The crew of 'Mama's Madhouse' was keen to let the folks at home see them in blue posing with their Lanc. Keen that is except for mid-upper gunner 'Chuffy' Hodgson. Time and time again he resisted, and so the crew decided that a spot of deception was called for. By some means they succeeded in 'persuading' him to meet the crew at dispersal one crisp day in December 1944, a day when they were not on the battle order. Faced with such collusion, he finally relented, even forcing a smile for Harry Ross's camera. No one seemed to notice that 'Chuffy' was wearing a raincoat rather than a battle dress like everyone else present, including some of the erks who looked after their kite and who were invited to join them.

Because of his legal training he was frequently called upon to attend disciplinary proceedings, and on the day in question he was called to Hemswell Station Headquarters, there to sort out a dispute with local traders. As a result he was still in his best blue uniform when taken to dispersal by another officer, who passed him a raincoat.

Above right:
A number of snapshots were taken that winter's day, including one of Harry Ross the 'driver' in the cockpit of 'Mama's Madhouse' (BI PD206 'TC:B') but barely had the prints dried when fate stepped in. Within days they were registered among the missing from a night attack on Gelsenkirchen, 29/30 December. All were killed.

Again within days their place in No 170 Sqn was taken by a fresh crew direct from training. Equally, a new Lanc soon arrived at Hemswell to replace 'Mama's Madhouse'. Frances Thompson

Right:
In the crew group, identities are: standing, left to right: flight engineer: Sgt George Faulkner; navigator: Flt Sgt Jack Stevenson; ground crew: unknown; rear gunner: Flg Off Jack Hawdon; ground crew: unknown; wireless operator: Flt Sgt Ken Barnett, RAAF; mid-upper gunner: Flg Off 'Chuffy' Hodgson. Squatting: ground crew: unknown; bomb aimer: Flt Sgt 'Bernard' Shaw. Would that we knew who the erks are.

How do we know all this? Through Frances Thompson, the girl 'Chuffy' Hodgson left behind, and who never got over his death. She never married and devoted her life to the care of others until her own dying day. A remarkable lady, from a generation rich in womenfolk of such character and whose sacrifice cannot be gainsaid. Frances Thompson

SLEEPING WARRIORS

'...The Padre came in looking across at the battle order...'

One Lancaster crew man, given to penning his feeling, his conviction that he would not survive to see his home and those dear to him again, wrote that they who took their Lancs into battle with the enemy were prodigals... that life was merely a present to them... with no future. And, he added, what of the future should, by some fluke, there be any? What were they who survived going to do in the postwar world? Were they all going to settle down into model husbands and fathers and live out the meaningless, humdrum lives that most had lived before the war... eaten away by the same old daily routine... the same old annual holiday... the worry about ways and means... the whole mediocre, drivelling bag of tricks.

He went on to consider mothers and wives, writing that women did not understand the game of flying and the glory of not being dead. That all a wife knew was the waiting... wondering whether the next man who opened the garden gate would be her husband coming back, or some poor devil, feeling like hell, calling to tell her that he wasn't coming back any more. Mothers, he wrote, seemed to take it worse than wives... that their grief didn't seem to heal up again in the same way... that perhaps it was a good thing so many shifted their own sadness on to the shoulders of the dead... not realising that a man's tragedy wasn't a tragedy for him... the tragedy

was for the living. The hard thing was to survive, not to end up as pieces of charred flesh and bone to be laid in a box and labelled and put in the earth... o be a ghost only... a fugitive image in the eyes of those who had cheerily waved him off... his delicate roots ripped out of the minds and the hearts of those who loved and remembered him...

Sobering, thought-provoking stuff.

How many of the dead, the still-missing-without-trace warriors of yesteryear, thought this way? How many survivors, alive to read these words, can honestly say they also had a fatalistic outlook — if briefly?

Quite a number we suspect.

How too many ended up... their broken and burnt bodies scattered all over Germany and occupied Europe as well as in mainland Britain?

Above:
Barely a month went by without there being a funeral procession like this at the Newark cemetery... each coffin containing a Pole from No 300 'Masovian' Sqn, Faldingworth... a son of Poland who would not see the land of his birth again. Six coffins?... the seventh?... a survivor? H. Dixon (formerly Szwagierczak)

Left:
Long after they who had survived, dispersed, adjusted to life in a world once more at peace, the unenviable task of accounting for those less fortunate continued. Hurriedly dug graves like this one, erected by the Germans, were not uncommon. P. H. George

AN INSIDE TALE

'...No phone call had come through to say that 'E-Easy' was safely down...'

When the inevitable happens and each Lancaster aircrew survivor of the air war reaches his allotted lifespan and takes his leave of us, he takes with him a slice of history unique to his crew, unique to him.

Most of what he can tell you, show you, will not be found in once-secret files now available for public scrutiny (given that some documents known to exist are withheld, for whatever reason, and are unlikely to be released).

Such as the full story behind the internment in Sweden of Lanc III PB379.

And what a fascinating, unique story it is to be sure!

It all began routinely at Binbrook on 29 August 1944 when Aussie Flg Off Peter Aldred and his mixed crew of like-Australians and British from No 460 Sqn RAAF set off for Stettin, their longest trip to date since beginning their tour with a visit to Sannerville in daylight on 18 July.

What transpired is best related by the Skipper who, shortly after, apparently returned to 460 and gave a talk to an attentive audience. Here are extracts from a transcript of his account:

'Our course took us straight across the North Sea to a point just south of Esbjerg, on the west coast of Denmark. As we crossed the eastern coast of Denmark we were attacked by an Me109 which the gunners claimed to have hit.

'Things went fairly smoothly until we approached the target area, where another fighter attacked, but once again he didn't do any harm. We continued our run up to the target at our briefed altitude of 17,000(ft) until the master bomber ordered the stream to basement 12-thou, so we orbited to the left, and came in on a second run up at 12,500(ft).

'The flak was thick as hell, as it always is at Stettin, and when we came in on our second run, I noticed a thin layer of stratus above us at 13-thou, which broke clear just over the target area ahead of us. During the run I noticed that there weren't any kites between us and the cloud but just after my bomb aimer gave the 'bomb doors open' order, the clouds broke and I noticed several above and slightly ahead of us, flying at about 17,000ft. By this time, however, our bombs were going, and I had no choice but to keep on my bombing run. As the bomb aimer gave me the 'bomb-doors closed' order we were hit by several incendiaries from one of our kites I had noticed above us.

'I copped it on the right hand and leg. Another one came through the Perspex windscreen in front of me, hitting and disabling the control column, whilst another landed on my platform, taking the flap lever with it, and finished up in the bomb aimer's compartment, fortunately none of them exploding.

'We then went into a rather violent dive, but my right hand being pretty well useless and my other not being strong enough to pull the kite out, necessitated the engineer to trim right back, and between us we levelled out again at about 10,000ft. I might add that all my instruments were U/S so we set course again by the nav's compass.

'Whilst all this was going on, the gunners did a hell of a good job giving me instructions to avoid searchlights, because I couldn't see a bloody thing with the air rushing through the hole in the Perspex, and boy, oh boy, was that air cold!

'However, we were coned by five or six searchlights, which directed a good deal of flak on to us, but we got out of this lot after diving to about 8,000(ft), although not before we received a direct hit, which U/Sed all the hydraulics and the ammunition lines to the rear turret.

'After what seemed hours, we finally crossed the Baltic coast, and I checked up to find the rest of the crew all OK, although the rear gunner had his turret jammed on the beam as a result of the hydraulics going. His parachute was still in the fuselage, and I realised then and there that I was not in a position to bale the crew out even if the situation finally arose.

'My hand was by this time beginning to bleed very badly, so the bomb aimer cut away part of my clothes and applied a tourniquet. He also gave me a shot of morphia, and rugged me up in all the blankets he could. I'm afraid I just can't speak too highly of him; he was absolutely wizard right through, and I'm sure if it hadn't been for his efforts, well, I doubt if we would ever have made it.

'Anyway, after our first-aid session, the engineer informed me that there was a hole about 5ft long inside the starboard wing, at about the position of No 1 petrol tank, and that this was probably accounting for the heavy consumption of fuel from that tank. He also estimated for me the flying time remaining with the revs at 2,600, plus 5¼lb of boost, and from this gen I asked the nav to calculate if we could reach England by maintaining our present airspeed which fluctuated between 95 and 100mph. He reckoned that we would run out of juice a little beyond the west coast of Denmark, so I had no alternative but to ask for a course to Sweden.

'So with the flaps and undercart hanging down, the rear turret U/S, no instruments, and half of my control column shot away, we set course over the Baltic for Sweden, and just prayed that no Jerry night-fighters would pick us up.

'The crew were absolutely wizard. There wasn't a bit of panic from any of them. For some reason, everyone seemed confident that we'd get through OK, although I must admit I had some pretty doubtful moments! I passed out a couple of times, and woke up on each occasion to find my bomb aimer hanging on to the controls like grim death.

'Anyway, we stooged up the east coast of Sweden about five miles out to sea, as far as Oland, where we sent out a brief distress message asking for permission to land, and also that an ambulance be ready when we landed.

'The Swedes replied, giving us permission, but they didn't give us any clues on the exact location of their airfields.

'We stooged around looking for a lighted runway somewhere, but couldn't find any, although we sighted what appeared to be a large field near Kalmar, so I decided to wait for dawn light before attempting to land. We circled for three-quarters of an hour while the crew demolished all our secret equipment, although briefing instructions were that in the event of landing in Sweden it wasn't necessary to destroy the kite itself.

'Eventually it became lighter, and at 2,000ft I was surprised to find that it was a small fighter airfield we were circling, but without runways. However, I made a careful examination of it before putting down, and the

Opposite:
PB379 'AR:E2', hemmed in by barbed wire at Kalmar, is admired by Swedish Air Force personnel. The observant will note 'Village Inn' (AGLT) radome below the rear turret (removed prior to the ferry flight). Also the gas detection 'disc' (a mustard-yellow in colour, with dull red surround) on the nose, unaccountably standard on No 1 Group Lancs right to the end of hostilities.

Prior to Stettin, PB379 had made one operational sortie: Kiel, 26/27 August 1944 — another long flog — again with the Aldred crew. Her flying hours, as recorded on the aircraft record card now held by the Ministry of Defence Air Historical Branch, totalled a mere 24.

Unusually for a Lanc built so late in the war, her Merlin 38s still drive pointed-blade props instead of the by then more standard paddle-blades. M. D. Thieme

Above:
Snaps of PB379 taken on 7 October 1944. The Lanc had been very neatly repaired though the flap lever had become a very Heath Robinson arrangment. This had been jammed in the 'down' position by the same incendiary which had wounded the pilot, but it worked very efficiently, as did everything else during the air test on the morning of 7 October 1944. As Don Thieme would further write almost 40 years later to the day, the afternoon flight to Linkoping was accompanied by fighters, which could have shot them down had they decided that Linkoping didn't really appeal! Later, one of the fighter pilots admitted that he and his colleague in a second machine had difficulty in keeping up with the Lanc, comfortably doing 220mph. Note blacked-out roundels and fin flashes.

So far as we can determine, PB379 did not take to the air again and apparently she was scrapped after plans to convert her for use as a flying test bed fell through.

As a postscript we can add that of the three Lanc skippers involved, only Don Thieme returned to operations. Forming a new crew (but with his original navigator Sgt Harry Vine included), he returned to No 576 Sqn (by now stationed at Fiskerton), only to be shot down during a raid on Duisburg, 21/22 February 1945, and became a POW. Vine (along with two others of the reconstituted septet), did not survive. R. C. Hawkes/M. D. Thieme

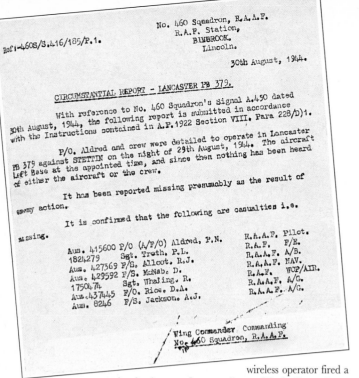

wireless operator fired a couple of reds to confirm our distress. We finally made a cross-wind landing at about 04.35, and I remember nothing from that point until I woke up in hospital next day!

'The rest of the crew have since told me though, that as soon as we landed we were surrounded by Swedish army types armed to the hilt with Tommy-guns, and when the boys started shouting "Doctor, doctor, wounded man very bad," one of the Swedish types grunted, "Ambulance come".

'Anyhow, I was shot off to Kalmar hospital where I stayed five or six weeks, while the rest of the crew were taken to an internment camp, and I joined them later after my release from hospital. The camp was an absolutely wizard set-up, consisting of a couple of hotels overlooking a lake, which in peacetime was one of Sweden's finest country resorts. We had a really wizard time; the treatment at the hospital was bang on, and — oh boy — are those Swedish nurses the shot! During the period I was in hospital I received a short notice from 'Bomber' enclosing a piece of DFC ribbon, because he said I might find it hard to get in Sweden!

'Anyway, when I came out of hospital, I joined the rest of the crew in internment, and they'd been having a hell of a time. There were a couple of other British crews beside ourselves, but quite a number of Jerries were there. We were all in together irrespective of nationality, and we had some quite interesting talks with the Jerry types, some of whom were really decent bods, but others, of course, were the typical Nazi jobs. One thing they couldn't understand was why we Australians were all volunteers. They were all under the impression that Empire servicemen were conscripted by the British Government.

'One of the Luftwaffe pilots we spoke to landed the same night as ourselves and we worked it out that he was probably the chap who attacked us over Denmark, so coincidence is rather a strange thing. He reckoned we had damaged him badly enough to prevent him from getting back to Denmark or Germany, so force-landed in Sweden.

'Life in the camp itself was very pleasant. We came and went pretty well as we pleased, the internees spending their time skiing or fishing, although I wasn't there very long because the British Consul in Stockholm appointed me Air Attaché to the legation. The Swedish people themselves were mostly very good to us; some were obviously Nazi sympathisers, but we just steered clear of them.

'When my hand fully healed up, some Swedish Air Force staff officers came to see me and asked if I would give them a demonstration flight in our Lanc, because it was the first to have landed intact in Sweden. They assured me it had been patched up and made airworthy again so I agreed, and arrangements were made for the flight to take place the following week.

'Well, when we got out to Kalmar aerodrome I found the whole of the Swedish Air Staff and God knows who else, waiting for us there! The pilot of one of the interned RAF crews agreed to come up with me and act as engineer. Anyway, we climbed aboard and started her up; everything seemed fair enough, so we taxied around and took off. The airfield was

practically surrounded by a pine forest and we had to struggle like hell to get her off the shortened runway and over the trees, because apart from the condition of the field, the motors had 'had it', so we only did one circuit and landed again. The old girl just had no guts left at all, added to which, several of the patches they had stuck on the holes in the fuselage and starboard wing started to peel off. It was just about as dicey landing again as it was taking off because we had to dip in over the top of these trees, and when we did get down, we found the brakes had also packed up. Anyway, we raced like hell across the field and finished up against a couple of trees on the other side of the field, which really wiped the old kite off.

'That night we were given a banquet by the Swedish Air Force, and I can assure you the RAF type and I were the envy of our crews when we saw them the next day and told them all about it.

'I wasn't in Sweden very much longer after that, being spirited away one very cold, dark and early morning...'

And here the story becomes a little confusing. Perhaps not unnaturally, others involved have presented a slightly different version of events.

Regrettably, Peter Aldred (who, when last we heard, still kept in touch with all his former crewmen) has resisted invitations to add to his remarkable story; as has his Scots engineer Peter Troth, known to be aboard PB379 when she made the flight for the benefit of the Swedish Air Force officials.

The 'RAF type' Aldred refers to was, it transpires, one Flg Off Don Thieme who, as captain of Lanc I ME800 'UL:W2', from No 576 Sqn, Elsham Wolds, also tangled with the Stettin defences on the night of 29/30 August 1944 and baled out, along with all his crew.

Sadly, Don is beyond our reach (he died in 1989) but his log book (made available through his son Michael) clearly records two flights being made — both on 7 October 1944, both with him as captain. The first was the air test, lasting 30min, and records a Flg Off Hawkes and Flt Sgt Allcott (the name Aldred being crossed out) (* see footnote 1) in the column headed '2nd pilot, pupil or passenger'. The second was the ferry trip lasting 45min, with Sgt Troth and Lt Ercranz accompanying. To add to the confusion (also illustrating the pitfalls awaiting us who attempt to chronicle such events decades later), Canadian Bob Hawkes (Skipper of No 626 Sqn Lanc I ME742 'UM:B2', also downed as a result of the Stettin attack), traced within recent years, has this to say about the ferry flight:

'...An English pilot, Flg Off Thieme, and an English flight engineer, Flt Sgt Troth, and myself were taken to Kalmar under escort. On arrival we were taken to the Lanc for inspection... the field was very short and the Aussie pilot showed great skill landing that Lanc at night, even though badly wounded, and not putting a scratch on his aircraft.

'After inspecting the aircraft we decided it was OK to fly, but we had some concern over the length of the field and the high grass. Before take-off we were advised that we had only a limited amount of fuel — in fact just enough to get us to Linkoping; we would also have a Swedish Air Force officer, Lt Encranz, to ensure our good behaviour.

'We took off from this short field — again credit the great performance of the Lanc — and set course for the Swedish base, any and all ideas of diverting to England dashed when we were joined by a couple of Swedish fighters called the B-17. Our arrival at Linkoping was great fun, as on our flight we engaged in some pretty low flying and then saw a large military turn-out as a welcoming party, so we did a bit of a beat-up. But after landing we sadly left 'Echo 2'. The Air Force then put on a party for us, and to this point I will certainly confirm they really know how to party as it was several days before we had fully recovered. We were returned to Falun under escort... I was repatriated on 27 October 1944...'

FOOTNOTE 1:
'Sandy' Allcott, Aldred's Aussie bomb aimer, was subsequently awarded a well-merited DFM.

FOOTNOTE 2:
All told, 20 Lancs ended up in Sweden. Of those, apart from PB379, only BIII PB842 'PG:Y' from No 619 Sqn, Strubby, and BI RA542 'JO:Z' from No 463 Sqn RAAF, Waddington, landed intact.

A BRIEF ENCOUNTER

'...He was pulling the stick back into his stomach to gain a few more precious feet of height before the bastard began his second attack...'

Try telling some survivors that Lancasters were a delight to fly, were queens of the sky, and they will cast you a quizzical glance. For them there are memories of clapped-out kites at Heavy Conversion Unit, or Lancaster Finishing School, even on their squadron. They were never to know a factory-fresh Lanc, still smelling of new paint and dope, still a little stiff on the controls.

All through OTU on Wimpeys or Whitleys, then HCU on Halifaxes, or Stirlings, or Lancasters — even Manchesters — they had grappled with worn-out crates well past their prime. As if they did not have enough to do — learning their trade, moulding together as a fighting team — there were the frustrations and dangers presented by tyre creep and buckling undercarts, glycol leaks or coring, engine fires and twisted fuselages to contend with. And there was the ever-changing weather to do battle with!

Always there was the prospect of their very own spanking-new Lanc when they began their tour. And invariably they were disappointed to find that, as new boys, they had to take the oldest kites, until the flight commander was satisfied they 'had the makings', had served their apprenticeship, were deserving of a new one. Too many crews failed to come through that so-called apprenticeship.

Consider what befell Flt Lt Bill Blott and his worthies, posted to No 15 Sqn at Mildenhall on New Year's Day 1944, freshly converted to Lancs at No 3 LFS, Feltwell, having earlier endured the HCU course at Wratting Common, whose ground crews deserved a medal for continually patching and mending No 1651 HCU's Stirlings.

Horror of horrors, Blott found himself allocated Lanc I W4355 'LS:A', a real 'banger', whose F700 was itself tattered and oil-stained, ready for the rubbish heap!

She rattled... she leaked... she was a sluggish climber... and, within days of arrival at Mildenhall, Bill Blott was bitching to his 'A' Flight Commander, Sqn Ldr Pete Lamason from New Zealand — to no avail.

Came 25 February 1944 and there on the battle order was ED473 'H' — another veteran — with, alongside it, the Blott seven listed as being ready for their baptism of action. Augsburg was the target that night — always a stinker — but they never got there as loss of the port-inner forced them to abort. A good start!

Atrocious weather throughout February continued to thwart operations and it would be the night of 1/2 March before Blott and his tenderfoots could prove they indeed had the makings. Despite W4355's shortcomings they made it back from Stuttgart without undue problems.

Then off they went on leave, only to find their names on the battle order on 15 March, target: another crack at Stuttgart; another long haul in the creaking W4355.

Whilst it was not unusual, the route that fateful night took them over Switzerland. They did not actually know they were within its borders when their tour came to an abrupt end. Suddenly there was one helluva racket and they knew they had a problem! Within no time they were going down, 'A-Apple' vibrating like mad, literally falling to bits. They assumed it to be a German night-fighter which got them, it, too, trespassing in neutral skies.

Not the first, nor last, crew to bale out without seeing their adversary, they lived to tell the tale, finding their Swiss 'captors' generous to a fault. But that, as they say, is another story.

Above:
The wreck of W4355 'LS:A' at Golaten. Note ops' tally immediately behind the rear door — unusual on a Lanc. That is unless she served on a squadron formerly equipped with Stirlings. Because of their height from the ground, erks found it easier to paint on their kite's ops score near the tail, continuing the practice when Lancs took over. As W4355 initially served with No 97 (Straits Settlements) Sqn, before moving on to flog the circuit with No 1661 HCU (and totting up 700-plus flying hours), we can but suppose her No 15 Sqn ground crew transferred her impressive offensive sortie log from nose to tail-end? Or did they? Swiss Air Force

UNEASY LIES A QUEEN

'...And there was nothing on the map to show the great barrier of searchlights, the fighters, and finally the flak over the target, seeming to fill every inch of sky...'

A question for you. If it is acceptable for the uniform, sword and medals worn by, say, a Royalist captain who fought at Edgehill, to be sold at public auction, how do you feel about a dealer selling the log book, uniform and medals of a Lancaster air gunner through a postal catalogue or shop?

You must be the judge.

Before making your judgement be aware that increasing numbers of artefacts are being sold only because some veterans, or their widows, are struggling to survive as pensioners. A sorry state of affairs.

Also disturbing is the trend towards the sale of replicas at car boot sales and other outlets. If it does not anger you, fill you with dismay, learning of replica medals and uniforms flooding the market, what about shrapnel, often complete with dried blood on it! Is nothing sacred? How lacking in respect for the dead, the maimed, can one be? How would *you* react were you disabled, scarred mentally if not physically through being a victim of flak?

Flak! The very mention of the word will cause many a survivor to shudder... recall his own survival... call to mind colleagues less fortunate. Survivors the like of New Zealander Roy Calvert, whose closest encounter of many encounters with flak he would recount in vivid detail some 32 years later:

'On 9 November (1942) we were briefed for Hamburg. Plt Off Sears, my navigator for 19 trips, had finished his first tour of ops and had been replaced by Flt Sgt Medani. We had had one very successful trip to Genoa and we had every confidence in him. Also, my flight engineer stood down this trip and we took along Plt Off Power (an American pilot who had trained in Canada) in his place for experience. My bomb aimer Sgt Gray had also finished his tour and was replaced by Sgt Wilson. The weather forecast was for cloud over Denmark but breaking over the target area.

'Approaching the coast of Denmark at 10,000ft, I realised we couldn't go over the towering clouds, so we went through them. We hadn't far to go before turning south in order to make our run from east to west across Hamburg, then a direct run home. The cloud was far more extensive than had been forecast and we couldn't see anything to help identify our position.

'I dropped down a couple of thousand feet hoping for a clear patch but found to my horror we were icing up and my airspeed registered zero. We turned for our run to the target by dead reckoning and I dropped down lower still, hoping for a break in the clouds. Then we broke through into a clear layer between 6 and 7,000ft and my airspeed began to register again, giving me renewed confidence; but I was faced with the decision whether to risk going through the thin layer of stratus below and making ourselves a

beautiful target against the searchlight-lit clouds, or staying where I was and hoping for a break in the clouds, when the time came to bomb. I inched my way up into the top cloud once more but immediately began to ice-up — so dropped down again to 6,000ft.

'Medani had just informed me that our ETA-target was up when, through a small break in the clouds to starboard, I spotted a large blue light on the ground. I immediately thought, "railway marshalling yards", swung the kite 90° to starboard and asked Sgt Wilson to get ready to release our cargo.

'A few seconds later there was a crack off our port wingtip and we were sprayed with shrapnel. It sounded like a handful of gravel thrown on to a tin roof. In the cockpit a top forward panel of Perspex and the starboard blister were shattered and our intercom went dead. Then another shell burst on our port, closer this time. Poor old 'S-Sugar' shuddered violently and we were sprayed with shrapnel once again. I felt something hit my left arm and my face was sprayed with small pieces of Perspex. The aircraft was difficult to control so I ordered Plt Off Power to tell the bomb aimer to release our load, then to check up on the rest of the crew.

'The plane was flying left wing low and aileron trim and rudder bias were unserviceable. Then Power yelled in my ear that John Medani, just behind me, was badly wounded in the elbow and was losing a lot of blood, so I told him to put a tourniquet on it, then to check on the rest of the crew and tell them all to come forward in case we had to 'abandon aircraft'. Sgt Wilson came back after releasing the bombs and helped to make John comfortable. It was very cold and noisy in the cockpit. I only hoped we could get back in time to save John who would already be cold through loss of blood. He managed to give me a course of 250° for home but I decided to go further north to clear the flak area of the Elbe estuary and get out to sea as quickly as possible before heading westwards.

'Power came back and informed me that Lewis Austin had been killed and the gunners were coming forward. Just about everything was U/S: wireless receiver; DR compass; Lorenz, IFF; and GEE had been hit and blown up. However, we staggered on. I had already decided we were going as far as possible, as long as we could remain airborne. I then turned for home and lost height to 3,000ft and found we were over the sea. Shortly, some islands came up on our port so I turned on to 270° and dropped down to 1,000ft thinking there would be less chance of fighters getting on to us; also it was warmer. I found that if I increased speed over 190mph the aircraft vibrated alarmingly so I dropped back to 180.

'After leaving the islands behind I turned on to 250° and sat back to await sight of the English coast. Extensive cloud ahead and to the north

Top left and centre left:
Gasp as you cast your eyes over the battered but unbowed wreck of R5702 at Bradwell Bay, whose station photographer was well used to crawling over many a lame duck.
R. O. Calvert (port)/B. Lewis (starboard)

Left:
With Skipper Flg Off Roy Calvert and navigator Flt Sgt John Medani in hospital, the able-bodied members of the crew stand in line, showing no ill-effects after their night of high drama.
Left to right: Sgt Alan Connor, Sgt Don Wilson, Plt Off Al Power, Sgt Gordon Cruikshank.
Within a few months both Wilson and Power were dead. As captain of his own crew Al Power (by now Flying Officer) went down on Cologne, 2/3 February 1943. B. Lewis

Top right:
Press call for Roy Calvert and some of his No 50 Sqn contemporaries at Skellingthorpe a day after the daring daylight/dusk attack on Le Creusot on 17 October 1942.
Left to right, back row: Flt Lt 'Jock' Abercromby, Sqn Ldr 'Mick' Moore DFC, an Australian in the RAF, 'A' Flight OC, Sqn Ldr Hughie Everitt DFC, OC 'B' Flight. Left to right, front row: Flg Off Drew Wyness, Flg Off Roy Calvert DFC, RNZAF.
Against the odds, Messrs Moore, Everitt and Calvert survived the war. As OC No 83 Sqn, 'Jock' Abercromby DFC and Bar was killed raiding Berlin, 1/2 January 1944; as a flight commander with No 617 Sqn, Drew Wyness, DFC and Bar, met his death attacking the Rhine Barrage on 7/8 October 1944. Not forgotten by those who knew them...their worth appreciated by us who wish we had known them. R. O. Calvert

decided me to turn southwards towards a large group of searchlights, promising clearer weather there. I spotted the coast as we approached, a conjunction of rivers indicating the Harwich area.

'The next problem was to find an aerodrome willing to have us. I headed further south towards a cone of three searchlights and, sure enough, spotted a flarepath laid out in the middle. I circled round, flashing the downward recognition light and received a 'green' to come in and land. We lowered the undercarriage with the emergency air system and, with Plt Off Power bellowing our airspeed into my ear, I lined up on the flarepath.

'It wasn't till we were about 200ft up that I realised there was a ground fog. The flarepath lights disappeared except for two 'money' flares at the start of the runway. Suddenly, the runway was there. We were a shade too steep with our approach so I applied power and pulled back on the stick, then cut the throttles. The wheels hit and collapsed and we skidded along on our belly, gradually turning to starboard, pulled by the revolving props until we slid on to the grass and stopped. I switched everything off: we were home! On my way out I said goodbye and thanks to poor old Lewis Austin, my friend and wireless operator for many trips. He had been killed instantly.

'As it turned out we had landed at Bradwell Bay, from where John Medani and I were taken off to hospital whilst the rest of the crew went to be debriefed.

'After a short stay in hospital I visited John and found him progressing well (he rejoined the crew a month later and we did two more ops together). Then I went out to Bradwell Bay to pay my last respects to poor old 'S-Sugar'. She was a sad sight, spattered all over with shrapnel, elevator and rudder control rods ¾-shot-through in three places. But she hadn't let us down for 24 ops, over France, Germany and Italy, surely reason enough for my love of the Lancaster. Shortly after, I said goodbye to 50 Sqn, having completed my first tour of 33 ops. I left with fond memories of many fine men.'

What, you may ask, subsequently happened to men and machine? Surprisingly, despite her battered state, 'S-Sugar' (BI R5702 'VN:S') was

'stripped to her underwear' and virtually rebuilt. In turn she served with Nos 460 and 100 Sqns before being hived off with the latter's 'C' Flight to form the nucleus of No 625 Sqn, opening for business at Kelstern with effect from 1 October 1943. Still she soldiered on... but her days — or rather, nights — were numbered. In the hands of Sgt R. W. H. Ashurst and his old hands she attempted one operation too many and Berlin 15/16 February 1944 was her undoing. Given that 51 Februaries have slipped by since then, can we hope sole survivor, ex-Flg Off H. J. Proskurniak is with us still... never forgetting his remarkable survival?

Roy Calvert moved on to spend most of 1943 instructing at No 1660 HCU, Swinderby (adding a highly prized green endorsement to his DFC and BAR) before getting away and forming a new crew. Succeeding in pulling in his former mid-upper gunner as wireless operator, Plt Off Alan Connor, RAAF, and rear gunner, WO Gordon Cruikshank (both worthy recipients of the DFM), he headed for No 630 Sqn at East Kirkby, soon to take over 'B' Flight. Completing a not uneventful second tour, he would return to his native land bearing the ribbons of no less than three DFCs on his chest. Alan Connor and Gordon Cruikshank also saw the war out.

THE TIME TO LIVE IS VERY SHORT

'...They kept glancing at the night's battle order...'

In these times of counselling for members of the armed forces, huge monetary awards for one reason or another, it is sobering to remind ourselves how many next of kin were virtually left to fend for themselves when sons, or husbands, or brothers made the ultimate sacrifice all those years ago.

How many mothers and fathers, widows and sisters struggled to come to terms with their loss, rebuild shattered lives? How many never fully recovered... were forced to sell log books and medals, even letters... went to their own graves feeling betrayed?

We must not forget them.

Equally, we must not forget the men and women whose thankless task it was to sort out those log books and medals and letters, and despatch them to

holding centres before being handed over to families near and far.

Typified by Kath Barfield who, as a WAAF not yet 'given the key of the door', found herself working for the Committee of Adjustment at, first, Bottesford, later East Kirkby... and who remembers with all too vivid clarity as a pensioner granted contented retirement... with time to reflect.

Here is one of several artefacts in Kath's keeping... a touching letter penned by Australian Flg Off Michael Skarratt from No 460 Sqn, RAAF, Binbrook, before he headed Lanc III PB255 'AR:X' for the Nippes railyards at Cologne on Christmas Eve 1944 and who, along with his crew of five countrymen and a British flight engineer, faced a violent death. Kath Lock

Below:
Not infrequently, all that remained to point to a man's existence on his squadron was his motor bike or car. And not infrequently they would be auctioned in the Mess — the Standard 10, third left in our line-up at Downham Market, among them — the proceeds sent to grateful families.

As a postscript, it is tempting to wonder what became of the Wolseley Daytona, MG Sports, Morris 8 and Panther (let alone the Standard 10), long after their No 635 Sqn owners moved on. J. P. G. Baines

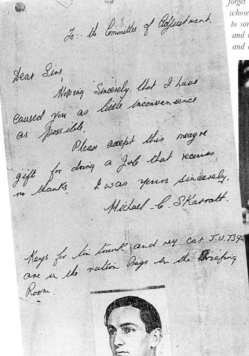

NO MEDALS FOR THEM

Ask any surviving Lancaster aircrew veteran what he thinks of the ground staff who kept his aircraft serviceable, available for when Group said she must be... packed his parachute... supplied his maps and escape kit... and he will, as likely as not, readily admit that without them he and his fellow crewmen, his contemporaries on every squadron on every airfield throughout the Command would have been lost, unable to prosecute the war, week in, week out; month in, month out.

He will doubtless go on to mention those who beavered away behind the scenes without fuss... the likes of radar mechanics... instrument repairers... spark plug testers... armourers... cooks and all who kept him fed... the list of trades is impressive and long.

And he will, no doubt, express regret that he did not get to know them better during his time on the station... did not get to pump more hands, buy more drinks... even though he feels sure they understood... understand now in old age looking back... those still in the land of the living.

And if that same survivor decides to satisfy his curiosity and attend a reunion of his old unit he will soon be disappointed that so few such one-time stalwarts turn up; are even members of his Squadron Association.

Little wonder considering the scant mentions they get when historians record the story of the air offensive, histories of squadrons and aircraft; film producers likewise considering them little more than background props.

And how shameful it is that a grateful nation did not reward them by striking a Bomber Command medal! As with the aircrew, they were shunned by a government which turned its back on them... as it did on their revered leader 'Butch'.

Hands up those of you who, never having worn air force blue in wartime, can say you know that to support any station's establishment of Lancasters it took around 2,000 or so personnel... ranging from the humblest clerks in the orderly room, the military policemen who manned the guardroom and picquet posts, to camp barber and tailor, to the 'old man' himself, the Station Commander. All played their part.

Here are a few of them:

For those hardy souls who can stomach it, breakfast is still being served in the Messes when the first erks, in ones, twos or in groups, pedal their way to dispersals near and distant, there to begin vital daily inspections (DIs). The aircrew have total trust in them, and when the Skipper will later do his own obligatory internal and external checks before accepting his charge by signing the F700 (the kite's log book), he will know that signatures already entered by a succession of tradesmen testify to a skill, a pride, a dedication without equal.

Park your bike and join them at (*Opposite top*) Elsham Wolds (Nos 103 and 576 Sqns) one crisp morning during the winter of 1943/44; and (*Below*) Wratting Common a year on, No 195 Sqn's veteran BI NG162 'A4:W' 'Willie the Conk' holding centre stage. *G. S. Morgan/R. T. Newberry*

THE FLIGHT MECH

He wears a suit of faded blue, no badge upon his breast,
You'll find more streaks of dirty oil than medals on his chest.
He wields a hefty spanner and piece of dirty rag,
While other fellows shoot the Hun and add a fighter to their bag.
He works in sleet, in mud and rain, and curses the blinking war
And wonders ninety times a day what he joined the Air Force for.
He's only a Flight Mechanic, nothing more or less,
With a greasy suit of overalls in place of battledress.
But he strikes a blow at Gerry, with his honest British skill
As sure as the pilot who delivers the bombs
Or the gunner who makes the kill.
So when you read of bombings or a Messerschmitt shot down,
When you've covered flying heroes with honour and renown,
When you've given all the DFMs and DFCs and such
Just think of the Flight Mechanic — he does not ask for much.
Just shake him by his oily hand and tell him he did a lot
To make those roaring engines safe for the man who fired the shot.

Anon

Opposite page, top:
Like this one, snapped, we believe, at Ludford Magna (No 101 Sqn and No 14 Base Major Servicing Section) a year later, looking in on erks in happy mood, taking a breather... having a swig... as is their right... but which can just as easily be their vigil awaiting return of their kite, their crew, from a daylight venture.

No need to worry about a likely charge for being incorrectly dressed out here, far from the gaze of mandarins who stalk the corridors of Station Headquarters. E. D. Evans

Left:
We may now all take photography for granted, and will usually note details on the back of prints, or in the album; but in the days when cameras were generally of the Box Brownie type, and colour beyond the reach of the 'man in the street', so few anotated their snapshots with names, let alone locations and dates. Thus it was that ground staff who laboured to keep any crew's Lanc in good working order rarely had their names recorded on the reverse side of photos (other than as 'Jock', 'Chalky', etc).

Like this gem, taken at Syerston during the late spring/early summer of '43, our mystery man finding himself the centre of attention as he snatches a few moments of rest while his mates continue to work on No 61 Sqn's BI W4900 'QR:Q', the mount of Canadian Ward Parsons and his cohorts. He'd probably dismiss as 'wishful thinking' any notion that his charge would survive the war, such was the reality of expectations at that time; but — survive she did, latterly with several HCUs, not being SOC until October 1945. W. C. Parsons

Centre left:
Like this one of an NCO who, in our files, has been studying his record book for more years than we care to remember and is deserving of a name. We don't even know for sure where it was taken, though judging by a serviceability board on the wall (listing serials and identity letters of Lancs operated by No 300 Sqn Polish Air Force), it could be Faldingworth. More likely it is the Instrument Section of No 14 Base's major servicing facility at Ludford Magna. Any offers? E. D. Evans

Bottom:
Like this capital 'take' of two worthies more intent on the job in hand — battling with the Zeuss fasteners which hold down the wing leading edge panels — than consciously posing for a probing camera wielded by one who takes BIII NE170 'AS:I' to war.

This is a No 166 Sqn dispersal, circa July 1944, at Kirmington, once as much a part of Lincolnshire as the city of Lincoln itself... 30 years later to be renamed South Humberside by bureaucrats oblivious to feelings of pride and tradition, yet, 50 years later reverting to its rightful Lincolnshire roots.

We know that NE170 was a virgin Lanc when allocated to Flg Off Ivon Warmington and his fellow knights errant and, suitably adorned with a mischievous Lincoln imp astride a bomb, and named 'The Imp Rides Again!', she saw them safely through their tour.

We know that NE170 was brought down by flak during an attack on V2 rocket stores located at Agenville on 31 August 1944, a successful daylight, but which saw 166 lose two of the six Lancs and crews lost (Canadian Flg Off Frank Elliott and crew in NE170; Flg Off Brian Tutty and fellow youths in ND635 'AS:M'). We do not know what became of her earthbound cadre beyond demob. Who does? J. F. Clark

THE GIRLS IN BLUE

Just as they did in the 'war to end wars' — namely World War 1, 1914/18 — our womenfolk answered the call of King and Country in their thousands during the second major conflict.

Conspicuous among that number were the girls who served in a wide range of duties within the structure of Bomber Command and who so rarely get a mention in histories, documentaries and such. Just as it was a culture shock for the majority of lads who exchanged civvies for RAF blue, so it was for many girls who, before enlistment, had never left home, had generally led rather sheltered lives.

And, barely had many a male 'regular' recovered from the shock of encountering boys fresh from school or apprenticeships flooding the squadrons as fully-fledged aircrew sergeants and more, when the fair sex entered the scene, to their total amazement, and more than a little resentment.

One can picture 'old sweats' who had taken up to 20 years to reach the revered rank of sergeant or warrant officer, having to work with — even report to — WAAFs with a mere 12 months' or so service! But any resentment soon turned to respect and admiration when witnessing slips of girls driving tractors towing Lancasters, packing parachutes, talking down crews, and performing these and other vital tasks with total dedication and obvious pride.

Here, look in on a few of the lasses the like of whom could be found on any Lancaster station. We salute them all.

FOOTNOTE:

The Ewens crew's tour spanned the period from Stuttgart, 7/8 October 1943, to Oslo Fjord, 28/29 April 1944, and all went on to act as screens before several began second tours. Russell Ewens DFC, on completion of his tour went as an instructor at 1661 CU Winthorpe. He eventuallly transferred to Transport Command, and later to BOAC, continuing to fly Merlin-engined types (Yorks, Lancastrians and Argonauts) well into the 1960s, before converting to the jet fleet, retiring as a senior instructor captain on VC10s with 20,000hr in his log book. Comfortably retired, he lives in 'airline pilot country' in Surrey.

Russell Ewens was one of many aircrew (pilots in particular) who, in the last few months of the war in Europe, were to establish their futures in flying, by responding to appeals put out on Bomber Command notice boards, and through the grapevine, for pilots, flight engineers, navigators, wireless operators to transfer to Transport Command. Initially, this was to establish the capability to supply 'Tiger Force' for the war on Japan, with the additional 'carrot' of eventual employment by the airlines, which were expected to re-emerge and expand after the war — BOAC, BEA, Skyways, British South American and the like. For pilots and engineers the minimum criteria were said to be two tours of ops, or 1,000hr on multi-engined types. No degrees required in those days, just the right skills and experience. After initial selection, the aircrew would transfer to special training units which were established, such as 6 LFS at Ossington, near Newark, with Yorks and Lancastrians. After a spell on Transport Command from bases at Hurn, Full Sutton, Lyneham, etc (as co-pilot for a while in the case of pilots), they would eventually be given a command and many would pass on to the airlines quite quickly: pilots such as Rod Rodley, Ron Munday, Bob Knights, Tony Iveson, Ken Beauchamp, Geoff Hall, Dennis Millar (a New Zealander), Gerry Fawke, to name but a few. Some of them dated back to Hampden days (Tony Iveson to the Battle of Britain as a sergeant pilot on Spits) and would have long and distinguished flying careers. Commonwealth airmen, too, such as Dan Cullen and Art Whitmarsh from No 460 Sqn (RAAF), both of whom flew into the 747 'Jumbo' era.

All round the world on airlines — British, Commonwealth, foreign, until the late 60s/early 70s, you'd see many civil aircrew proudly wearing DSO, DFC and DFM ribbons beneath their company airline wings. Such things are a great rarity these days.

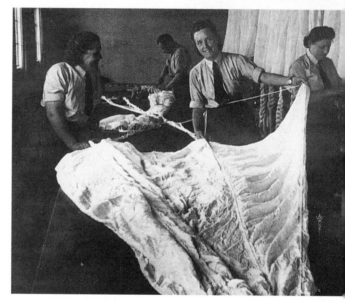

Top:
Many a lass served in the intelligence role, as here, an early morning interrogation at Fiskerton during the winter of 1943/44. It was a task requiring a sharp intellect, mixed with tact and patience, and to which the Air Ministry felt that women were particularly well suited. Tired crews, more intent on breakfast and sleep, were not always enthusiastic about answering seemingly endless, pointless questions as required by the Operational Research Section of Bomber Command.

It is tempting to wonder what memories the No 49 Sqn crew skippered by Flg Off Russ Ewens have of the WAAF who so often faced them from across the trestled table? What does the lady herself recall of her time at Fiskerton — whoever she is? Has she, in common with others of her ilk, felt the tug, only to encounter near total dissolution, an indefinable sadness?

In our eavesdropping study, identities of the Ewens crew in view, foreground are (left to right): Navigator: Flt Sgt Joe Pitcher; Bomb aimer: Flg Off Bob Grainger; Mid-upper gunner: Sgt Jim Lees; Rear gunner: Sgt Maurice Laws; Pilot: Flg Off Russ Ewens. (See Footnote.)
D. C. Tritton/Sheffield Star

Above:
Virtually every Lancaster crewman who survived baling out owed his life to one or more of the WAAFs who packed his parachute. Early in the conflict, before WAAFs made their appearance, the duty was performed solely by men. No job was more vital and, whilst every girl prepared the 'chutes she was responsible for with a care unmatched, invariably each aircrew member kept to his own pack for the duration of his tour.

The parachute room at Faldingworth, here pictured, exists now only in the mind's eye of those who knew it in wartime, but can we hope that a threesome from Poland are still in our midst? So also their male colleague, here barely visible in the background.

And how many parachutes are to be found — albeit masquerading as wedding dresses and underwear — in the countries of Holland, Belgium, France all these years on? In such war-torn lands many a discarded 'chute was secreted away and later suitably 'modified' by grateful brides-to-be. Polish Sources

Right:

Stand in the shell that is the operations block at a largely intact Bottesford over two score and ten years after this picture was taken — the early hours of 2 March 1943 — and you can almost hear the laughter, echoing round this and adjoining rooms, now overtaken by an all-engulfing blackness. On hand to dish out hot tea to lads of the largely Aussie-manned No 467 Sqn is a well-remembered WAAF, who remains anonymous, as do all others with her, save for pilot Flt Sgt Freddy Wilmott, right foreground. Düsseldorf 11/12 June 1943 was to be his last trip and he became one of 282 Australians killed in action with 467. Freddy's young life was brutally cut short, but we hope the lady in blue returned to civilian life and fared well. Marie Claridge

Below right:

If pedal-power bicycles abounded on any Lancaster station, hardly less so it seemed were the motorised vehicles to be found in their dozens, ranging from motor bikes and staff cars to petrol bowsers; and all maintained by the MT section. Prominent among drivers were no small number of WAAFs who, whilst in the main natives of Great Britain, included in their ranks a fair sprinkling from distant lands.

And what a grand job they did! No task was too difficult and many a girl who, though prior to enlistment had never sat behind a steering wheel, took to the role like a duck to water despite an initial dread of starter handles and double-declutching.

Almost as varied as their accents were the types and sizes of vehicles they drove. Motor bikes and ambulances, gharries and lorries of 15,30 hundredweight or more (no metrics in those days!)... they handled them all with skill and dedication. And the list of makes was equally impressive. Recalling manufacturers like Bedford and Guy, Austin and Commer, Dodge and Ford is akin to a Who's Who of an industry soon to undergo radical changes, and which would see the demise of several household names in the decade or so postwar. Most of the names have all but disappeared completely from our roads now.

In our snapshot, taken on a No 103 Sqn dispersal at Elsham Wolds late 1942/early 1943, we see SACW Muriel Mansfield in the cab of her Commer Q15. Where are you Muriel? Your one-time colleagues long to hear from you. The annual Elsham Wolds reunion would welcome you. Mary Smith

Below:

Few who served at Ludford Magna stepped inside the No 14 Base Operations nerve centre, or even knew what went on in there. Controlling three stations (Faldingworth, Wickenby and Ludford), it was a windowless, supposedly bomb-proof structure manned by hand-picked individuals.

How many historians and students of the bomber war consider at length the vital work done by the teams who set up raid after raid without fuss and ceremony night after night, day after day?

Wading through wads of signals and other documents that once chattered their way through noisy teleprinters (and which are held in perpetuity in the nation's archives) tell us little of the human toil that went into their preparation. It needs the human element to put 'meat on the bone' and it is warming to note that a number of surviving mortals have, within recent years, stepped forward to relate their experiences while memories last.

One such is 'Nancy' Mackie and here is one of her treasured reminders of times past.(Left to right) Sgt Joan Ellis, Wng Cdr Peter Ward-Hunt, Sgt Pat Robinson, Sgt 'Nancy' Mackie, Flt Lt Harry Beckett. Nancy Mackie

PICKING UP THE PIECES

How many, we wonder, would have spared a thought for the salvage and recovery parties, who could be called out any time of the day or night, whatever the weather, whatever the location, whether it be farm field or bog, river or fen, mountain or moor. If it happened, you went. It demanded a special breed of discipline and dedication. Britain was basically split into a few large geographical areas, each with its own specialist maintenance unit, each with a large complement of airmen from all the basic trades, all of whom would be kept very busy during the war. As soon as an accident occurred, out would go a working party, to picquet the site and make an initial inspection and assessment, to recover bodies, make safe any war load, recover/protect remains for crash investigators, and salvage whatever parts might be reusable, however large or small. Numerous Lancasters flew again made up almost entirely of salvaged parts and sections.

The parties worked in teams usually comprising an SNCO, plus four or five airmen, including perhaps two engine mechanics, plus an electrician or armourer, depending on the job. The NCO usually drove the lorry carrying equipment and tools, with the gang on board. Low-loaders and cranes were available when needed. It could be a tough job, calling for tough men and good leadership, with plenty of initiative and basic know-how.

Our focus is on No 58 MU, which was stationed not on an airfield, but on an industrial site taken over by the Air Ministry at Newark, out on the Lincoln Road. It was in the thick of 'Bomber Country', covering eastern and central England from the Humber, down the centre as far as Wellesbourne (Warwicks), across to Cambridgeshire, Suffolk, up to Norfolk and all Lincolnshire. Count the number of RAF aerodromes, including bomber stations, in that! No 58 MU probably handled more Lancasters than all the other MUs combined. It came under the control of HQ 43 Group, which was at RAF Hucknall, near Nottingham. It was a WAAF section officer there, who took it upon herself to visit a number of No 58 MU's working parties actually in the field on a variety of tasks. Her observations prompted Greta Wilson to report on her findings and thoughts, which we are very pleased to be able to reproduce below, as we feel she says it all:

To be distributed to all members of salvage parties the Cinderella of the services
by S/O Greta Wilson
HQ 43 Group

It's time someone thought up a better word for 'SALVAGE' — one thinks immediately of old bones dug up from the dog's burying ground, tin cans, rubbish and generally the sweepings of the highways and byways. This article is not concerned with Salvage in its usual sense, but with the salvage and — shall we say — *resouling* of crashed aircraft by that drudge of the RAF, the Salvage and Repair organisation under Maintenance Command.

Booklets are written, photographs published and films made of the activities of the more spectacular Commands, and rightly and honourably so. But it is time someone beat the big drum for that lost and forgotten tribe, the Salvage Gangs and Repair on Site parties. Theirs is one of the toughest jobs in the Service, for which they get neither ballyhoo nor braid. So little is really known of what they do that these men, working all the time exposed to the four winds of heaven and everything they send, are practically last on the offical list for the issue of War Service Dress.

An aircraft crashes in some lonely spot miles away from her base. She lies helplessly there, perhaps with her back broken, perhaps only needing minor attention to bring her back to useful life. In any case, she has got to be moved, and you cannot just pick up a Halifax, say, and put her on a lorry. You need mobile cranes, you need transportation equipment, you need these strange craft which have somehow or other acquired the odd name of 'Queen Marys' — the long low-loaders. And you need the skilled men to dismember the prostrate monster and get her away somewhere where she can be worked on and 'reconstructed' in one way or another, either back into the air as a whole ship, or taken to pieces to make spares for her sister ships, or in the extreme cases, to be rendered back into the metal from whence she came.

One has only to go out and see the terrain on which these unsung heroes fight their battles to realise a little of the skill, patience *and* courage that is needed to rescue a crashed aircraft, whether it be a whole unit, or in handpicked fragments.

The torn carcass of a Lancaster in some lonely ploughed field in East Anglia, with the cold rains of February clogging the ground to make a nightmare labour of manual toil and effort — a maimed Fortress on Skiddaw; the party must be as agile as goats and with the same ability to live on anything for days at a time — the graceful shell of a Spitfire on some southerly seashore, washed by the tides and only accessible between them, man has to fight man's oldest enemies, time and tide — a Halifax bogged down on the Yorkshire moors, the gang digging desperately against a constant and heartbreaking seepage — these things are part of the daily life of the Salvage crews. They fight the elements just as surely as the bomber crews in the airconditioned cabin, to give back to that crew or its successors their ship in one form or another. Their working hours are the hours of daylight, all of them. No NAAFI break wagon can reach them, they get no tender mercies from the WVS, they have no shelter tents, no Music While you Work, no bonuses. They can't strike, they can't expect any gongs or any glory.

It stands to reason the the NCO I/C Salvage has to be an exceptional fellow. He is a sort of Vagabond King; once he and the gangs have reached the site of the crash the whole responsibility for operations from then on becomes his. He is cut off from his base unit; telephones do not grow on bushes. This means that he has to take his own decisions — and they can be very tricky. How to manoeuvre a heavy crane across a rustic bridge that will scarcely support a horse and cart, how to get his 'Queen Marys' into a field separated from the road by two other fields, with as little damage as possible to the farmer's crops, how to make the best of what equipment is available at the time, how to improvise if the right equipment is not forthcoming, and above all, how to keep his men cheerful in conditions of wet, snow, frost, mud and general misery. Hollywood has not yet made a film character of the NCO I/C Salvage, yet you could not find a tougher Tough Guy, and if he goes out into the howling wilderness, it is not because his girl loves another, it is because some bloke has been careless enough to prang his kite there.

These men deserve the greatest respect for their technical skill and its application; they and those under them deserve admiration for their handling of difficult jobs in difficult situations, and praise for the way in which they stick on until they have done what they are meant to do — help keep the Air Force flying.

No body of men in the Service has contributed so much to the Motto 'Per ardua ad astra' with so little recognition.

Greta Wilson

Opposite:

We are fortunate, too, to have found one of those 'NCOs I/C Salvage' about whom Greta writes — a 'Tough Guy' as she so aptly describes them, though he, like most involved at the time, would be surprised at that title, like so many others, 'just doing his job'.

Ron Makinson had joined the RAF in 1938 at Cardington, 1st Direct Entry, and went to Halton (though not as a 'brat' apprentice), becoming an airframe mechanic. He was posted to No 56 Sqn (Hurricanes) at North Weald as war broke out, later did a fitters' course, was posted to Sutton Bridge, still on Hurricanes, then to Pershore, 23 OTU, where he had his first experience of bombers (Wellingtons). There he was promoted to sergeant, and after 2 1/2 years in the pleasant Worcestershire surroundings he was posted abroad to the Middle East, followed by Italy, to various MUs, repairing and rebuilding Spitfires, later as a stock inspector at an MU at Brindisi. With the war in Europe over, he volunteered for 'Tiger Force', and one day in August 1945, was a passenger aboard a Lancaster (one of five or six) which had taken off eastwards from Pomigliano (near Naples), carrying a contingent for the Far East. About an hour into the flight (actual destination still secret) the navigator came back down the fuselage to announce to the passengers that 'The War is over — Japan has surrendered', upon which the Lanc turned, pointed its nose northwest, and some eight hours later landed them at Glatton (near Peterborough), all still in their KD.

It was then on to a London staging unit, a spot of leave, and a transit camp near Blackpool, there to learn of his next posting — to Iceland! The night before his departure, he happened to be chatting in a local pub to a corporal who worked in Administration. On learning of the posting, the corporal told Ron the rules about a three month reacclimatisation when going from 'hot' to 'cold', and — good as his word — got it, and several others changed to a 'home posting' — No 58 MU, Newark, for which he and a colleague were quite thankful. The two of them set out on the long and rather tortuous cross-country train journey from Blackpool to Newark, arriving there late evening, no transport, having to hump their kitbags etc the mile or so to 58 MU, to be told on arrival by the Ministry police at the gate — 'You've missed 'em. They moved to Skellingthorpe yesterday.' So, it was up with the kitbags again, to thumb a lift to Lincoln, followed by another long hike back to 'Skelly'.

Though the war was over, the MUs were, it seemed, as busy as ever with hundreds of aircraft standing round all over the area, awaiting their fates, surplus to requirements. The airfield-based MUs at such as Llandow, Aston Down, Silloth, etc were full to capacity, and many aircraft were being dismantled in situ. There were still plenty of prangs taking place, and during his period with 58 MU, Ron kept a log of aircraft which he attended, numbering over 300, types including Tiger Moths, Tempests, Hurricanes, Lancs, Lincolns, Spitfires, Albemarles, Horsa gliders, Meteors — the list is endless. The working parties continued to roam far and wide, dealing with not only wrecks, but, at the other end of the scale, aircraft such as Lancs which had only a few hours flying on them from new. The working parties would break up aircraft into main sections after removal of engines, and which would then be carted back as several 'Queen Mary' loads to Skellingthorpe. Each working party would spend a week back there in rotation, further dismantling main sections into smaller components, preparing items to be saved (such as engines) for despatch elsewhere, with the remains taken into Lincoln to be loaded into railway wagons at Holmes Yard, to await their final journey to scrapyards at Newcastle-upon-Tyne. Similar things were happening countrywide as we disposed of our unwanted war surplus.

Ron Makinson and his team were ordered to Scampton on 1 July 1947. Their job: to dismantle three Lancasters and reduce to E2 category (ie scrap). To him, as SNCO, and his lads, it was just another routine job, which was to take them two weeks, following their usual drill — remove engines, tail and fins, outboard wing sections; then split the fuselage — nose and cockpit/centre/main fuselage and tail, and off they'd go on the Queen Marys to Skelly. This particular job is recorded in Ron's log book thus:

1.7.47 Job No 96 ED932 LANC SCAMPTON E2
10.7.47 Job No 97 ED906 LANC SCAMPTON E2
15.7.47 Job No 98 ED909 LANC SCAMPTON E2

Whilst he'd realized at the time, due to their unusual bomb bays, what they had been used for (ie the Dams raid), he and his team had given it no more than a passing thought, and their dismembered remains went the same way as all the others being processed by 58 MU at that time. It was only in later years that he was to recognise their significance, in particular that of ED932, which had been Guy Gibson's own 'AJ:G', the others having been flown on the raid by David Maltby (ED906 'AJ:J') and Mick Martin (ED909 'AJ:P'). Of the three, two — ED906 and ED932 — had done a few special ops after the Dams attack, as related elsewhere in this book (see 'The Inseparables'), but they were only of limited use, having been so extensively modified, their hydraulics in particular. They were held in reserve for some time at Metheringham, Coningsby and Woodhall, flown intermittently, and used for odd tests as also mentioned elsewhere in this book, but in early 1945 were flown up to 46 MU at Lossiemouth for open storage. They were revived in 1946 and flown down to Scampton to take part in 'Operation Guzzle', for disposal of the stock of bouncing bombs which remained in store, and which after over two years were becoming leaky and unstable. The three 'Provisioning Type 464s' were the only ones capable of dropping them. Over the period August/December 1946, the three Lancs, flown by Lincoln crews brought in on detachment from Nos 617, 9, 101 and 61 Sqns, took their unique loads well out into the Atlantic, and dropped them from medium level, most exploding on impact. Ironically, not long into 'Guzzle' numerous inquisitive Russian 'trawlers', all bristling with sensors and listening gear, started to congregate in the dropping zone, obviously thinking they were witnessing some new weapon being tested! Forty-four bombs were disposed of, plus another, a late discovery, in June 1947.

ED932 had reappeared at Scampton in January 1946, and was flown on a series of altitude an equipment tested in bad weather by the station's Test Flight (mainly by No 83 Sqn crews, who found its heating systems sadly lacking). It seems to have been at this juncture that she received her 'YF:C' codes (ie of Scampton Station Flight) to replace her latter-day No 617 Sqn markings of 'AJ:V', having lost her Dams Raid identity of 'AJ:G' (G-'George') soon after the raid itself. It seems that after these tests 932 returned to Lossiemouth, and came back to Scampton in August 1946 for 'Guzzle' accompanied by ED906 (which had assumed the mantle of 'AF:G' from 932 and ED909, which was still 'AJ:P' ['Popsie' as Mick Martin had always called her]). Before 'Guzzle' had started, it was found that ED932 needed all four engines changing, and, in the event, only flew on three of the 'ops', of which the first two were flown by

Flt Lt Steve Nunns on 23 and 31 October 1946. On the 3rd, piloted by Flg Off R. C. Norris on detachment from No 12 Sqn, she flew into a large flock of birds on lift-off from Scampton. In ducking down to try to fly beneath them, the part-retracted wheels struck the runway, and would then neither retract nor extend — a difficult situation with five tons of explosive dangling below. So Norris elected to continue the sortie, and the bomb was dropped in the Atlantic. He made a fine landing back at Scampton after a nail-biting 6 1/4hr trip, using emergency air to get the wheels down, but the crew not knowing if they were locked. ED932 was towed back to dispersal, being considered unsafe to taxy, and was declared Cat AC. It is not thought that ED932 flew again. (For this information we are very grateful to Dennis Mills, who was Flg Off Norris's flight engineer, doing 15 'Guzzles' with him, plus one with Steve Nunns.) The grounding of ED932 left 906 and 909 to carry on with the remaining disposals through November and December 1946, and they progressively became 'YF:A' and 'YF:B' respectively. It is thought that 906 did the final 'Guzzle' sortie in June 1947 flown by a No 61 Sqn crew. After that the days of the trio were numbered, and Ron and his team moved in to perform the final act.

That such historic aircraft should have been broken up without thought is incomprehensible to the preservationists of today. But that is how things were in 1947, and for nigh on 20 years to follow. However, all was not lost — quite. One man did do something to save a few small pieces of history...A. C. (Sandy) Jack, who has been mentioned earlier in this book, and who would have dearly loved to have preserved ED932. Despite his very senior position as Chief Inspector of AVRO's Lancaster Group, even he could not prevent the inevitable. However, he was aware of ED932's presence at Scampton, and on hearing on the grapevine (no doubt through one of the outworkers based at the AVRO repair depot at Bracebridge Heath) that she was being dismantled there, Sandy arranged to have certain items removed from ED932; the pilot's control column, and the quadrant housing the throttle, pitch and fuel cock levers, for posterity.

The dismantled remains of the three Lancs were taken to Skellingthorpe for final break-up, and it was probably there that the parts were removed for safe-keeping. Ron Makinson cannot recall it happening at Scampton. Whatever — the three Lancs' final journey to Newcastle inevitably followed, and that was the end.

'Big Ron' (picture above) became an acting flight sergeant, eventually moving with 58 MU to Newton, then for his last six months in the RAF returned to Scampton as an instructor, until demob in July 1950. Having married a Lincoln girl (May), he has remained in the area, working as a production (rather than 'destruction') supervisor at Ruston Bucyrus until retirement in 1982. Our thanks to Ron, for at least keeping his job records; and to Sandy Jack who departed this life a few years ago. Is Greta still going strong?

Bottom left, and below:
COVER STORY

The salvage heroes did have their moments of 'glory', being prominently featured in Picture Post of 18 September 1943, as seen in these photos, B1 and B2, struggling in adverse weather with a Lanc of 1660 HCU, Swinderby. The recovery of the machine itself was featured in the first volume of Lancaster at War, but these two pictures illustrate graphically the human effort required, the faces of the two lads from 58 MU, Newark, telling the story better than any words ever could. In the (Left:) picture, up to his knees in 'you-know-what', our hero has just secured the sling for lifting an inboard engine. Picture Post

Top right:
BOMB DUMP

A salvo of 2,000lb semi armour-piercing bombs falls away from a Lanc over Cardigan Bay, May 1946. Disposal of thousands of surplus bombs, which were becoming unstable after a few years in storage, was a useful task for those squadrons which continued to fly the Lancaster postwar, on such operations as 'Guzzle' and 'Wastage', the latter starting almost as soon as the war in Europe had ended. The North Sea was also a designated area, though the fishermen got a bit upset. In the 1950s, thousands more tons of surplus 'iron bombs', including 4,000lb Cookies were dropped by Lincolns in the campaigns against the communist terrorists in Malaya, and the Mau Mau in Kenya. The Lanc in this picture is a Mk I, PA332 'PH:S' of 12 Sqn, Binbrook, Vickers-Armstrong (Chester)-built, a near-contemporary of the RAF's flying example, PA474. Thought to be flown on this occasion by a crew from 101 Sqn, also at Binbrook, the two units frequently flying each other's aircraft, numbers of which had been cut right back by that time. '332 had started life with 57 Sqn, April 1945, eventually passed from No 12 to 300 'Masovian' Sqn, and was scrapped in March 1948. G. H. (Mick) Bridger

Right:
DEATH'S DUEL

Scenes like these were commonplace to the MU salvage gangs, never short of work right through to VE-Day and beyond. This is the wreck of No 227 Sqn's BIII PB610 '9J:O' on the grass at Balderton after return from Sassnitz 6/7 March 1945, and from which all on board escaped with but minor injuries to two of them.

As was not unusual, there was more to such a prang than a brief summary in the squadron's record book, as navigator Eddie Foster would relate with vivid clarity when, in retirement, recalling his war years.

Flg Off Eddie Foster DFM, an experienced navigator on his second tour (his first had been with No 467 Sqn RAAF, Bottesford in 1943), was approached one evening in the Mess by Flt Lt M. W. Bell and invited to join his crew on a temporary basis. His regular navigator, Flt Sgt P. T. Edwards, was away on a short kitting-out leave, having been recently commissioned. Eddie readily agreed. He'd been impressed by Northeasterner Bell, considering him a solid, conscientious pilot who would one day be an asset to a civil airline.

And so he went as spare bod navigator with his 'adopted' crew to Bohlen, 5/6 March 1945, and was duly accepted as an honorary member. It was a long, tiring outing of almost 10hr and there had thankfully been no navigational problems.

Barely, it seemed, had he slipped into blissful sleep when, just a few hours after landing, he was awakened by one of Bell's crew and again 'invited' to join them for another operation! Sassnitz, a small port on the island of Rügen in the Baltic, was to be the target, another nine or 10hr drag of a trip, which, in their present state of weariness, was hardly an appealing prospect. As it transpired, opposition from flak and fighters was negligible, but the long ride home seemed to go on for ever.

Perhaps Bell, after two long night trips at the controls was the most tired man aboard PB610, and could be excused the heavy contact with the ground when landing back at Balderton? The second bounce was followed by an alarming tilt to port as the tyre burst when the Lanc swerved violently off the runway, on to the grass. At some 80mph the port undercart then collapsed, causing the wingtip to carve up the drome as the tortured kite performed a screeching, shuddering cartwheel.

Despite holding grimly to any available structure, Eddie's head was still in transit when the forward motion ended abruptly and collided violently with the H₂S set. Momentarily stunned, he sat quite happily feeling that a sore head and a trickle of blood from under his helmet was a small price to pay for yet another entry in red in his log book.

Skipper Bell and his two up-front colleagues seemed to have other ideas as they scrambled hastily rearwards. Foster, in his bemused condition, could not understand their rapid retreat, but was grateful when they propelled him before them in the direction of the escape hatch. As he emerged through the top emergency exit the reason for their alarm became apparent. Half of the port wing was ablaze, the fire spreading towards the fuselage.

After 10hr flying, the petrol remaining was in the inboard tank and, conscious of the fact that this could explode at any time, he responded to the thrusting hands at his backside before leaping from the wing root to the ground and commencing a cross-country sprint, narrowly avoiding the arriving fire tender.

All the crew had managed to scramble clear and gather together at a safe distance to discuss their lucky escape. Rear gunner Sgt G. F. C. Stevenson had made a swift evacuation by turning his turret to one side and 'baling out' backwards in the approved manner. This resulted in mild concussion, and he and Eddie Foster, the only casualties, were taken, protesting, to the station sick quarters. A couple of aspirins and a piece of sticking plaster was the only medication the navigator required and he later joined the crew in the Mess for breakfast. Later that day they inspected the wreckage of PB610 and were shocked to see the fuselage in two separate sections, with all the Perspex turrets melted like toasted cheese.

Eddie did not fly with Bell and his boys again. Just a week later they were dead, shot down during a raid on Lützkendorf on the night of 14/15 March 1945. The last contact with them had been the transmission of their estimated wind from a position between 10° and 11° east and later it would be learnt that all were killed. C. Watson via E. Foster

Lower centre right:
Eddie Foster often reflects on his good fortune when looking at himself posing with one of the smashed-up Merlins from PB610. C. Watson via E. Foster

Bottom right:
Had not regular navigator Flg Off P. T. Edwards' commission come about when it did, Eddie would have been at the plotting table when Flt Lt M. W. Bell hauled BI PA214 '9J:P' off the runway and headed for Lützkendorf, never to be seen again in life. The whole crew, as seen here, is buried in the beautiful setting of the war cemetery at Durnbach, high in the mountains of Bavaria, where a reported nine out of ten graves are the resting place for young blades of Bomber Command. J. P. Holmes Collection

WINTER'S IRON FIST

Next time you join the milling throng at an air display on a summer's day, the afternoon sun beating down from a benign sky of blue, with here and there fleecy cotton-wool clouds, look about you. As likely as not, that old gentleman with a walking stick appearing to stare into space, as if in a trance, is a survivor of the bomber war, recalling days and nights of long ago when airfields were, too frequently, grim places to behold.

There were days, and nights, when hard-pressed ground staff found it well-nigh impossible to stand, let alone work on engines or fuelling or bombing-up, due to incessant winds howling like an army of banshees. There were days, and nights, of dense, choking fog or torrential rain, or cloying mud that meant more gritting of teeth... and there were the numbing frosts, the ice, the snow to do battle with as and when; each testing men, and women, and machines, to the limit of endurance, determination, often beyond the call of duty.

Snow, when it fell, was particularly troublesome. Such snowploughs as were available could not clear runways, dispersals and peri-tracks quickly enough and it befell the lot of all personnel, aircrew as well as erks, officers as well as NCOs and WAAFs, to turn out and take a turn with shovel, whatever was handy.

Take a gander at a quintuplet of snowbound settings far removed from traditional yuletide card canvasses.

Top left:
An ice and snow-bedecked No 156 Sqn Lanc at Upwood, Christmas 1944. An almost Dickensian setting... soon to be transformed... alive to the scraping of shovels as the graft to clear overnight snow must begin. J. B. Nicholls

Centre left:
On a day when most of Skipton-on-Swale's humanity is wisely indoors, doing its best to keep warm, Canuck Flg Off Don Sanders and his merry men find themselves on the duty roster, down for another bind of an exercise.
It is January 1945 and the 'Tigers' (No 424 Sqn RCAF) must continue to battle against time, and the elements, so as to complete its conversion to their newly-acquired Lancs before the month is out.
At first somewhat reluctant to give up their trusty Hally IIIs, which had seen them through 18 trips, Don and his brood soon came to appreciate their new steeds and successfully completed the last 15 ops of their tour on Lancs. S. D. Sanders

Bottom left:
A ground crew corporal balances precariously as he sweeps snow from BIII PB838 'OJ:M' of No 149 'East India' Sqn, Methwold, January 1945. Better him than us! H. Birch

Below:
Blizzard-hit Fiskerton looks more like a wilderness than an aerodrome. Snow-clearing teams in action and facing exhaustive, back-aching toil before No 576 Sqn Lancs can leave their bays. Another chilling reminder of how harsh it was during the last winter of the European war. E. K. Pollard

Inset:
Not exactly in the mood for having their picture taken is this trio, getting to grips with a Merlin at a freezing Binbrook or Ludford Magna dispersal. Study the character in their faces... visualise yourself out there, grappling with nuts and clips and pipes ice-cold to the touch... stamping your feet in a vain attempt to keep warm... cursing the Chiefy, the powers-that-be calling for a maximum effort... wishing that damned NAAFI van would hurry. Remember chaps? E. D. Evans

FOR OUR NEXT NUMBER...

Naturally, there is a tendency for those who wore air force blue in time of war — they who returned to civilian life and are now in the autumn of their lives — to recall the good times they had, to shut out the privations, the misery, the waste of human life. At no time in their lives have they enjoyed such comradeship, such simple pleasures. Seemingly, everyone accepted their lot, be they cook or adjutant, fitter or air gunner, be they volunteer, conscript or regular.

Morale was an important factor in fighting a war, and authority, alive to the need for providing a safety valve whereby personnel had sufficient time off in which to indulge in leisure pursuits, made certain each aerodrome had the necessary facilities. Who among men and women long since grandfathers and grandmothers can ever forget the frequent dances, parties and shows? Very orderly they were, too, and rarely did anyone step out of line, cause trouble, bring the service into disrepute. In a force where discipline was strict, if low key, and everyone knew the dividing line between familiarity and respect, self-pride was ever present, even when the beer flowed and actions became rather lively. Halcyon days and nights!

Here, a quartet of memory-joggers.

Top left:
Hear the strains of the Spilsby Station Band as it entertains assembled WAAFs and airmen. Perhaps it is early on in the proceedings? Certainly the girls will not remain 'wallflowers' for long. S. Burch

Centre left:
Or take a turn on the polished floor of the Wickenby NAAFI, the soothing tones of the band sounding every bit as good as maybe Roy Fox, perhaps Ambrose, forcing out thoughts of what might be happening in the world outside. Inevitably, many a romance flourished at such gatherings and it is warming to record that no small number of subsequent marriages are still intact 50 years and more on. A. E. Coles

Left and above:
With it being physically impossible to have ENSA and its like touring companies perform at other than irregular intervals, it was left to each station to organise its own home-grown entertainment. There was no shortage of volunteers, and here we see a Christmas 1944 concert in full swing at Waltham. At the microphone, ever-ready with a ditty, is No 100 Sqn Bombing Leader Flt Lt 'Ziggy' Zagerman; but who are the lads accompanying him on piano and banjo? K. Morland

"ONE CAME BACK"

'Vic' Huxley

The crest of the bat, widely known as the official badge of No 9 Squadron could well be adapted to the sign that now greets you as you ponder on what used to be the copse accommodating hundreds of airmen in quarters, the NAAFI and the Sergeants' Mess in this part of the bleak Lincolnshire countryside during the height of the 1939-1945 bombing offensive: Bardney.

It was with mixed feelings that late in September 1980, some 35 years after, whilst returning from a holiday in the Yorkshire Dales with my wife we chose to take a left turn off the A1. Soon we found ourselves approaching the prominent spires of Lincoln Cathedral, well-known to hundreds of aircrew as a familiar landmark on their return from bombing operations over occupied territory during the dark, anxious days of the war.

Finding bearings was somewhat difficult with all the additional roads, roundabouts and new developments; but eventually, on leaving Lincoln, keeping the city on our left, I began to realise I was on a familiar road — a road along which I had pedalled many times on an old RAF-issue green Hercules cycle for a "night on the town" in Lincoln with various old pals of 9 Squadron.

We had not travelled far before another familiar landmark appeared on the horizon — Bardney sugar beet factory!! I knew then I had come back.

Arriving in the village over the old iron bridge on a crisp, sunny September afternoon one was made aware that this little Lincolnshire village had seen many changes over the years. But, ah yes, there was the "local", the old cottage, the shop, still there; but above the tranquility of the afternoon one thing was distinctly absent — the roar of Merlin engines!

Approaching the old airfield one noticed a proud, solitary, silent building. Alone but still prominent, the old watch office looked out over what had once been a hive of activity but was now stilled — a building that, could it talk, would have vivid memories of bomber crews taking off, landing, and all the allied "chat" which passed over the intercom.

And, lo and behold, there in the far distance, the remains of "A" Flight dispersals. My mind immediately went back to the many dark, freezing-cold nights spent out there with the lads, all insulated in issue underwear, battledress, greatcoat, leather jerkin, Balaclava and woollen mitts to stave off the cold; the arrival at dispersal of wagons with the aircrew; the old coke stove ablaze in the hut, on which a few slices of bread would be toasted when the crews were airborne.

More memories crowded in: the tractor that refused to start; the cries in the night so often heard:
"Who's got the blue torches?"
"Who's for supper?"
"Where's my bike?"
These and many more memories of days and nights long past danced before my eyes.

A few yards further on, in the stillness of the afternoon I stood and gazed and pondered: there stood the old guardroom, the hangars and once vibrant crewrooms, the HQ block — all apparently put to good use by some contractor, and ideal offices for the present tenants.

Yet, beyond my thoughts I was aware of a feeling of sadness: here so very long ago the place was alive with dispersal wagons and petrol bowsers, fire tenders and ambulances; and, of course, all those issue Hercules, all going about their routine with the clockwork efficiency which made No 9 the squadron it was, and is I believe today.

Still reflecting, with a lump in my throat, I gazed to my right and there

in the distance was the copse, now far more mature, but still proudly surveying the field, the remains of — could it be — the mess, the NAAFI or cookhouse? All just a series of derelict Nissen huts, they had served their purpose.

As we proceeded along the crumbling road I was aware that, yes — this was the track leading to the mess, the billet or the NAAFI; but here I came upon the sign: 'No Admittance, Bird Sanctuary.'

Still having trouble with the lump in my throat, I could not resist the temptation! As one of the Bats of Adolf's Belfry surely this entitled me to a fleeting glimpse into the past?

My wife, obviously aware of my feelings, allowed me the privacy of strolling down the well trodden track alone whilst she waited in the car.

As I strolled through the copse the eerie silence was broken by the distinct repertoire of a blackbird. A flight of starlings flew overhead as I came upon the derelict framework of a few Nissens, once a part of everyday life here. One could reflect: here was the NAAFI, here was the mess. In the silence a lonely robin perched on the decaying framework unaware of my presence: what a difference to when the place was alive with the hustle and bustle associated with take-off time back in those autumn days almost 40 years ago.

The blackbird departed; then the robin looked down and as if to say "I'll leave you alone with your thoughts," likewise disappeared.

I was alone — alone with my thoughts to reflect. Yes, down this very road I had seen them come and go; new crews, new friends, new faces. I could almost hear them reply "Morning Sarge" as I recalled the chat to and from the mess:
"Morning Tav;"
"Hi'ya Pinky;"
"Goodnight Bill;"
"Hurry up Titch, your late, all the cocoa's gone. No bread left for toast and the NAAFI's shut!;"
"See you later Jacko."

Familiar names — and faces — kept coming back, and like the flight of the starlings that disappeared over the hedgerows, I was reminded of the Merlin sound, of kites "L for the Lady in Red," "G for George", "N for Nora" and "W for Winston," all disappearing into the night sky over the Lincolnshire countryside and asking oneself: "How many will return?"; but keeping such thoughts to myself.

Here was I, alone, pausing awhile to remember those who returned to Bardney, and those who did not. Realising my wife was still waiting, I turned to walk away and continue our journey; but as I ambled back along the track in the silence of the late afternoon, a well-known verse* with a slight alteration went through my mind:

"They shall grow not old,
As we that are left grow old.
Age shall not weary them,
Nor the years condemn.
But at the going down of the sun
This September
I came back to remember them."

*Footnote: From Laurence Binyon's poem "For The Fallen."

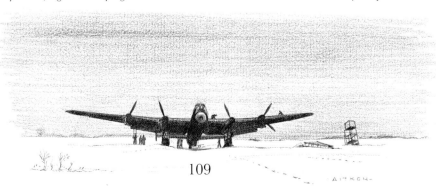

NO ESCAPE FROM MY PAST

'...These and many more memories of days and nights long past danced before my eyes...'

How often have we heard it said that our schooldays were the happiest, the most carefree years of our lives? Maybe they were, though we did not think so at the time! Equally, it can be argued that for those worthy souls who rallied to the clarion call in their youth, their years spent wearing air force blue were the most rewarding of their lives. Again, they may not always have thought so at the time!

There were times when they wished they were anywhere but their squadron, their station. For ground staff in particular there was substandard, ill-prepared food to stomach... seemingly endless petty restrictions to contend with... the all-too-frequent periods of boredom. Yet, was it not a time of unique friendship, a camaraderie never again experienced, enjoyed? Was it not a time of purpose and pride, honour and trust... far removed from the world of today where envy and greed, deceit and insincerity too often dominate the headlines?

Like so many before him, 'Vic' Huxley never forgot the years he spent serving his country. Finally, he could no longer resist the temptation to see again *his* place of the spirit. And, inevitably, his return was a mixture of rediscovery and disappointment, despair, sadness.

Below:
No rumble of Merlins coming from Lancs like 'Rosen Oboe' (BI ME757 'WS:O')... nor sign of No 9 Sqn's 'B' Flight earthbound bods who kept her in working order until the Hun claimed her when Brest was a daylight target on 13 August 1944 and seven braves led by Flt Lt E. H. M. Relton provided more unwanted work for Bardney's Committee of Adjustment. J. W. Allinson

Inset:
Not a trace of his pit (his bed), little different to this one. Not a brick, nor rusting remnant of corrugated iron could he find. E. D. Evans

SLEEPING ACCOMMODATION (apart from S.H.Q.).

The next question, apart from any way to the nearest Pub, is where to spend the night. The simplest thing to do is to phone the N.C.O. in charge of Number 2 Picquet Post and ask him what accommodation has been allotted to you. This will save a lot of unnecessary travel because although the various sites, in any of which you may find yourself, are quite near as the crow flies, as the Erk walks they are quite a tidy step, especially if the "Red Lion" is taken in on route.

Especially if the "Red Lion" is taken in on route.

Once in the correct hut, and equipment dumped, you can go over to 2 Site to collect your bedding. You will most probably view your new quarter with a somewhat jaundiced eye at first, however remember that your Hut-mates have come to regard it as their home and expect it to be in an habitable condition. So do your bit to help to keep it clean and tidy.

THE IMPRINT OF MAN

'...Here was I, alone, pausing awhile to remember those who returned to Bardney, and those who did not...'

A Bardney 'Vic' Huxley never knew... a mixture of the old and the new, rows of modern-day broiler houses steadily advancing along two of its runways, an abandoned postwar Thor missile site still well in evidence.

By air is now the most rewarding way to view, explore where once the Lancs sought flight... into a storm of sound, of blinding light, of deadly, whirling metal... and to which some returned to roost when night or day was done.

No stretch of the imagination could transport we who followed in their slipstream, from the relative comfort of an orbiting single-motor Cessna, into a Lancaster within which seven bone- and mind-weary blokes longed to pancake, sleep for a week.

It was one thing to be aloft from a not-so-distant Wickenby one golden autumn morning 42 years after the last Lancasters left Bardney; it was quite another to see ourselves as bleary-eyed aeronauts on return from up to nine hours airborne in a petrol-reeking, juddering Lanc, eager for a glimpse of white smoke rising from the sugar beet factory, or peering into the gloom for the bead-necklace of light that heralded the circuit. R. A. Davis

TWO OF THE MANY

'...I was reminded of the Merlin sound, of kites...all disappearing into the night sky...'

Anyone who served at Bardney will surely instantly recognise the work of Jackie Pattison, who was kept ever-busy gracing No 9 Sqn's Lancs with the female form (undeniably his favourite!), but who was equally at home applying Disney characters, whatever was requested by crews, with effortless ease.

'Tav' Tavener (who as flight sergeant bossed 'A' Flight ground staff) would remember BIII ED666 'WS:G' 'Goofy' were he still with us. He departed many years ago, and is sorely missed, but how many of his bods made it through to well-earned retirement? Can 'Smudge', 'Lofty' and the rest tell us about nursing 'Goofy' through 29 ops (including a Group recall and an abort when a motor went duff soon after take-off) during her five months of service? Do they remember that empty feeling finding her dispersal vacant when 6 September 1943 dawned... learning Plt Off T. H. Gill and his crew had not come back from Mannheim?

Do they recall posing for this picture a day or so after Sgt Gill (as he then was) had steered her to and from Peenemünde, 17/18 August 1943, the nose of ED666 suitably adorned? We could fill a book with such pictures. S. L. Huxley

GOOFY

GOOFY

JOE · JACK · TAV · SMUDGE · LOFTY · TWH

Above:

Certainly 'Vic' Huxley does. Here he is seen in the cockpit of BIII JA852 'WS:L', 'The Lady in Red', giving a typically Churchillian gesture. Do 'Dunnit', Bill, Joe, 'Darky' and 'Tich', his trusty erks, also remember? How many of you are still with us? Vic awaits your call. And what about artist 'Jackie'? How often do you find yourself leafing through yellowing prints you must have by the dozen, reminding you of your artistry? Studying the figures, legends and symbols you painted on No 9 Sqn kites has been fascinating.

On JA852 we know that two ice-cream symbols represent trips to Turin on 12/13 July and Genoa on 15/16 July 1943, both undertaken by Flt Lt Dickie Bunker and crew. We realise that a palm tree (barely discernible next to the second ice-cream cone) tells us that, when the intended target of Reggio Nell Emilia could not be located due to adverse weather that night of 15/16 July, Bunker opted to bomb Genoa (despite losing an engine) and went on to land in North Africa.

Are we right to assume that an RAF eagle and crown with 'OHMS' underneath indicates the carrying of a high ranking official, for we know Bunker skippered JA852 through Gibraltar on the way home a week later? Intriguing! Are any of Dickie Bunker's crew still around to fill us in?

And who suggested the legend 'Allez en haut d'escaliers!', which needs but little translation!

Like so many of her breed, JA852 did not survive long, going down on Mannheim, 23/24 September 1943, flown by Sgt R. C. Ord and his fellow freshmen (it was only their second operation). We will add that compilers of unit ORBs were not averse to making mistakes and on this occasion recorded JA852 as ED399 — a Lancaster never built! J. Gaskell

LAUNDRY SERVICE.

This is a bit of a bind, but still you had better read it, if only to get some idea as to what happened to your laundry between the time you packed it up and failed to have it returned.

All laundry is to be made up securely in bundles and accompanied by a label supplied by the contractors (they are called this because of their habit of shrinking everything they lay their hands on) bearing your Station, No., Rank, Name, Hut number, and Site number, all in CAPITAL LETTERS.

Eight articles may be sent and no more, these eight may be selected from the following.

R.A.F.

Collars	Vests
(2 count as one article)	Drawers
Handkerchiefs	Shirts
(3 to count as one article)	Towels (hand)
Socks	Gym shorts, Gym vests

W.A.A.F.

Shirts	Collars
Belts	(3 to count as one article)
Knickers	Brassieres equals 1
Pyjamas	corselette
(1 suit to count as one article)	Pantees
Towels	Stockings
Ties	Cardigans

One article may not be substituted for another. For example :—Two shirts may not be included in the place of one pair of socks and one towel. If more than eight articles are included in the bundle, the Contractor will return the whole bundle unwashed (Decent of him) and in addition there is a possibilty of the excess items being mislaid. The total number of articles is to be placed in the space at the foot of the label.

All garments are to be marked with your number and name. Bundles are to be handed into the Picquet Post. The latest time for this will be given to you on application when you collect your clean laundry. Newcomers must just ask one of the old stagers.

All queries regarding laundry must be accompanied by the label which was submitted with the bundle, and should be raised the day following receipt of laundry by the Picquet Post, in order that action may be taken with the Contractor.

The above is mainly all theory, in practice it is found simpler to wash your smalls yourself.

WE WHO DO NOT KNOW, AND CAN NEVER KNOW

There is, we feel, far more to the study of the Lancaster than recording its development and production, its operations telling of the aircrews who flew this symbol of defiance, this means of hitting back at him and his fiends who would terrorise and overrun Europe.

It is as much about civilians whose lives were either directly or indirectly touched by it, be they staff and shop floor workers at the factories, so proud of their involvement, or farmers and villagers living within the shadow of aerodromes, so tolerant of the blue-uniformed 'invasion' which dominated their community.

There are, too, those then-too-young to have served their country in time of war, but who could not resist what was happening at the aerodromes beyond their villages, their towns, and who still today take an active interest in all matters concerning the Lancaster. And there are the then-unborn who have followed in our wake, and who have chosen their own paths of discovery.

Come with us and share the experiences of two who, like your two chroniclers, *do not know and can never know* what it was like to go to war in Lancasters, nor indeed support them from the relative safety of the ground.

"PICTURES IN MY MIND"

John Delanoy

I stopped the tractor, climbed down and walked onto the very spot where 'IL:A' had stood. Oily stains could still be seen. Some skid marks were visible and a cycle clip showing signs of the onset of rust, was lying, doubtless where it had fallen months earlier. Tenacious weeds were already forcing their heads between the joints in the tarmac, giving notice of Mother Nature's determination to take charge once again. Where lately there had been a mighty roar, now there was an eerie silence. It was a lonely place. My friends had gone away, never to return. For their sakes I was glad, but I could not suppress a feeling of deep sadness. What was 'IL:A?' Who were my friends? Where was I?... 'IL:A' was a great Lancaster bomber, my friends were its crew and I was standing on the dispersal pan which had been the recent home of this magnificent aeroplane. As I returned to my ploughing alongside this hardstanding, I pondered the Freudian elements: There was I, haunted by a thousand memories, helping as it were to turn swords into ploughshares (I hit the odd concealed runway light base, and so needed a few of the latter anyway!) with the sound of the mighty Lancasters still ringing in my ears.

Roger Sykes, a schoolfriend of mine who was seeking a career in farm management, had taken a job with a local farmer, to learn the trade, as it were. One of his first tasks was to plough up the now-agricultural acres of Witchford aerodrome. He came to see me and asked if I could help, since he had at his disposal two Caterpillar tractors and only one driver: himself. The interests of a perpetual schoolboy most certainly embrace an activity such as this and I accepted his invitation with great enthusiasm, fascinated to find myself there on the very airfield from which my favourite aeroplane had so recently flown.

I was born in King's Lynn, Norfolk in November 1930 and from a very early age it became apparent that I was indeed destined to be a lifelong schoolboy. Any mechanical device that actually moved was like a magnet to me, and to this day, nothing has changed! Coasters, entering and leaving the port of King's Lynn, caught my attention from the very beginning, and if the docks' tug had a head of steam... well! When a steam lorry passed by on the main road I had to drop everything and rush to admire its leisurely progress, and I was ecstatic if the steamroller happened to be working in the district. On the local pond, skilled model-makers sailed their home-built yachts. I found these irresistible. The pond was long and narrow, like a section of a river, and the modellers worked in pairs, one on each bank, sailing their vessels across to each other. On one occasion, the ice-cream vendor (on his tricycle) appeared on the far bank and sold his wares to both sailors. One wafer was then ceremoniously placed in the hold of the yacht. I recall that to see a cargo thus borne across the water was a concept which truly appealed to my imagination. (The coins representing the cost of the ice-cream had been sent across on the previous trip.) Predictably, any activity on the railway was also guaranteed to command my full attention and I was especially interested in the shunting operations in and around the docks, the little 0-6-0 tank engines with long strings of trucks being firm favourites.

All of the foregoing, however, paled into comparative insignificance when an aeroplane put in an appearance. For me, the aeroplane represented the pinnacle of mankind's achievement, eclipsing even the steamroller! The sound of an approaching aircraft was the trigger which sent my brother and me rushing to scale the heights of the coal bunker in the garden, in order to get the best view of the 'plane as it passed by. In those days this was not a regular occurrence and so each manifestation caused great excitement. Vigorous arm-waving was directed towards each aircraft, regardless of whether it was flying at 1000 or 10,000 feet!

Then one day there came to town what was the forerunner of the modern air show. The redoubtable (Sir) Alan Cobham brought his "circus" to King's Lynn. Because my father's job involved access to the dock area, he was able to obtain permission for us to secure an elevated vantage point atop a storage tank which was adjacent to the chosen flying field. No doubt by modern standards this early display would be regarded as a rather tame affair, but to me it represented the highlight of my life to that date. I could talk of nothing else.

From about this time onward, air activity began to increase, keeping pace with the gathering of distant clouds of war. For Christmas my uncle gave my brother and me each a traditional balsa-and-tissue paper flying model, ready-built by his air-minded brother-in-law. Mine was my prize possession until a heavy-handed grown-up picked it up to inspect it and in so doing crushed all the ribs and stringers aft of the trailing edge of the wing, thereby rendering it a constructional total loss! At about the same time, my brother's model suffered a heavy crash and was also written off. I was shattered, but my brother, unperturbed, began building his own balsa models. I followed suit, though I remember that my early efforts left a great deal to be desired.

War came, and in 1941 my father was called-up. He did not return. Our family moved to Ely in Cambridgeshire (which was where my mother's parents lived) and there I spent the remainder of the war. Nearly ten years old when war broke out, I was old enough to be fascinated by the whole business, but too young to realise the tragic aspects of the conflict. Ely emerged almost totally unscathed at a time when, at only 70 miles distance the London blitz was at its height. On many a dark night the German bombers droned past towards the large industrial towns which were their targets. Ely did suffer the odd bomb or two and we heard a few doodlebugs but I realise now how lucky I was. All that would excite a schoolboy was there, minus the horror ingredient.

For the innocent lover of aeroplanes, East Anglia was then the only place to be. The building of the massive concentration of wartime airfields in this area has already gone in to the history books as one of the greatest-ever achievements in the field of civil engineering. The staggering numbers of aircraft which could be airborne at one time from these bases presented an awesome spectacle to those privileged to watch. As a schoolboy I counted, in a single morning, 2,175 aircraft comprising Fortresses, Liberators, Mustangs, Thunderbolts and others, which roared by in successive waves. As it happened all of these were American, and one wonders just how many Allied planes in total could have been fielded in any exercise to launch everything that was airworthy.

AITKEN

As thrilling as it was to see these great armadas in the sky, I nevertheless yearned to see them on the ground. But a problem which could not be appreciated by youngsters today was that of wartime communications. My only means of practical local transport then was my pedal cycle. To those now used to uncensored local and national radio and TV, local and national newspapers plus a comprehensive telephone service, and who can also pop out in their cars to tour the locality. To them it must seem incredible that there were several airfields within my not-inconsiderable pedalling range, the existence of which did not become known to me until after the war.

I believe it was in 1942 that work began on an airfield to be located at Witchford, a mile or two from Ely. I knew about that one! As the work progressed, my excitement grew! In 1943 the airfield was ready for use. Wellingtons appeared, followed by Stirlings, but at first the planes were, to my disappointment, concentrated centrally and were difficult to see clearly from the public road. Then in November the Lancasters arrived. The first ones were of the Mark II radial-engined type, and in keeping with the new policy of dispersal these were more widely spaced. Many were plainly visible from vantage points on the roadway, and some of the hardstandings, to my delight, were surprisingly close. The nearest of these was alongside the Ely-Witchford road and it was there that, over many months, I spent numerous hours entirely absorbed in watching all the comings and goings. Attending school was a terrible nuisance!

The Lancaster was to the bomber what the Spitfire was to the fighter and it followed that it had to be my favourite four-engined aircraft. For as long as daylight permitted, my routine did not vary. As soon as I arrived home from school a hasty (rationed) meal was consumed; out came the trusty bike and then off to Witchford to monitor the war's progress! when the Lancasters were warming-up prior to take-off for a raid, they could be clearly heard from my home: It was the signal for another cycle sprint record to be broken! I would watch enthralled as the bombers taxied to their take-off positions. My earlier fascination with the yacht and its waterborne cargo of ice cream extended equally to the aeroplane's ability to become airborne with its cargo of bombs. Observing the heavily-laden machines struggle into the air was unbelievably exciting to a youngster who at that time was totally unaware of the feelings of the crew, hoping and praying as they no doubt were that they might, against all the odds, survive.

It must have been in the spring of 1944 that the radial-engined Lancasters were replaced by Rolls-Royce-engined ones. The somewhat harsher note of the in-line engines was for me an even louder clarion call, and no aircraft movement escaped my notice. A particular aircraft was allotted to "my" hardstanding. It's identification letters were 'IL:A.' I cannot remember how many pilgrimages I made to see 'IL:A' but I do recall that in my household it became a password, symbolising the entire Bomber Force! It never occurred to me for a moment that one day it might fail to return, and mercifully it never did. Such was my confidence and faith that, if it was not in position, I always assumed that it would shortly reappear; and it always did so.

Meanwhile, construction of model aircraft (begun when the fragile Christmas presents came to grief) now gathered pace. Materials were restricted to low-grade balsa and obechi wood. Balsa cement was often in short supply and we frequently used some dubious-looking yellow glue which we heated on the obligatory "Valor" pipe-shaped stove, the latter in the winter serving also as the sole source of heating. The room used was a spare downstairs bedroom which today would probably glory in the name of "study", though such niceties were not fashionable in the '40s. I remember that my brother and I each had a worktable on opposite sides of the room. Imitating then current Air Ministry practice we used to devise a build-specification for a particular aircraft. (It was normally a very simple formula such as 'Maximum span 24" for long-range' or 'Maximum span 18" for high speed'.) We would then each build a free-lance model to this agreed specification. Neither would peep at the other's efforts until the great unveiling ceremony. When inactivity at Witchford permitted, assembly proceeded at a feverish pace. The only allowable interruption was the then-frequent dash outdoors to identify every overflying aircraft. My brother, who was by that time showing all the signs of oncoming technical brilliance, installed a sophisticated early-warning device in the shape of a microphone and reflector at the top of a tall aerial pole situated in the garden. The associated receiver/amplifier occupied pride of place in the model-making room. As I recall, we heard more Starlings than Stirlings but it was all part of the fun!

When the latest "secret" prototypes emerged, there followed the inevitable competition to see whose plane would be the winner. My brother's models were precisely built and well finished. Mine were the reverse of this, being rather floppy and having glued joints which did not always bear close inspection. My brother usually won the speed events and I the duration contests. Probably the lack of rigidity in the wings of mine produced an ornithopter-like effect which helped to prolong the flight!

My mother, hearing of nothing but the legendary 'IL:A,' suggested that I might like to write to the crew. Although rather shy about the whole idea, I gladly did so. Apparently, upon receipt of the letter the Flight Commander, with mock ceremony sent for the skipper who, receiving the unexpected summons, was frantically searching his conscience! In due course I received a reply: A letter signed by the entire crew. This letter is now one of my most treasured possessions.

Shortly afterwards, the captain and the wireless operator (both Australians) paid a visit to my home. They were intrigued to see the modelling den, the walls of which were covered mainly with pages from an aircraft recognition

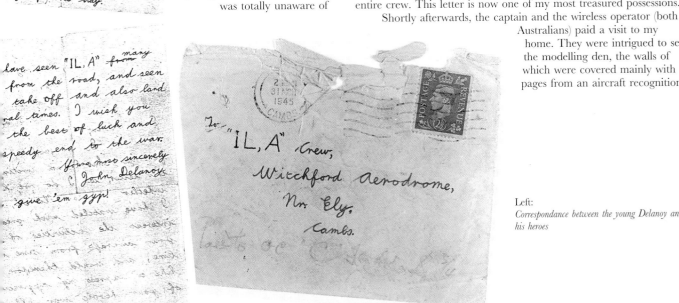

5, Railway Terrace,
Ely,
Cambs.
30. 3. 45.

Dear Crew,

It is with mixed feelings that I am writing this letter, as I do not know whether it is allowed, but I have watched with great interest the activities of ... aircraft from time to ... and would therefore ... to express my appreciation ... our heroic war effort. Although I am only a ... boy, I hope to become a ... myself one day.

... have seen "IL, A" from many from the road, and seen take off and also land ... times. I wish you the best of luck and speedy end to the war.

Yours most sincerely
John Delanoy

... give 'em gyp!

To "IL, A" Crew,
Witchford Aerodrome,
Nr. Ely,
Cambs.

Left:
Correspondance between the young Delanoy and his heroes

publication, *The Aeroplane Spotter*. I would be safe in saying that every service aeroplane then in existence was displayed somewhere in that room, and in most cases portrayed many times over. Among the collection was one of those magnificent "ghosted" drawings featuring the Lancaster bomber. At about that time, although not old enough to join the Air Training Corps, I had an opportunity to have a shot at their aircraft identification tests. I scored 100%, but the less said about other scholastic achievements the better! Although with one or two exceptions our model aircraft were on the small side, output in common with full-sized aircraft at this time, was very high. Evidence abounded of volume production at every stage.

Completed planes, some showing crash damage, hung from the picture rail while wings, tailplanes and partly completed fuselages littered the tables. Under wraps (quickly removed in honour of the guests) were the latest designs conforming to the most recently-formulated specification. From what I remember, my aircrew visitors were quite impressed by what they saw, and they generously asserted to my mother that they had learned more about aircraft during that visit than they had absorbed over all the preceding years!

I fear that I was completely overawed by their presence. These men to me were Gods. There before me stood the very crewmen who took those mighty aircraft to Germany and back. On numerous occasions I had caught glimpses of the aircrew at their stations within the aircraft. That alone was a great thrill for me; but there they were "wings" and all, and in the same room! Perhaps the passage of time has removed the schoolboy adoration aspect of this encounter, but the admiration and the awe remain.

The two Aussie crew members of 'IL:A' were, at the time of their visit, rapidly approaching the end of their tour of operations and in consequence they were more than usually apprehensive about the prospects for their remaining sorties.

At the every next opportunity, I was in position on my favourite spot. 'IL:A' was absent, and so were most of the other aircraft. I did not worry. Suddenly there was a familiar sound, distant at first but growing louder. Four Lancasters appeared. They approached the circuit in turn. The windsock had already told me that the bombers would be landing virtually over the top of my head. Lovely! They began to "put their boots on," as other squadron aircraft appeared on the horizon. With a succession of thunderous crescendos the Lancasters passed a few feet above me to make their landings. I am sure that members of one particular crew were in their last operation on that occasion, for the rear gunner gave a quick squeeze of the firing mechanism. The four Brownings burst into life and volumes of shredded cabbage erupted from a nearby field! It was, I felt sure a gesture of "joie de vivre." Ever faithful, 'IL:A' joined the circuit and landed in great style, taxiing the long way back to its hardstanding. By that time, the daylight was beginning to fade but I could nevertheless see my own enthusiastic waves reciprocated by the crew members. That particular operation had, of course, been a daytime raid, and its very execution bore witness to the complete air supremacy gained by the Allies by that time.

It would have been in early April 1945 that the two Australians came to see me, and according to the airfield's recorded history the final raid carried out from Witchford took place on April 24th 1945. Apart from the dropping of food supplies to the unfortunate Dutch people, no further operations took place.

'IL:A' had survived. Praise-be!

Thereafter, to my disappointment, the aircraft were taken from their dispersal areas and grouped at the centre of the airfield. Hope of further contact, and of a crew photograph then faded rapidly, especially since the aircraft were again barely visible from the public roads.

The wheel had turned full circle.

The airfield was closed down in March 1946.

Forty years have passed. I still make aeroplanes and my intense interest in flying machines has never diminished. In 1972 I realised a burning ambition to "have a look up there" when I took up the sport of gliding. I gained a qualification known in gliding circles as a Silver C and thereafter obtained a private pilot's licence. I held this until 1986, when rising costs and falling income forced me to abandon my much-loved hobby. The Auster and the Piper Cub were the nearest "wartime" aircraft that I got to fly, but in dabbling about in the skies over East Anglia (STILL the place to be for flying!) visual evidence of many of the old wartime airfields never failed to bring back a flood of poignant memories.

Above:
THE AGES OF MAN
'...Time will run back, and fetch the age of gold...'
Milton's words seem appropriate when pondering on John Delanoy's memories of youth. Here he is seen as a schoolboy aged about 12, looking remarkably composed, if revealing an impish smile. Not so different when in his 50s, content with life in his beloved East Anglia. J. W. Delanoy

Left:
A schoolboy's dream come true! The reply from Skipper and crew of Lanc IL:A

116

Above:

IN HEREWARD'S WAKE*

'...It was in 1942 that work began on an airfield to be located at Witchford, a mile or two from Ely...'

Witchford: as clear an aerial view as you are likely to find and taken one fine day in August 1945 when resident No 115 Sqn (whose Lancasters are here visible on their hardstandings) was preparing to pack its bags and depart for Graveley, another war-emergency aerodrome not many miles distant.

Thereafter, save for the odd Oxford and Anson lobbing in, Witchford was devoid of aircraft, though the station did not officially close until March 1946, abandoned despite government assurances made during the war that all such airfields would be expunged and the land fully restored.

Ask any of the locals — villagers and farmers alike — who remember those days and they will regale you with stories associated with clearing the area and constructing yet another of the springboards from which Bomber Command could 'Strike Hard, Strike Sure'.

Despite warnings about it being the Isle of Ely and an appreciable slope likely to cause drainage problems (borne out in no uncertain manner), work went ahead.

Working round the clock the construction gangs overcame more than the odd obstacle (a story in itself, not without humour!) and by June 1943 Witchford was ready for use.

First unit to move in was No 196 Sqn with Wellingtons but its stay was short, leaving in November, by then equipped with Stirlings.

Barely had the sound of Hercules radials died down when No 115 Sqn with its like-engined Lancaster IIs arrived in the early hours of 27 November 1943, having taken off from its former base Little Snoring and bombed Berlin (though crews had, of course, familiarised themselves with their new home a day or so earlier).

It was in April 1944 when the first Lancs with in-lines flew in and thereafter the raucous growl (dare we say music!) of Merlins became an accepted intrusion, as much a part of rural life as the cawing of rooks, the chugging of farm tractors.

Note that no attempt has been made to camouflage the acreage, the runways (the main runway, west to east, measuring 2,000 x 50yd) in particular disfiguring the landscape, then and for aeons to come, albeit in steadily reducing form as farmers set about tearing up concrete and an industrial park developed on the former technical site. Some hangars and buildings still remain, and the site is now bordered by the Ely bypass. A. K. Holt

* Footnote:

Almost 1,000 years ago, Hereward The Wake put up an heroic defence against William The Conqueror in nearby Ely.

Right:
COME ON IN!

'...East Anglia was then the only place to be...'
Witchford, at work and play, as a dwindling,
privileged band of mortals will remember it.
A rare glimpse inside the watch office showing
the flying control staff at work. Observe how
spartan the room is, how basic the furniture —
far removed from the sophisticated equipment to
be found in control towers (as they are now
called) at Royal Air Force stations today and
where quite a number of the fair sex are still
on active duty!

Half a hundred years ago, throughout
bomber country — indeed the RAF as a whole
— WAAFs by the score did a job second to
none as watch keepers (their official trade title).
To tired crews returning from mind- and
sinew-sapping operations the soft, yet
authoritative, tones of a WAAF coming over
the R/T, giving stacking heights and landing
instructions, was the most wonderful sound.

For those on the ground, fortified by
innumerable cups of tea, coffee, cocoa, the
sitting, pacing, waiting, wondering, well into
the small hours, would take its toll on the
nerves. Many of the sweet-voiced WAAFs
would have boyfriends, fiancés, even husbands
up there, not knowing when — or if — their
call-sign would crackle out of the speaker, or if
they would become another gap in the 'returned'
column of the ops board, with hopes gradually
fading when all diversions had been accounted
for.

Does anyone recognise a face in our picture?
Where are such unsung stalwarts now — those
still among us — all these years later?
J. N. M. Heffer

Right:
'EWS.' A striking example of what men of
initiative and enterprise could do to improve
their lot. Who suggested modifying twin
emergency water supply tanks on this Witchford
communal site is long forgotten, but it was
certainly an inspired idea, and doubtful if Air
Ministry approval was sought!

The general motley collection of the huts of
the domestic and admin sites in the background
bear more than a passing resemblance to those
of the POW camps to which many aircrew
were consigned.

How many of these young fellows, now
grandfathers in the autumn of life, wish they
still weighed in at 10 stones wringing wet?!
S. Wood

BATH ARRANGEMENTS.

Showers, and constant hot water are situated on No. 1 Communal Site. (You lucky people). Well anyhow the tap's got "HOT" written on it.

"The taps got "HOT written on it."

PRIVATE CALL TELEPHONE SERVICE.

There is one private telephone call box on the Station, this is located on No. 1 Comm. Site. The Queue ends somewhere near the N.A.A.F.I.

118

Left:
ONE FOR THE ALBUM

'...I fear that I was completely overawed by their presence. These men to me were Gods...'

Aussie Flt Lt Jim Robson and most of his 'C' Flight No 115 Sqn crew pose in line before their trusty steed, BI HK698 'IL:A' at Witchford. Their last op — Kiel, 9/10 April 1945 — is behind them, the war in Europe is over, and soon they will enjoy a final drink together, share a last yarn and joke before dispersing, never to meet again as a group.

With, daily, the Sqn's Commonwealth men being posted home there is a hurried call for a crew picture. But already it is too late for all the crew to be present. Rushing round the Mess, the gunnery section, it is a case of grabbing who is at a loose end, who is willing to help out. Standing in for regular rear gunner Sid Stromquist will be a gunner whose name will be quickly forgotten, whilst mid-upper Len Alger's place will be taken by one Les 'Nick' Carter who frequently flew with them as a mid-under gunner (HK698, in common with other 'C' Flight Lancs, being fitted with an extended bomb bay and rather basic under-gun position).

Identities and crew duties, left to right: navigator: Flt Sgt Les Rossiter; mid-under gunner: Flt Sgt 'Nick' Carter; spare mid-upper gunner: Name unknown; wireless operator: WO Don Looker, RAAF; pilot: Flt Lt Jim Robson, RAAF; flight engineer: Sgt Wally Hallatt; bomb aimer: Flt Sgt Sid Adamson.

What happened to HK698? Within six months her days of usefulness were over and she was flown to the huge graveyard set up at No 20MU, Aston Down, there to be scrapped during November 1945. J. T. Robson

FOCUS ON MY YOUTH
Then-and-now glimpses of Witchford.

Centre left:
One of the few dispersals still identifiable is this one — possibly the very one on which 'IL:A' was parked — now a handy storage area for a farmer's hay. J. W. Delanoy

Below:
A setting similar to the one John Delanoy would have known so well. This 'spectacle' dispersal supports Lanc I HK790 'KO:Y' from No 115 Sqn's 'B' Flight during the same period. Note how featureless the terrain is. S. Wood

'...I stopped the tractor, climbed down and walked on to the very spot where 'IL:A' had stood...'

Jim Robson and his boys would find little to recognise at Witchford five decades on from when last they saw it, knew its every twist and turn as much from the air as they did from the ground... knew it as well during their few months there as they would the village or town, their home in boyhood or retirement.

Pictures in their minds would, understandably, be confused, fragmented. True, there on the skyline would be the towering presence that is Ely Cathedral, beckoning them as old men, just as did it beckon them in their youth. But where was the airfield, its once familiar black hangars, ugly and incongruous, the girderwork-supported water tower hardly less so...?

That bypass was not there in '45 and, were it not for roads named 'Stirling Way' and 'Lancaster Way' they would not know where the technical site had been. Too many years had passed.

Above:
PASTORALE

'...and some of the hardstandings, to my delight, were surprisingly close...'

Like all war-emergency aerodromes, Witchford truly blended into the landscape. Our vista, taken perched atop the starboard-inner of No 115 Sqn's 'KO:H' (possibly B III ND790 or successor, BI LM127), clearly illustrates how rural they were.

For much of their perimeter all that separated them from adjoining farms, villages and woods were hedges and fences. Topped with coils of barbed-wire seemingly laid without enthusiasm, they posed little challenge to enterprising aircrew and ground staff intent on slipping in or out of the airfield unnoticed.

After all, during a lull, who could resist tea and home-made cakes at the farmhouse little more than a stone's throw from dispersal!

With perimeters so readily easy to penetrate, security did occasionally cause a stir. Whilst there were few incidents of sabotage by agents — none at Witchford that we know of — more worrying were forays by diddicoys and their like who stealthily removed equipment large and small at the dead of night. Certainly Witchford had one or two wheel/tyre assemblies from trolley accs 'lifted'. Such guards as were posted at night, ill-equipped as they were to tackle an intruder, usually slept part of their duty in the kites!

Points to note in our summer 1944 picture are the de-icers directly in front of the cockpit windscreen, and control column locking bar on 'KO:H'.

For the purist 'KO:G' was BI ME692, new in March 1944, which went down on Wilhelmshaven 15/16 October 1944 (the last major attack on the port by Bomber Command) with Flg Off J. P. Perry and crew. ND790 was a casualty on the successful but costly night raid on Chevreuse, 7/8 June 1944, Skipper Plt Off S. F. Francis and his boys joining five other No 115 Sqn crews failing to make it back to Witchford. All told, 17 Lancasters and 11 Halifaxes were lost. LM127 fell victim to the enemy on the night of 26/27 August 1944, Plt Off J. E. Morgan and company setting out for Kiel on a one-way ticket. A. R. Ashley

THE FICKLE HAND OF FATE

'...The daylight was beginning to fade...'

To John Delanoy the Lancasters of No 115 Sqn's 'A' Flight, dispersed away on the far side of Witchford, would have appeared as little more than a blur. He was not to know that one hardstand — that of 'KO:E', BI HK555 — was the habitat of a Lanc destined to become the unit's top scorer, a veteran which returned time and time again and seemed certain to reach her century. It was not to be. On the night of 4/5 April 1945, target Merseburg and at least the old girl's 98th op, she collided with another Lancaster (BI RA533 'XY:P' from sister Sqn No 186, Stradishall, with Flg Off J. A. G. Beck, RAAF and crew aboard) over Giesh, Belgium when returning, taking to their deaths the final crew — Skipper Flt Lt Tom O'Halloran — lost by 115 in World War 2.

Equally unknown to our schoolboy enthusiast was the fact that the press corps made regular visits to Witchford. Such an occasion was 12 March 1945, a day when No 115 took part in a massive 1,000-bomber daylight/dusk assault on Dortmund. Among a score or more of pictures taken during a near-24hr stay were these two:

Top:
Tom O'Halloran and company on their return.
Even if HK555's ground crew were a day or two behind painting on the latest bomb symbols, she still reveals an impressive 90-op tally. Identities are, left to right — Rear gunner: Sgt Tommy Buckley; Mid-upper gunner: Sgt Ernie Sheavills; Navigator: Flt Sgt Gordon Carr; Bomb aimer: Flg Off Bert Adams; Pilot: Fl Lt Tom O'Halloran; Wireless operator: Flt Sgt Gordon Saville; Flight engineer: Flt Sgt Eddie Marchant.
via C. L. Petty

Above:
With the shadows beginning to lengthen as the day wears on, the welcoming crackling and popping of Merlins, the rhythmic threshing of propellers break the silence as 115 returns. via J. T. Robson

121

REMEMBER

Remember us, we would ask you, through dawn
And the break of day
And recall us then with your quiet prayers,
In the lofting sun's first rays.

Know that we ensured your freedom,
But grieve not at the cost.
For better far pay the final price,
Than to suffer your future lost!
Then ever an airman's honour, but
Never an airman's shame.
For we gave all for freedom's call; and
Died in our country's name.

Remember us, we would ask you, through sunset's
Last red glow
Then salute us all with the bugle's call; for
The dawns that we'll never know.

John Roy Walsh November 1985)

THRESHOLD

Do you gather here ready for take-off
Through soft dusk, as the day slowly dies?
Are you forlorn and forgotten in anguish,
Bound for battle in long empty skies?

I sense your brave souls all about me;
Though your conflict is long past and gone;
While your home base crumbles around us,
Do you still hear the Merlins' great song?

Must you come sadly here in pale twilight
Through soft dusk, as the day slowly dies?
Are you alone and forgotten, just shadows
Or still airborne in the dark silent skies?

I can feel your courage around me.
Do you still haunt this old airfield site?
Maybe watch me unseen as I visit,
Do you still fear that very last flight?
When that swift Shining Sword was your weapon;
And a thirty Op' tour your crusade,
Now Lancaster men still remember
And honour brave sacrifice made.

John Roy Walsh (September 1985)

DRAWN UPON THE WIND

Once more we come together as those days of yore,
To stand here in the sighing wind, as we'd done so oft' before.
Empty bleak dispersals, blank reminders of our past,
No armed-up Lancs for us to crew, but we've returned at last.
No Browning guns or dinghy drills, no tension in our guts;
Nor massive props in silhouette, nor draughty Nissen huts.
With vivid memories of Berlin's hell, or Essen, or Cologne;
Of Squadron crews who'd got the chop, on ops we all had flown.
We few now walk in silence where once our Lanc sought flight;
Bombs and petrol, men and fear, borne swift by Avro's might.
Recalling Hercs or Merlins, four engines at full cry;
Across this runway broad strong wings, courting lift to fly.
We brothers from a time gone by, bound by memory's freeze,
Seeking echoes of a gallant band, faint voices on the breeze.

John Roy Walsh (June 1986)

QUESTIONS

Where do they bide, those heroes
Those bods who never flew home?
Are they out of sight in the still dark night
And is there peace where their spirits roam?
Or do they still haunt deserted dromes now
To beseech aid midst the chatter of Morse?
Will they still ride the sky as the years rush by
In hope of their final course?
Where did they die and how then;
Quick and clean in the searing blast?
Maybe time to pray as life slipped away,
With the fierce cruel flame roaring fast?
What of their thoughts in those moments,
When they knew that they must die?
As the Lanc' screamed down was the reason found
Why brave men venture so high?
Did they cry for home I wonder;
And call one last brief farewell,
Or did they grin as their kite spun in;
Then laugh in the face of hell?

John Roy Walsh (March 1986)

"GREMLINS ON MY SHOULDER"

Rob Davis

"Well?" asked Den eagerly, when we left the Watch Office the following morning. His expression conveyed a mixture of apprehension and admiration. Craig and I looked at each other. We had exchanged no word of the sharp edge of fear which had brushed us during the dark hours we had stayed in the front upstairs room, but we each knew that the other had been afraid.

"We saw nothing untoward," I replied gravely, and Craig smiled at the expression. It was true: we had actually seen or heard nothing out of the ordinary. But the human mind works in frantic overtime when it is in a place reputed to be haunted, and can often sense a deep presence of the past even when no knowledge of a location's history is known.

The watch office, or what would today be called the control tower, at the former Bomber Command aerodrome at East Kirkby, Lincolnshire, was famous for its ghosts even before Doug Smith's and Jack Currie's excellent television programme. I had heard some months before about the odd happenings there and was determined to make an overnight stop to judge for myself. With the owners' consent we installed ourselves on camp beds and blankets in the front upstairs observation room late on a hot afternoon in summer 1984. It was the second or third such overnight trip I'd made and the first to an old aerodrome known to have "odd occurrences."

Wandering around the site during daylight presented no problems. As any schoolboy student of horror films will immediately tell you, sunshine dispels supernatural influences; and so it was only during the dark hours that we felt the presence of the past leaning on us. It was a bit of a giggle at first, if the undertone was serious; but once we had locked ourselves in, made a late night drink, experimented with a new flashgun and laid down, the whole affair took on a new significance.

I wasn't exactly scared. It was just an old wartime building, wasn't it? "Fear" would be an overstatement, surely? But it was a completely different matter when Craig had slipped down to the toilet and left me alone; and then I really was edgy, then apprehensive, then — yes — frightened of what I had come all this way to experience. Whether it was the actual atmosphere or the knowledge of what had been seen and experienced there by others which was working on my mind, I can't say. I will say this, though; there was no way I would have stayed there on my own.

We had approached this little expedition with open minds on the subject of the supernatural. Whilst I had experienced "atmosphere" in the past at other aerodromes, I had never actually seen or heard anything definite.

The awful stillness, the moonlight slanting in through the uncurtained windows and the smell of concrete dust are permanently etched on my memory. Neither of us slept much; we were far too keyed-up looking for what we hoped we would not see but had gone to so much trouble to find.

In the morning we compared notes. We both said we thought there was a definite presence in the old building. Interestingly, Craig's views coincided with my own. I remarked that I thought we'd been examined by the spirits of East Kirkby and that they'd decided we were sympathetic to them and what they had done in the dark days of Bomber Command. But it was as if they could not resist winding us up and making us aware of them in a sort of jokey way. If you like to think of it like this; we had had our legs pulled.

I am often asked why I wander the aerodromes. Some people would say that it is an attempt to reach back into the past and try to be part of something I am not, like those odd folks who dress up in wartime uniform or flying-kit (complete with unearned wings and medal ribbons) and who go to aviation film shows and meetings. I won't agree with this; in spite of thousands of photos of the old aerodromes and many scores of visits and experiences, I am only too well aware that I was not there at the time the deeds I have read

and heard about were done. It cannot be merely curiosity about hauntings which impels me, because I have spent far more time on old Air Ministry concrete in daylight than at night.

So I can't explain what drew me into the offbeat hobby of "Aerodromology". There was an unfathomable force which gave me a peculiar restless itch until I had seen for myself some of the places I had heard about: Elsham Wolds, Wickenby, Fulbeck and dozens more. It was not sufficient to read about them, I had to go there and feel "the wind coming clean and free over the last earth touched by our wheels" to quote Don Charlwood, where the Australian, a former No 103 Squadron navigator recounts his trip back to Elsham in 1958.

Since 1979 I have explored the crumbling concrete of the mighty Lion which was once Bomber Command and these years have been punctuated by frequent photographic excursions and less frequent overnight trips. History is by necessity retrospective and today's aerodrome historian, and even the layman, can sometimes pick up vibrations from the past, sensations of human courage and endurance, fear and triumph, which have been absorbed by brick and concrete.

My personal theory is that a location has just so much — a finite quantity — of *atmosphere*, and that each visitor takes away a small part of it. Finally, a location with a once fully charged atmosphere becomes drained, as is a car battery when the lights have been left on all night.

What began as a peek into the past has grown into a great aerodrome trek. Whilst concentrating on the Bomber Command ones, I have not resisted others when the opportunity has been there. I find the Bomber stations nearest to my heart but have felt the tug of emotions at such far flung places as Dale, in Wales, where the Atlantic breeze slaps over the clifftop dispersal pans and sweeps the empty runways; at Holme-on-Spalding Moor with the sad atmosphere of its Operations Block; and at Bottesford, where the watch office and ops block reached out and spoke to two of my companions.

I won't fall into the trap of listing my visits and giving a synopsis of each one. There are too many; each of the memories are as different as the aerodromes, and such a dissertation would be shallow, empty reading. Instead, I'll tell you of the ones which made the most impact on me.

It was Elsham Wolds, without doubt, which affected me most. In both its decline and decay it reached out to me, craving understanding of the deeds done from there. When I visited it for the nth time and found that it had been bulldozed, I was moved to tears. It had been eradicated with such completeness that only the black arch-roof J-type hangar now betrays the original identity of the once bustling bomber station.

Even with my knowledge of the site and dozens of photographs taken when it was largely intact, it was almost impossible to orientate myself with sufficient accuracy to take "then and now" photos. Such was the degree of thoroughness employed to slay the aerodrome known as Elsham Wolds.

Gone now is the half-burned-out watch tower with the sound of phantom chattering Morse code and its sad but benevolent ghost. Only the airborne can see the true layout, as from the ground it is unrecognisable. May it rest in peace with its thousand dead, marked by the excellent memorial and the tireless efforts of its very own Elsham Wolds Association.

I discovered Elsham in late summer 1979. I was returning from delivering documents to Hull, the weather was glorious, and I felt as one with my motor cycle. I rode Don Charlwood's "incredibly long way" from Barnetby village to the main gate. The aerodrome lay crushed under the hot afternoon sun, the overgrown paths and peeling concrete-skinned buildings conveying an odd feeling of dormancy, as if the site was simply asleep, requiring only the firing of a red Very flare or the crackle and snort of Merlin engines to revive it.

The ops block imposed a more sombre atmosphere, a taut, heavy sensation, the focal point of the aerodrome's strength. The roof with its ventilation trunking and briefing rooms left no doubt that what had soaked into the Air Ministry brickwork was a powerful presence of the past. The whole building was alive with it.

On another trip and in the small hours of the morning when heavy fog had collected over the Humber Estuary and crawled silently over the aerodrome to blanket the station in grey miasma, the place took on a totally different and far more tangible presence. My companion had insisted on being told nothing about the site, wishing to tackle the overnight trip with a clean mental slate. As we walked from guardroom to main stores, parachute room to bombing trainer, time yawned, the atmosphere became charged, and the ground gave up its ghosts.

We sensed the presence of others watching us and summing us up, assessing our motives for intruding on their preserve. It was like smoking in church, shouting in a library, being stared at in horrified fascination. Every bush seemed to be a figure in blue battledress and wearing the full gleam of sergeant's stripes and to be watching, waiting… the long walk around the perimeter track, hand torches probing the wall of fog, wondering if that bit of concrete was a runway end — a road — a dispersal pan — or the back of the Moon?

Finally came the relief of the next morning, when sunshine washed away the fear, leaving behind just a derelict aerodrome. It was that day we found the incredible graffiti on the lavatory wall in the Sergeants' mess. Pencilled scribblings, covering most of the easily reachable wall, showed a fierce squadron pride and were quite free of foul language. These priceless cameos from a man's most private moments are now demolished, but preserved on film for both posterity and the curious.

There is a B1-type hangar at Wickenby, left abandoned in a field with only the old shooting butts for company. Today it is thriving in its new life as a transport depot, but when I saw it first in 1983, it had been left high and dry by the retreating tide of war and its echoing walls and roof had a sharp eeriness all of their own.

Enter then, Bomber Command's steel cathedral, and marvel at it. Ignore the havoc wreaked on the structure by fifty or more years of barometrical anarchy, and reach out with your mind. From here, men worked night and day patching and repairing battered bombers, so that other men could drop bombs on foreign lands. The high vaulted metal roof and tired walls shout this straight into your mind with neither preamble nor apology.

I had intended to walk the length of this silent, brooding place, but such was the concentration of force, so overpowering was the presence of the past that I was quickly pushed outside and back to my parked motor cycle. Does an odd energy watch over such places still, preserving them when other buildings have succumbed to the bulldozers?

Apparently not so in the case of the crew rooms and flight offices at Syerston. Escorted by an at first bored but later highly interested young aircraftman, Mike Garbett and I followed in the footsteps of the Nos 61 and 106 Squadron crews, taking accurate then-and-now photographs and succeeding in touching some of the tension which would have abounded in the long Maycrete huts in that awful time between briefing and take-off.

Only days after our visit, the buildings were destroyed in a fire-fighting exercise.

Yet the curious thing is that on so many thoughtlessly destroyed aerodromes, it is the watch office and often the parachute store which can still be found by the roving historian. Do the Black Magic symbols daubed on Wigsley's unique three-storied watch office guard against more than meets the eye? Do the shades of the crews killed there in the course of training take offence at the desecration? I, untarnished by personal memories, certainly did.

It was at Fulbeck that the message struck me with unprecedented clarity. I was exploring the derelict watch office, camera in hand. As I went from room to room I could feel the gremlins on my shoulder all right. Suddenly I felt as if I'd been grabbed by the scruff of the neck. "This was an operational station. Some good boys died flying from here." It was so sudden, a startling electric punch. I fled up the metal exterior staircase to the roof, where I stood for a long time in the lengthening shadows, turning from horizon to horizon.

In the late afternoon it did not take a very great feat of the imagination to visualise the black Lancasters crouched over their hardstandings, bomb doors agape, cockpit and turrets tarpaulined. I could picture the long lines of laden trolleys being towed from bomb dump to dispersal, calls for whoever and whatever over the Tannoy, and hordes of blue-clad humanity going about Air Force business.

Suddenly I turned and saw my modern Japanese motor cycle parked on the nearest hardstanding. The anachronistic sight made me feel really uneasy again and had me scurrying away from the frowning ghosts, down the perimeter track, and heading for home.

I went back again though, and one bleak January afternoon I was showing Fiona around. To both my relief and disappointment, the powerful presence I had detected before was not in evidence; the only chill feeling came from the winter wind rocketing in through the shattered windows. Fiona took refuge in the lee of the building, under the front balcony, whilst I went round with my camera and photographed what I'd missed on the previous trip.

Suddenly she called me. She had seen two uniformed figures walking along just to one side of the watch office. I knew that the site was used by the army for training purposes and as I had written permission to be there, I wasn't worried about being stopped by the military. Fiona said that one of the men had been dressed in dark blue battledress with a forage cap; the other one in best blue with an officer's hat. The two figures had walked behind a bush, deep in conversation.

On further discussion it transpired that the two men had been walking along, apparently up to their knees in a ploughed field. As my photographs show, the curved concreted path around the back of the watch office is not there. Not now, anyway. We waited and waited for the men to reappear from behind the bush, but they never did.

"Never go back" is what they tell you; but if you do go back, beware, lest you find more than you seek.

124

Above:
SOUL GUARDIAN
'...It was at Fulbeck that the message struck me with unprecedented clarity...'
Beneath an empty bowl of milky blue sky on a day of high summer the derelict watch offices dotted across the counties of Yorkshire, Lincolnshire et al are, to passers-by, little more than deserted structures drained of all emotion save for a spark of curiosity. But, when the mists descend or darkness falls those same neglected ruins of brick, steel and concrete take on a totally different ambience. It is then that each seems to sink back into its 50-year-long sleep, as if trying to hide its ugliness in shame and shadow, yet giving out the sharp ache of loneliness, of sadness, behind which is somehow stored the presence of mortals who worked there, laughed there, cried there.

How many of these watch offices will survive into the second millennium is debatable. Most have survived only because landowners hitherto found it too costly, too labour-intensive to demolish them; but with advances in technology within recent years, machines are now capable of making short work of such constructions and each year sees one or two more reduced to rubble. Thankfully, a handful have been saved, even restored to house museums depicting the war years. Some still serve as control towers at active airfields, Wickenby for one. Moves are afoot to encourage English Heritage to take more interest in preserving vivid slices of history.

Fulbeck, August 1981. Note T2 hangar in the distance.
R. A. Davis

125

BOMBER COMMAND PASSED THIS WAY

'...Ignore the havoc wreaked on the structure by 50 or more years of barometrical anarchy, and reach out with your mind...'

Be there warriors out there who, in old age, yet feel the urge to return to the haunts of their youth spent wearing uniform, they may be put off making the pilgrimage, when learning how little remains of the war-emergency dromes half a century on.

For many — perhaps most — collecting their demob suit was the severing link with a way of life so divorced from the harsh reality of Civvy Street. In the austere postwar world there was no room for sentiment, dwelling on the past, though inevitably, thoughts drifted back to a time of unique purpose and pride and comradeship. Half a century!

The RAF Public Relations Book 1995 records that 'over 1,000 airfields were used by the RAF in the UK during the Second World War, so it is not without some justification that Britain was referred to as a "vast aircraft carrier anchored off the NW coast of Europe!". By the end of the war some 36,000 acres of land had been occupied by airfields, and a staggering 160 million sq yd of concrete and tarmac had been laid down.'

Landowners cannot live on sentiment and, once the aerodromes were sold off by the then Air Ministry, the demolition gangs began to move in and the ploughs set-to. The likes of runways, perimeter tracks, dispersals and buildings survived only if functional, if they suited a purpose for their postwar owners, and many miles of concrete and tarmac have been sold as hardcore for motorways, roads, etc.

And so, five decades later, precious little is on view to the veterans, or the curious, intent on touching the world that was Bomber Command.

Right:
With barely a nod to the 1990s, a sleeping Nissen at Little Staughton, 1981, lurking in the undergrowth, the shadows... as silent as a tomb... sanctuary for an untold drift of memories... an oasis of quiet were it not for the occasional swinging of a steadily disintegrating door on its oil-starved hinges... the crunch of broken glass underfoot... To stand amid the weeds and rubble is to step beyond the frontier of another world... to experience a drugging of one's senses, a massaging of the heartstrings.
B. Goulding

Below right:
How they were. Living site Nissens at East Kirkby in 1944, each little more than a concrete slab base with brick or wood end-walls and corrugated iron shroud. Which trembled in the winter winds that came raw off the fens, whining their weird requiem, rising intermittently into high-pitched screams. Which all too often became intolerably fuggy and stuffy due to cigarette smoke, the stoked-up, fume-belching pot-bellied stoves, sweaty bodies sleeping in close proximity. Which now — the few that remain in time-fogged ruin — seem wearied by the passing years.
For we who attempt to chronicle the events of yesteryear there has been an undiminishing compulsion to stand where once the Lancasters crouched on oil-stained dispersal pans... walk where once they staggered skywards, Germany-bound. In daylight, and at night, in fog and mist and rain, as well as when the weather was kind, we have meandered and clambered, stood and listened and searched... attempting to 'tune in'... to 'feel' what has gone before.
F. Foster

Left:
Was that really a modern-day combine moving slowly along avenues of wheat once runways straight and true... not a contractor laying tarmac or concrete at a still-unfinished Ludford back in the summer of '43?; with Lancasters already in situ; with brand-new David Brown tractors waiting to do their bit towing aircraft, equipment, bomb trolleys; with the Foden tipper carefully feeding the Barber-Greene machine, which would look little different today other than for more driver comforts; with, back to camera, steam roller driver Jim Proctor keeping his eye on things, having already spent much of his time during this war away from his home at East Bridgeford, near Syerston, on airfield construction work — a dedicated 'civvie' who'd also answered the call. (Passed away 1990.) E. D. Evans

Below:
Was that really a Lightning jet squatting on a hardstanding, not a No 460 Sqn RAAF Lanc having a spot of bother, having her starboard-inner fixed at nearby Binbrook during the same year? E. D. Evans

Inset:
Were those distant figures resting between grass-cutting one day in 1987, standing in for Nos 12 and 626 Sqn' aircrews awaiting arrival of the crew buses that would take them to their war-horses at Wickenby back in '44? A. E. Lowry

BROODING SECRETS

'...Enter then, Bomber Command's steel cathedral, and marvel at it...'

Though time is running out, it can yet be a rewarding experience discovering what remains of Bomber Command's presence in the counties of Yorkshire, Lincolnshire and their like. In particular, it is those airfields kept by the Royal Air Force after hostilities ceased which offer the most tangible evidence. True, the onset of the jet age, bigger and heavier aircraft, advances in technology, all forced changes; but those huge hangars, watch offices (now known as control towers), station headquarters, etc, have stayed little changed during five decades; but their future is decidedly uncertain. As the RAF contracts ever more, the bases that served it so well are being steadily vacated, some handed over to the army, others to developers.

Typical of those still in RAF hands are Leeming and Syerston; the former very much a part of the present jet scene, the latter a gliding centre. Each has its share of mouldering relics, long abandoned to Mother Nature's will.

Above:
PRIVY TO THE PAST
'...We sensed the presence of others watching us and summing us up...'

Rob Davis, snapped whilst sheltering from biting winds during a never-to-be-forgotten day spent exploring Dunholme Lodge.

That day — 22 January 1986 — saw him once more reaching out... letting his imagination take wing... attempting to open Pandora's Box... one part of him feeling an interloper as he traced the footsteps of long-gone, long-dispersed, blue-clad mortals... walked a brooding Lincolnshire acreage once host to the Lancasters of Nos 44, 619 and 170 Sqn. R. A. Davis

Right:
Freeze-framed in semi-ruin, sort of shrine to a bygone era, stand remnants of bomb dump girderwork at Leeming, North Yorks.
M. F. Chandler/M. A. Garbett

Below:
A fusing shed at Syerston, Notts. Where once daily the air was shrill with the whirring of pulleys and chains hoisting bombs and incendiary cans aplenty, the voices of blue-clad humanity at work, near silence now reigns.
R. A. Davis

AITKEN

REQUIEM

'...Old men forget; yet all shall be forgot,
But he'll remember with advantages
What feats he did that day...
...This story shall the good man teach his son;
...From this day to the ending of the world,
But we in it shall be remembered, —
We few, we happy few, we band of brothers;
For he to-day that sheds his blood with me
Shall be my brother...'

So did William Shakespeare have King Henry V say before the Battle of Agincourt; but how easy it is to imagine Sir Arthur ('Butch') Harris delivering such stirring words to his volunteers of tender years before they manned their Lancasters to dice with death over Germany, wherever they were directed. Equally, with but the odd change of word, he could have been addressing the earthbound men and women who made it all possible. And so, to close this dip into a treasury of unforgettable scenes and happenings of yesteryear, let us join two ageing pilgrims unable to resist scratching the good, and not so good, scars of youth... willing to unleash — yet somehow fearful of unleashing — a riptide of memories... memories that can turn into nightmares.

"SKY OF MEMORIES"

Sid Giffard

Going back to the Conversion Unit had been rather a let-down. Ghosts of the past would not gather unto themselves substance among the brick buildings, so familiar but — not so. The residents were not of that time; this was peacetime and the intangible aura of a war-footing station would not be conjured up.

I stood at the main gate for only a few minutes. I made no attempt to go in for that would have superimposed new memories and forever afterwards the originals would have lost their clarity. Whilst walking beside the airfield amid the non-urgency of the present I'd have been hard-pressed to recall pictures of Halifaxes and Lancasters launching themselves down runways with the awesome sound of magical Merlins. Those thoughts would have been out of place among the frenetic scream of jet engines and aircraft of so different aerodynamic shapes.

No — let memories remain untarnished. I returned to my car and sat awhile, remembering what had been — so very long ago.

There, I saw, was one of the many small offices inside a hangar. It was crowded with pilots and flight navigators. The pilots needed an engineer to complete their crews, so this was the occasion to "sort yourselves out."

The tall young skipper approached and invited: "Would you like to be my engineer?" And that was that.

"Circuits and bumps" followed, daytime and night-time ones. Then cross-country training flights as we learned about four-engined aeroplanes. These were good times to remember. There had been the Link Trainer Unit where I had spent many hours flying courses and recovering from simulated spins in preparation for an emergency when I would be required to take over a Lancaster's controls. Funny how unavailing it was to prove not so very long afterwards.

Christmas 1943, and we went on a few days' leave. Returned to find the station's aircrews in disgrace; some fathead had removed the Air Officer Commanding's flag and deposited it in a dustbin. There followed a week — or perhaps it was ten days — of strenuous physical training as penance. We were exempted as we were not on station precincts at the time of the offence.

I had suffered from airsickness until the Medical Officer prescribed certain pills. They cured me almost immediately. Then I followed up with a violent attack of boils which caused me to miss a night's cross-country flight. My crew, with a stand-in engineer, encountered an electrical storm which rendered vital instruments inoperative. So, in an unfortunate position, the exact whereabouts of which was quite unknown to them, they were obliged to call upon "Darkie" to get them home safely. Not their fault, of course, but nevertheless a great deal of ribbing ensued. Ah, happy days and nights! These and other memories were to remain untouched by today.

But now — across the Yorkshire border and into that part of Lincolnshire once so well-known, from the air at least. How would it appear now, twenty seven years on? Would I recognise the terrain.

Early September gloom threatened rain so I stopped for a brief time in Market Rasen to ask the way. All around the greyness seemed in sympathy with my mood; somehow a golden afternoon would not have suited — it was that kind of pilgrimage.

A signpost directed left, off the main road and a lesser one led to a small hamlet which announced itself as my destination, but not quite journey's end.

I drove on through, slowly, as a feeling of unreality pressed in on me and apprehension tightened my stomach in strange anticipatory waves. Would the years have left anything to recognise or would they have engulfed all that wartime's urgency had built? The watch office maybe? It was to be hoped for, as I would need a datum-point to try to pick out landmarks. Perhaps it would seem that all that had been had never existed. Perhaps — but over there on the wide grass verge, rising some three or four feet from a double-tiered stone platform of similar whiteness, I saw a memorial plaque with a Royal Air Force crest near its top.

I drew on to the opposite verge and walked across to this stone plinth with its legend-bearing column and read the engraved word which would perpetuate the memory of a long-gone bomber squadron. Beneath the crest, and simply: "625 Squadron Royal Air Force October 1943 – April 1945. We Avenge."

Yes, I suppose in our own way we did avenge, but now those of us who are left can but say — "We remember."

I returned to my car and looked back once before driving off down a side lane towards the few skeletal remains of buildings; and very few indeed were they. Then, several hundred yards away to my right I saw my datum-point. Not as I remembered it though, for the ravages of time were apparent, but the old watch office still commanded the flat terrain, now returned to agriculture.

My lane passed across the weed-encrusted remains of a still distinguishable runway, so once more I drew on to a roadside verge. But this time my steps were even slower as I stepped upon the runway — for this then was truly "journey's end."

I looked towards the watch office and could see it as it was; no longer desolate and crumbling, but vibrant with life along with the entire station area. I saw long-gone hangars and admin buildings, mess-huts and all the other similar Nissen huts which went to make an air-station. All corrugated metal constructions which had proclaimed their probable impermanence; but then it had LIVED.

The Sergeants' Mess held a particular memory which alone made its demise so very sad. A Canadian had undertaken the monumental task of drawing a vast colourful Lancaster on one of the inside walls. I wondered if he had managed to complete it, for it was a creation of sheer beauty, which showed how we all felt about our aeroplane. Sadly, the way things went with the squadron, it was to be doubted if he finished his task. But now it was only to be recalled to my mind's eye.

Now just a moment — was it not the same Canadian whose other pride and joy was a little bulldog puppy? Only a few weeks' old was Butch, and by way of being the mess mascot. Ah, little Butch, you too have gone, along with your master and his wonderful picture, and his mess too.

We had been part of that scene, had been to our briefings, had carried out our air tests and had been part of the "Battle Orders." A strange battle indeed, the like of which had not been experienced before. And would never be seen again.

I raised my eyes to where had been our "circuit," that aerial path surrounding each airfield, and which, due to congestion of airfields was overlapped by others. The fact that each was at a different altitude should, in theory, have eliminated the danger of collision. It was not foolproof, especially at night, as we discovered on return from Stuttgart. We were actually in the "funnel" prior to landing when a four-engined job passed several feet above us on an opposing course. A very shaky do was that.

130

We went around that circuit on the occasion when we did our scheduled "dawn patrol." It had been a matter of honour that we took off at the specified time. No earlier, and no later. We lifted off dead on time.

I conjured back the many dispersals set off the perimeter track and saw crew lorries disgorging aircrews. I saw the scene shortly afterwards as, nose to tail, the Lancasters made their slow, ponderous way around this peri-track towards the beginnings of the runway. This runway on which I now stood.

It was but a mind's flicker to put me up there in my old place as our Lanc wheeled onto the runway to await the green light. To my right a naval chief petty-officer stood waving with a line of other well-wishers. His brother was operating this night.

Looking across to port I saw, standing near the mobile, chequer-board-patterned caravan another group bidding us farewell.

Then the green light committed us and we drew full power from our four Merlins and sped away along the runway.

Back again on the tarmac I watched us lift off and soar above the then snow-covered fields at the beginning of a circle through space and time. That circle was now made whole by the only survivor.

I turned away from desolation and saw a small triangular-shaped copse still gracing a gentle rise about two miles away. I remembered that. Nature at least was unchanged.

And then my skin crawled, as faintly but seemingly not of this day, I heard voices. I stared all around, but saw no-one.

But again, and yet again they came. The sensation was eerie — beyond description, although not alarming, for if the shades of long ago were around me I was among friends.

Then, as yet again they came I guessed they were probably far-off agricultural voices I was hearing. The present was as one with the past.

Once more I looked to where the Lancaster was traversing its ghostly circuit with its crew of seven young men.

A few gentle raindrops touched my upturned face as though the lowering clouds wept for them — and so many others.

I turned away and left Kelstern behind me.

Above:
PLACE OF A SKULL
'...I conjured back the many dispersals set off the perimeter track and saw crew lorries disgorging aircrews...'

A picture certain to cause the hairs to rise on the back of Sid Giffard's neck is this one of No 625 Sqn's 'CF:K', 'Himself King'. To Sid it does not matter that she cannot be BIII ND596 which last he saw in daylight on the afternoon of 18 March 1944... last knew by feel and sound and smell that night... knew every inch of... that only he escaped from when a night-fighter destroyed her during an op to Frankfurt.

To we who never knew Kelstern in wartime, it is little more than a camera's eye glimpse of the drome when the few trees were bare, the winds persistent and perishing: a picture of winter, perhaps of spring. To Sid it is full of movement... of noise... of laughter... of sadness as he sees himself, Skipper Plt Off 'Mac' MacMaster, and others of his clan, chatting, smoking, before climbing aboard to earn their keep with an appointment over Stuttgart, 15/16 March 1944, as daunting a début on the operational stage as it is possible to have. To his dying day he will carry with him the image of his Skipper in near-silhouette but a shoulder's distance from him... will ever hear the voices of his pals on the R/T... before their right to live was so rudely violated.
W. H. Theaker

Above:
SOMEWHERE-ON-THE-WOLDS
'...How would it appear now, 27 years on? Would I recognise the terrain..?'

'Somewhere-on-the-Wolds' is about as precise an answer as you are likely to get if you ask the whereabouts of Kelstern. Even on the flight up from Norfolk to photograph the sparse remains of this remote aerodrome from the air (April 1995), the weather clamped in, as it tends to do without warning atop the Lincolnshire Wolds, a veil of thick cloud seeming to appear from nowhere on an otherwise perfect sunny day over the rest of Lincolnshire, and contrary to any forecast from Humberside Airport not far distant. Fairly typical of Kelstern, as anyone who was based there will tell you.

Apart from these dispersals, and stretches of taxi-rack angling round the southwestern end of what remains of the main runway, there is virtually nothing else to be seen. Two of the Nissen-type huts on the near dispersals are wartime relics, the others modern counterparts. The close proximity of the 'spectacle' dispersals to the late Tom Brooks' farm is evident — a common feature on numerous airfields of wartime construction. A small copse offers the only screen for the farmer and his family from the daily and nightly hubbub of a bomber base.

Tom's relatives still reside at Julian's Farm, as it has been known for many years, having taken its name from the sun god Julian, there still being traces of the worshipping site nearby. Julian certainly didn't work his magic very often during the war! Parts of the farm are still referred to as 'bomb dump field' and 'shooting range'.

Kelstern had been the site of a World War 1 flying field too, 1916/1918, slightly nearer the village. The new airfield's first modern-day occupants were No 625 Sqn, which formed there in October 1943, to stay until leaving for Scampton in April 1945. It was to be a one-squadron station throughout its active life, apart from two weeks in October 1944, when No 170 Sqn was formed out of 'C' Flight of No 625, moving quickly to Dunholme Lodge. There were always difficulties with Kelstern's circuit, which virtually overlapped those of Binbrook and Ludford Magna, the three dromes being situated in a triangle, each only three or four miles apart.

Kelstern, along with Ludford, became inactive in October 1945 and officially closed on 4 August 1946, its call-sign 'Peak Freen', and that of 625 ('Himself') by then already long-silenced.

It became what is thought to have been the first former bomber airfield to have a memorial erected to its wartime occupants, the stone being dedicated as long ago as 25 October 1964, annual remembrance ceremonies continuing to be held there to this day.
Brian Goulding

THOROUGHBREDS FOR HIRE

'You love a lot of things if you live around them. But there isn't any woman and there isn't any horse, nor any before nor any after, that is as lovely as a great airplane.

'And men who love them are faithful to them even though they leave them for others... and if it is a lovely airplane... there is where his heart will forever be.'
Ernest Hemingway (Extract from a quote displayed on the wall of a museum at Galveston, Texas, courtesy of Johnny Spiegel.)

'...It was a creation of sheer beauty, which showed how we all felt about our aeroplane...'

Nostalgia, it is said, can be dangerous... an open invitation to indulge in sentimentality, a cosy longing for the 'good old days'. Who was it who said that he suffered from nostalgia like some people suffered from heartburn; that they instantly turned food into painful acids... not so much because the past was painful, but painful for being past? True? It depends on so many factors, dating back to our childhood, our upbringing, what we have done with our lives, how we have coped with difficulties, dealt with challenges along the way.

We may never know how the men, and women, as yet untraced, or now deceased, would look upon their time in and around Lancasters. We *do* know a goodly number — from Australians to South Africans, from the eminent as well as the humble — have, at varying stages of their lives postwar, reflected on their involvement. Never have we come across any with a bad word to say about the Lanc. Quite the opposite. Even the eyes of those whose quality of life was forever changed for the worse as a result of baling out or being dragged from crashes, light up when discussing Roy Chadwick's thoroughbred.

So, let us take an imaginary journey through time and call in at a few of the dromes spread far and wide throughout the stretch of England that was Bomber Country. Let us look over a few of the Lancs which battled their way to and from targets near and far, by day as well as by night.

Opposite Top:
Coningsby, Lincs, summer of '44, and Aussie gunner Flt Sgt Vic Robley takes time out to snap his kite, BIII ND979 'OL:G' 'Gremlin Junior', pride and joy of Flt Lt Harry Foote and companions, and a worthy successor to their first 'OL:G', BIII ND494 (lost Gennevilliers 9/10 May 1944: Flt Lt J. A. T. Meredith and crew). Beginning Brunswick, 22/23 May, ending Stuttgart, 12/13 September 1944, the Foote septet completed at least 15 ops in ND979 before being declared tour-expired and splitting up. Later becoming 'OL:K', ND979 soldiered on until crashing on 14 August 1945. Subsequently dumped at No 22 MU, Silloth, she was a memory by May 1947.
V. J. Robley

Left and opposite:
Croft, North Yorks, February/March 1945. Stand in line with Canadian flight engineer Flg Off Mike Bachinski as his camera records BX KB837 'SE:X' running up her Packard-Merlin 224s. She brought Flt Lt George Percival and his six like-Canucks of No 431 ('Iroquois') Sqn, RCAF back from 13 targets (Dresden, 13/14 February through Wangerooge, 25 April 1945, in daylight) before collecting 24 former POWs from Juvincourt on 10 May. Then it was a case of awaiting the signal which resulted in them flying KB837 back to Canada, which they did beginning 6 June 1945, leaving mainland Britain via St Mawgan. First stop in Canada was Yarmouth, Nova Scotia, and by September 1945 she was at Claresholm, Alberta, a holding/maintenance unit, and not known to have worked again.
Ultimately scrapped August 1950.
M. Bachinski

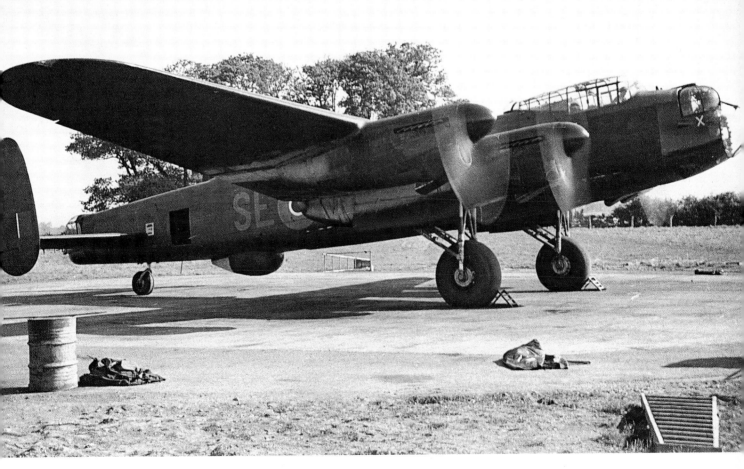

Opposite top:

Tibenham, Norfolk, 2 September 1945. Barely had the locals again settled down to a daily life free of engine noise following departure in May 1945 of the B-24 Liberator-equipped 445th Bombardment Group, when Tibenham briefly played host to Lancasters as 'Operation Dodge' got under way. Here we see redundant pathfinder '6O:J' from No 582 Sqn, Little Staughton, Beds, taxying in having brought some two dozen soon-to-be-demobbed soldiers from Italy. Just eight days later (a little over 17 months since its formation), the unit disbanded and Little Staughton went into slumber soon after companion No 109 Sqn's Mossies left for Upwood in late September 1945. M. F. Hudson

Opposite below:

Mepal, Cambs, September/October 1944. Adding scale to No 75 (New Zealand) Sqn Lanc III NE181 'JN:M' is 'C' Flight Commander Sqn Ldr Nick Williamson's Hillman pick-up. Then well into his second tour (his first had been with 214 Sqn, flying Stirlings), New Zealander Nick took over NE181 prior to engaging the enemy over Stettin, 29/30 August 1944, liked the feel of her and called her his own for the remaining six trips of his tour, which ended with a night assault on Duisburg, 14/15 October.

Succeeding 'C' Flight boss, Sqn Ldr Jim Bailey, RNZAF, had the satisfaction of piloting the old lady on her official 100th operation — Krefeld, 29 January 1945 — and soon moves were afoot to fly her out to the land of the Kiwi for preservation. Sadly, it came to nothing, and she languished at Mepal until transferred to neighbouring No 514 Sqn at Waterbeach in July 1945 before joining row upon row of like-Lancs 'surplus to requirements' awaiting attention from the scrap-metal gangs at No 5 MU, Kemble. She was finally broken up during September 1947.

Would that someone with a sense of history had salvaged her nose panel. At least, because 'Just Jake' could be found among other cartoons in a daily newspaper, the Daily Mirror, we know what colour paints were used when an artist (as yet unidentified) got to work at Mepal. Or do we? Did he have to use such paint as he could scrounge? N. A. Williamson

Right:

Does Nick Williamson's navigator, Flg Off John Watts, RNZAF (here seen posing for his picture) remember? His skipper couldn't when we asked.

For sure they, and others who knew Mepal in time of war, will scratch their heads in disbelief if they attempt to locate where NE181 stood. Not only has virtually all trace of their drome been expunged, even sleepy Mepal has been bypassed by a new A142 Ely-Chatteris road Was hereabouts really inhabited by 2,000 or so blue-uniformed souls who truly dominated the locality? N. A. Williamson

Below:

St Eval, Cornwall, 19 August 1942. No 61 Sqn's BI R5679 'QR:O' showing signs of damage to her port wing after an argument with flak during an attack (from 3,000ft) on a tanker 30 miles northwest of Cape Oretago by Flt Sgt Norman Turner and his brood the day before. Along with others from their squadron they were on detachment from home base Syerston, Notts, engaged in Atlantic patrols and shipping strikes. All told, R5679 carried them through 17 ops, starting Bremen, 25/26 June, finishing Bremen, 13/14 September 1942, before she failed to return from a gardening foray near Stettin on 24/25 September 1942 (Captain: Sgt L. W. Morrison), by then an old campaigner with 165 flying hours to her credit. (See footnote.) T. L. Cass

FOOTNOTE:

R5679's Skipper, Norman Turner, who had joined the RAF in 1939, had a much longer career, completing an unusually long tour of 38 ops (230 flying hours) in mid-October 1942. (Had someone forgotten to count the eight they'd done from St Eval!) After instructing on Lancs at 1660 HCU, he did a second tour of 20 ops with No 61 Sqn, August 1943/April 1944 then became a test pilot, attached to Vickers at Squires Gate testing Wellingtons (and the prototype Viking) until the war's end, followed by a variety of types at AVRO's Woodford, 12 Ferry Unit, Transport Command Dev Unit, etc, including Lancs, Lincolns, Lancastrians, Tudors, Dakotas, Liberators, Warwicks, until demob in 1946. He rejoined the RAF in 1949 flying Wellingtons, Halifaxes, Hastings and Neptunes, but went back to Lancs in July 1954 as a staff pilot at the School of Maritime Reconnaissance, St Mawgan, until May 1956, only five months before the last Lancs in RAF service were retired from that unit (in October 1956). His last flying tour was as staff pilot at Luqa (Malta), flying Meteors, Pembrokes, Vikings *and* Shackletons — the 'last of the line' on which he'd first flown in 1941 (ie the Manchester). A remarkable record. After 10 years as an air traffic controller, Flt Lt Norman Turner DFC, DFM, retired from the RAF in late 1969, and took up a banking career. Norman died of a heart attack on Easter Sunday 1995, aged 75. The surviving five members of his second-tour crew held an *'in memoriam'* with his widow, Joan, and family shortly after. An all-too-familiar occurrence these days.

Above:

Wickenby, Lincs, June 1944. Ever-ready with his camera was Canadian Bob Bennet, skipper of BIII PA990 'UM:R2' 'Bennet's Beavers'. Here is one of many studies snapped during his tour with No 626 Sqn: BI LL961 'UM:S2', flown by Plt Off T. E. Newton and crew (and probably 'on camera' lounging near her tail-end). Before taking over LL961, they had done 13 trips in BIII EE148 'UM:S2', lost Mailly-Le-Camp 3/4 May 1944 with Plt Off N. J. Fisher and crew, while they were on leave. Taking over LL961 from new, they blooded her by visiting Dieppe, 10/11 May, then went on to complete a further 15 ops in her, to end a 'good' tour with Vaires on 27/28 June 1944. Next day they passed ownership of 'Sugar 2' to Plt Off 'Timber' Wood and his lads.

They, too, would leave Wickenby with a successful tour behind them, but LL961 was destroyed in still-undetermined circumstances whilst climbing through cloud above the Soissons area en route to Munich 7/8 January 1945. The official report states that another aircraft collided with LL961 but two of her surviving crew still wonder if American AA fire may have brought about her demise. At this distance in time it is impossible to come to a positive conclusion. Regardless of the cause, Canadian captain Flg Off 'Marsh' Smith and rear gunner Sgt Bill McLean tragically died. Maureen Bennet

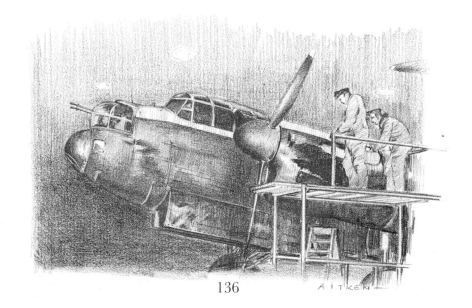

MOMENTS IN TIME

What brought me back it's
so lonely
Was it really from here that
I flew?
From here that I skippered
those youngsters?
Those laughing young warriors
I knew.
But this is where it all ended
so many long years ago
Right now it seems only moments,
but my eyes tell me this can't be so.

For there's corn where once there
were runways!
Though there should be by now
I suppose,
For I've moved on in Time through
my memories
And these days are not urgent,
like those.

Where Lancs flew just the wind and
the birds now
With but clouds in the vast
silent sky.
Though the snarl of those Merlins
still lingers,
To be heard just by us, you and I.

One last poignant glimpse of the
old days,
Those grim days of war that we knew,
recall tension and fear; and raw
Courage
with light hearted moments
spent Too!
But come my old friend let us leave
now, our battle skies fade with
the Past,
As we take our memories with us;
this Old warrior's tears
gather fast.

John Roy Walsh (November 1985)

ARE YOU ALL RIGHT JACK?

Are you all right, Jack? I'm asking
For you're often in my mind
As you journey on do you ever think
Of the pal you left behind?

I often think of you, Jack
Do you ever think of me?
Do you still recall the good old times;
The days that used to be?

We met as little kids at school:
We hit it off at once
Though you were such a bright lad
And I was such a dunce.

Apart from my old widowed Mum
I hadn't any kin
And I loved you like a brother:
My pal through thick and thin.

We went through school together;
The glad days and the sad.
You shared with me the good times
And cheered me through the bad.

And then we went as 'prentices
On the local factory floor
And I know I took for granted
We'd be pals for ever more.

We finished our apprenticeships
With old Hitler coming strong,
So we upped and joined the RAF.
We went to 'right the wrong'.

We did our Morse together;
Our guns and OTU.
We joined the self-same squadron;
The very self-same crew.

I well recall those lively times
Though they're so long ago;
When you were our mid-upper
And I was tail-end Joe.

Our tour was nearly at an end
We thought we'd won the race.
When another man went missing
And you'd to take his place.

Of course, I went to see you go;
You grinned and winked your eye.
I never thought as you went off
We'd said our last goodbye.

I grieved for you a long time.
The days seemed bleak and drear
And I know I still remember
Every day of every year.

It's been a lonely road since then
But I've conquered every hill.
There was a time I wouldn't fight
But you gave me the will.

You have 'no known grave', Jack;
And little claim to fame
But on that wall at Runnymede
I know they've carved your name.

I sometimes sit and ponder
For only God can tell
But you always were a man, Jack
And you made me one as well.

Are you all right, Jack? I'm sure you
are
For you're often in my mind
And I know you're up there waiting
For the pal you left behind.

Victor Cavendish (Vic Cuttle, ex-No106 Sqn)

IN THE FRAME

'...Once more I looked to where the Lancaster was traversing its ghostly circuit...'

Not surprisingly, all the pictures that follow have, like the vast majority of others in this book, come from men only too willing to 'open the hangar doors', share their mementoes, their experiences of life with the Lancaster. How many other vivid slices of history are beyond our reach because their owners have died; or have yet to be traced; or are embittered; or believe that it serves no useful purpose to scalpel into memories of their youth spent flying or supporting Lancs? These and other reasons, for the in-depth study of an aircraft like the Lancaster is also the study of human nature. There is no pattern. You will find those who had a reasonably 'good' war having no wish to dwell on their youth spent wearing uniform; and you will come across those who had a rough time of it — like Sid Giffard — with no 'hang-ups'.

But the sands of time are running out whereby hitherto uncontacted battle-scarred war-horses can add to our coverage in word and picture... our store of knowledge... our understanding relative to a remarkable aircraft and its associated mortals. Here's hoping...?

Just to select a handful of snapshots of Lancs in their natural element is to prompt questions.

Opposite top:

Which No 44 (Rhodesia) Sqn rookie crew was it who, detailed for a daylight training exercise in BIII RE132 'KM:G' one unrecorded, best forgotten day in '45, decided to show an 8th USAAF Liberator what a Lanc could do? Unbeknown to them, the 'Lib' was being flown by the CO of the B-24 Bomb Group, who took a dim view of the proceedings and reported them! Result: after a severe wigging from Spilsby's Station Commander, the Lanc crew was promptly posted. We know it was not RE132's usual 'owners' — Flg Off Pete Young and his troupe, here seen engaging in a cross-country stooge, spring 1945. They completed five ops in RE132 (Nordhausen, 4 April — Cham, 17/18 April 1945) before Germany was finally overrun. Continuing to fly RE132 during those early heady days of peace, they were posted to No 617 Sqn for 'Tiger Force' duty in June. After further service with Nos 75 and 207 Sqns, RE132 was deposited at No 20 MU, Aston Down for scrapping (effected August 1946). R. J. Nelson

Opposite middle:

Is this evocative study of No 150 Sqn's BI NN742 'IQ:U' in formation over Lincoln, the work of he from Hemswell's photographic section who had going 'a nice little earner' taking pictures 'on the quiet' for crews with their aircraft out on dispersal? What did he do with all those 'spare' prints we know he kept, took home with him when his demob number came up? How long did they reside in a dark corner of his attic? How long was it before he dumped or burned them, as others of his trade did as each succeeding year postwar forced out a need to cling to what was past, beyond recall, of no further value?

Perhaps because he had cheated death so many times, rear gunner Aubrey ('Bob') Drinkwater kept his photo of NN742 taken that day spent droning above a Lincolnshire countryside bathed in sunshine. He and his fellow confidants — Canadian Skipper Flg Off A. R. Roffe and the rest — came through 14 bombing ops in her without a scratch (opening with Hamburg, 22/23 January, closing with the daylight on Berchtesgaden, 25 April 1945), followed by two satisfying 'Manna' food drops: Valkenburg 29 April; The Hague 30 April 1945.

Whilst the enemy failed to destroy NN742 during her near-six months spent dodging flak and fighters, the breakers had no problems in reducing her to scrap metal at No 38 MU, Llandow during May 1947. A. Drinkwater

Opposite below:

As their equivalents did here in the UK, so German fighter units and flak regiments displayed, on the walls of their Messes, 'trophies' recovered from aircraft brought down over their homeland. One such trophy was the charred and bent nose panel (on which were recorded at least 114 ops) from No 100 Sqn Lanc III ND644 'HW:N', downed during a trip to Nuremberg, 16/17 March 1945 (Flg Off G. A. Dauphine, RCAF and his kindred spirits). When last seen, the near-5ft square item of war booty was being strapped beneath the roof of the bomb bay of a No 100 Sqn Lancaster specially sent out from the unit's then base of Elsham Wolds around July/August 1945. What became of it? Which German unit was forced to hand it over? Who knows the details of an intriguing story?

Our air-to-air features 'Nan', snapped by South American skipper Flt Lt Owen Lloyd-Davies from the cockpit of a sister Lanc from No 100 Sqn, Waltham, during a daylight sortie a week or two before her destruction. Note how a year of squadron service (close on 800 flying hours) has resulted in chipped and worn paintwork, nacelles heavily coated in deposits of lead from engine exhausts. G. A. Vickery

Opposite inset:

This is surely BIII ND756 'AA:M' from No 75 (New Zealand) Sqn, Mepal, last heard rather than seen, taking off at 22.00hrs, 28 July 1944, headed for Stuttgart and death for pilot Flg Off I. E. Blance, RNZAF, and three of his crew.

As the three survivors would later relate, their Lanc was attacked by a fighter when on the homeward leg over France. All four motors were rendered useless by the fighter's very first bursts of fire; then it came in again, raking the fuselage, killing both wireless operator and mid-upper gunner, and wounding the navigator. Closing in for a repeat attack, the Hun met determined fire from the Lanc's rear turret Brownings and it went down a flamer.

But ND756 was doomed. Blazing furiously, she began to go down out of control. By a supreme effort, Blance arrested the downward plunge just long enough for three of his crew to bale out safely; but he (along with his bomb aimer) was unable to leave. Ironically, both hunter and hunted crashed within half a mile of each other. J. K. Aitken

Below:

As always, every picture tells a story, and this one of BII DS713 'OW:J' from No 426 'Thunderbird' Sqn RCAF, Linton-on-Ouse, taken on 16 August 1943, does so on more than one count. Operating the durable Wellington from Dishforth since its formation on 15 October 1942, 426 was selected to be the first Canadian No 6 Group squadron to re-equip with the mighty like-engined Lancaster II, moving further south in Yorkshire to Linton-on-Ouse in the process. Despite an intensive conversion programme, provision was made whereby air-to-air photographs could be taken, both for historical record and public relations purposes, ie keeping the Canadian public informed, by word and picture, as to how their boys were contributing to the blitzing of Germany.

Newly posted in, and yet to do an operation, Flt Lt Bob Epps, RCAF and his crew found themselves detailed to carry an official cameraman. However, the first attempt, on 14 August 1943, was abortive due to a constant speed unit going U/S on take-off. It proved to be quite an occasion for, after completing a circuit, the Lanc pranged in the middle of the runway. Undaunted, they tried again two days later and many worthy studies were taken that afternoon from BII DS651 'OW:A'. But who was that photographer? What became of the pix he took, for just two have come to light? Which crew cavorted around the sky in DS713?

Next day — or rather the night of 17/18 August — it was back to the deadly business of war, 426 taking its BIIs into action for the first time by raiding Peenemünde. Epps and his team of six flew in DS713; as it turned out their only trip in her. Theirs was to be a protracted tour spanning 18 months — due in part to the Skipper's promotion to flight commander by November 1943, in part because 426 converted to Halifax IIIs during April 1944.

Düsseldorf, 3/4 November 1943, proved to be an op too many for DS713 when Plt Off D. W. Ditzler, RCAF and crew disappeared without trace, in the Unit ORB so bluntly recorded as 'Nothing has been heard of this aircraft since time of take-off, 17.10'. E. C. G. Jones

WHERE DO WE GO FROM HERE?

One who experienced that unwanted 'surplus to requirements' feeling was former 106 Squadron flight engineer Gilbert Gray, who had done a tour of 34 ops from Metheringham, May/August 1944, 'in a hectic 103 days', as he relates in his splendid book *Green Markers Ahead Skipper* (Newton Publishers 1993). Gilbert has very kindly allowed us to quote from his book on his emotions at that time of, in effect, living in a vacuum, with the war over, and having been shunted out to India, serving as a clerk, and finding himself caught up in the Hindu/Moslem troubles which led to the partition of India and Pakistan:

'The return of the services to a peacetime footing brought much that was unacceptable and, to me, trivial and insensitive. I had enlisted to fly and had completed a tour of operations over enemy territory, being lucky to survive what so many comrades had not. By and large, while the war was in progress, the public had recognised the part played by the flying men of the Royal Air Force — "the Brylcream Boys"!

'Now there was a growing awareness on my part, conveyed in my letters, of the contempt in which young aircrew senior NCOs were held by many "Regular" NCOs in the Sergeants' Mess. This was something new to me. On the flying units at home, I was aware of an intense mutual respect between those on the ground and those in the air. We depended so much on the skill and conscientiousness of the men and the women on the ground while they, only too often, waited in vain for their aircraft and equipment to return.

'I consoled myself by assuming that the chaps who held us in disdain had never been on an operational flying unit, but had grown bitter and weary at slogging out their service year after year in work which was humdrum and confined to offices of one kind or another.

'Authority, too, was imposing more and more petty regulations. "Airmen below Commissioned rank must not walk in front of the Officers' Mess", was one. In the Sergeants' Mess it was decreed that there was to be no noise in the afternoon... lest those that preferred to sleep were awakened, I suppose.

'Most of all, I remembered that, when remustering at Catterick, posters proclaimed that redundant aircrew could be assured of retaining rank, pay and status — or words to that effect. These promises disappeared into thin air on 1 July 1946. An edict from the Air Ministry regraded aircrew who did not have 7½ years service as aircrew (counting time up to 1.9.45 as double time) to "Aircrew II".

On paper few wartime aircrew had little chance of being anything other than "Aircrew II" and retaining their rank. My rank now became Sergeant Engineer II and my Warrant Officer rank was forfeit.

'It was a most degrading experience and on 337 MU did little for one's status. It was a particularly insensitive way to treat ex-operational aircrew who had been "through the mill". Particularly unfortunate was the fact that the "demotion" was not universally applied and it was frustrating, to say the very least, to see aircrew junior to myself still sporting their Flt Sgt and WO insignia in public.

'A new Pay Code was introduced at the same time. At home, the Press were indicating that the forces had been given a pay rise, but my letter to my father on 3 June 1946, tells a different story.

'By it I lose 2/- a day Jap. Campaign pay, and 1/6d War Service Increment. On top of that we are now under UK Income Tax (much higher) and we have lost the special forces concessional rate of Rs 15 per £1. It is now Rs 13.4 to the £1. So where is the increased pay coming in?

'These events, and the refusal of the Authorities to grant the Aircrew Europe Star to aircrew of my era, led to considerable disenchantment with the RAF as it was now functioning.

'I was home for Christmas.

'My final posting was to Swinderby, of all places, where I had spent a year training new crews for Bomber Command. Now I was a "pen-pusher" there — in the Equipment Accounts section. I remembered the lovely sound of the Merlin engines in my ear; the squeal of rubber on tarmac at touchdown; the exhilaration of floating smoothly in peaceful space at night with the full moon hanging motionless against a backcloth of awesome star-studded blackness. That more than compensated for those night skies torn and illuminated in the belligerence of war operations.

'There, for a few weeks, I worked under the scathing eye of the Flight Sergeant in charge of the section. One of my colleagues was Wolfgang, a German prisoner of war, still wearing his uniform of dull crimson battle dress with blue circular patch on the back of his tunic.

'I took final leave of these new colleagues on 17 February 1947 and the last person to wish me "Godspeed" was Wolfgang. Perhaps there was something symbolic in that.

'At No 101 PDC (Personnel Despatch Centre) at Kirkham, I was presented with a new uniform — navy blue pinstripe suit, grey raincoat, shoes, tie and trilby hat to carry me into "Civvy Street". I also carried my Service and Release Book with its travel warrant which I would need should I be recalled to service from the Reserve of the Royal Air Force to which I was now relegated. Such a recall would entitle me to a contingency sum of 5/- payable by the Post Office.'

FOOTNOTE:

After demob in February 1947 Gilbert Gray got an Honours Degree in Geography in 1951, became a teacher, and retired as Headmaster of a Grammar School in 1986. He is now living a healthy and happy retirement in his native Scotland.

Above:
WHERE DO WE GO FROM HERE?
Suddenly, it was all over, May 1945. The lights were coming on all over Europe and the squadrons began to wind down. Men — and women — by the hundred found themselves in a sort of vacuum. The brief spell of euphoria which followed victory in Europe and during which it seemed, everyone headed for York or Lincoln, Cambridge or London, had given way to days of anti-climax, even boredom. No longer was there a purpose and, save for the selected few destined for the Far East where Japan still fought on fanatically, the many aircrew and ground staff — yesterday's heroes and heroines — found themselves 'surplus to requirements', posted to such diverse penguin jobs as drivers, clerks and orderlies.

First to be posted away were the men from the Commonwealth. Within weeks most of the Canucks, Aussies, Kiwis, and all the rest from around the world, said their goodbyes and headed for the holding units prior to boarding the ships laid on to transport them home. Ahead lay mixed fortunes, for not all were warmly welcomed...but that is another story and not for comment here.

Presented is an intimate shot taken at Rufforth, 1945, with Canadians 'in limbo', awaiting posting notification with equanimity. W. R. Weir

VIEWS AND CLUES

Almost as sobering an experience as having survivors relate their recollections of being shot down in action with the enemy, is have them recount tales of crashes when in training or engaged in non-operational flying duty on their squadrons.

Given that statistics make dull reading, and are misleading... given that figures can never reflect cost in human terms... it may surprise you to learn that for every 14 Lancasters lost on operations, one was written off on non-operational duty. Weather... tiredness... 'friendly' fire... oxygen failure... sabotage... carelessness... inexperience... metal fatigue — the list is wide-ranging — all contributed to losses of valuable aircraft and even more valuable men... and it was not always the inexperienced crews who bought it.

And an end to hostilities in Europe did not mean an end to the crashes... the maiming... the loss of life.

Dangers aplenty awaited the squadrons engaged in bringing back former prisoners of war ('Operation Exodus')... the build up of 'Tiger Force' (for there was a war yet to be won in the Far East)... bringing back the British 8th Army from Italy ('Operation Dodge')... the need to maintain a strong bomber force due to the menacing shadow cast by a Russia now controlling much of Europe.

Here are a few misadventures during those early months of peace.

Above:
Liberally covered in foam and left to burn herself out is this No 300 'Masovian' Sqn Polish Air Force Lanc at Faldingworth. What can ex-Flt Sgt J. Gryglewicz and his fellow Poles tell us of their two mishaps? We know that on 14 March 1946, they made a three-engined approach in BI NG283, swung in the air due to a cross-wind, and belly-landed. We know that on 7 May 1946 they had the undercarriage of BIII RF262 collapse on take-off, resulting in a swing and resultant fire. But there is far more to them than brief, blunt one-liners! A. Gorski

Left:
Someone, somewhere knows details of this prang in Germany, likely to be at a one-time Luftwaffe base, and certain to evoke vivid mind-pictures for those who knew the fear, the terror of fire.
W. J. K. Endean

Bottom:
Another puzzler is this one, known to be a kite from No 429 'Bison' Sqn RCAF and which may turn out to be BIII RF253 which, on return from dumping bombs in the sea, had two engines cut out on approach to home base Leeming, 26 June 1945 (Captain: Flt Lt L. Bawtree, RCAF); or she could be BIII RF259 (Skipper: Flt Lt J. N. Snelgrove, RCAF) which came to grief on 14 February 1946 due to inadvertent retraction of her undercart before getting airborne.

Along with sister unit at Leeming — No 427 'Lion' Sqn RCAF — the 'Bisons' had discarded Hallies for Lancs as late as March 1945 and stayed behind when most of the No 6 Group Lancaster squadrons flew home to Canada.
H. G. Bowles

141

MEN LIKE THESE

For those who returned home to resume civilian life there was much hand-shaking and back-slapping. Be they from village or city or farm, there was generally a warm welcome, ranging from quiet family reunions to street parties. And what a strange period it was! After being away from home for several years, locked in to a way of life so very different, many suffered restlessness, total bewilderment, now that the daily sense of purpose which had for so long ruled their very existence was no more.

There was no guarantee of a job either, and many found themselves undertaking menial, routine tasks. Some had a trade to return to; others had no skills, having joined virtually straight from school, or had interrupted apprenticeships to volunteer for service. It was difficult for most to 'come down from the clouds' and adjust to the seemingly dull routine of normal life again, especially in a world where people wanted to forget the war and everything to do with it, including yesterday's heroes.

There was no counselling in those days and it was left to family and friends to rally round as best they could.

If it was a trying period for those who had had a relatively 'good' war, just imagine what it was like for the veterans who were scarred mentally and physically for the remainder of their allotted span on planet Earth — a span too often abbreviated; old age, well-earned retirement denied them.

Our pictures portray two extremes whereby survivors were appreciated during their period of rehabilitation.

Top right:
Despite inclement weather the citizens of Melbourne turn out to honour their countrymen on Anzac Day 1947. Well in evidence is the Nos 467 and 463 Lancaster Squadrons' contingent. Both Squadron Associations (and that of No 460 Sqn) remain very active throughout Australia, and many of their members have made regular pilgrimages back to their former bases, and for crew reunions. Likewise, they have hosted hundreds of their former air and ground crew colleagues from Britain and the Commonwealth who have visited Australia in more recent years. Melbourne still has its trams, too.
E. K. Sinclair

Centre right:
Stage and screen luminaries join the reverie during a Christmas 1945 party held at the legendary East Grinstead Burns Unit. Sir Archibald McIndoe (the 'Boss') — himself a legend — sits alongside the pianist. Fourth left standing with hat on is the redoubtable 'Guinea Pig' Reg Hyde who, having completed a gruelling tour with No 49 Sqn as a Lanc navigator, would survive an horrific crash in a Wimpey when instructing. He would subsequently endure more than 70 skin-graft operations with unsurpassed courage and fortitude. Kent and Sussex Courier

Bottom right:
Far from feeling bitter, the Guinea Pigs to a man did not lie down, retreat from the world in shame, anger, despair, even though a distinctly uncertain future stretched ahead of them. And who better to represent such men of resilience, such indomitable spirit, than Alan Morgan, by coincidence another No 49 Sqn crew member.

Alan joined the RAF in December 1942, aged 19, qualified as a flight engineer through No 4 S of TT, August 1943, by then a sergeant. He crewed-up at 1660 HCU, Swinderby with Jack Lett and his boys, sergeants all, joining No 49 Sqn at Fiskerton in early December 1943. Their first op was to Berlin, 16/17 December. Their eighth was to Stuttgart in Lanc BIII JB421 'EA:K' (their third in her), 20/21 February 1944, taking off 18.20hrs, the evening of Alan's 21st birthday! Just after dropping their load, the rear door was blown in by a flak burst. The wireless operator went aft to try to close it, but passed out through lack of oxygen. The Skipper sent the engineer back to help, and Alan rescued Frank Campbell by connecting him to the main oxygen supply, having to remove his gloves to do so. Alan then tried to close the door, but his portable oxygen bottle packed up, and he passed out. Jack Lett dived from 22,000 to 10,000ft, Alan gradually being brought round and helped forward by the bomb aimer, Sgt MacKew. He had, however, suffered severe frostbite in his hands, and had left much of the skin from his fingers adhering to the frozen fuselage interior. They diverted to Ford, in Sussex, and Alan was rushed to Chichester Hospital, eventually moving to East Grinstead in the care of Sir Archibald McIndoe, spending almost a year under repair. All his fingers were amputated, right down to the hand joint and small stubs were created by cutting down into the hand itself, thus giving Alan some use of his hands. Through Sir Archibald's dedicated care and genius, and his own great fortitude, Alan passed a special medical board in late 1944, and went back to flying duties as a flight engineer at the Empire Air Navigation School, Shawbury, flying Halifaxes. Then came VE-Day, and Alan, by then a flight sergeant, was demobbed, getting his release in the very first batch, grey suit, cap, and all.

After the war he became a fully qualified and highly proficient precision toolmaker. As he

says, 'Thanks to the skills of Sir Archie', as the New Zealander surgeon was so affectionately known by all who passed through his hands.

Jack Lett and crew continued to operate with a replacement flight engineer, but the crew was to suffer another setback when the bomb aimer, Flt Sgt Gerald ('Mack') MacKew was killed by a flak burst on an op to Brunswick, 22/23 April 1944. The remaining crew completed their tour. They did not fly JB421 again after the Stuttgart incident. It went down on 7/8 May 1944.
Jack Lett DFC in 1991.

Alan and Ella Morgan pose for the camera on their wedding day at St Mary's Church, Droylsden, 10 June 1944, Alan's hands still bandaged nearly four months after the eventful return from Stuttgart. The happy couple celebrated their Golden Wedding in 1994. Both are still busy fundraising for the McIndoe Trust and Guinea Pig Club. Alan & Ella Morgan

BEGINNING OF THE END

The defeat of Germany did not mean an end to the Lancaster 'at war'. Far from it. Plans were already well advanced whereby a mixed force of Lancasters, and its successor, the Lincoln, would operate alongside the B-29 Superfortresses of the 20th USAAF from the Marianas. 'Tiger Force', as it was codenamed, was to include in its order of battle a reconstituted No 5 Group, initially comprising Nos 9, 57, 75 (NZ), 83, 97, 106, 460 (RAAF), 467 (RAAF) and 617 Sqns, not forgetting No 627 with Mosquitos. A similarly re-formed all-Canadian No 6 Group would begin operations with Nos 405, 408, 419, 420, 425, 428, 431 and 432 Sqns. Barely had the Canadian Lanc squadrons left for Canada in June, preparatory to intensive training, when the resident UK-based No 5 Group Units began gearing up in earnest.

The dropping of the atomic bomb changed everything and, in the event, only Nos 9 and 617 Sqns 'went out East'. Initially sent to India to replace Liberators (which had to be surrendered under the terms of the lend/lease agreement), the Lancs and crews of 9 and 617 soon found themselves on a war footing, standing by at the request of the Indian Government when there was a revolt by some Royal Indian Navy units. Thankfully, the Lanc crews were not called upon, and both squadrons settled down to a pleasurable detachment until flying back to England in April 1946.

OUR GRAPHIC SNAPS SHOW:

Above right:
Ein Shemer early 1948. Escorted by Palestinian policemen, captured members of the notorious Stern Gang file past No 38 Sqn Lanc III ME380. Originally a BIII with No 514 Sqn, she was converted to ASR standard and saw service with No 6 OTU before passing to No 38 Sqn. 'Put out to grass' at No 38 MU, Llandow, she ultimately succumbed to the scrap men in September 1951. R. Bannister

Centre right:
No 38 Sqn was to spend much of its working life in the Middle East hotspots, both during the war from 1940, flying Wellingtons, and eventually, by a succession of squadron reshuffles, found itself the operator of Lancaster ASR IIIs, such as RF323 seen here on air test by Sqn Ldr Arthur Barden and crew after collection from No 135 MU, Gebel Hamzi, 23 May 1946, complete with underslung airborne lifeboat. She was first issued to No 621 Sqn, a little-known, short-lived Lanc unit, renumbered No 18 Sqn in September 1946 at Ein Shemer, and disbanded only two weeks later, to be absorbed into a No 38 Sqn detachment from Malta. A. G. Barden

Bottom right:
Ein Shemer again, and RF323 'RL:C' with nose section completely gutted, not, as might be supposed the result of a terrorist mortar attack as reported in the local press at the time, but due to having caught fire during refuelling, 28 March 1947. Flg Off Glyn Huyton and two of his No 38 Sqn colleagues ponder the scene. The squadron detachment eventually moved back to Malta, April 1948, from where it continued to operate the Lancaster on MR/GR duties until December 1953, becoming the last front-line Lanc unit in the RAF, and then converting to the Shackleton, which it flew until 1967, an unbroken run of over 20 years with the AVRO piston-engined genre. A. G. Barden

It was un unsettling period none the less. Apart from the threat posed by Soviet Russia, there were rumblings of discontent in countries under British control in the Middle and Far East and Lancaster squadrons were frequently on standby, such as No 7, which flew out to Singapore in January 1947 ('Operation Red Lion'), some 15 months before the Malaysian emergency began (and in which Lincoln squadrons became heavily involved).

But it was in the Middle East that Lancaster squadrons really became embroiled in conflict. Saddled with the burden of the Palestinian Mandate, it was Britain's thankless task to act with impartiality until control was relinquished in mid-May 1948. It was an impossible situation. The Lanc crews became the eyes of the Royal Navy, intercepting boats laden with Jews intent on illegally moving to the 'Promised Land', and by their actions the RAF became a target for activists.

LEND AN EAR

No two air forces enjoyed as much co-operation as did the American 8th Army Air Force and the multi-national Royal Air Force. Whilst, inevitably, there were disagreements on policy and other issues (the province of senior officers), there was much liaison and good-humoured rivalry down at grass roots level.

When the two 'sides' mingled in pubs, dance halls and hotels, jibes about our warm beer were countered with quips about Flying Fortresses flying at 40,000ft with a teeny-weeny bomb, and so on. Rarely did such exchanges become serious, though it might sometimes depend on how much ale had been consumed and what influence any female companions had!

On a more official footing, any Lanc crew which found itself diverted to a Fort or Lib field experienced hospitality quite overwhelming...a respect for all that the RAF stood for, and was doing in the round-the-clock pounding of Germany, and of targets vital to its war effort located in occupied lands.

And there was the food on offer... the stuff of dreams, seen only on celluloid at their RAF drome's 'Astra'.

Some fortunate souls managed to book their places on liaison tours which took in one Yank Base after another, typified by a select group of veterans and specialists manning BI R5868 'PO:S', sort of on loan from No 467 Sqn RAAF, Waddington... an old girl with as impressive a tally of recorded ops (137) as any adorning a B-17 or B-24. No less impressive was the Lanc's 33ft bomb bay... and, of course, the 'music' of four Merlins running in unison, certain to turn heads, draw a crowd.

Below:
Maybe a few time-worn aviators will be moved to tell us about our two pix? All we know is that the snap of R5868 entertaining a gathering of American airmen with Merlins in full song was taken at Ridgewell, where resided the Fortress-equipped 381st Bomb Group.

Are they aware...surprised...interested that she exists to this day, 'lording it' over all in the Royal Air Force Museum at Hendon, a taxi ride from the nation's capital?
E. W. Keene (starboard view)/R. A. Freeman Collection (port view)

FOOTNOTE:
Behind the Lanc in the lower picture is a London Transport AEC Regal bus, one of a batch commandeered during the war, and converted to a mobile canteen for use on USAAF bomber stations, manned by the Red Cross, named 'Clubmobiles'. Most were returned to service with London's Green Line after the war.

144

BOMBER BASES: A LAMENT

Of the 70 or so aerodromes from which Lancasters flew during the war, only a handful remain operational, or even in RAF hands, the most secure, perhaps, being Waddington, with its mighty Boeing E3 Sentries (AWACS) airborne control stations. Paradoxically, these directly succeeded, in 1991, the last of the 'Lancaster line' in the RAF, the AVRO Shackleton, the remaining five of which were sold at auction in London. Thus ended an association of 52 years with the breed (ie through from Manchester/Lanc/Lincoln), much of the 'Shack' itself being of basically Manchester design and construction, still retaining that classic outline.

Coningsby, a few miles to the east of 'Waddo' appears reasonably secure as a front line station (fighters now — Tornados); also home of the Battle of Britain Memorial Flight, whose future seems far from secure, particularly its Lancaster PA474 in these days of perpetual cut-backs.

Legendary Scampton, a few miles to the north through Lincoln, is doomed to close in 1995. The RAF without Scampton? Almost unthinkable to anyone with Bomber Command connections and memories. We can but hope that some small part might be preserved as a shrine to the events which took place from there; and that Nigger's grave and headstone will be protected — by removal to an appropriate, secure site in Lincolnshire if necessary, and surely not abroad as has been suggested by some. (Thankfully the decision on that appears to be in the hands of the RAF, not the politicians.) Finningley is also doomed to closure.

Leeming continues to fly the jack-of-all-trades, master-of-none Tornado; Linton the noisy, busy-bee, inelegant, Brazilian-designed Tucano; but Wyton looks set to lose its active airfield status and become an administration centre for the RAF at a cost of many millions. Feltwell is a radar site. Mildenhall should continue as a base for the USAF tankers etc for the foreseeable future at least, though the American forces are being pruned just as savagely as the RAF in the wake of the Cold War thaw.

Upwood and Syerston are RAF gliding centres, but even their future must be doubtful in the medium term, as more RAF activities are 'privatised'. No doubt cases are being made for the abolition of cadet forces such as the Air Training Corps in any case, inevitably to the ultimate benefit of much less honourable, and infinitely less character-building activities. Swinderby, which provided the first taste of RAF life for entrants this past quarter century has succumbed and awaits its fate, its runways sometimes smothered with new cars built under the badges of another former adversary.

A few of the bases have fortunately survived fairly intact in private hands (including watch offices and administration buildings in some cases), with active flying clubs and small commercial operations: Wickenby, Bourn, Langar (School of Parachute Training), Sturgate, Breighton; and even the delightfully-named Wombleton and Little Snoring. Gransden Lodge has recently reopened a small strip for gliders; at Strubby there are gliders and helicopters, the latter on North Sea gas support duties. Metheringham and Graveley have microlight operations (better than nothing, but what a comedown!); and the army operates helicopters out of Oakington and Waterbeach. Lindholme, Stradishall are prisons! Faldingworth remains fairly complete, its recent history and present status being detailed in one of the captions.

Two former Lanc stations have achieved 'International Airport' status — Kirmington and Middleton St George, and now masquerade under the titles of Humberside and Teesside.

Many have now become virtually unrecognisable as former airfields from the air, having been largely returned to nature by farmers, some still marked as disused airfields on the CAA half-millionth flying maps, Chedburgh and Wratting Common in particular, being barely discernible, as are Kelstern and Ludford Magna. Bardney, Fiskerton, Spilsby, Wigsley, still stand out quite clearly from above. Elsham Wolds is an industrial estate bisected by a motorway with nowhere for even a light aircraft to land, as is Waltham (Grimsby).

Skellingthorpe completely disappeared long ago under postwar housing estates, the only visible mementoes being a memorial, the inclusion in the village sign of a Lancaster, a display in the former railway siding weighbridge building, and a few crumbling blast mounds marking the former bomb dump through which the Lincoln bypass now runs.

Winthorpe is still active for gliding, and as home of the well-established Newark (Notts and Lincs) Air Museum, which has the fuselage centre section of W4964, 'WS:J' on display, plus many other Lanc-related exhibits. Similarly, East Kirkby houses the Lincolnshire Aviation Heritage Centre, established by the Panton brothers, Fred and Harold, its centrepiece being former French Navy Lancaster NX611 which is being nursed back to life, and will surely fly again one day from the splendid mile-long runway nearby, which the Americans built postwar.

This is in no way intended to be a complete list, merely examples of what has happened in general in the postwar period.

Some of the disused dromes have in recent years even been excluded from the aviation maps altogether: Downham Market, East Wretham, Mepal, Dunholme Lodge, North Killingholme, Tuddenham: beautiful, euphonious names, as British as Britain can ever be, almost totally anonymous to much of the population before their new neighbouring airfields took their names during World War 2, and now gradually receding again into comparative anonymity off the beaten track.

Even as this is written (April 1995), it is announced in the press that the Ministry of Defence is putting 20 airbases up for sale, covering 20,000 acres, and expected to fetch £300 million. They include Scampton, Binbrook, Swinderby. It would be too much to hope that sale proceeds might be channelled into providing pensions or comfort for those who served in some way, but instead, no doubt the powers-that-be have already earmarked which drain it will go down.

An efficient M.T. Section.

DEEP IN THE HEART OF FENLAND, or THE " INNS " AND OUTS OF SPILSBY.

True to type and security any relation to Spilsby Town and R.A.F. Spilsby is purely coincidential. The new arrival must therefore bide himself with patience and accept the fact that the nearest railway station is Firsby, the nearest village Great Steeping, and the phone number Scrimby (XYZ). However, for those who arrive by rail, the efficiency of the M.T. Section solves immediate confusion by whisking the weary traveller off to the Guard Room, where a welcome will be awaiting him, and further information regarding his immediate future given.

AERIAL ASPECTS

As photographed by Rob Davis, 1985/1987, reminders of a conflict now long past, but far from forgotten.

Below:
Metheringham... the Sergeants' Mess as seen from the water tower. Once a second home, a place of refuge, relaxation, laughter and tears. Now crumbling, succumbing to nature, but still clinging to life, still in use by farmers. But for how long? Those bleak winds off Martin Moor and Blankney Fen are gradually winning the last battle. Many would barely recognise their former base, of which little remains visible at ground level, though the water tower still provides a source of orientation. The watch office, part demolished, still stands — just — but is a ruin beyond redemption. There is a memorial to No 106 Sqn on the eastern edge of the airfield, and a small heritage museum has been established at the southwest end of the drome on the former No 4 communal site, in what was the ration store. Its curators Peter and Zena Scoley are always pleased to welcome former inmates. R. A. Davis

Opposite top left:
Faldingworth... once home to many-a-hundred Polish airmen of No 300 'Masovian' Sqn. A sole BI hangar stands black and silent, no doubt once used for repair and inspection of Lancs, the former throb of activity, ringing of metal on metal, long since stilled, its last flying residents (No 305 Sqn's Mosquitos) having departed in early 1947. Some 10 years later it reopened, becoming a top security establishment to do with nuclear weapons and missiles, surrounded by high fencing and orange lights, remaining a brooding, forbidden place, even following its closure in 1972... closure on the surface, that is, because the site is still in use by the British Manufacturing & Research Co (BMARC), involved in the production and testing of armaments, with large underground facilities. Its main runway and peri-tracks remain largely intact, though increasingly weed-strewn, with a sadly neglected, greying air. R. A. Davis

Opposite top right:
Hemswell... quite high up on the Lincoln Edge, with grand views of sunsets west over the Trent Valley and Gainsborough, and sunrises east over Ermine Street and the Wolds; south to Lincoln Cathedral on the horizon, and north to somewhere-on-Humber. Its origins as an RAF station date back to June 1918 — as old as the Service itself. It was enlarged in the 1930s expansion plans, and reopened in 1937, constructed to the new RAF station standard, with four large hangars built on a graceful curve, to house the front-line bombers of the time — Blenheims, Hampdens, Wellingtons, later succeeded by the Lancasters of Nos 150 and 170 Sqns. It was always a busy station, lots of comings and goings, residents postwar including Mosquitos, Lincolns, Canberras, even Thor missiles. Once the Lincolns left in 1958 it was never quite the same. The views over the airfield from the Gainsborough road of them lumbering off into the dip beyond the runway's end were unforgettable. The Canberras left a year later, the missiles in 1963; gliding continued for a time, and the married quarters were to remain in use for some years for the Scampton overspill in the halcyon days of the V-Force, when we still had some proper bombers made by AVRO. After final closure in 1967, its hangars were put to various uses, even to housing refugees, but in latter years as grain stores for the European Community. The former administration and domestic sites, SHQ etc are still there off to the right, some housing light industry, but a sad, shabby atmosphere prevails. At the top end still stands a T2 hangar, a grain silo complex alongside. Also in good order is the watch tower and its postwar extension (centre). The runways have virtually disappeared. A museum and memorial commemorate once-great days. But where are those Merlins which boomed out around the hangars for so many years?
R. A. Davis

Opposite inset
Sturgate... a few miles southwest of Hemswell, a name not even on some larger-scale road maps of today. Completed in late 1944, too late to become operational before the war ended, it provided a relief landing ground for 1662 HCU's Lancs and Hallies. It then became home to Nos 50 and 61 Sqns' Lancasters from June 1945 until January 1964, but fell vacant until 1954 when a squadron of USAF Thunderstreaks briefly used it as home, finally closing in 1964. This view shows clearly the differing layouts of dispersals, typical of the wartime construction. The piles of gravel on the end of one of the runways indicate that much of its length and that of the taxiways have been plundered as hardcore for roads and construction sites. The Lincs/Notts airfields which closed down after the war contributed greatly in this respect to the numerous large power stations built along the Trent. The almost inevitable bales and stacks of straw stand out in the late afternoon sunshine, many farmers, too, having put the airfields to wide use. Fortunately, Sturgate still has a good length of runway, and some wartime buildings, which remain in use by local flying groups. R. A. Davis

Opposite below:
Woodhall Spa... place of legends. Bordered here on its north side by woods where Robin Hood reputedly roamed. The T2 hangar, still in use by the RAF, is about all that remains of No 619 Sqn's former territory, which was taken over in April 1944 by the Mosquitos and crews of No 627 Sqn, whose former briefing rooms and flight offices have all but disappeared under the encroaching trees and shrubbery. Also still used by the RAF is the complex of buildings across from the T2, the largest of which is the Tornado engine repair and servicing bay. To the left of this is the engine test bed with outlet tower. The twin-span building to the far right is the spares store for the RAF Memorial Flight's Lancaster, Spitfires, Hurricanes, Dakota etc, based at Coningsby, just a stone's throw away. These modern structures were built on the site of four former dispersals used by No 627 Sqn's Mosquitos, the one under the very centre of the complex being that from which Wg Cdr Guy Gibson VC, DSO, DFC, taxied out for his last op (in a Mossie), from which he FTR, the night of 18/19 September 1944.

Soon after VE-Day, Woodhall's illustrious main residents (No 617 Sqn) split up and left with its Lancs for pastures new, to be followed soon after the fall of Japan by the Mosquitos. The station then fell quiet, went into slumber, until 1959, when it became a base for Bloodhound missiles, soulless objects which were supposed to render aircraft obsolete. They stayed until the 60s, when they, too, went to the scrap heap.

Not a lot remains of the airfield itself, runways and taxi-tracks having all but given in to gravel extraction pits, though the RAF has created a small golf course in between the craters. Along the western perimeter, beside the Woodhall–Tattershall road, several wartime buildings, including Nissens, remain. Some are being restored by a local aviation historical group for use as a World War 2 museum. Imagine standing beside those same sparse buildings fifty and more years ago, watching the sunset, listening and feeling the thunder as not only Woodhall's resident 20 or so Lancs run-up at dispersal before taxying out, but also another 150 or more from other bases, within earshot!... Coningsby, Metheringham, Bardney, East Kirkby, Spilsby. Did it all really happen? R. A. Davis

"PER ARDUA AD ASTRA... IN LANCS"

Desmond M. Chorley

Undersides painted night bomber matt black, broad wings spread wide. Four silent Rolls-Royce Merlin engines jut from the wings' thick leading edges. Dusk creeping across the barely undulating, chalk-flecked Lincolnshire farmland of The Wolds.

Having carved an immortal niche in military annals as a superb night bomber, the best of the war, at dusk the Avro Lancaster always looked premiére classe, strangely ominous and stubbornly reliable. Ah yes, that would be exactly the right time and place to renew acquaintances with the Lanc.

Alas, such was not to be.

Forty-one years had slipped by since the Second World War ended and the same number since I'd last seen an Avro Lancaster on a Royal Air Force aerodrome in Lincolnshire, the county of wartime England known as Bomber County because of the myriad RAF Bomber Command airfields that polka-dotted its 2,600 square miles, and clustered so closely in some locations that circling Lancs often nerve-rackingly trespassed into a neighbouring drome's circuit.

The RAF Battle of Britain Memorial Flight based at RAF Coningsby, Lincs, had invited me, a Canadian civilian, to climb aboard its Lancaster, on a Sunday, when it would make a memorial flight over the ancient village of Ludford Magna.

Below, 101 Squadron Association oppos would have just completed attending a service in the Ludford parish church of St Mary and St Peter, and placed a wreath at the inscribed polished granite pillar that ex-101ers worldwide had made contributions to have sculptured. It was dedicated in July 1978.

The overflight would not be a simple sentimental journey but a symbolic, nostalgic salute, not only to personnel who served with 101 Squadron at Ludford Magna, but to all of the 100,000 men, of many Allied nations, who flew in Bomber Command during the Second World War — every one a volunteer and more than half of them meeting their deaths doing it. God knows how many of the survivors were injured, some maimed for life.

As for my visit, fate stepped in and it became impossible for me to be in the United Kingdom for what would have been an unforgettable flight. But, about a year later, I *was* in England and paid fitting homage to the BBMF Lanc at Coningsby, 18 miles south of Ludford Magna.

101 Squadron was based at RAF Ludford Magna at the end of the war in Europe. Crews, arrayed in front of a weary, paint-peeling Lanc were photographed there on peace-bringing VJ Day, August 15th, 1945.

We all look wet behind the ears.

Regardless, a print of that historic shot (of which I have a negative) reportedly hangs in the Boucherette Tearoom of Robinsons Farm Café at Ludford (endearingly remembered as Mudford), where wartime aircrew late risers could buy an off-the-base breakfast, and commissioned and noncom flyers could mingle — without RAF-favored class distinction, and regardless of rank — to shoot wizard lines over jugs of hot char.

Arriving at Coningsby, welcoming rain slashed across the airfield. That right sharply brought back authentic memories.

Panavia Tornadoes were neatly sprinkled along the flight line, canopies up, guaranteeing clammy offices for the next pilots to fly them.

Wartime Lancs — deafening, cold, draughty and ceaselessly vibrating — were even less endearing steeds when beads of moisture clung visibly to their spartan interiors. No one ever accused a Lanc of being comfy. Vibes turned the aircraft into a well-remembered all-shudderingly eager beast, an aerial Mack truck designed to haul bombs, bullets and fuel, and — just incidentally, you understand — a seven- or eight-man crew. Cold, cacophony and the shakes don't fuss BBMF.

Rounding the end of the drab olive green camouflaged hangar at the northwest corner of the airfield, the high black underside of a rounded starboard wingtip became visible.

Four decades of misting memories were about to be spanned in seconds after a few more sashaying, squishy steps across the well-trimmed, sodden lawn.

Two huge bulbous tires chocked for a just-completed engine run check, hefty undercarriage legs wide apart, there brooded the, then, world's lone surviving and currently flying Lanc.

Think about that — one out of the 7,377 built, 430 of them in Canada at Malton (where I'd been graduated from No 1 Air Observer School as a qualified aimer and dropper of bombs; try and turn those skills into a peacetime vocation). Malton is today's Toronto International airport.

About 3,800 Lancs were lost, all but 10% in action.

And, the BBMF example looked exactly what it was, and how it's always remembered as... a very large and formidable four-engine bruiser of a heavy bomber.

Its role: Destruction and death. Category: World's best.

Standing there in ominous rain-spattered majesty, its lordly appearance evoked legendary staying power, enormous airframe strength, the ability to absorb incredible amounts of punishment from flak and fighter, and to pull well over maximum G ratings in violent evasive action.

Also evoked: Much of the glory that so many laughing, all-volunteer, piece-of-cake, dicey-do, P/O Prune-worshipping, barely post-pubescent crews bought it during their frightening, meat-grinder tours of bombing sorties, ops mostly at night and often in the cruddiest of weather.

No wonder indomitable (and still — incredibly — officially unsung!) Air Chief Marshal Sir Arthur T. Harris, commander in chief, Bomber Command, so fondly nicknamed Butch.

It was the superbly strong Lanc, albeit in fierce resistance, that sorrowfully took many of Butch's bomber boys to their death. And with a casualty rate consistently below that of all other bombers, resolutely brought many back to safe, if sometimes soul-sapping, landings.

Seven men used to crew an ordinary squadron Lanc and, from the night of October 7/8th, 1943 (the night of a 343-Lanc raid on Stuttgart) eight aboard numerous specially-equipped aircraft on 101 Squadron. They carried normal bomb loads and an extra German-speaking crewman to operate hush-hush, multi-aerialed 'Airborne Cigar'. Two ABC antennae stood like goal posts ahead of the mid-upper turret, one jutted below the bomb aimer's hatch. ABC's fiendishly tricky job was to ear-piercingly jam the enemy's radio signals and hornswoggle prowling Luftwaffe night-fighter voice communications with phoney commands.

"During the war, 101 Squadron had a higher number of casualties on operational sorties than any other squadron in Bomber Command, and, until recently, much of the activity of 101 Squadron has been covered by the Official Secrets Act," BBMF stated at the time of my visit.

"That's why the BBMF Lanc is in the markings of an aircraft of 101 Squadron − SR," said BBMF's then commanding officer and Lanc pilot, Squadron Leader Anthony F. Banfield.

"Call sign is simply 'Lancaster'," quote Tony. "If queried, 'THE Lancaster'."

As chocks were pulled free, the Lanc, a Mk 1 built in 1945 that never was bloodied by enduring ops, was pushed back into the hangar. Its 102-foot wingspan seemed to crowd the walls, and its glasshouse cockpit, with astrodome zit, to scrape the ceiling.

Memory waved some flags.

Black sides and underbelly? Correct.

Authentic wartime camouflaged upper sides and top surfaces? Dead right.

Paint finish? Not on, not the way it used to be. The whole proud aircraft gleamed magnificently, reflecting hangar lights and glistening with rain droplets on its glossy polyurethane paint. In the war is had been a dull finish above, matt black below. To aid survival.

148

And where was the peardrop for H_2S, the airborne map-reading radar? It should snuggle under the belly, just about beneath the Elsan chemical toilet and ahead of the rear turret.

Gaping 33-foot-long bomb doors displayed the dark cavern into which were stuffed bomb loads heavier than any other wartime aircraft could carry. A typical mix of goodies: a 4,000lb Cookie, three 1,000 pounders, twelve weighing 250lbs each and six unfriendly incendiary canisters.

Even so, for the 26-foot, 22,000lb Grand Slam, the bomb bay doors had to be removed, the terrifying bomb's 46-inch girth bulging beneath the fuselage. No other aircraft could carry that monstrous earthquaker.

Gazing up at the immense product of British aeronautical designer Ray Chadwick's imagination, it was a mite difficult to credit that one man — Alex Henshaw, chief test pilot for Vickers-Armstrong Ltd — intentionally had barrel-rolled every Lanc that came off the Castle Bromwich factory's production line.

Swapping lies with an Air Canada captain, one day, I mentioned Mr Henshaw's routine rolls.

"Before joining Air Canada, I flew Lancs in the RCAF, long after the war, and was never able to complete a roll," said this-is-your-captain-speaking. "Now, with the centre thrust of the [Douglas] DC-9s I'm driving..."

"Piece of cake?" I offered.

A noncommittal smile.

The spirit lives.

Once the hangar doors were closed, overhead lights turned the four-gun turret and the twin-gun mid-upper and front turrets into twinkling baubles before adhering rain droplets evaporated.

Beckoning, on the rear starboard fuselage, was the square-hole crew access door, with inside step over rear turret ammunition trays.

Ah, to be privileged to climb aboard and nose about in once-familiar, crowded space that smelled of chromate, hydraulic fluid, high octane av gas, dankness, a toilet, the strange earthy smell of Lincolnshire mud that had adhered to flying boots, and the sweet/sour aroma of that funny oil with which the gunners used to clean their guns — all, of course, experienced following a traditional nervous good luck piss on the single rear wheel.

But this time the RAF said no. Heritage, you know.

Ah then, to fly in the old kite for maybe 15 minutes of its precious, stringently rationed 75 airborne hours a year.

Again, despite the intrepid writer's 6,000-mile roundtrip pilgrimage, another not-on answer.

Arrgh!

But oh, what it would have been like to get comfortably prone once more in the bubble-nosed bomb aimer's hatch, to recline transfixed during the unequalled exhilaration of low flying and to listen on the intercom while the rear gunner bellyached about salt water gun barrel corrosion as four Merlin-driven propellers churned quadruple frothing wakes in the North Sea.

Next day, the SR-D was bound for Cologne. As an invited guest. Reason: To strut some nostalgic muscle stuff before an audience that half a century previous used to parade some pretty formidable military hardware itself.

How many times had other Lancs gone there in the early 1940s? At night. Never by invitation. But always receiving a memorable reception.

In wartime its identifier and call letter, D, would have been D-Dog. Nowadays its a more phonetically demure D-Delta. Seems we often flew in, what was it? Ah, yes — N^2, Nan Squared. That would be prosaic November-Two today.

Shush!

It was cathedral-quiet in the hangar. No boyish nervous laughs, no overly loud guffaws of youths suddenly made men. Just the odd thump from a young airwoman tin basher working at a corner bench.

Lanc SR-D looked down on BBMF's hangarful flock of tiny Spitfires and Hurricanes that cluttered the place. Compressed air cylinders, frighteningly reminiscent of 1,000lb bombs, were parked on the floor beneath Delta's port wing.

Outside, there was a moderndday cacophony tuning up: An angry double-barrelled rumble as an English Electric Lightning spooled. A Tornado screeching into low-hanging, drenching clouds. And a McDonnell Douglas Phantom just plain growling. All of them, way off key, never did get it together.

"That's noise," said engaging Warrant Officer Barry Sears, BBMF's engineering officer.

"This —" he indicated the Lanc, "is music."

To that music in wartime, 101 Squadron flew 4,895 sorties in Lancs, losing 171 aircraft, as well as 33 in crashes, according to *The Bomber Command Diaries* (Martin Middlebrook & Chris Everitt, Viking).

But for the legendary Lanc, of which the BBMF classic showpiece bomber was then the last one flying, inexplicably fond memories persist. The Lanc did it all, you see.

Bombing prowess aside, a few unconnected anecdotes hatch in something of its fun side... without, that is, mentioning Lancs that scooted under the Firth of Forth bridge because it invitingly was there, and zorched wave-top low alongside North Sea fishing boats out of Grimsby (just north of Mudford), all three gun turrets getting off exuberant bursts at the buoys marking the nets and occasionally, 'tis said, earning enthusiastic return fire from a single bridge-mounted Lewis gun.

War wasn't always hell, you understand.

It might be hard to evince such a remark from certain crews manning United States Eighth Army Air Force Boeing B-17 Fortresses or B-24 Liberators. Airborne of an early morning, a great flock of them was busily engaged in assembling one of the Yanks' magnificently stepped-up, thrashing-great formations. Down Norfolk way. Before pressing on to plaster an enemy target.

The sky was starred with gracefully arching Very colors they kept firing to identify squadron levels and to pull in stragglers.

On a P/O Prune, finger-in-to-second-joint, dead-steady straight climb to test a recalibrated George, the automatic pilot, a lone Lanc found itself chummily amid its orbiting, formating, bewildering allies. Friendly like, the Lanc crew took great interest in this dead serious, awe-inspiring aerial ballet and co-operatively worked through its supply of Very cartridges, popping off the colorful mix quite indiscriminately. The Americans could not have been amused, and maybe were in fact confused, by such a cavalier pyrotechnical festoon.

To crew a Lanc, many a time, could cause laundry bills to grow. Even when the war in Europe had ended.

F'instance. Crews for all of 101 Squadron's Lancs were briefed for one of the shortest flights any of them would log. Target, er, more properly, destination, the permanent peacetime aerodrome of RAF Binbrook. Its circuit just about overlapped Ludford Magna's.

Drill was: Take off with minimum spacing between aircraft and once established airborne, call for landing sequence at Binbrook which would then become the new home of the squadron. No silly-bugger beatups or suchlike immature aeronautical antics.

Prudence aforethought, and somewhat annoying to the crews, the brass ordered all guns removed from all aircraft. So — but, of course, you silly brass hats — some gunners and bomb aimers promptly armed their turrets with stolen government-issue brooms and mops.

Ludford and Binbrook were beaten up. Ludford was 'windowed' with playing cards and lightly bombed with toilet rolls. Lancs hairily jostled in from all directions. A proper rabble. But oh what jolly good fun!

Who was in our crew? Stephen A. O'Brien, a crack shot rear gunner, who always used to complain about the proximity of the malodorous Elsan and was scared stiff in his first postwar flight aboard a commercial airliner.

"I sat facing forward," he told me.

Steve became City Clerk of Devizes. He died October 7th, 1977.

C. Frank M. Saunders, the lanky mid-upper gunner, used to claim his turret wouldn't accommodate long legs. Frank, age 20, was killed July 30th, 1945, flying with another crew. And Stanley Lilley, who replaced him, also had unkind things to mutter about the lack of cushioned accommodation. Stan shaped his postwar career in engineering.

Clifford W. D. Wood, navigator, moved to Zimbabwe to become a wheel in insurance and died there August 7th, 1988.

Pilot Donald Lord's short legs made him stretch for the rudder pedals. William Taylor was flight engineer. After the war, Don went to Nigeria to keep cotton mills spinning, and Bill to Wales to guide newspaper circulation.

Wireless operator Robert C. H. Lander, Royal Australian Air Force, was posted back to Sydney while we were at 1660 Heavy Bomber Conversion Unit, RAF Swinderby. His replacement, Geoffrey Ryder, was plumb lost track of.

I segued to Canada to write for a living. And in Canada, a few years ago, was once again able to kick a Lancaster's tires and to crawl around in its entrails. But not to pee on its tail wheel...

Shortly after stroking the wondrous beast again, it was high blue, contrailed and warm on the last Saturday in September, 1988.

They flew in all morning.

Nestled together off the runway at the west end of the airport, they constituted a colorful flock of just under 200 general aviation aircraft, fine representatives of the myriad species that Canadian Owners and Pilots Association members fly.

Curiosity and respect had brought most of the pilots and passengers and me to Hamilton's Mount Hope Airport, Ontario. But for many of us gals and guys with gray or white or little hair, the tug of tumbling memories was the irresistible draw.

About 15,000 other aviation buffs, and just plain curious folk, had also arrived... from as far away as Hong Kong, Europe, and across the United States and Canada. Airport parking and grassland spaces bulging, cars, vans and trucks were parked bumper-to-bumper on roads up to five miles from the aerodrome.

This was a once-in-a-lifetime gathering. Impossible to re-enact, impossible to forget.

These people had an abiding desire to see and hear the dedication and inaugural flight of Canada's superb flying memorial, a meticulously restored Lancaster.

Nobody, repeat nobody, was disappointed.

The public address system was busy babbling all morning, connecting veterans with their past.

"Anyone from 101 Squadron who flew on *Operation Dodge*", boomed the loudspeakers, "please come to the announcer's trailer." Hey, that's me! At the trailer I was met by a former Desert Rat who had finished his war in Italy and was flown home from Pomigliano by a 101 Squadron Lanc.

"When we landed in England," he said, "we were whipped off so fast I never got a chance to thank the crew. That's what I'm doing now... after 43 years."

A Hawker Hurricane and a Supermarine Spitfire completed their aerial *pas de deux* and gracefully exited to the west, stage left. As the sheer music of their Rolls-Royce Merlins faded, the public address system also trailed off into silence after announcing "...this is a salute just for you."

Stage right, at the end of runway 30 Left, the Lanc was in position. Its four Packard-built 12-cylinder Merlins were turning over in a cherished melody of long ago. Part growl, part crackle, the unique sound transfixed an expectant crowd.

Pressed against a restraining fence, one spectator held a radio tuned to tower frequency. The knot of men, women and children around him were privileged to eavesdrop on some crisp historic words.

"Lancaster cleared for takeoff."

Growl-crackle changed key. Now it was a deep-sweet pulsating whir-drone, a powerful voice of commanding authority and throatiness.

Completely quieted, the crowd remained hushed until first the tail wheel had daylight under it, and seconds later, the main two wheels parted with the runway.

The inaugural flight was airborne.

Spontaneous cheering and clapping broke out. Many faces were wet with the tears of reminiscence. Palpable waves of nostalgia inundated all those who — ladies and gentlemen — back in the Second World War, had built, flown in, fixed, serviced or been based with Lancs.

Grandly, the mightiest bomber of yore retracted its undercarriage and majestically climbed away in a gentle bank, the sun suddenly shafting off its four-gun rear turret.

The brilliant reflection from the turret's gleaming Perspex helped conjure a flashback to the night of June 12/13th, six days after D-Day, 1944...

A Royal Canadian Air Force 419 'Moose Squadron' Lanc took off from its base in England. It was the crew's thirteenth mission. Target: the rail yards at Cambrai, France.

Shortly after crossing the enemy coastline, a Luftwaffe night-fighter attacked. Both of the Lanc's port engines became useless blowtorches. Hydraulic lines to the rear turret were blasted apart and the fluid ignited. Pilot Art de Breyne ordered the crew to bail out.

The rear fuselage of the Lanc was an inferno. Pat Brophy could not escape from his immobilized rear turret.

Mid-upper gunner Andrew Charles Mynarski, 24, of Winnipeg, desperately making for the rear escape door, realized Brophy was deathtrapped. All other crew members had left the blazing, falling and doomed aircraft.

On hands and knees, Andy Mynarski crawled through the fire to rescue his fellow gunner.

Although his flight suit was ablaze, Andy Mynarski heroically fought to release Brophy. But his courageous actions were in vain and, reluctantly, he finally obeyed Brophy's insistent order to jump.

"Backing through the flames he stood up and, before parachuting, saluted," Pat Brophy told me, his voice breaking.

The Lanc crashed at a shallow angle. Two of its 20 bombs exploded. Miraculously, Pat was thrown clear, uninjured.

"My watch stopped at 13 minutes after midnight. It was the very early morning of Friday, June 13th," Pat continued. "Andy died of burns within hours of floating down to safety."

Posthumously, and with the rank of pilot officer, Andy later was invested with the Victoria Cross.

So, how fitting it was that the Avro Lancaster taking off from Hamilton was painted exactly — and with the same squadron code letters, VR-A — as was the bomber in which selfless Andy Mynarski won his VC.

Restored to flying condition during the course of nine painstaking years by the Canadian Warplane Heritage and the CWH Lancaster Support Club, it took about $1.5 million and thousands of volunteer hours to do the job, Dennis Bradley, CWH president, estimated.

Attending the inaugural flight ceremonies, besides Pat Brophy, of St Catherines, Ontario, were four surviving members of Andy's crew:—

Art de Breyne, pilot, St Lambert, Quebec; Bob Bodie, navigator, Vancouver, British Colombia; Ron Vigars, RAF flight engineer, Guildford, England; and Jim Kelly, wireless operator/air gunner, Willowdale, Ontario.

The remaining crew member, Jack Friday, bomb aimer, of Thunder Bay, Ontario, was attending the wedding of his son that memorable Saturday, otherwise, he too, would have been there.

There was always give-and-take rivalry between British and American forces during the Second World War, often involving comparisons of the merits of Lancs and Forts. Maybe one more anecdote will encapsulate the spirit of the Lancaster at War.

Robert S. Raymond, a Lanc pilot with 44 Squadron (at the time bossed by South African J. D. Nettleton, VC), wrote home on November 21st, 1942:

"I dived on an unsuspecting Flying Fortress the other day, but he wouldn't play, so I came up alongside, stopped one propeller, and passed him."

The fact that Dr Raymond was an American who won a Distinguished Flying Cross and completed a tour of operations flying Lancs with the RAF, seems to lend the story an added poignancy.

Per ardua ad astra... in Lancs.

Right:

ONE LAST LOOK

'...Dusk creeping across the barely undulating, chalked-flecked Lincolnshire farmland of the Wolds...'

The cathedral cities and seats of learning of Eastern England have much to offer the curious, eager to retreat from the commercial realism of the 1990s and dip into the ethos, the distinctive character, spirit, even attitude of people who lived there, died there in centuries past...

Cambridge, Norwich, Ely and the like... and York, ranging from its castle and minster to railway and Viking museums, there is even a walking tour of haunted sites within its ancient walls.

But it is the road to Lincoln you must head for if you have a mind to take advantage of council-encouraged coach and car tours, set up within recent years for the purpose of visiting some of the aerodromes from whence Bomber Command took wing to do battle with the Third Reich.

As inspired, as admirable as they undoubtably are, too many years have slipped by for much to loom within range of searching eyes, wide-angle camera lenses. Too many time-fogged years have come and gone for you now to make yourself known to landowners, farm and estate managers who would, in times past, have been willing to grant access, if a trifle puzzled why you should have wanted to wander through hangars and parachute stores at Kelstern and Metheringham and Skellingthorpe, all long since gone.

Too many long-ago summers of memory denying you the challenge of suppressing your nerves and maybe climbing the rust-encrusted Braithwaite water tower which used to dominate the skyline at Ludford Magna; no opportunity for inspecting crumbling radar huts once nestling within its shadow. Nora Palmer

STICKLEBACKS

'...Two ABC antennae stood like goal posts ahead of the mid-upper turret, one jutted below the bomb aimer's hatch... Memory waved some flags...'

Shrouded in secrecy were the unique Lancs flown by No 101 Sqn from Ludford Magna. Few of the personnel on the station knew what was going on, felt disposed to enquire, for it did not pay to ask questions. It was an era when those in the know kept what they knew to themselves and even now, half a century on, only a small number of those involved in 'Airborne Cigar' will talk openly on the subject. Moreover, it comes as no surprise to learn that much of the technical and operating details remain under lock and key, though probably due more to officialdom not bothering to declassify rather than a need to preserve secrecy.

Inevitably, No 101's 'cloak and dagger' activity has collected its share of myths over the years. Certainly the specially trained operators carried on operations had to be German-speaking, capable of understanding and intercepting instructions from German controllers to the Luftwaffe night-fighter force; but the operators were not, as might be supposed, university professors, nor linguists, nor supermen in any way. Most simply volunteered because the rather vague 'invitation' on a notice board provided an escape from the daily routine of teaching, whatever. Their entry into the world of aircrew was itself unique. Not for them courses at OTU, HCU, LFS: they invariably went straight to the squadron, some never having stepped inside an aeroplane let alone having flown in one! And even when on the squadron and not flying they were generally kept apart from the basic crew. Thus few formed close relationships.

As the air war moved into its final phase there was a steadily reducing requirement for the eighth man. Apart from the decline in the Luftwaffe's night-fighter force effectiveness, the work of No 100 (Special Duties) Group increasingly took over the work of deception and interference. Few special operators remained on 101's strength when war in the west ceased. Thus ended a contribution to victory largely unsung, unrecognised, and it is to be hoped that one day their story will be told in full.

Left:
An autumn 1943 setting for 'SR:O' showing to advantage the under-nose-mounted aerial.
P. G. Davys

Below:
An illicitly taken picture of BI DV302 'SR:H' in 1945. An old warrior, joining No 101 Sqn from new in November 1943, she is complete with paddle-blade props but still retains her original Frazer-Nash rear turret (most of 101's Lancs were fitted with the Rose twin 0.5in Browning-mounted machine-gun turret from the summer of 1944). With a total of 121 ops to her credit, she was retired to No 46 MU, Lossiemouth and broken up in January 1947. C. F. Brown

Right:

NO SIGN OF FIDO NOW

'...Ludford was 'windowed' with playing cards and lightly bombed with toilet rolls...'

Ludford Magna, once home to 'secret service' unit, No 101 Sqn, with its 'Airborne Cigar' Lancs, shrouded in secrecy and mystery to some extent even to this day. Seen here April 1995, looking south are (foreground) the remains of the Technical Site, on which only two wartime huts still stand (lower right). The large stack of hay stands not on the base of a hangar, as one might assume, but on where once stood a busy complex of offices, workshops, etc. So little is left, it was identifiable from a wartime aerial photograph only by the 'kink' in the road running upwards in the picture, just left of centre, to the curve of the peri-track. Centre right of the junction between the two stood the watch tower.

The pattern of the three runways is still discernible, the almost E/W one standing out as a concrete track straddled by former Thor missile sites, which from 1959 to 1963 somehow seemed to perpetuate Ludford's rather clandestine image, and making it again very much a prohibited place. The other two runways can just be made out through the top soil, the main one running virtually N/S (01/19) making an intersection with the third (NW/SE) near the top centre of the picture. Disappearing southwards, off to the top right of centre is the B1225 Caistor to Horncastle road, the stretch seen in the photo once having passed between 'C' Flight's large complex of dispersals and 14 Base site (top right). On a nice day, it is a delightful route along the edge of the Wolds, with Lincoln Cathedral sometimes visible on the horizon 18 miles to the southwest. But don't drive too fast, or you'll miss Ludford; and if you've gone beyond the 1900ft Stenigot TV mast, you have missed it anyway!

Ludford's secondary runways were actually laid out the wrong way round, hence their circuits conflicting badly with Binbrook's. The village from which the aerodrome took its name stands in unusually close proximity at its northern fringe. In the village is a memorial to the wartime days.

Ludford opened for business on 15 June 1943, with the posting-in of No 101 Sqn from Holme-on-Spalding Moor, 101 being its only operational residents until departure for Binbrook in October 1945. From 15 December 1943 it was home also to No 14 Base which formed there, and which encompassed the three airfields in the 'triangle', ie Ludford, Wickenby and Faldingworth. Ludford's call signs were 'Bookshop', later changed to 'Brylcream', possibly for security reasons (no doubt the Germans knew them all anyway), but more likely to avoid confusion with 101's, which was 'Bookworm'. Fido was installed in 1944.

Flying ceased when 101 Sqn left, the station being put on a Care & Maintenance basis, and its land handed over to the Ministry of Agriculture until 1958/9 when the Thor missiles raised their ugly heads. With their demise in 1963, it lapsed militarily into permanent disuse.
Brian Goulding

Opposite below:
YOU HAD TO BE THERE
'...Four decades of misting memories were about to be spanned in seconds...'

'PA474' flagship of the RAF's Battle of Britain Memorial Flight, in 1995 celebrating her 30th year in preservation, and her 50th birthday since delivery by Vickers-Armstrongs. She remains the greatest crowd-puller at any airshow. Seen here in her early post-restoration 44 Sqn colours, still bereft of mid-upper turret, doing an impromptu 'fairly low' flypast at Waddington in the hands of Sqn Ldr John Stanley about 1970/71. In the background, more AVRO thoroughbreds — Vulcans. PA474's livery is changed periodically, currently (1995) representing 9 Sqn as 'WS:J' 'Johnnie Walker'. A book about '474', A Lancaster at Peace, by Sqn Ldr Ray Leach is available, published by Lincolnshire's Lancaster Association, PO Box 474, Lincoln, LN5 9ES.
Lincolnshire Echo

Above:
'FM213': The doyen of all privately-preserved Lancasters on the very point of taking to the air again for the first time in public in 25 years, on 24 September 1988 at Mount Hope, near Hamilton, Ontario, after a restoration project spanning a decade. What a proud moment for the Canadian Warplane Heritage Museum, and its Lancaster Support Group. What a proud moment for its Captain, Stu Brickenden, who had flown Lancs in the '50s in the RCAF; and his co-pilot Bob Hill, ex-RCAF of a later era, both becoming commercial aviation captains. What a proud moment for Norm Etheridge, an English aviation engineer, who had supervised the restoration over the final, crucial five years from 1983 to fruition. A proud moment, too, for the team of restorers, many of them volunteers, some with prior experience of Lancs as both ground and aircrew. What a proud moment for the many wartime veterans present — none more so than Art de Breyne and the survivors of his wartime crew, whose aircraft KB726 'VR:A' of 419 ('Moose') Sqn RCAF, FM213 has been chosen to represent by its markings. And surely none prouder than Stephanie Holowaty, guest of honour on the day, and to whose brother, the late Andrew Mynarski VC, the Lanc had been dedicated as a tribute to his heroics in KB726 on that night, 12/13 June 1944, when their Lanc had been shot down by a night-fighter on only its 4th op — the crew's 12th. Proud moments, too, for the tens of thousands of people who had attended to see that first 'official' flight, packed into Mount Hope Airport, and jamming roads for miles around. Who could fail to be thrilled... moved...? Certainly not any of those who were there that day.

FM213, a 10 MR, had been retired by the RCAF in November 1963 after service with 407 Sqn (Greenwood, Nova Scotia), and 107 Rescue Unit (Torbay, Newfoundland), and in mid-1964 was flown to Sky Harbour airfield for preservation as a memorial by the Royal Canadian Legion, Goderich (Ontario). She was mounted on three pylons in flying pose, with wheels retracted. In 1977 it was bought by the CWHM for its collection, with distant thoughts of possibly getting it flying again one day, and by 1979 it had been dismantled and moved to Mount Hope. Though some restoration work was soon started, it was 1983 before full-scale efforts began under Norm Etheridge, and finally came to fruition in September 1988 — the 11th to be precise, when 213 made her maiden flight in the hands of Sqn Ldr Tony Banfield, who had then recently relinquished his job as CO of the RAF's Battle of Britain Memorial Flight. Since its rebirth, the Mynarski Lanc has flown some 400hr (to end of 1994).

An excellent book detailing FM213's history, its restoration, and the experience of Art de Breyne and crew, written by Bette Page, entitled Mynarski's Lanc (Boston Mills Press, 1989) is available from Canadian Warplane Heritage Museum, Mount Hope Airport, Ontario, Canada, L0R 1W0. Brian Goulding

Below:
GREAT LEADER — THERE BY RIGHT
'...No wonder indomitable (and still — incredibly — officially unsung!) Air Chief Marshal Sir Arthur T. Harris, Commander-in-Chief, Bomber Command, so fondly nicknamed "Butch".'

How appropriate that this picture was taken by the widow of a former Lancaster Skipper, Canadian Bob Bennet DFC, of 626 Sqn, Wickenby.

Maureen herself was a Wren during the war, moving to Canada postwar with her husband, to start a new life.
Maureen Bennet

SURVIVORS

Of the 7,377 Lancasters built, how many survive? By our reckoning, less than a score; we think 18 to be in a reasonably complete state, plus three nose sections, and a few remains in Canada. Of the 18 preserved, only four are known to have flown operationally in World War 2: R5868, W4783, KB839 and KB882.

Odd additional Lancasters have tended to 'turn up' over the years, and it has been rumoured that the Argentine Air Force *may* have one somewhere (in addition to the Lincoln on display in Buenos Aires), but no one has yet tracked it down. There *may* be a forgotten horde buried somewhere under the fields of north Lincolnshire as has been suggested in the Press in recent years, but not yet authenticated. There *may* be a hidden cache in Canada, though this now seems unlikely, as an extensive trawl for parts was made when FM213 was being restored. Who knows, perhaps even the French *may* still have the odd one hidden away from among their once-large fleet. It is thanks to the generosity of the French in any case that at least three Lancasters are still very much with us in museums round the world, plus the one they themselves are restoring.

We have commented in previous chapters (and, indeed, in our previous books) on how inconceivable it is that such a once-huge population of Lancasters, and all types of aircraft used in the greatest aerial conflict ever known, came to be virtually wiped out. But, that is the way of the world, no matter what, particularly in relation to erasing all traces of war and its remains and reminders as soon as possible after any such events.

Nearly 20 years had passed since the end of World War 2 before the decision was made to preserve a second Lancaster in this country, R5868 'S-Sugar' having been considered quite sufficient to represent the breed. But 'Sugar' was not going to fly again; that was perfectly clear. As it was, PA474 was saved, in flying condition initially, after a lot of pressure from private individuals, but after being flown in to Waddington in 1965, it was immediately grounded and its future became uncertain. There was even talk of it being scrapped, or at best put into a museum. It was the efforts of a private group (Bill Fisher's Historic Aircraft Preservation Society) to fly Lancaster NX611 back to this country from Australia in May 1965, and to keep it flying for the next few years, which prompted the authorities to get their act together on PA474 to save it from stagnating; it was thanks also, it must be said, to some admirable local initiative by RAF Waddington to get her flying again, and from which she has never looked back. But it was a close-run thing at the time, every sort of old excuse having been put forward against it flying. Even this past year there have been rumours that PA474 might be grounded due to 'lack of funds', etc, etc, as it needs a re-spar. Fortunately, it now seems it should continue to thrill the crowds at airshows until well into the next century, provided some government minister doesn't red-line it in the interests of ever more 'economic cut backs'.

The Canadian Warplane Heritage Lancaster Support Group has done a magnificent job by private enterprise in getting its Lancaster FM213 airborne again after a 10-year restoration project. Long may it continue to grace the skies. It started off as a 'basket case' after initial recovery from years on open display at Goderich, but since its first reborn flight in September 1988, it has filled hundreds of thousands of people with pride and pleasure across Canada, and North America too, bringing home to many Americans that there *was* another bomber in World War 2 other than the B-17. (Many Americans don't know of the B-24 either!)

Once the project got under way, it was amazing how help materialised, not least from the aircraft industry and airlines, as well as the private sector. The job was undertaken just in time to benefit from skills and knowledge which still existed — but which will not last for ever, take note!

It is the Canadians who have the largest share of the preserved Lancaster population, at 12, two thirds of the total; not surprising,

perhaps, as by the time the Lanc was retired from the RCAF in April 1964, the preservation movement was getting into gear, and some good examples were saved. It must be said, however, that Canadian awareness was already well ahead of most others, probably due to the American influence in the preservation field.

It is a great pity that so many preserved Lancasters are incarcerated in museum buildings from which they are unlikely to escape. They are purely 'dead' exhibits, none more so than the three 'Down Under' (two in Australia, one in New Zealand), which for one reason or another — mainly money, of course — were allowed to stagnate and decay for more than a quarter of a century. This is not to belittle the efforts of those who eventually got them under cover and have undertaken good cosmetic restoration, particularly the former French machines at Perth and Auckland. The latter was kept in 'engine-running' condition for some years.

As for W4783, 'G-George' at Canberra, was it really beyond the ken of the Australians to have found it a hangar at one of its bases, and to have kept it reasonably active, if only to taxi; or later to have housed it somewhere within the AWM where it could still have been pulled out and run-up on special days? To see these fine aircraft locked in so apparently irrevocably, crowded by other exhibits, is truly dreadful. The Canadians *have* shown what can be done by getting one of their Lancs airborne, with possibly one or two more to follow in due time.

A 'live' Lancaster is a wonderful sight and sound to behold, and in Britain, the Panton brothers, Fred and Harold, are also showing what can be achieved, by bringing NX611 back to taxying status at their Lincolnshire Aviation Heritage Centre, after the aircraft had been so shamefully allowed to deteriorate by successive owners and custodians post-1970, to a point where it could have been scrapped. If any other Lancaster owners want proof-positive of the drawing power of a 'live' Lancaster, witness the crowd of nearly 3,000 who turned up at remote East Kirkby in the most atrocious weather, when NX611 was taxied publicly for the first time for 23 years on 22 April 1995. Compare that with the few dozen a day which such a museum could normally expect.

Perhaps the Imperial War Museum should take note. It unveiled its Lancaster, Canadian-built KB889, at Duxford 7 November 1994, with due pomp and ceremony. A nice job done over some years, but why wasn't it taxying that day? With all the resources at its disposal, the IWM's Lanc should surely be brought up to at least that status, with ample taxying facilities, and a good runway even! What a crowd-puller it would be, moving under its own power. If Duxford-based private enterprise can achieve what it did with a Blenheim (twice!), why not the IWM with its Lanc? The attendances which a 'live' Lanc would attract surely would justify the expenditure. Why stop part-way? Merlin engines are in reasonable supply now (thanks largely to the Americans). Why not invite adoption of the Lanc by someone such as Richard Branson; and what about the National Lottery in this Victory Year? Many Spitfires and Mustangs have been made airworthy again in recent years; why not Lancasters, particularly in Britain, the country in which this masterpiece was conceived, and all but a few produced?

FOOTNOTE:
In describing the squadrons with which the Canadian Lancasters served, we have omitted the 'RCAF' suffix and individual titles, which are:
405 (Vancouver) 407 (Demon) 408 (Goose)
419 (Moose) 425 (Alouette) 428 (Ghost)

Above and left:

A GHOST GOES WEST

We wonder if the movie film being shot by the airman atop the van survived? The aircraft did — or at least part of it! Lanc X KB848 'NA:G' 'Fightin' Pappy', of No 428 'Ghost' Sqn, RCAF, Middleton St George about to depart for Canada, 31 May 1945, with Flt Lt G. Cox, RCAF and his worthies, no doubt looking forward to getting home. They would arrive at Yarmouth, Nova Scotia, via the Azores, on 8 June 1945. Their mount had done a number of ops with the 'Ghosts' from February to April 1945; her nose insignia (left) would suggest 30. She was later modified as a 10 DC (Drone Carrier) with pylons under the wings on which were carried Ryan Firebee pilotless target drones until withdrawn in April 1964.

Her nose section is now on public display at the Canadian National Aeronautical Collection, Rockcliffe, Ottawa. We wonder, too: did her nose insignia survive? Did someone at the plant where she was converted for her postwar role think to save a piece of history? There were dozens of RCAF Lancs similarly adorned. Northen Echo via R. G. Beaton

155

SURVIVORS: CANADA

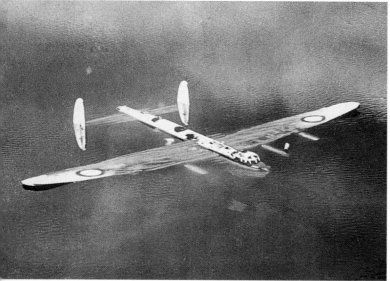

Left:

KB999 10 MR (Maritime Reconnaissance) of No 405 Sqn, RCAF Greenwood, Nova Scotia, resting on a sand bar in a lake 162 miles WNW of Churchill, Manitoba. Piloted by Flg Off T. A. R. Staners, RCAF, it had run into severe electrical storms late at night on 22 August 1953, and was finally forced down in atrocious conditions, hitting an incline, bursting into flames and slithering into the lake. The crew were missing for several days until found by a search-and-rescue Dakota, following which they were dropped supplies from Lanc FM213, also then of No 405 Sqn, and which is now flying again. The crew were flown out a week after their crash in a DH (Canada) Otter. KB999 was the 300th and last Mk X off the Canadian production line, and became the 'Manufacturer's Presentation Aircraft', named 'Malton Mike'. It saw brief service in England with 419 and 405 Sqn, mid-1945, but was too late for ops. It was still known to rest in the lake in 1984; recovery was planned, and salvage rights granted, but a progress report would be welcomed. Winnipeg Free Press

Below left:

FM212 on display at Jackson Park Sunken Gardens, Windsor, Ontario, as photographed in 1972. Quite what the colour scheme and markings were meant to represent is not known, but there were moves afoot to repaint it more authentically. It was still then carrying the special nose and cockpit mods for its postwar role with the RCAF as a 10 P (Photographic) with No 408 Sqn, until retired to Dunnville early '60s. From there it was tranported by barge. It is not recorded as having flown to Britain in 1945. Jack McNulty

Inset:

KB882, one of the four preserved Lancs known to have been operational in World War 2, albeit with only a few raids, March/April 1945 with No 428 Sqn as 'NA:R', returning to Canada in June 1945. Later much modified as a 10 AR (Aerial Reconnaissance) as seen here when still in service with 408 Sqn, Rockcliffe, with whom she continued until early 1964, when she was retired to the RCAF's Dunnville (Ontario) storage facility. Purchased for preservation by the City of Edmunston, New Brunswick for 1,500 Canadian dollars (complete), and flown into the city's St Jacques Airport in July 1964 for outdoor display. In recent years she has been restored to more normal configuration with front turret, etc. Being largely complete, might she, we wonder, fly again? Nick Wolachotnik

Below:

FM159, 10 MP (Maritime Patrol) now preserved at Nanton, Alberta. Based in England, spring 1945, too late to operate, it remained at MUs until returned to Canada in September 1945. It served with No 405 Sqn, Greenwood, and No 407 Sqn, Comox, before retirement in mid-1959. Bought 1960 by three private owners, it was towed 25 miles behind a farm tractor to Nanton, and sat beside a highway near the local airport for 30 years. Nanton Lancaster Society was formed in 1986 to rescue and restore it, and in 1990, repainted in bomber colours, and dedicated to the memory of Sqn Ldr Ian Bazalgette, an Albertan, who won the VC (only one of two Canadian bomber crew to do so, both posthumously, the other being Andrew Mynarski, who is likewise commemorated by Lancaster FM213). FM159 bears the codes of Bazalgette's Lanc 'F2:T' of No 635 Sqn PFF. She was moved under cover into a specially-built hangar in 1991, complete overhaul under way, and it is hoped to get the first of her engines running again during 1995. Seen here about mid-1956, one of three RCAF Lancs visiting RCAF 30 Air Materiel Base, Langar, Notts, when still in service with 407 Sqn, flanked by FM136, also now preserved, caught by the camera of long-time Lancaster buff Chas Waterfall, who himself worked for AVROs at Langar for some years. Only a few miles over the hill in this picture lies Melton Mowbray airfield, where 159 was flight-tested at No 12 Ferry Unit by Flt Lt Norman Turner DFC, DFM, before her return flight to Canada in August 1945. C. S. Waterfall

SURVIVORS: CANADA

Above right:
FM136, Calgary, Alberta. Having been plinth-mounted at McCall Field for many years, shown here in July 1992 being removed to the Calgary Air Museum. The undercarriage was specially lowered for the removal, and she was towed into the museum building on her own wheels — a good sign. Restoration is under way. Will she fly again? When first put on display, was given the markings 'VN:N' (50 Sqn), but later changed to 'NA:P' of No 428 Sqn. Had been to England mid-1945, but too late to operate, and held at MUs only until return. Became a 10 MR, and served with No 407 Sqn on patrol and reconnaissance duties from Comox, BC, visiting Britain on joint exercises on occasions, and seen in the picture of preserved FM159 at Langar in mid-1956; retired 1961. Art Roberts

Right:
FM104 — A superb sight as she climbs away from RAF Cottesmore, September 1962, after appearing at Battle of Britain Day, probably the last visit by a RCAF Lanc to the UK operationally. As a 10 MR she was to remain in service with 107 Rescue Unit, Torbay, Newfoundland, until withdrawal in 1964. Soon afterwards, she became a plinth-mounted exhibit at the Canadian National Exhibition Grounds at Toronto, beside Lake Ontario, in wartime bomber colours, but open to the extremes of the elements and to vandalism. She had been ferried to England in early 1945, and flew with Nos 408 and 428 Sqn before returning to Canada, but is not known to have operated. What is her future we wonder? MAP

Below right:
KB839 'Daisy', RCAF Base, Greenwood, Nova Scotia, June 1988, as preserved by the RCAF. She is one of the four Lancs with wartime operations to have been saved, from the bomb tally on the nose, apparently having done 29 ops during her 'tour' in England, most, if not all, with No 419 Sqn at Middleton St George. Of these, 13 were flown by Plt Off (later Flt Lt) P. H. Tulk RCAF and crew, Tulk's name appearing below the cockpit window on both sides. Below his name is that of Flg Off Simmons, who may have been one of her postwar skippers on No 408 Sqn from Rockcliffe as a 10 AR (Aerial Reconnaissance), and with whom she served until WFU April 1964. The name 'Daisy' was certainly carried on her nose during her operational career, as shown in Lancaster at War (Vol 1, page 63). 839's engines were donated to the CWHM to help get FM213 airborne again. Anthony J. Goulding

Below:
KB944 as seen shortly after withdrawal from service, still in 10 S (ie Standard bomber) form, one of the first Lancs to be preserved in Canada, held by the National Aeronautical Collection in its Rockcliffe Museum, Ottawa. At quite an early stage of preservation was dressed up in wartime camouflage, complete with bomb tally and nose art as 'NA:P' of No 428 Sqn. She had seen service briefly in England at Linton on Ouse, with No 425 Sqn at Tholthorpe as 'KW:K' but too late to operate. Now a static exhibit only, together with the Museum's nose section of KB848, which is also on view to the public, and which was an operational Lanc with No 428 as already related. via Ron Clarke

SURVIVORS: AUSTRALIA

Above:
W4783 Mk I 'AR:G' 'G-George', No 460 Sqn RAAF, is second only to the RAF Museum's 'S-Sugar' of the four operational Lancs to have been preserved, completing 90 sorties, December 1942/April 1944 surviving one of Bomber Command's toughest periods. Seen here magnificently displayed in the Australian War Memorial Museum, Canberra, with 4,000lb Cookie, and 'manned' by a full replica crew. She was still in excellent condition, and being taxied occasionally, until incarcerated in the late 1950s, and is now purely a static exhibit, more's the pity. The Australian War Memorial, Canberra, ACT, Australia, has produced a very comprehensive illustrated history book entitled just 'G' for George. Australian War Memorial

Left:
NX622 Mk 7, formerly WU16, one of the former L'Aéronavale trio presented by the French Navy for preservation. Delivered to Perth Airport (Western Australia), 1 December 1962, being escorted in by three RAF Vulcans which happened to be visiting nearby RAAF Richmond. Plans to keep her flying fell through (almost inevitably) and she stood in the open at Perth. Her code letters in this picture indicate an interest reportedly acquired by the Confederate Air Force, Aussie branch, but which came to naught. In 1978 she was moved to Bull Creek, near Perth, home of the Royal Australian Air Force Association Aviation Museum of Western Australia. In March 1994, a team from RAAF Richmond completed a repaint in bomber colours, as 'JO:U' of No 463 Sqn RAAF. Now purely a static exhibit, seemingly irrevocably locked into the museum building. MAP

IN REFLECTION:
50 YEARS ON

by the Reverend Canon James A. Day DFC, AKC, a Canon of Lincoln Cathedral; himself a former Lancaster pilot on No 156 Sqn, and who was shot down on 24 February 1944 to become a POW. Only the pilot and flight engineer survived.

I have been asked to write a short article for the fifth volume of *Lancaster at War* which I gladly do, as it offers me the opportunity to pay tribute to the gallant men of Royal Air Force Bomber Command, who in their thousands suffered and died in order to achieve victory in World War 2.

During the 50 years that have elapsed since the end of the war in 1945 much has been written about the role of Bomber Command and we have been criticised in certain quarters for the devastation that was caused. It is no part of my purpose to provide an evaluation of wartime bombing policy, but I have to say that I consider a great deal of the criticism to be both ill-informed and unjustified. At the time when thousands of young men volunteered for aircrew duties, this country was still under the threat of invasion and, for four long years after Dunkirk, there was no way of carrying the war to Germany other than from the air.

If the Nazi system (now revealed in all its horror) was to be defeated, the massive armaments production and industrial potential of Germany had to be destroyed. Night bombing was resorted to only when it was realised that casualties from daylight attacks would have been unacceptably high, but, until the formation of Pathfinder Force, night bombing on a large scale was impossible. Even with target marking, the existing navigational aids did not allow for pinpoint accuracy and, with bombing often taking place through total cloud cover, considerable peripheral damage to cities was bound to occur. The enemy defences were powerful and highly organised and hundreds of aircraft were shot down as their crews pressed forward courageously to their objectives. It should also be realised that the successful Normandy invasion owed much to the disruption of enemy communications by Bomber Command and, had it not been for the destruction of the rocket establishment at Peenemünde, who can tell what the consequences would have been for this country?

To end on a more personal note — I have written as a Pathfinder Lancaster Pilot (No156 Sqn) shot down on my 32nd mission on the way to attack the ball-bearing works at Schweinfurt. As a result of my experiences in a Prisoner of War hospital at Metz my vocation to the priesthood was established and I say Mass regularly in Lincoln Cathedral for all those who have suffered and died as a result of war, especially those who flew in the Royal Air Force. We must pray always for peace and reconciliation. My aircraft crashed on Briey in France and when I returned last year (the 50th anniversary) I was received with great generosity of spirit by the people of that town.

AFTERWORD

By David Shepherd OBE, FRSA, FRGS

I am delighted and indeed honoured to add a few words to this further book on the classic bomber of World War 2, by two friends of mine who probably know more about the Lancaster than anyone else, Brian Goulding and Mike Garbett. Brian and I became friends 40 years ago. I had just completed a painting from life of NX739, 'Q for Queenie', an ex-617 Squadron Lancaster which, at that time, was based at Blackbushe Airport, in Hampshire, and which was used for air-to-air photography by the Ministry of Defence. A few weeks after completing the painting, she flew down to Wroughton and, in a matter of days, was reduced to scrap with five other Lancasters. Brian sent me a photograph of the six Lancasters all lined up as if on parade, awaiting their immediate destruction; a tragic example of how much we cared about our heritage in those days.

Many years later, I came to realise at first hand just what the Lancaster meant to those brave air crew, supported by their dedicated ground crew. During the course of research for my painting, 'Winter of '43, Somewhere in England', I spent five days with the Battle of Britain Memorial Flight at Coningsby and had the thrill of flying in PA474, *City of Lincoln*, the sole remaining Lancaster that still flies in this country. Indeed, she is one of only two in flying condition anywhere, out of more than 7,000 built. After flying in her, I was allowed to go into the hangar by myself, after dinner in the Officers' Mess.

I was given the keys by the Station Commander and told not to 'touch the Phantoms'. I didn't want to. It was *City of Lincoln* that was the object of my attention. She was standing under the dimly lit hangar roof and the Merlins were still warm and ticking after their afternoon flight. Like Brian and Mike, I was a schoolboy during the war (in north London), and in those exciting days I lived through the same experiences of which the authors have written in this book — air raid shelters, listening to the drone of the German aircraft overhead, and watching the aerial fighting on my way to school. So, as I stood by myself in that hangar, looking at the Lancaster, my emotions welled up inside me. I could then well understand why those who flew this classic aircraft felt so much for her.

When I flew in PA474, it was to participate in a Lancaster World War 2 Squadron Reunion, on an airfield in the northeast of England. Dressed in my Royal Air Force overalls, I was simply an anonymous member of the crew and, as we landed, I stood aside and watched the reverence with which the Lancaster was treated when these brave men touched her; trying to get in the back door, one gentleman said, 'I baled out of that in 1943; I can't even get in it now!'. It was altogether a most moving experience in which I was honoured to participate as an outsider.

Just occasionally, man designs a 'perfect' machine, whether it be a steam locomotive or an aircraft. I firmly believe as an artist in the old adage, 'If it looks right, it is right'. The Lancaster was designed as a weapon of war, but Chadwick managed to create a beautiful design; of that, surely there can be no doubt.

Brian and Mike have done a great service in their series of books, 'Lancaster at War'. First of all, their writings and photographs keep alive the excitement and interest felt by so many young people who were not even born during the war, but who flock to air shows to see, in many cases, 'their' favourite aircraft, the 'Lanc'. More important, I believe that these books keep alive for all time the memories of not only those who flew in this wonderful aircraft, but also give further emphasis to the shocking lack of recognition given to those vast numbers of brave men who failed to return from 'ops' or who were lucky enough to come home.

David Shepherd

Above:
David Shepherd with Sqn Ldr Rick Groombridge, Officer Commanding the Battle of Britain Memorial Flight, at Coningsby in July 1995 alongside the RAF's last flying 'Lanc' PA474.
Brian Goulding

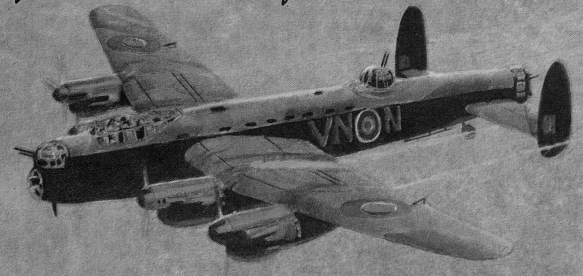

SURVIVORS: NEW ZEALAND

Top right:

NX665 Mk 7, WU13, seen in its L'Aéronavale Pacific all-white colours, taxying in at Whenuapai (near Auckland) on 15 April 1964 after arrival for presentation, straight out of service. Now housed at the Museum of Transport & Technology, Western Springs (Auckland), where for some years she was on display outside, and her engines were run quite regularly. Now permanently static indoors, she has been restored cosmetically to a high standard in bomber colours showing No 75 (New Zealand) Sqn markings (starboard) and 101 Sqn (port). She is in the process (1995) of having mid-upper moved from the 'Mk 7' (forward) to the standard position, with a fairing to be fitted. How nice it would be if John Barton (former navigator on 101) and his dedicated restoration team could get her out into the open again on occasions and give her engines some exercise. We can but hope. A very detailed and well-illustrated book is available from MOTAT entitled Lancaster NX665, by Mervyn Sterling and J. D. Duncan T. W. Collins

FRANCE

Right:

NX664 Mk 7 WU21, Austin Motors-built, as are all four of the preserved NX series, all former French Navy survivors. This one was lucky to do so, having suffered a landing accident in a storm at Hihifo Airport, Wallis Island, a French Protectorate in the Pacific, 500 miles NE of Fiji in 1963. When seen here in April 1979, she was gradually being overgrown, said to be 'home to a million mosquitos and ants', by airline pilot Captain John Laming AFC, who took the picture when staging through in his Air Nauru Boeing 737. He'd flown Lincolns in the RAAF for many years, and had spotted the Lanc quite by chance. John and other airline personnel offered to form a consortium when an Australian colleague obtained salvage rights in 1983 with a view to restoration, but then the French decided to rescue it themselves, and it was shipped back to France by the French Navy in 1984. Now under restoration at Musée de l'Air et Espace, Le Bourget Airport (Paris). John Laming

AMERICA

Below right:

KB976 — Surely the most tragic of all Lancaster preservation stories must belong to this once-proud machine, which had served briefly with No 405 Sqn at Linton-on-Ouse, mid-1945, but did no ops. It became a 10 AR variant with 408 Sqn postwar, and was not withdrawn until April 1964, after which it became a water bomber with civil registration CF-TQC. It was bought by Sir William Roberts and flown from Canada to Scotland in May 1975 to join his Strathallan Museum. When that was wound up, the Lanc was purchased by property developer Charles Church in 1986, and in August 1987 was at Woodford (the former AVRO Lanc assembly sheds) for survey with a view to making it airworthy again, when part of the roof fell in on it, with the results as shown in the photo. Church was tragically killed soon after, flying a Spitfire, and eventually the salvageable parts were acquired by a leading American preservationist, Kermit Weeks, and taken to Florida. There the plan is to marry them to the fuselage of another Canadian Lanc, KB994 (previously held by various preservationists over many years), plus some pieces from Lincoln RF342 (allowed to fall into disrepair at Southend). Hopefully, the end result will be a complete, flyable Lancaster. Quite a prospect which, if it materialises, should boost the flow of British and Canadian tourists to Florida. KB976 was featured in our Volume 3 of Lancaster at War, including a picture of it in its wartime guise. Dick Richardson